several years, in a country where wood is in greater plenty,
than large capitals, ~~large enough to~~ ~~whichever~~ spare a sufficiency for a more permanent but more expensive erections. — In the first place
a number of round logs are lapped together to the length of
the wharf on the edge of the Water. the angles are returned
by other logs, with diagonal pieces; and ~~pieces~~ are dove-tailed onto the front logs to serve
as land ties. This machine being made, ~~it~~ is carried into the ri-
ver where it floats. —
Another is then made

River

exactly of the same size & construction & being laid upon it, is fixed
with treenails (Trunnells). A third & fourth succeeds, and as the
Wharf sinks it is pushed further and further from Shore.
At last it finds the bottom at the [depth] intended, & the
back is then filled up with Ballast [wharfwood],
that is, young first trees of ~~about~~ 4 or 6 inches [cut] into lengths
of 8 or 12 feet & laid parrallel across the ties. — The lower logs,
which are either sunk in the mud or constantly covered with
water last a great number of Years without injury, but those
that are alternately wet & dry, are devoured by the Worm in the
course of 7 or 8 Years, & the Work is to be done over again. The Wharf
then assumes the most irregular twisted appearance imaginable
and the Warehouses erected upon it nod in unison with their

support. — These wooden
Wharfs are said to have been
the invention of Mr Owen, a Welchman. He was a drum

The Papers of Benjamin Henry Latrobe

Edward C. Carter II, Editor in Chief

SERIES I

Journals

The Virginia Journals of Benjamin Henry Latrobe, 1795–1798

Benjamin Henry Latrobe, c. 1804. Portrait by Charles Willson Peale.
White House Collection.

The Virginia Journals of

Benjamin Henry Latrobe

1795–1798

Edward C. Carter II, Editor

Angeline Polites, Associate Editor

Lee W. Formwalt and John C. Van Horne, Editorial Assistants

VOLUME I

1795–1797

Published for The Maryland Historical Society

by

Yale University Press, New Haven and London

1977

The Papers of Benjamin Henry Latrobe has been generously supported
by the National Endowment for the Humanities and the National Historical
Publications and Records Commission. These two volumes are published
with the financial assistance of the National Historical Publications
and Records Commission.

Designed by John O. C. McCrillis and set in Baskerville type. Printed in the
United States of America by The Murray Printing Co., Inc., Westford,
Massachusetts.

Published in Great Britain, Europe, Africa, and Asia (except Japan) by
Yale University Press, Ltd., London. Distributed in Latin America by
Kaiman & Polon, Inc., New York City; in Australia and New Zealand by
Book & Film Services, Artarmon, N.S.W., Australia; and in Japan
by Harper & Row, Publishers, Tokyo Office.

Library of Congress Cataloging in Publication Data

Latrobe, Benjamin Henry, 1764–1820.
    The Virginia journals of Benjamin Henry Latrobe, 1795–1798.

    (The papers of Benjamin Henry Latrobe: Series I, Journals)
    Includes index.
    CONTENTS: v. 1. 1795–1797. — v. 2. 1797–1798.
    1. Latrobe, Benjamin Henry, 1764–1820. 2. Architects — United States
— Biography. 3. Virginia — Social life and customs — Colonial period.
I. Carter, Edward Carlos, 1928–   . II. Maryland Historical Society.
III. Title. IV. Series.
NA737.L34C37   720'.92'4 [B]   77–76301
Library of Congress Cataloging in Publication Data
ISBN 0-300-02198-4

Contents

VOLUME 1

THE JOURNALS

VOLUME 2

Contents

Introduction

1. Benjamin Henry Latrobe: Architect and Engineer (1764–1820)

THE PROGRESS OF AN AMERICAN PROFESSIONAL

On 24 January 1798 Benjamin Henry Latrobe wrote to a friend in Philadelphia about his life in Richmond:

> I have purchased of Mr. [Bushrod] Washington an island in the midst of the Falls of James river. It is a beautiful, fertile and romantic spot. It contains about 80 acres of good land, and its scenery would not disgrace the magic rivers of Italy. . . . I have half ruined myself by living in this expensive city upon my own moderate capital. I mean therefore to be independent, and shutting myself up in my island to devote my hours to litterature, agriculture, friendship, and the education of my children, whom I hope to see here this Spring. And yet if I thought that in any part of America my talents, my acquired knowledge, and my honest intentions (of all which I have learnt to think myself possessed, from seeing the want of these qualifications in those who are here confided in) would meet with moderate respect, I believe I should be happier in the *active* pursuit of professional reputation. Indeed I am here truly unhappy. My only friend is Washington. He can feel with me, and I believe loves me. But yet he is only a Lawyer, and I have the itch of Botany, of Chemistry, of Mathematics, of general Literature strong upon me yet, and yawn at perpetual political or legal discussion especially conducted in the cramp, local manner in which it is treated in Virginia.[1]

Thus less than two years after his arrival in America, the English-born professional was becoming discontented with his life in Virginia. Today Latrobe ranks as the father of the American architectural profession and the most important engineer of his day, but at that moment his first major American commission, the Virginia State

---

1. BHL to Dr. Giambattista Scandella, 24 January 1798. For the full text of the letter, see pp. 336–43 below.

Penitentiary, progressed unsatisfactorily, and Latrobe was highly sensitive to the criticism directed toward him. More important, he realized that the limited economic resources and provincial taste of Richmond would not support the public work he desired to execute. Nor was there a sufficient demand for his services as a domestic architect to hold him much longer in Virginia.

Although he had made valuable and even loyal friends in Virginia, Latrobe was frankly becoming bored with the traditional hospitality, the talk of horses, and the discussion of politics and law. A man of culture and intellectual curiosity, Latrobe was seized not so much by a sense of superiority to but estrangement from the merchant and gentry circles in which he had found friendship, entertainment, and, on occasion, even enlightenment. Basic to this state of mind was the gnawing loneliness that plagued him. Foremost, he sorely missed his two young motherless children who had remained in England in the care of relatives when Latrobe departed for America in November 1795. Indeed, no man required or profited from the affection and security of family life more than Latrobe. Painful as the years were between the death of his first wife in November 1793 and his remarriage in May 1800, they proved to be the exception in a life distinguished by unusually close and rewarding family relationships. It was not that Virginians had treated Latrobe poorly or that he had not profited in many ways from his sojourn in that state. Rather Latrobe sensed it was time to move on, and throughout 1798 he was ever watchful for an opportunity to do so.

In March Latrobe visited Philadelphia for the first time for the stated purpose of pursuing penitentiary business and seeing his American relations, the Antes family. On his arrival, Latrobe wrote Thomas Jefferson, then vice president of the United States, presenting a letter of introduction, noting his current employment while implying that his association with Virginia republicans lessened his chances for governmental preferment, and requesting an interview the following morning. Latrobe concluded with the observation that "since my arrival in America, it [has] been my very anxious wish to become known to you, and to improve an old acquaintance with, and admiration of your works, into a personal knowledge of you."[2] This meeting initiated a relationship that profoundly affected the cultural life of the nation.

More immediately, Latrobe found in Philadelphia the professional opportunity he sought in the person of Samuel M. Fox (1763–1808), the president of the Bank of Pennsylvania, whose institution required a new building. After ascertaining Fox's requirements, Latrobe proposed a design for the bank and then returned to Richmond assuming that nothing of advantage would materialize from his northern trip. But in

2. BHL to Thomas Jefferson, 28 March 1798. For the full text of the letter, see p. 366 below.

autumn, Latrobe learned from Fox that his design was accepted and his presence was required to carry the work forward. On 30 November Latrobe informed Governor James Wood (1750–1813) of his imminent departure; a few days later he was back in Philadelphia and the career of America's first great professional architect and engineer at last was firmly on course. It is not known whether Jefferson had advanced Latrobe's cause with Fox, but the gifted amateur's own Roman temple-form capitol at Richmond provided a prototype for the bank that shortly thereafter arose in Philadelphia on Second below Chestnut.

The man who had hurried northward stood six feet two inches tall, and in his thirty-fifth year was approaching the height of his intellectual and physical capabilities. During the next two decades he would travel the route between Washington and Philadelphia many times pursuing his profession. Fortunately, Latrobe was endowed with strength and endurance, for he observed that those qualities were nearly as important to a practicing engineer's success as professional competence itself. He had had outstanding professional training, first studying engineering and then architecture. Prior to that, in the Moravian school system in England and Germany, he had acquired not only a sound classical education but also a knowledge of several modern European languages (German, French, Italian, and Greek), modern history, theology, mathematics to calculus, physical science, and natural science (biology and geology). Latrobe also was an accomplished musician, a talented watercolorist, and was not without literary ability. The reasoned clarity of his technical reports and his scientific papers were valuable elements in his professional advancement, but, as his journals so brilliantly demonstrate, writing also afforded him great personal enjoyment and proved to be an important means of self analysis and reflection. Writing with great verve and wit, Latrobe experimented with a wide range of writing styles and modes of expression, all of which were made more enjoyable by his keen ear for dialect and his perception of life's risible qualities.

Although there were limits to his natural sociability, Latrobe made friends easily and those relationships generally were of long duration—some even surviving financial and professional disagreements of considerable intensity. Naturally there was a darker side to his personality and character, although it was more than offset by the architect's natural charm, kindness, and generosity. Latrobe did not suffer fools gladly. His frank judgments, sometimes brutally direct, would earn him serious enemies—some of whom he scarcely knew, such as Oliver Evans (1755–1819), the inventor of the high-pressure Columbian steam engine. Members of corporate and public bodies and important politicians were treated injudiciously when he thought them incapable of comprehending pressing technological or artistic problems. Conversely, Latrobe could be extremely thin-skinned, particularly when fatigued, and take unwarranted offense at legitimate inquiry and criticism. Mingled with his physical and mental strength was an element of psychological fragility that made him prone to bouts of depression and contributed to Latrobe's two nervous breakdowns—one following his first wife's death in childbirth, the other twenty-two years later when his Pittsburgh steamship venture collapsed.[3]

Latrobe's accomplishments in Philadelphia were imposing. Within three years, he established himself as the most imaginative and professional architect and engineer in the country, settled happily into a new marriage, and was reunited with his two children. The Bank of Pennsylvania (1798–1801) was designed and built with seeming ease and an absence of friction between architect and client.[4] American and foreign visitors alike admired and praised the completed building, which Latrobe considered his finest work. As his major biographer, Talbot Hamlin, has explained, "In the new country it was the first building to be erected in which the structural concept, the plan conceived as a functional agent, and the effect both inside and out were completely integrated, completely harmonious."[5] Latrobe conceived of the building as a domed banking hall forty-five feet in diameter, encased in an amphiprostyle temple, which housed the subsidiary rooms at either end. He executed the whole in fireproof masonry construction, his great contribution to American structural engineering. For the porticoes he introduced the Greek Ionic order into American architecture. A major artistic achievement, the bank set a theme on which Latrobe played variations throughout his career.

Even as the bank rose, Latrobe directed the erection of the Philadelphia Waterworks (1799–1801), a sophisticated technological project employing two steam engines and requiring heavy capital investment. Several years of yellow fever epidemics, which many thought were caused by impure water, had forced the Philadelphia city councils to finance a public water utility to replace the polluted backyard wells. Latrobe's system tapped the Schuylkill River on the west side of the city. First water flowed into a settling basin, and then into a canal and tunnel cut into the rocky bluff. At the end of the tunnel a perpendicular shaft led to the first engine house on the top of the bluff. A pump raised water up the shaft and it flowed through an

---

3. Hamlin, *Latrobe*, pp. 34, 143, 433–36. The first breakdown was mentioned in BHL's English obituary, "Memoir of Benjamin Henry La Trobe," (Ackermann's) *Repository of the Arts*, 2d ser. 11 (21 January 1821): 31–32, and also in a letter written by his elder to his younger brother. " . . . the loss of his first wife, a Miss Sellon, had quite deranged his affairs and almost his mind." Christian Ignatius Latrobe to John Frederick Latrobe, 18 September 1821, John Henry de La Trobe Collection, Hamburg. Christian Ignatius apparently provided much of the information on BHL's early life for the obituary.

4. Dates given for BHL's architectural and engineering projects specify those years during which he and his staff were associated with the work.

5. Hamlin, *Latrobe*, p. 157.

underground brick conduit to the Centre Square Engine House nearly a mile away. There a second steam engine pumped the water up to a reservoir from which it drained by gravity into a network of 30,000 feet of wooden pipes.

This was the first comprehensive American steam-powered waterworks. The settling basin itself was an impressive technological achievement, and the tunneling and hydraulic masonry had no American precedent. By late January 1801 Philadelphians had fresh, clear water. However, the system when completed did not function perfectly, encountered serious financial difficulties, and was eventually replaced by a new system, the famed Fairmount Waterworks. Despite its shortcomings, the Philadelphia Waterworks demonstrated that innovative European technology and organization could provide a solution for one of the major public health problems facing America.

In domestic architecture, Latrobe produced America's first Gothic Revival house, Sedgeley (1799), built on the banks of the Schuylkill just above the city. When further commissions failed to materialize, he accepted an appointment as engineer for the survey and improvement of the Susquehanna River (1801–02), which facilitated river navigation from Columbia, Pennsylvania, to tidewater below the Maryland border and drew Latrobe into regional transportation planning. His successful completion of this undertaking led to his appointment as surveyor and engineer of the Chesapeake and Delaware Canal (1803–06), which was financed by Pennsylvanians. Its purpose was to direct the state's agricultural products to Philadelphia for consumption, processing, and reshipment to European markets.

In the midst of this professional activity, Benjamin Henry Latrobe married Mary Elizabeth Hazlehurst (1771–1841), the daughter of a Philadelphia mercantile family. Mary Elizabeth Latrobe, a woman of great charm, affection, and strength of character, thoroughly understood and appreciated her husband's genius, aspirations, temperament, and need for emotional security. On one level she provided Latrobe with the social milieu comparable to that of his London years; indeed, their Washington home was to be both in affluent and hard times a salon where Americans and foreigners of intellect, talent, and taste gathered. More important, neither professional failure nor poverty nor sickness shook her resolve to provide a warm and secure environment for her family. Nor was she merely a worthy helpmate, for in 1815 Mary Elizabeth paved the way for her husband's reappointment as architect for the U.S. Capitol by pleading his case with President James Madison while Latrobe lay emotionally exhausted and dispirited from the Pittsburgh fiasco. Three of the six children born to the Latrobes reached maturity: John Hazlehurst Boneval (1803–91), Julia (1804–90), and Benjamin, Jr., (1806–78), each of whom proved to be artistically talented.

By the end of 1802 Latrobe's career was entering its more well-known stage. At President Thomas Jefferson's request, he prepared plans for an innovative covered drydock at the Washington Navy Yard together with a scheme for extending the Potomac Canal across the city to supply sufficient water for the facility's operation. Even though Congress found the cost excessive, the president was greatly impressed with the project's technological sophistication and its author's professional skill and energy. Jefferson, confronted with the task of finishing the Capitol and planning and constructing additional federal buildings in Washington and elsewhere, appointed Latrobe surveyor of the public buildings of the United States in March 1803. The architect and the statesman entered into an artistic partnership that—although occasionally strained by the incompatibility of the two men's architectural ideas—produced two major results: the U.S. Capitol drew nearer to completion at the highest level of professional competence and taste; and Latrobe absorbed, refined, and translated a number of Jefferson's architectural concepts into his own work, most notably in the Baltimore Roman Catholic Cathedral (1804–20).

The considerable technical problems Latrobe faced in completing the Capitol were increased by the lack of cooperation and the hostile criticism of Dr. William Thornton (1759–1828), whose designs for the building had won the competition early in the 1790s. The president supported Latrobe in his attempts to effect certain necessary alterations of the original plans and also regularly defended the architect against congressional charges of excessive construction costs and delays.[6] While many authorities have judged the Capitol to be Latrobe's greatest achievement, the architect up to his death generally claimed for this work only the merit of "la difficulté vaincue." Yet despite the imperfect realization of his ideas and the devastating drain on his psyche, this great commission gave him a unique opportunity to exercise his maturing talents.

Latrobe's first term as architect of the Capitol was from 1803 to 1812, followed by a second term from 1815 to 1817. Starting his first building campaign, Latrobe faced formidable obstacles to success: an immense, imposed plan; the paucity of a resident, trained labor force and of the material resources necessary to build monumental architecture; the lateness and uncertainty of congressional appropriations; and the aggressive hostility of Thornton. During this campaign Latrobe constructed an improved version of the South or House Wing including the chamber of that body. (Unfortunately, Jefferson insisted that the space be roofed by a glass-and-timber system modeled on the dome of the Halle au Blé, the Parisian grain market he so admired. The result aesthetically and functionally was an unhappy compromise.)

6. The following passages on the U.S. Capitol and the Baltimore Roman Catholic Cathedral are based largely on information kindly provided by Charles E. Brownell, assistant editor for architectural history, who also collaborated in the evaluation of BHL's contribution to American architecture set forth below.

Latrobe also successfully rebuilt the North Wing's western side (including vaulted ceilings) in masonry, invented his famed cotton and corn orders as national alternatives to the Greek orders, and planned numerous unexecuted features, such as a formal west entry which could have anchored the architectural mass to the hill.

In his second campaign following the 1814 fire, Latrobe worked with a freer hand to create an entirely new Hall of Representatives—a magnificent interpretation of the Greco-Roman theater theme—and reconstructed much of the North Wing as an enhanced version of the pre-fire design. His resignation in 1817 deprived the Capitol of his architectural abilities as they reached their height.

The range of Latrobe's Capitol work was impressive, for he had faced and solved daring structural problems, shaped subtly lighted spaces into monumental units, composed them in sequences on the analogy of the natural landscape, united an amateurishly conceived architectural mass with its site, and evolved imaginative systems of ornament. Fortunately he was allowed to demonstrate fully his mature artistry in another great commission undertaken almost simultaneously with the Capitol—the Roman Catholic Cathedral of Baltimore.

The cathedral has long been recognized not only as Latrobe's masterpiece, but also as one of the chefs d'oeuvre of American architecture by scholars such as Fiske Kimball, Talbot Hamlin, Sir Nikolaus Pevsner, and Henry-Russell Hitchcock. At the outset Latrobe exposed the Baltimore congregation to the great tradition of Western ecclesiastical design, but even as he developed his conceptions for the building with the counsel of Archbishop John Carroll (1735–1815), his own understanding deepened. In the end, out of solid, uncompromised masonry he created a brilliant fusion of a rotunda and a Latin cross. The original masterful lighting of the cathedral demonstrates how he had profited from his years at the Capitol: mysterious illumination filtered into the rotunda through the crown of an inner masonry dome from an outer skylit dome directly modeled on that of the Halle au Blé. Thus American Catholicism received the full resources of the central tradition of Catholic ecclesiastical architecture, fittingly modified by Latrobe's exposure to such Americans as Jefferson and Carroll.

Latrobe's other work included almost every kind of building. Some of these building types, such as houses and modest churches, were familiar to Americans. Others, such as government offices, arsenals, banks, exchanges, academic buildings, and public monuments represented the newer needs of an emergent society. Buildings designed by him were constructed along much of the Atlantic seaboard and as far west as Kentucky, Ohio, and Louisiana. Latrobe consistently volunteered his services to nonprofit institutions, asking only to be reimbursed for his expenses.

Latrobe's engineering work was less celebrated than his architectural achievements but was of great significance. His work was characterized by an adherence to current European practice and theory, energy and innovation, and a facility for transmitting professional knowledge and standards throughout the nation by example, training, and publication. Appointed engineer of the United States Navy in 1804, Latrobe supervised the construction of the Washington Navy Yard. His introduction there of steam power in 1810 to drive a sawmill, a forge, and a blockmill made it a modern industrial facility. Latrobe's use of steam engines at the Philadelphia and New Orleans (1809–20) waterworks, the Navy Yard, and his promotion of steam power for industrial use mark him as America's first great steam engineer.

He commissioned, designed, and on occasion actually built engines, thereby serving as an invaluable disseminator of technology. The lure of steam power's economic potential drew him to Pittsburgh in 1813 and set in motion a chain of events that nearly resulted in Latrobe's ruin. He became the agent and engineer of a company building Robert Fulton's steamboats for Ohio commerce. After a promising start costs rose, funds became scarce, and Fulton turned against Latrobe, who foolishly attempted to continue the work on his own credit. In the end Latrobe incurred debts that eventually forced him into bankruptcy in 1817–18. The suspension of the Chesapeake and Delaware Canal Company's operations in 1806 had only reinforced Latrobe's belief that proprietorship, rather than professional practice, was the surest path to affluence for an American engineer. Accordingly, after negotiations with Congress, the Louisiana territorial legislature, and the New Orleans City Council, he obtained in 1811 a charter to construct and operate a waterworks in that city. Henry (1792–1817), his son by his first marriage and a talented architect and engineer of unusual promise, was placed in charge. Then in 1817, as the project was regaining momentum lost by wartime delays, the younger Latrobe suddenly died of yellow fever. Grief-stricken and faced with the prospect of few commissions in Washington and Baltimore, Benjamin Henry Latrobe departed for New Orleans in December 1818 to finish the waterworks in hopes of insuring his family's security.

It was a new beginning. He was fascinated by the sights, sounds, and populace of this most cosmopolitan North American city. More important, he was well received by men of station, influence, and wealth, the much-needed waterworks progressed satisfactorily, and architectural commissions materialized and others were promised. Convinced that his future lay in New Orleans, Latrobe sailed to Baltimore, wound up his business in the East, and returned with his family in April 1820. He was swept up in his work on the waterworks and the central tower of St. Louis Cathedral. The stifling summer heat descended upon the city and the fever returned. The level of the Mississippi fell and the waterworks suction pipe had to be pushed further into the river bed than previously planned. This required more digging by Latrobe's fever-decimated work force, which he supervised. Suddenly the great architect and engineer was stricken with yellow fever and died on 3 September 1820. By the cruelest coincidence, it was the third anniversary of his son's death.

Latrobe's contribution to American architecture was vast. His buildings set a wholly unprecedented standard for accomplishment because Latrobe comprehended the future of good architecture as the union of fitness to purpose, construction, and decoration, and because he possessed a gifted professional's means to those ends. Latrobe, by personal example and through the agency of his students, hastened the acceptance by American professionals of standards such as precise architectural rendering and fireproof, vaulted masonry construction. Among his pupils were his son Henry, Robert Mills (1781–1855), William Strickland (c. 1787–1854), and William F. Small (1798–1832), whose works embellished places as diverse as Philadelphia, Charleston, Nashville, Baltimore, and New Orleans. Aside from his pupils and associates, at least three generations of architects of every persuasion studied Latrobe's works, and his influence was felt down to the Civil War. Most appropriately, his favorite creation, the Bank of Pennsylvania, proved to be the greatest conduit of Latrobe's influence: the building was studied and imitated across the land. By recasting Jefferson's revival of the Roman-temple form according to the Greek taste, Latrobe had established a direction that reshaped the architecture of early nineteenth-century America.

In engineering, Latrobe's influence was profound during his lifetime. As the nation's first major steam engineer, he prepared the ground for Philadelphia to become the early center of that mode of industrial power. The capital expenditures of his engineering projects were not matched until the great era of canal building (1820–50); the range and variety of his technological accomplishments were not approached until the advent of the large office engineering firm. His experience, grasp of technological and scientific theory, and high-level European education allowed him to solve a wide range of problems and see possibilities inherent in the nation's developmental requirements that escaped the educated laymen and even those who claimed the title of engineer.[7] What Latrobe brought to the American scene were the latest English architectural principles and practices, an unusual organizational capacity, an ability to locate trained personnel at all levels of expertise, and a natural educator's inclination for nurturing the creative impulse of young technologists. Some of his assistants and students such as Mills and Strickland became

7. BHL's knowledge of geology was beneficial to his work on the Philadelphia Waterworks and certain river improvement and canal projects. His comprehension of geological formations, hydrology, and topography were utilized in making his survey estimates concerning tunneling, excavations, channel alterations, seepage, building material resources, and water availability at lock levels.

leading engineers during the era of canal building, although they, like their preceptor, are generally thought of as architects. Thus Latrobe not only helped produce the first generation of native-born engineers but also eased the way for future generations of engineers by establishing professional engineering standards and continually informing entrepreneurs and politicians alike of the heavy cost, technical complexity, and economic and social benefits of sophisticated large-scale public works. As part of this effort he helped Secretary of the Treasury Albert Gallatin (1761–1849) draft his famed 1808 report on internal improvements, the first intelligent, orderly, well-documented plan of an integrated national transportation system.

What then is the measure of Benjamin Henry Labrobe's life? To his elder brother, Christian Ignatius Latrobe,[8] it was a grievous misfortune that the architect had "resolved rashly to quit his own Country, and go to that receptacle of all that is restless, visionary and bad," where he found but one thing of value—an excellent wife. In September 1821 Christian Ignatius bitterly described Latrobe's American career and untimely death to the youngest of the three brothers, John Frederic (1769–1845), then practicing medicine in Livonia:[9]

> Our Correspondence had just grown very brisk, and his letters were most entertaining. He was a man of an uncommonly clear head, and superior talent. He served the United States with great fidelity and spent his talents upon them. His buildings as Architect and Surveyor of public Works have established his character as a first rate man in that line, and they are Monuments erected to his honor. But he met with the usual fate of servants to a Republic. Most ungratefully was he treated, and at length superseded by an old fool,[10] who had interest enough to direct the favor of a cabal: on which Benjamin threw up his commission.

If Christian Ignatius's judgment was harsh, it did not lack substance, for despite Latrobe's unmatched contributions to the betterment of American life and culture

8. Christian Ignatius Latrobe (1758–1836) was born at Fulneck and educated in Moravian schools in Fulneck and Silesia, as was BHL. Upon Christian Ignatius's return to England in 1784 he was ordained a Moravian minister and in 1787 became secretary to the Society for the Furtherance of the Gospel. He had much musical talent, and produced many sonatas, anthems, and chorales. He was the editor of the first English edition of the *Moravian Hymn Tune Book* and of *Selection of Sacred Music from the Works of the most Eminent Composers of Germany and Italy*, 6 vols. (London, 1806–25). *DNB*.

9. In 1821 Livonia was one of the three Baltic provinces of Imperial Russia. Today it occupies what is now the southern portion of the Estonian Soviet Socialist Republic and the eastern section of the Latvian Soviet Socialist Republic. The following quotation is from Christian Ignatius Latrobe to John Frederick Latrobe, cited above in n. 3.

10. Samuel Lane, the commissioner of public buildings who oversaw construction of the Capitol during BHL's second campaign.

his family found itself nearly destitute at his death. Yet as Talbot Hamlin has so properly cautioned,

> The tragic irony of Latrobe's death should not obscure the triumphant richness of his life—rich in friends, in family, in the joy of creative work. From whatever abyss of despair, he always emerged—chastened though victorious—to pursue his unique destiny in the country's growth to maturity and to enrich it with further fruits of his indomitable idealism and his creativity.[11]

Surely little more can be asked of any man's life.

YOUTH, EDUCATION, AND EARLY CAREER, 1764–1795

The journey that ended so tragically in New Orleans began fifty-six years earlier in Fulneck, Yorkshire, near Leeds on 1 May 1764 with the birth of the second son of the Reverend Benjamin Latrobe (1728–86) and Anna Margaretta (Antes) Latrobe (1728–94). The original Latrobes had been French Protestants who had settled in Ireland at the close of the seventeenth century; the elder Benjamin was born in Dublin, educated at the University of Glasgow, and upon returning home helped organize a Moravian congregation of which he later became the minister.[12] Because of his persuasive preaching, administrative talent, and erudition he was sent to Fulneck, at that time a newly established center of Moravian activity, to serve as both minister of the congregation and head of the now famous boys' school. Benjamin Henry Latrobe's mother was a third-generation Pennsylvanian whose father, Henry Antes (1701–55), proved to be a staunch friend and supporter of the Moravians who established Bethlehem. In 1743 she went to England to complete her education. In due course she became first a teacher at and then headmistress of the Moravian girls' school in London. The school was transferred to Fulneck, and there she probably first met her future husband. The year after Latrobe's birth the family moved to London, where his father became the widely respected minister of the Fetter Lane Chapel (a post later filled by his son Christian Ignatius), and also assumed the general superintendency of all Moravian institutions in Great Britain and Ireland.

---

11. Hamlin, *Latrobe*, p. 530.

12. Over the years members of the Latrobe family have spelled their surname in various ways. Originally in France the family apparently used the form "Latrobe." Later in Ireland and England "La Trobe" (sometimes spelled "la Trobe") was used. The Livonian (now German) branch of the family adopted the form "de La Trobe" which continues in use today. BHL apparently adopted the original French form early in his professional career (c. 1790), and his American descendants have followed this usage. For the sake of conformity, references to family members in this edition will use the spelling "Latrobe," except in direct quotations from manuscript and printed sources and in reference to living members of the family using variant spellings.

With the death of Count Nicolaus Ludwig von Zinzendorf (1700–60), the man most responsible for the reconstitution of the Moravian Church—the *Unitas Fratrum* (Unity of the Brethren or United Brethren)—and the passing of the movement's other early leaders, the Reverend Benjamin Latrobe's influence increased steadily throughout the church and beyond. He became president of the Society for the Furtherance of the Gospel, established and maintained good relations with the leaders of other denominations, and wrote and translated histories of the church and its missionary efforts that dispelled much of the prejudice against the Moravians and helped establish their reputation throughout the Atlantic world.

While the Reverend Benjamin Latrobe was greatly admired for his intellect and charm, basic to his unusual accomplishments was his character. Because of his natural kindness and good humor, charitable tolerance, and exemplary conduct, he was thought to be a truly Christian man by persons of all ranks and persuasions. Thus he was widely known in London society, counting among his numerous friends those two eighteenth-century luminaries Dr. Samuel Johnson (1709–84) and Dr. Charles Burney (1726–1814), the organist and music historian. The Moravian minister, who was a knowledgeable musician in his own right, was said to have assisted Burney with the translation of German musical sources and commentaries.[13] Thus Benjamin Henry Latrobe was born into an impressive world—one that was international in scope, filled with music, books, and good conversation, and characterized by both a devotion to ethical behavior and a comprehension of human frailty.

At the age of three Latrobe was sent to boarding school in Fulneck; then, in 1776, he left England to enter the Pedagogium, or high school, at Niesky in German Silesia. Christian Ignatius, who had arrived there five years before, soon completed his course and became a teacher at that institution. Latrobe must have contemplated entering the ministry, for he next proceeded to the Moravian seminary at Barby near Halle in Saxony. Latrobe's academic education was both impressive and strikingly modern, for the Moravians stressed not only biblical and theological studies but also classical languages and a whole range of disciplines that today constitute much of a liberal arts curriculum: mathematics, geometry, algebra, modern foreign languages, history, geography, and fine arts (drawing). Judging from the expertise he had acquired a decade later, Latrobe may well have started his study of natural and physical science in Germany although neither field was officially taught at the Pedagogium. Certainly he traveled widely in the eastern German states, for his

---

13. For a brief discussion of Dr. Burney's work and BHL's probable knowledge of it, see the editorial note on "Jottings on the Opera 'Alceste,' " pp. 225–27 below.

knowledge of the region's geography was precise, and he must have been acquainted with civil engineering works that were then being planned and executed.

There is an indication that Latrobe's first engineering experience was gained while working briefly on a river improvement project in Saxony when he was about seventeen. Latrobe was profoundly impressed with German hydraulic engineering throughout his professional career. He applied its principles and techniques to specific technological problems and attempted to keep abreast of its developments after his arrival in America. Having rejected the ministry as a possible career, Latrobe journeyed leisurely homeward in 1783 on a Grand Tour of Germany and France, an itinerary that naturally included Paris. Among the buildings in Paris which impressed him were the Halle au Blé and the anatomy theatre at the Ecole de Chirurgie.[14] He also traveled to Italy, probably on this tour, or perhaps on a second trip in 1786. He visited Naples and Rome, studying such cardinal monuments as the Pantheon, a building whose architectural and acoustical qualities he greatly admired.[15] It is not known whether Christian Ignatius and Benjamin Henry Latrobe traveled together, but by the summer of 1784 both brothers were back in London: the elder soon to be ordained, the younger working as a clerk in the Stamp Office.

The length of Latrobe's service in the Stamp Office is not known, though there is evidence that he was working there as late as May 1788.[16] By then, Latrobe had begun his professional training under John Smeaton (1724–92), England's most renowned engineer.[17] Little can be said of his experience in Smeaton's office (c. 1787–88) except that Latrobe arrived in America extremely well versed in the technical and theoretical aspects of advanced English civil engineering, having worked at some

14. Later BHL noted that "Joseph the second [1741–90] visited the Madhouse in Paris [April 1777]—a few years before I was there." BHL to Alexander James Dallas, 27 August 1816, Latrobe Letterbooks, *PBHL, microfiche ed.*, 132/G13. BHL considered the anatomy theatre to be "one of the most beautiful rooms, and perhaps the best lecture room in the world for speaking, hearing, and seeing." BHL to [Thomas Parker], "Remarks on the best form of a room for hearing and speaking," [c. 1803], American Philosophical Society, Philadelphia, *PBHL, microfiche ed.*, 157/E10.

15. There is no doubt that BHL visited Italy, but when he was there is unclear. For references to Naples, see p. 475 below; for Rome, see BHL to [Thomas Parker], "Remarks on the best form of a room for hearing and speaking," [c. 1803], American Philosophical Society, Philadelphia, *PBHL, microfiche ed.*, 157/E10. BHL's presence in Naples in 1786 is suggested in his journal entry of 22 May 1797 (p. 223 below). He later wrote, however, that he was in England from July to November of 1786. BHL to Isaac Hazlehurst, 15 September 1805, Latrobe Letterbooks, *PBHL, microfiche ed.*, 44/A10.

16. BHL to Arthur Young, 22 May 1788, The British Library, *PBHL, microfiche ed.*, 140/A1.

17. The following account of BHL's English engineering and architectural careers is somewhat conjectural, as it is based largely on scattered references in BHL's American correspondence. It alters the standard account found in Hamlin, *Latrobe*, pp. 26–28, 41–48 by extending BHL's engineering activities to c. 1789 and placing him in Samuel Pepys Cockerell's architectural office from c. 1789 to the end of 1792, when he established his own office.

time between 1788 and 1794 (probably 1788–89) as a resident engineer overseeing section work on the Basingstoke Canal under the direction of William Jessop (1745–1814), a famous Smeaton protégé.[18] Perhaps it was in Smeaton's office that Latrobe learned to produce the magnificent architectural and engineering delineations that so distinguished his later American career. His most important English engineering work was to be an unexecuted commission for the Chelmer and Blackwater Navigation (1793–95) in Essex, which consisted of deepening and straightening the Blackwater's channel between Maldon and the sea, and improving and partially canalizing the Chelmer River above the busy port town. Thus, before leaving England, Latrobe's engineering skill was sufficient to earn him the direction of a regional canal and river improvement project.

Latrobe's engineering training soon led him to develop his interest in architecture. Formerly it was not uncommon for one man to function as an architect-engineer, but this practice was dying out by 1790. However, it is not surprising that an architect such as Samuel Pepys Cockerell (1754–1827), who was then engaged in designing public works such as the house for the First Lord of the Admiralty in Whitehall, would have welcomed a promising young man possessing engineering experience and drawing skills. Latrobe entered Cockerell's office in about 1789–90, and there gained invaluable experience and rapid advancement, for by his own account he "conducted" or managed the office in 1791–92. By this association Latrobe was immediately drawn into the orbit of England's three most advanced architects: Cockerell himself, George Dance the younger (1741–1825), and Sir John Soane (1753–1837). Latrobe was greatly influenced by the latter man's work. Years later in America, Latrobe, long out of touch with the English scene, independently produced brilliant solutions to sophisticated design problems that were strikingly similar to those Soane arrived at when faced with similar challenges.

Near the end of his service with Cockerell, Latrobe was made a surveyor to the London police (c. 1792). This minor official appointment required him to oversee the renovation, alteration, and repair of a number of existing buildings used as district police stations. About this time he opened his own office; enough work—mostly alteration jobs—came his way that he took on at least one student apprentice. Latrobe's

18. BHL probably worked on the Basingstoke Canal during its initial years of construction. There is an indication that in 1787 he had worked under Jessop on some harbor improvements at Rye, and it seems logical BHL would have followed the chief engineer from one job to another in the typical pattern of apprenticeship training of the period. BHL, who was living in London then, might well have combined office work with this type of nearby seasonal field experience.

reputation grew and he received commissions for new residences, two of which still survive: Hammerwood Lodge (1792) in Sussex, and Ashdown House (1793) in Berkshire. Both houses, if somewhat awkward in execution, demonstrate a certain boldness of design and an interesting use of Greek orders that foreshadow his later work.

This factual recital of Latrobe's early professional progress must be balanced by some mention of the social, cultural, and intellectual world in which he moved. In late eighteenth-century England skill alone was rarely sufficient to guarantee initial success in any calling; family background and connections played a large role. When Latrobe and his brother returned to London from Germany in 1784, they rejoined a well-known and highly regarded family. The Reverend Benjamin Latrobe was on exceedingly good terms with Dr. Johnson and the two were in each other's company frequently in the final years of the great man's life.[19] There is a hint in Benjamin Henry Latrobe's 1796 journals that he may have met Johnson before his death in December 1784.[20] But it was his father's friendship with Dr. Burney that allowed Benjamin Henry Latrobe access to that circle wherein the lines of art, literature, scholarship, politics, and society intersected. Both Latrobe brothers became admirers and frequent guests of the great musicologist and his talented family. The two young Moravians were more than welcome, for not only were they gentlemen and intelligent conversationalists, but both, like their father, were accomplished musicians well versed in German and thus able to assist Dr. Burney in his work. There is no doubt that both became intimates of the Burneys and members of their circle. When Dr. Burney's wife died in 1796, he "wrote to those friends who, having been entertained through the years at his home, best knew Mrs. Burney," one of the three being Christian Ignatius. The following year his daughter Fanny (1752–1840), Madame d'Arblay, the famous novelist and diarist, included Benjamin in a list of prospective husbands for her widowed sister Charlotte Ann (Burney) Francis (1761–1838).[21]

Latrobe, with his love of books and music, must have flourished in such an atmosphere; judging from the evidence of his literary and scientific knowledge that is scattered throughout his surviving papers, he was a prodigious reader. By the time

19. For the Rev. Benjamin Latrobe's probable role in bringing William Cowper's (1731–1800) 1782 volume of poems to Johnson's attention see Maurice J. Quinlan, "[Benjamin Latrobe:] An Intermediary Between Cowper and Johnson," *Review of English Studies*, 24 (1948): 141–47. On Latrobe's supposed view of Johnson's religious state of mind as death approached see Quinlan, *Samuel Johnson: A Layman's Religion* (Madison: University of Wisconsin Press, 1964), pp. 59–60, 188–89.

20. See p. 167 below.

21. *The Journals and Letters of Fanny Burney (Madam D'Arblay)*, ed. Joyce Hemlow (Oxford: Oxford University Press, 1972–73), 3: 205n; 4: 257–58.

he left England in November 1795, Latrobe had gathered together a 1,500-volume library containing many professional books; this was lost in transit to America, and he spent years unsuccessfully attempting its reconstruction. It seemed inevitable that Latrobe would try his hand at some literary or historical genre, and in the late 1780s he translated from German and edited two historical works of contemporary political interest.[22] At the same time he was involved in preparing the first volume of James Bruce's *Travels* for publication. The African explorer thought of Latrobe as merely a well-to-do amanuensis who should work for prestige rather than pay. Latrobe saw matters differently and legal proceedings followed; in 1817 he was to tell Thomas Jefferson that the entire text of the volume and all the illustrations were his work.[23] This dispute must have made some splash, even in London's contentious literary circles.

It was a young man of good background, considerable achievements, and much promise who on 27 February 1790 married Lydia Sellon (c. 1761–93), the daughter of a wealthy and well-known Anglican clergyman, Dr. William Sellon.[24] It was a love match and the marriage was one of great happiness, mutual interests, and shared experiences. They had two children: Lydia Sellon Latrobe (1791–1878) and Henry Sellon Latrobe (1792–1817). Then in November 1793 Lydia died in childbirth along with their third. Shortly thereafter Latrobe's mother also died.

Latrobe kept his small family together and for awhile carried on professionally, although the renewed French war had economic consequences that limited his architectural and engineering prospects. But according to Christian Ignatius a financial crisis did not unsettle his brother, for "he was in the way of promotion and places of Emolument were offered him—but the loss of his first wife . . . quite deranged his affairs and almost his mind.[25] His major commission, the Chelmer and Blackwater Navigation, did indeed come to a standstill in May 1795; throughout June and July the promise of work in Ireland flickered on the horizon like a summer storm only to vanish in August.

These two dismal years had brought Benjamin Henry Latrobe one bit of good

---

22. *Characteristic Anecdotes, and Miscellaneous Authentic Papers, Tending to Illustrate the Character of Frederic II, Late King of Prussia, with Explanatory Notes and Observations* (London, 1788), chiefly translated and compiled from "Anekoten und Karokterzüge aus derm Leben Friedrich des Zweiten"; and *Authentic Elucidation of the History of Counts Struensee and Brandt, and of the Revolution in Denmark in the Year 1772* (London, 1789), translated from the original by S. O. Kalkenskjold (Germanien [Kempten], 1788).

23. James Bruce (1730–94), *Travels to Discover the Source of the Nile in the Years 1768–73*, 5 vols. (London, 1790); BHL to Jefferson, 12 August 1817, Latrobe Letterbooks, *PBHL*, microfiche ed., 137/E4.

24. For BHL's extraordinarily sympathetic and satirical sketches of the Reverend Dr. Sellon and members of his family, see pp. 201–12 below.

25. Christian Ignatius Latrobe to John Frederick Latrobe, cited in n. 3 above.

fortune—the land in Pennsylvania which his mother had left to him. He determined to start life anew in America, bade farewell to his two small children who already were living with relatives, and journeyed to Gravesend from where, late in November 1795, he sailed for America.

THE ATLANTIC VOYAGE AND THE VIRGINIA YEARS, 1795–1798

Latrobe characterized the fifteen weeks spent reaching the United States as a "voyage, in which everything that deserves the name of anxiety had been experienced."[26] Indeed, the passage had been an arduous but not an unusual one for the period. The *Eliza* spent two weeks beating her way out of the Channel in foul weather, then sailed slowly southwest through storms past the Azores, until on 21 January the first breath of the northeast trade wind announced the start of the voyage's great western leg; by mid-February the ship was able to head north to the mouth of Chesapeake Bay and Norfolk. For long periods the winter passage was made miserable by a combination of unwholesome and on occasion insufficient food, exceedingly cramped and filthy quarters, rough weather, poor seamanship, and a lack of proper ballast. Yet almost daily under these trying circumstances, Latrobe perceptively—and often humorously—described his Atlantic voyage in his journal and sketchbook; the combined result is a unique account of eighteenth-century sea travel.[27]

Here in his earliest major graphic creations, we see two of his most salient qualities: a talent for precise observation and an unchecked engagement with life. Latrobe skillfully recorded the varieties of human character and behavior both satirically and sympathetically, and when he turned his attention to the world of nature the results were often even more remarkable. Latrobe saw beauty everywhere, not only in the sensuous form of the fishes and whales but even in the uncomely Portuguese man-of-war. At the same time, he was curious to understand each organism's way of life. He wondered about natural causes, and only those, searching for neither allegorical meaning nor divine purpose in his subjects. Latrobe was simply eager to appreciate each living thing for itself.

Like many passengers before and since, Latrobe hungered for diversion from the

26. See BHL's 7 March 1796 journal entry below, p. 70.

27. Some twenty years later Christian Ignatius Latrobe, when visiting South Africa, sailed courses similar to the southwestern portion of the *Eliza's* voyage. It is extremely interesting to compare the two brothers' descriptions of porpoises, flying fish, dolphins, the changing weather, the sighting of the mountainous Atlantic islands, and the arrival of Neptune on board. The elder brother's passage was by far more comfortable and safe, but BHL's account was livelier, more vivid and amusing. See Christian Ignatius Latrobe, *Journal of a Visit to South Africa in 1815 and 1816 with Some Account of the Missionary Settlements of the United Brethren, Near the Cape of Good Hope* (London, 1818).

physical discomforts, abrasive personal relations, and boredom associated with ocean travel. It was his curiosity about the natural world that provided him with a much-needed form of escape (indeed the study of a single jellyfish afforded an entire day's diversion). His delight in this escape is evident in the beautiful watercolors of his subjects. As the *Eliza* sailed west, he recorded and speculated upon that which naturalists before him had observed: floating *Sargassum* with tiny crabs living on it, flying fish escaping into the air from pursuing bonitos and dolphins, and sharks accompanied by pilot fish. He filled his journal and sketchbook for his own pleasure, yet in his attitude toward nature Latrobe represented the best science of his time.

Latrobe was by nature an open-minded man. He was also knowledgeable about the United States. Yet the *Eliza* and her boorish, inept master (both American) may have led him to question his decision to leave England. The voyage itself was not an experience likely to have enhanced the young republic's reputation for good seamanship and technological proficiency. But during the final month of the passage, a number of other American vessels were encountered whose beauty of design and skillful handling by their captains favorably impressed Latrobe.

Landfall was made near Cape Henry on 3 March, but first a calm and then a sudden, violent winter storm which drove the *Eliza* out to sea delayed Latrobe's landing in America by perhaps a week. A fortnight later, on 23 March 1796, having recovered from his Atlantic voyage and having observed Norfolk's town plan, architecture, wharves, and sanitary problems, Latrobe committed his thoughts to paper, thus commencing his Virginia journals.

Quite naturally Benjamin Henry Latrobe immediately attempted to take the measure of American architecture and technology. A major theme of his American career was his determination to transfer advanced European architectural and engineering practices and standards to the United States. That twenty-five-year uphill struggle began in March 1796 when Latrobe designed a house for Capt. William Pennock in Norfolk. Latrobe proposed a compact town house with an ingenious and elegant stair hall, for which he prepared a virtuoso rendering in perspective, but the local craftsmen spoiled the building in the execution. The Pennock House served as a portent of Latrobe's architectural work during his Virginia years. In 1797 he began building his only major Virginia commission, the state penitentiary at Richmond, a thoughtful but uninfluential essay in penal architecture which suffered severe modification after his departure in 1798. His principal domestic commission, the Richmond house that he designed for Col. John Harvie in 1798, likewise underwent thorough modification. With the Pennock House, the penitentiary, and the John Harvie House no longer extant, the architectural legacy of Latrobe's Virginia years are his architectural drawings, often of superlative quality, but which were sometimes unrealizable in the economic climate of Virginia. Of special interest are the albums "Designs of Buildings . . . in Virginia" (1796–99), which contains the drawings for the John Harvie House, and "Designs of a Building . . . to contain a Theatre, Assembly-Rooms, and an Hotel" (1797–98), which contains a project intended for Richmond.

Initially, however, it was Latrobe's engineering knowledge and skill that were in demand, for his arrival coincided with Virginia's first wave of internal improvements. His engineering work was largely devoted to canals and river improvement. Within three months of his appearance on the local scene, he was consulted by three companies: the Dismal Swamp Canal Company, the James River Company, and the Upper Appomattox Navigation Company. For the latter his work included a survey of the Appomattox River from Cumberland County to Petersburg. Through these consultation projects, his technological expertise became known to the gentlemen of eastern Virginia who interested themselves in internal improvements. A visit to Mount Vernon afforded an opportunity to discuss the state's transportation needs with George Washington; prior to Latrobe's removal to Philadelphia, he offered Thomas Jefferson his services in improving the Rivanna River where it passed through the vice president's lands near Charlottesville.

While no major engineering project was to result from Latrobe's Virginia sojourn, it was a period not without importance, for he made his basic judgments concerning the nature of American internal improvements. Latrobe observed the gap between the expectations and the financial and technological resources of the promotors of improvements, the importance of geological and geographical factors in successfully executing river improvements and canal projects, and the availability of trained or educable personnel. Above all he learned how, as a professional engineer, he should conduct himself so as to both advance his career and fulfill the technological needs of his adopted country.

Measured against his later professional activities and accomplishments, Latrobe was underemployed in Virginia, a circumstance that has proved to be posterity's good fortune. For with ample time at his disposal and the stimulus of a fresh environment, he was able to fill his journals with astute observations and luminous impressions on an astounding range of human activities and natural phenomena. Late eighteenth-century Virginia culture and society, architecture and technology, natural history, geology and topography, agriculture, rural and urban life, art, legal institutions, education, music, politics and economics, the unpredictable ravages of yellow fever, and numerous other topics were described and speculated upon by Latrobe. The sketchbooks which were integrated with the journals probably constitute one of the finest pictorial representations of the people, buildings, roads and rivers, harbors, towns and cities, landscape, and flora and fauna not only of contemporary Virginia but of America as a whole.

As Latrobe received no regular salary until his appointment as the architect of the penitentiary in June 1797, he most likely arrived in Virginia with both cash and some instrument of credit in hand. Also his mother's brother, Frederick Antes, aided Latrobe with funds evidently realized from a sale of some of his nephew's inherited Pennsylvania lands.[28] If Latrobe looked to his American relations for financial assistance, his journals after April 1797 dramatically reflect his deep emotional and intellectual dependence on the family and cultural world he had left behind in England. From that moment forward recollections of the past were interspersed among observations on the present; Latrobe's accounts of the Sellon family, the stories of Charlotte Hoissard and Tommy Rhodes, the tale of Sir Osbert, and the "Ode to Solitude" written after Lydia Sellon Latrobe's death not only inform us about his early life, knowledge, and literary skills, but strongly suggest that their author, who had been separated from his children for nearly two years, had fallen prey to something more unsettling than nostalgia. To a lesser degree, the sketchbooks echo a similar discord.

Latrobe wrote his journals, or memorandum books as he termed them occasionally, for his own reference and personal enjoyment and his children's future enlightenment. During the Atlantic voyage and some of his travels throughout Virginia, the journals served as diaries, being the record of his daily activities and observations. At other times they indeed were memorandum books into which Latrobe entered his descriptive notes and speculative thoughts on various biological and geological observations, some of which when later combined with sketchbook materials became the bases of published scientific papers. The journals also took the form of commonplace books in which the architect pasted newspaper clippings, and of letterbooks in which he drafted communications.

As an antidote to the press of business, boredom, or loneliness, Latrobe experimented with writing styles and literary conceits, composing Gothic tales or accounts of his earlier life. Thus the journals were a valued repository of his most important thoughts and reflections and also a catchall for notations and fugitive bits of information which Latrobe wished to retain.

28. For an accounting of funds BHL received from Antes as of 23 May 1796, see inside front cover of Latrobe Journal III, 10 June–24 July 1796, *PBHL, microfiche ed.*, 4/A3. Eleven years later BHL complained to Jefferson that his professional activities had consumed $15,000, referring to the liquidation of his patrimony of Pennsylvania lands. BHL to Thomas Jefferson, 18 February 1807, Latrobe Letterbooks, *PBHL, microfiche ed.*, 55/D11; BHL to Rev. William Dubourg, 12 November 1809, Latrobe Letterbooks, *PBHL, microfiche ed.*, 71/D6.

From a literary standpoint, the most impressive aspect of the journals is Latrobe's adaptive and visually suggestive prose. A man of contemporary as well as classical letters, Latrobe was well acquainted with the eighteenth-century English satirists and pre-Romantics and with a number of major European writers such as Cervantes and Voltaire. When seized by inertia or depression he sought relief in reading novels. While he experimented with a number of literary modes, particularly satire, Latrobe's style depended less on literary models than experience gained from his daily activities. As an architect and engineer, he was committed to careful observation and exact terminology; as an artist, he was sensitive to the picturesque in nature and man. Blessed with a good sense of humor, an unusual ear for everyday speech patterns, and a mimic's ability to reproduce national and regional dialects, Latrobe produced an invaluable portrait of Virginia's variegated society. All these factors resulted in a prose style distinguished by its analytical and descriptive clarity and facility to reproduce the color and emotion of a novel environment. Latrobe was a gifted story-teller, and a number of his accounts, such as the reading of his father-in-law's will, were minor masterpieces of social satire. His imagination was essentially earthbound, and seldom ventured far from the realm of measurable fact. His attempts at reflective, philosophical, or sentimental poetry were embarrassingly awkward. Language served Latrobe best when limited to an exploration of the workings of things and men.

Benjamin Henry Latrobe's skill as a draftsman and watercolorist is best represented in his fourteen volumes of sketchbooks. The capacity to make a pictorial record of experience, rare in the young nation, had spread through the literate classes in England during the later eighteenth century, when the complementary discoveries of the beauty of the natural landscape and the appeal of the visual arts promoted an unprecedented vogue among laymen for making watercolor drawings. Latrobe's graphic activity revolved around his love of natural beauty, which he recorded with the standard techniques of the eighteenth-century English topographical draftsman. He began with a pencil drawing, filled the outlines in with india ink, brushed in the modeling with blue-gray "dead color," and finished the scene with complex layers of deliberately calculated color washes. The completed drawings range from competent topographical studies to scenes of exceptional beauty. Latrobe applied his drawing abilities to the wide variety of subjects which interested his curious and well-stocked mind. His volumes contain genre scenes, portraits, still lifes, antiquarian matter, technical diagrams, and subjects from literature and from his own imagination. His interest in natural history accounts for a considerable number of the drawings.

Latrobe considered himself an expert naturalist, and a careful study of his writing shows that his own evaluation was not presumptuous. It would be interesting to know just what training in science Latrobe had received in Germany or England. Somewhere along the way he had the opportunity to carry on laboratory experiments in biology, for he later described in some detail those which he had performed to demonstrate the ability of the *Hydra* to regenerate lost parts.[29] Evidently he had a good grasp of the history of natural history, being well informed of the recent work of Linnaeus and others. He recognized the importance of classification, based upon accurate detailed descriptions and drawings, and made some important contributions to scientific literature along these lines. Whenever practical, Latrobe made his own observations on the natural phenomena he encountered. As a mathematician he appreciated the importance of measurements, and he recorded both the weights and the dimensions of the organisms he described. Some of his recorded statistical data is still of value. He drew excellent illustrations of his biological subjects which included the entire organism, specific small anatomical details, and in certain cases a portion of the organism's life cycle.

Latrobe was at his best as a naturalist when describing animal behavior. One measure of his skill was his ability to execute surprisingly accurate sketches from memory. He spent several hours profitably observing the activities of some ants with which he shared a rather unattractive room in a Richmond tavern. Entomology held a special attraction for Latrobe, and he wrote at length not only about ants, but also about wasps, bees, hornets, moths, butterflies, and particularly mud-daubers.[30]

The range of Latrobe's interest in nature can be gauged from the fact that he observed and recorded matters as broadly ecological as the conservation of wildlife and stages of plant succession on abandoned fields, and matters as detailed and specific as the presence of secondary parasites on the parasite of a fish. Very little seems to have escaped his keen eye in the world around him.

It was natural that he should have been fascinated by the opportunity to compare this new country with the familiar terrain of England and Germany. He was very much interested in the changes which had occurred since the coming of the white man. But Latrobe could pursue his natural history interest only so far in Virginia; he complained of a lack of access to scientific works (his own library having been lost in transit from England) and the seeming absence of any amateur scientists.

Latrobe found that sought-after scientific community in Philadelphia; in mid-

---

29. Although this is a commonplace laboratory experiment in biology courses today, it was only first described in 1744 by Abraham Trembley (1700–84), the Swiss naturalist.

30. For BHL's journal description and sketchbook illustrations of these observations on mud-daubers see plate 16 and pp. 239–42 below.

summer 1799 he was elected a member of the American Philosophical Society and thereafter became increasingly active in that body. On 7 February 1800 Latrobe read a paper entitled "A Drawing and Description of the Clupea Tyrannus and Oniscus Praegustator," which reported his observations made in Virginia on a parasite found in the mouths of fishes called alewives, a type of herring.[31] It was to be Benjamin Henry Latrobe's most enduring contribution to the literature of natural history. He made careful observations and drawings of both fish and parasite, and later consulted the works of Linnaeus, Gmelin, Fabricius, and others in Philadelphia. He discovered descriptions of similar parasites but was sufficiently accurate in his observations to doubt that his was identical. To his surprise Latrobe learned that the fish had not been previously described, so he set to work preparing a well-organized scientific paper that is considered excellent even by modern standards. Believing both the fish and parasite to be new species, he proposed names for them. Although his proposed generic names have been changed, the alewife is today known as *Brevoortia tyrannus* (Latrobe), and the crustacean parasite found in its mouth is *Olencira praegustator* (Latrobe). Thus in having his name designated as the first to describe them, Benjamin Henry Latrobe achieved what Peter Collinson once called "a species of eternity."[32]

While Latrobe's journals were not written with an eye to publication, those passages that dealt with his Atlantic voyage and Virginia experiences and observations naturally bore a certain similarity to the published accounts of other European visitors.[33] What distinguishes Latrobe's journals is his informed sympathy for American society and its stated principles, his intense curiosity, sense of topography, and an artistic ability to give a lifelike quality to the wide range of subjects described. That the journals and sketchbooks were created together made the former all the more vivid.[34] Among visitors' accounts, the Virginia portion of La Rochefoucault-

31. Printed in American Philosophical Society *Transactions* 5 (1802): 77–81, *PBHL, microfiche ed.*, 162/D2. The plate accompanying this paper was based on a sketchbook entry BHL made c. March 1797; see *PBHL, microfiche ed.*, 248/C1.

32. The preceding descriptions of BHL's fascination with marine biology, his writing style, and proficiency as a naturalist are based on materials generously provided by Mary P. Winsor, Institute for the History and Philosophy of Science and Technology, University of Toronto; Maxwell H. Bloomfield III, department of history, The Catholic University of America; and Edmund and Dorothy S. Berkeley, Charlottesville, Virginia, respectively.

33. For a critical bibliographical review of relevant printed travelers' accounts see Thomas D. Clark, ed., *Travels in the Old South: A Bibliography*, 2 vols., The American Exploration and Travel Series (Norman: University of Oklahoma Press, 1956), 2:73–165.

34. A relatively obscure foreign commentator who combined BHL's literary and artistic skills was his friend

Liancourt's justly celebrated *Travels* bears the closest affinity to Latrobe's journals in matters of coverage and attitude. The Frenchman arrived in Norfolk just two months after Latrobe and then followed an itinerary which, except for its latter portion, was strikingly similar to Latrobe's. It is unfortunate that these two men failed to encounter each other, for they had much in common and wrote about many of the same places, events, and persons.[35]

Benjamin Henry Latrobe's journals reveal the means by which a highly educated and literate European accommodated himself to a new society and became an American. Latrobe knew a great deal about the United States and the ways of his future countrymen before his departure. His mother, an American herself, had undoubtedly told him much about her youth in Pennsylvania, her immediate family the Antes, and her cousins the Rittenhouses.[36] Given the international composition of the Moravian church, Latrobe most likely had American schoolmates throughout his formal education. His father's home in London was a waystation for Moravian missionaries, ministers, and laymen who were continually traveling from North America and the West Indies to Germany by way of England. Presumably Latrobe had read Moravian historical literature, some of which considered the Brethren's activities in Georgia and in Pennsylvania where his grandfather, Henry Antes, had played such a vital role in

---

Pavel Svin'in (1787–1839), secretary to the Russian consul general in Philadelphia (1811–13). During his twenty months in America, he traveled from Virginia to Maine executing some impressive genre and landscape paintings and recording his observations on the similarities and differences between the two countries. On returning to St. Petersburg, the diplomat published his observations in 1815 under the title *Opyt zhivopisnago pŏteshestŭiia po severnoi Amerike* ("A Picturesque Voyage Through North America"). A number of Svin'in's watercolors, hauntingly similar to BHL's work, were published in Avraham Yarmolinsky, *Picturesque United States of America, 1811, 1812, 1813; Being a Memoir on Paul Svinin, Russian Diplomatic Officer, Artist and Author* (New York: Rudge, 1930). See also Abbott Gleason, "Pavel Svin'in 1787–1839," in Marc Pachter and Frances Wein, eds., *Abroad in America: Visitors to the New Nation, 1776–1914* (Reading, Mass.: Addison-Wesley Publishing Company in association with National Portrait Gallery, Smithsonian Institution, 1976), pp. 12–21.

35. François-Alexandre-Frederic, Duc de La Rochefoucauld-Liancourt (1747–1827), *Travels through the United States of North America, the Country of the Iroquois, and Upper Canada, in the Years 1795, 1796, and 1797*, 2d ed., 4 vols. (London, 1800).

36. Anna Margaretta (Antes) Latrobe had four brothers who survived childhood. Frederick (1730–1801), Revolutionary War hero, was active in state and local politics and later worked with BHL on the Susquehanna River improvement in 1801. William (1731–1810), a gunsmith and local politician in Philadelphia and Northumberland counties, moved in 1795 to the Genesee country in New York. Henry (1736–1820), Revolutionary War veteran, served as sheriff of Northumberland County. John (1740–1811), a jeweller and watchmaker, served for a time as a Moravian missionary in Egypt. After moving to Fulneck, England, he wrote *Observations on the Manners and Customs of the Egyptians, the Overflowing of the Nile and Its Effects; With Remarks on the Plague, and Other Subjects* (London, 1800). BHL to Christian Ignatius Latrobe, 7 March 1808, Latrobe Letterbooks, *PBHL*, microfiche ed., 64/A3; Edwin MacMinn, *On the Frontier with Colonel Antes* (Camden, N.J.: S. Chew & Sons, 1900).

establishing the church; in addition, he knew of the missionary work among the Indians.[37] Latrobe had read both Thomas Cooper's *Some Information Respecting America* (1794) and Thomas Jefferson's *Notes on the State of Virginia* (1785) while in England. If this knowledge helped prepare Latrobe for his new experience, so had his extensive Continental travels, which provided him with a basis for judging the relative sophistication and development of Virginia's society and economy. Latrobe had known in Germany places which were more desolate and backward than most of those he visited in Virginia. All this insured that Latrobe would not be overly patronizing in his attitudes toward Virginia and also suggests why he was neither unduly surprised nor disconcerted by situations or events encountered there.

Latrobe was well received in Virginia, and with the assistance of men such as Bushrod Washington he soon established himself in acceptable social circles. While he counted the Thomas Mann Randolphs of "Tuckahoe" and several other aristocratic families among his friends, he associated for the most part with members of the lesser gentry and the professional and merchant classes of Richmond. Yet while his journal observations on the manners and institutions of his Virginia friends were generally balanced and free of malicious satire, Latrobe was often moved to comment rather caustically on Virginia society. He was amused by the curious speech of Virginians and the ubiquitousness of their use of military titles, and he found fault with the eating habits of his hosts and with the Virginians' propensity for gambling, drinking, and horse racing.

On the subject of slavery it is hard to ascertain Latrobe's true feelings. He intended to send his friend Dr. Giambattista Scandella a statement of his views on slavery in Virginia, but unfortunately this account has never been discovered. While the slavery he observed in Virginia was not the grinding system of the West Indies, whose bitter effects the Moravians attempted to alleviate, Latrobe as a naturally kind and humane man must have found the institution disturbing. Indeed, Latrobe later partly attributed the "rough splendor, and wasteful hospitality" of aristocratic Virginia families to the presence of large slave populations.[38] It must be recognized however that Latrobe was not without that sense of racial superiority common to his class and time. In 1816 he offered to sell the remaining time of his black indentured servant partly

---

37. The Reverend Benjamin Latrobe translated, edited, and wrote a significant portion of this doctrinal and historical literature. The year before BHL's departure, Christian Ignatius Latrobe translated from the German George Henry Loskiel, *History of the Missions of the United Brethren among the Indians in North America* (London, 1794).

38. BHL to William James, 1 August 1812, Latrobe Letterbooks, *PBHL, microfiche ed.*, 101/D4.

because the man did not treat Latrobe's sons with the respect he thought due them.[39]

If the Americanization of Benjamin Henry Latrobe had started long before he stepped aboard the *Eliza* at Gravesend on 25 November 1795, it was completed in Virginia. The process was not totally free of friction, but on balance Latrobe retained his admiration for Americans and their ideals even though his initial enthusiasm was tempered by the experience of building the penitentiary. Extremely proud of his American heritage, he may have actually at first entertained the romantic belief that his mother's birth endowed him automatically with United States citizenship. He had come to stay and happily proclaimed himself an American republican. Years later in 1811, in a dispute with Thomas Moore over "the *prevailing practice* of trusting the execution of public works to *mere travelling Europaean Engineers,*" Latrobe denied the existence of the practice and reaffirmed his nationality with quiet eloquence:

> Your observation applies to me only as far as it is not known that my family for more than 90 years have been settled in Pennsylvania and that altho' I was educated in Europe, on the continent, and for some years practiced my profession in England, I am already an American of the fourth generation. I am therefore a *travelling Engineer* only by having *travelled home.*[40]

2. History and Plan of *The Papers of Benjamin Henry Latrobe*

THE STRUCTURE AND DISPOSITION OF THE LATROBE FAMILY PAPERS

Because of Benjamin Henry Latrobe's historical interests and lifelong involvement with publishing and editorial ventures, he took a serious interest in the preservation, ordering, and use of his personal and professional papers.[1] He once explained the purpose and nature of his journalizing:

> The practice of keeping a regular journal was recommended to me very early in life by my father, merely for the sake of acquiring a habit of writing down my ideas with ease and correctness: for he recommended at the same time, that I should, at the close of every Year, extract all the generally useful facts, and burn the remainder. I have followed his advice at intervals ever since

39. BHL to William Gadsby, 13 September 1816, Latrobe Letterbooks, *PBHL, microfiche ed.,* 133/B13. The servant had been BHL's slave since 1804, but BHL emancipated him at the age of sixteen in 1813 and bound him to serve until he was twenty-eight.

40. BHL to Thomas Moore, 20 January 1811, Mrs. Gamble Latrobe Collection, MdHS, *PBHL, microfiche ed.,* 83/A12.

1. Much of this section of the introduction is taken from material in Edward C. Carter II, "The Papers of Benjamin Henry Latrobe and the Maryland Historical Society, 1885–1971: Nature, Structure, and Means of

I was a boy, both in writing and burning my journals. Since my arrival in America, I have in a great measure altered my plan of a diary into a collection of observations and a record of facts in which my personal interests and actions were not immediately concerned. The great chasms which appear in the collection, are chiefly owing to *personal* activity which so filled up my time as to render it *out of my plan*, to record what was going forward. As Winter approaches, and leisure to look about me returns, it may be well to resume the practice.[2]

He concluded this passage with a line of Latin that translates "Let us therefore proceed to what, we hope, may be happy, favorable, and successful to me and to my children, to whom these books are dedicated!"[3]

Latrobe also kept polygraph copies of letters he wrote from 1803, when he first used the machine he had received from Charles Willson Peale, until a few years before his death in 1820. The polygraph probably passed into his creditors' hands during the Washington bankruptcy proceedings that lasted from December 1817 to January 1818, and with the loss of the copying instrument Latrobe's letterbooks ended. He often had occasion to refer to his letterbooks in professional and financial matters.

During the early period of his American career Latrobe repeatedly claimed that, because he possessed no professional books, it was necessary for him to rely on memory alone; but in fact he brought a small technical sketchbook from England, the pages of which were filled with his architectural schemes, drawings of classical orders, and quotations from Smeaton's writings which he utilized during that period. He also employed his American sketchbooks in various ways. Certain drawings, watercolors, and accompanying observations from those sketchbooks served as the bases of scientific papers which Latrobe presented to the American Philosophical Society and which were later published in the *Transactions*. On another occasion Latrobe drew on a journal entry dealing with the descendants of Pocahontas in giving a talk to the society. His hopes for publication focused mainly on his architectural and engineering drawings—plans, elevations, and perspectives—some of which were shown in the Pennsylvania Academy of the Fine Arts exhibitions of 1811, 1812, and 1818. Unfortunately, nothing came of several attempts to produce in England a handsome edition

---

Acquisition," *Maryland Historical Magazine* 66 (1971): 436–55 and his introduction to *The Guide and Index to the Microfiche Edition of The Papers of Benjamin Henry Latrobe*, ed. Carter and Thomas E. Jeffrey (Clifton, N.J.: James T. White & Company, 1976).

2. Latrobe Journals, 17 September 1799, *PBHL, microfiche ed.*, 12/C9.

3. *Quod felix ergo, faustum, atque secundum sit, mihi, et, liberis meis, quibus hi, dicati sunt libelli, pergamus!*

of engravings of his most notable work. If realized, this venture might have spared his reputation the near anonymity which clothed it in his native country until the 1950s. In 1817 Latrobe had solicited from his friend Robert Goodloe Harper a written legal opinion that his professional books, being analogous to a mechanic's tools and therefore instruments of his trade, were protected from seizure and sale. At the same time, he was careful to pack up his papers "and what I need not surrender under our Law" in preparation for the family's removal to Baltimore.[4] Latrobe's journals, letterbooks, sketchbooks, and many of his architectural and engineering drawings were then removed to New Orleans, where they were perhaps subject to sequestration when the architect died there penniless. They finally were returned to Baltimore when Latrobe's widow and children settled in that city under the generous protection of their old family friend, Robert Goodloe Harper.

For over a century and a half the Latrobes were faithful and intelligent custodians of these papers. That the materials have remained in such fine condition is a tribute to the care with which Latrobe and his descendants kept them. Although it is impossible to describe with certainty the structure and scope of the papers in Latrobe's possession at his death, we believe that the greater part were preserved and have passed from the family's hands into the care of the institutions where they now reside. The heart of this corpus was acquired by the Maryland Historical Society in 1960, when it purchased fourteen sketchbooks containing 310 watercolors and sketches dating from Latrobe's departure from England in November 1795 until his death a quarter of a century later; thirteen small journals; and nineteen bound volumes of letterbooks for the years 1803 through 1817, which contain more than 5,000 letters to a broad spectrum of individuals, including such notables as Latrobe's great patron Thomas Jefferson, James Madison, Dolley Madison, Aaron Burr, Albert Gallatin, Robert Fulton, Robert Mills, and Archbishop John Carroll. This was only a late chapter in the history of family donations and divestitures that began in 1885, when Charles H. Latrobe (1834–1903), a son of Benjamin Henry Latrobe, Jr. (1806–78), presented the Maryland Historical Society with the Susquehanna River Survey Map. Two years later, John H. B. Latrobe (1803–91), who had received a larger share of the papers than his younger brother Benjamin, Jr., gave a bound folio volume of drawings and plans of the Philadelphia Waterworks and the Bank of Pennsylvania,[5] together with a number of separate Second Bank of the United States drawings, to the Historical Society of Pennsylvania. Charles H. Latrobe then contributed five of

---

4. BHL to Robert Goodloe Harper, 27 November, 10 and 19 December 1817, Mrs. Gamble Latrobe Collection, MdHS, *PBHL, microfiche ed.*, 234/D8, 234/E4, 235/A1.

5. BHL inscribed the volume to his elder brother, Christian Ignatius Latrobe.

his grandfather's favorite architectural watercolor perspectives to the Maryland Historical Society in 1897. Eight additional journals were donated to the Society in 1918 and 1927 by John E. Semmes, Sr., and his family. Semmes had been both a law partner and the biographer of John H. B. Latrobe, from whom he apparently received the journals as a gift. Ferdinand C. Latrobe II (1889–1944), a grandson of John H. B. Latrobe, presented thirty-three Baltimore Cathedral drawings to the Archdiocese of Baltimore in about 1924. A magnificent gift to the nation was made in 1945, when Captain William Claiborne Latrobe, USN, Ret., a great-great-grandson of the architect, gave the Library of Congress three bound volumes of Latrobe's early architectural designs.[6] Fifteen years later the Maryland Historical Society received its aforementioned major collection from Mrs. Ferdinand C. Latrobe II, and in 1961 the Society rounded out its Latrobe holdings by purchasing the remainder of Charles H. Latrobe's share of the papers from Mrs. Gamble Latrobe, the widow of Latrobe's great-great-grandson.

Three characteristics of these collections require comment. First, there are very few letters addressed to Latrobe; most of the incoming correspondence is presumed to have been lost or discarded during his numerous changes of residence over the years. But because Latrobe often summarized in his letters the contents of his correspondents' previous communications, the letterbooks themselves provide a close approximation of his incoming correspondence.

Second, there are more missing items among the series of journals than among either the letterbooks or sketchbooks. Latrobe's own numbering system and internal evidence indicate that for the Virginia years seven of sixteen journals and one of two known journal appendixes are missing, and for the period 1818–20 one of eight manuscript journals is missing. No such estimate is possible for the years 1799 to 1818, as Latrobe, under the increasing press of work, journalized on an irregular basis and used several confusing serial systems.

Third, more than half the extant architectural and engineering drawings were clearly intended for presentation to particular individuals or groups. These presentation drawings served as gifts for friends and family members, progress reports to official bodies, promotional material for prospective clients, and a basis for possible future publication. The actual working drawings that remain raise valuable technical questions and are probably better guides to how a project looked when it was constructed than are Latrobe's presentation drawings. The latter, however, were of high

6. These were "Designs of Buildings Erected or Proposed to be Built in Virginia" (1796–99); plans for the Richmond theater, assembly rooms, and hotel complex (December 1798–January 1799); and the New York City Hall (1802).

artistic quality, ably demonstrating the overall concept of the specific work, and thus they were greatly valued and carefully preserved by their recipients.

PREVIOUS PUBLICATION AND SCHOLARSHIP

Writing from Washington on 3 April 1811, Latrobe informed his good friend Thomas Parker of Philadelphia, "I am employing my leisure in preparing for a publication of my works—a publication which I mean to be a useful, *practical*, book, as well as a showy thing on the shelf of a Library."[7] This project must have been taking shape in his mind for a number of years, considering that some of the pre-1800 Virginia architectural drawings were actually prepared for engraving. By 1816 Latrobe had completed the text of the proposed volume, for he requested Eric Bollman to negotiate with J. Taylor, the London publisher, promising to send him the following year two perspectives for inclusion as colorplates. Evidently nothing came of this, for just prior to his death Latrobe was in contact with Rudolph Ackermann, the famous art entrepreneur and publisher of the *Repository*, on the same matter. He intended to send copies of designs for the Bank of Pennsylvania, the Philadelphia Waterworks, the Centre Square Engine House, the U. S. House of Representatives, the Baltimore Cathedral, and the Baltimore Exchange. Ackermann's interest did not decline even after Latrobe's death. In vain he urged Mary Elizabeth Latrobe to send to London any of the drawings so that he might have them engraved, in hopes of producing "a work which would have given your dear husband pleasure."[8]

Copies of a few of Latrobe's watercolors were published shortly thereafter by John H. B. Latrobe, who had resigned from West Point in 1821 when he was a fourth-year man, entered the law office of Robert Goodloe Harper, and began contributing to the support of his family as best he could. Writing with skill and facility, he turned out biographies, novelettes, childrens' stories, and verse. He had considerable talents as a watercolorist and architectural draftsman and illustrated a number of books for Fielding Lucas, Jr., once in exchange for credit on his law-book account. Under the pseudonym Eric von Blon, he produced one of the first American drawing books, Lucas's *Progressive Drawing Book* (1827–28), later claiming to have drawn "all that it contains."[9] Actually, he copied at least eight of his father's watercolors for inclusion

---

7. BHL to Thomas Parker, 3 April 1811, Latrobe Letterbooks, *PBHL, microfiche ed.*, 85/A6.

8. BHL to Eric Bollman, 11 May 1816, Latrobe Letterbooks, *PBHL, microfiche ed.*, 130/C11; "Memoir of Benjamin Henry La Trobe," (Ackermann's) *Repository of the Arts*, 2d ser. 11 (1 January 1821): 31–32; Ackermann's request was conveyed by Christian Ignatius Latrobe to Mary Elizabeth Latrobe, 5 December 1820, Mrs. Gamble Latrobe Collection, MdHS.

9. John E. Semmes, *John H. B. Latrobe and His Times, 1803–1891* (Baltimore: Norman, Remington Co., 1917), p. 104. Carl W. Drepperd has stated about this work, "I regard it as the keystone of any collection of American

in this volume. John H. B. Latrobe became a vigorous promoter of his father's great achievements and ideas. Indeed, as Paul F. Norton pointed out in his invaluable critical bibliography of 1972, serious Latrobe scholarship started in the 1870s with, and was accelerated by, the younger Latrobe's articles, public addresses, and the memoir of his father's life that was used as an introduction to *The Journal of Latrobe* in 1905.[10]

This ill-executed collection of journal selections, published by D. Appleton and Company, passed for nearly half a century as the only example of Latrobe's published writings. A good deal of mystery surrounds the publication of this book; the editor's name is absent from the title page and the inclusion as an introduction of an essay written thirty years earlier by John H. B. Latrobe led many to believe that the entire effort was his handiwork. The publisher could not enlighten us concerning its editorship. There is a family tradition that a journalist gained access to the papers in the possession of Mayor Ferdinand C. Latrobe through the good offices of his two impressionable daughters, made his selections from among the journals and watercolors, and then presented them to the world as *The Journal of Latrobe*. A detailed study has shown that all the literary and illustrative elements—including the introduction itself—were taken from larger parts of the collection then in Mayor Ferdinand C. Latrobe's care.[11] The whole undertaking was haphazardly structured and unscholarly in nature. Several topical chapters lacked any chronological integrity; journal entries for different days were run together, omissions were not editorially indicated, and on occasion, chapter titles were irrelevant or misleading.

Some positive developments were unfolding at the same time however. Glenn Brown's *History of the United States Capitol* (Washington, D.C., 1900–03) contained many of Latrobe's architectural drawings. On the death of his mother, Ferdinand C. Latrobe II received his father's share of the papers, and thus finding his true métier, set to work organizing them, calendaring and transcribing the letterbooks, studying and photographing the sketchbooks, and in time allowing a few scholars limited access to the collection. Most important, he and his wife understood that their family

---

drawing books because it is so wholly and completely American." Drawn by a native, Latrobe, and colored by a native, Anna Claypoole Peale, "the major plates of scenery are American as American can be." Drepperd, *American Drawing Books* (New York: The New York Public Library, 1946), p. 8.

10. See Norton, comp., "Benjamin Henry Latrobe," *Papers of the American Association of Architectural Bibliographers* 9 (1972): 51–84.

11. The introduction was taken directly from John H. B. Latrobe's "Memoir of Benjamin Henry Latrobe, 1st" that exists in manuscript in the Latrobe Family Journal, a large ledger into which have been copied obituaries, genealogies, and a variety of family observations. The editor mistakenly included two New Orleans scenes by John H. B. Latrobe among the illustrations.

had a unique and priceless inheritance which had to be preserved intact if it were to promote Latrobe scholarship in the future. But by far the most critical factor in the progress of Latrobe scholarship was the birth of professional art history in America at the time of World War I.

Fiske Kimball, perhaps the first great American-born architectural historian, throughout his life pursued a passion for Jefferson, Monticello, and Charlottesville. His research into Jefferson's architecture led him in turn to a consideration of Latrobe's work in a series of ground-breaking articles starting in 1917. With them the flow of Latrobe-related scholarship began, and by 1950 approximately sixty-five articles had been published. Prominent were those by Talbot Hamlin, whose masterful study of the Greek Revival style in America had delineated Latrobe's dominant role in its establishment and evolution. Hamlin next undertook a full-scale study of the man and his works that culminated in the Pulitzer Prize-winning biography, *Benjamin Henry Latrobe* (New York, 1955). Not only had Hamlin been allowed to use the Ferdinand C. Latrobe II family papers, but he had available the recently published New Orleans journals which Samuel Wilson, Jr., had edited with modern scholarly exactitude and unusual imagination in 1951.[12] These two books, as Paul F. Norton pointed out in his Latrobe bibliography, "appear to have stimulated the writing of an enormous number of reviews and articles": more than fifty in the 1950s and at least thirty-five articles in the following decade.[13] Beginning with his 1952 Princeton dissertation, "Latrobe, Jefferson and the National Capitol," Norton himself has emerged preeminent among the second generation of Latrobe scholars.

In a real sense, however, the work of Hamlin and Norton brought the initial phase of Latrobe scholarship to its conclusion. By the 1960s historians were questioning the biographical approach as an instrument for probing the processes of American cultural, economic, and social change. Even before historians of technology came to the fore, a number of scholars complained justifiably of the excessive attention paid to Latrobe's influence as an architect at the expense of his role as an engineer. The next task was evident. As Louise Hall wrote in her perceptive review of Hamlin's biography, "Nothing but a full edition of the multitude of papers . . . can enable scholars to evaluate for themselves Latrobe's first twenty-two American years in the way that Samuel Wilson, Jr., made possible for the final two years."[14]

---

12. *Impressions Respecting New Orleans by Benjamin Henry Boneval Latrobe: Diary and Sketches, 1818–1820*, edited with an introduction and notes by Samuel Wilson, Jr. (New York: Columbia University Press, 1951).

13. Norton, "Benjamin Henry Latrobe," p. 54.

14. *Mississippi Valley Historical Review* 42 (1955–56): 744–46.

THE PRESENT PROJECT

The Maryland Historical Society acquired the collections of Mrs. Ferdinand C. Latrobe II and Mrs. Gamble Latrobe with publication firmly in mind, but several years of repair and restoration were needed first. The letterbooks were microfilmed for security, then repaired, deacidified, laminated, and rebound; the journals were laminated; the drawings and watercolors were photographed in color. Throughout the 1960s, four individuals formulated and promoted the idea of an edition of Benjamin Henry Latrobe's papers: two directors of the Society, James W. Foster and Harold R. Manakee, and two chairmen of the Society's Publications Committee, Charles A. Barker of The Johns Hopkins University and Rhoda M. Dorsey of Goucher College. When the long and exacting repair and restoration process was finished in 1969, the Publications Committee began a search for a scholar to direct the project. Edward C. Carter II was appointed editor in chief on 1 January 1970 and the office of *The Papers of Benjamin Henry Latrobe* was opened formally on 1 October of that year.

The first year was devoted to studying the Society's various Latrobe collections, conferring with several scholars and other editors on how best to proceed, assembling an editorial board, negotiating with potential publishers, seeking funding, creating a documentary control system, and starting our search for copies of Latrobe documents in other repositories throughout the United States and in Europe and Australia. News of the project's existence spread rapidly, encouraging both scholarly and financial support. The American Philosophical Society and the National Endowment for the Humanities made major grants in 1971 to support our work. These were followed by many such generous acts by numerous individuals, foundations, and sister institutions—all of which are gratefully acknowledged below. The same year Chester Kerr, director of Yale University Press, informed the Maryland Historical Society that the Press, after a thorough study of our collection and of our publication plans, wished to publish the selective printed edition of *The Papers of Benjamin Henry Latrobe*. That felicitous offer was eagerly accepted, thus beginning a working relationship between our two organizations that has been always characterized by a common devotion to high professional and artistic standards, sympathetic cooperation, and good fellowship.

By August 1971 the editor in chief had made two major decisions that were to determine the project's direction and the nature and scope of its publications program. The first was to publish as soon as possible a complete microform edition with a comprehensive guide and index containing all the Maryland Historical Society's Latrobe holdings together with the Latrobe documents from the repositories and private collections that might be gathered during our collection and planning phase just getting under way. The editor in chief, whose earlier research had been greatly facilitated by the microfilm edition of *The Adams Papers*, felt strongly that Latrobe's complete manuscript and published works, plus a sophisticated finding aid, should be made available to historians and other students of American life as quickly as possible. Such an action was doubly attractive because it allowed us to plan a selective printed edition of from ten to twelve volumes.

The second resolve was to start work on the microform edition and four printed volumes simultaneously. This necessitated a rapid buildup of our staff through the appointments of a microfiche editor, an assistant editor for architectural history, and an assistant editor for technology. Also it was evident that because of the unusual scope of Latrobe's professional abilities and intellectual and artistic interests, *The Papers of Benjamin Henry Latrobe* would require the services of a number of consultants. The search for personnel and the considerable funds needed to carry out this program began immediately.

The collection and planning phase of our work continued for two years until 1 September 1973. Letters of inquiry were sent to all possible holders of Latrobe material; in cases where the collections were large and complex, our staff members visited the repository. Arrangements were made with the major repositories for duplication and collection of their Latrobe materials. To locate the more elusive items, we placed advertisements in bibliographers' and book magazines, the major historical journals, and selected state and local historical publications. Our search uncovered more than 2,200 manuscripts, published works, drawings, and related material. A few minor Latrobe items may subsequently come to light, but we are certain that no large group of documents remains undiscovered. Preliminary editorial work proceeded concurrently with the collection of outside documents. All Latrobe's journals and sketchbook notes (approximately 1,100 pages of manuscript) were transcribed.

With the collection phase nearly completed, we turned our attention to the microform edition of *The Papers of Benjamin Henry Latrobe*. During the fall of 1973, negotiations were conducted with several microform companies and the comparative advantages of microfilm and microfiche formats were examined. After extensive study, we decided that our collection could best be reproduced on microfiche. James T. White & Company of Clifton, New Jersey, became our publisher and selected Princeton Datafilm to film our collection in October 1974. The microfiche edition of *The Papers of Benjamin Henry Latrobe*, together with *The Guide and Index*, was published in 1976.

The microfiche edition represents the first attempt ever made to film a large and complex collection of primary sources on microfiche. Less bulky and cumbersome than microfilm, the fiche format allows immediate access to each document. The microfiche edition contains 315 fiche cards with approximately 12,700 exposures. It was filmed in five series: Journals, Letterbooks, Manuscript Documents and Published Works, Sketchbooks, and Architectural and Engineering Drawings. Documents in the first three series appear in chronological order. The sketchbooks were filmed in their original sequence, with a catalog containing a detailed description of each sketch. The architectural and engineering drawings are grouped in geographical order by project and are preceded by a table of contents. A target card indicates the general description, date, size, technique, and repository of each drawing. The guide itself describes the history and nature of our collection, the types of materials available, and the arrangement of the microfiche itself. The comprehensive index provides the reader with dual access, by correspondent and by project, to the documents on the microfiche, with numerous cross references. *The Guide and Index* is not only a useful research tool when used in conjunction with the microfiche but constitutes a valuable bibliographic source in its own right.

Meanwhile editorial work was proceeding on four volumes of the printed edition: the Virginia journals in two volumes, the architectural drawings, and the engineering drawings. When the Virginia journals were sent to Yale Press in February 1976, the staff immediately began editing the final volume of post-1798 journals.

THE OVERALL PLAN OF THE EDITION

This edition of *The Papers of Benjamin Henry Latrobe* is both selective and interpretive. While these volumes focus on Latrobe's life and role as the leading architect and engineer of the young republic, we have no wish to become hagiographers. Latrobe's papers are broad gauged, and therein lies much of their great historical value. Materials are selected not only because they illuminate the development of American architecture and engineering, but also because they are crucial to our understanding of, among other things, the transfer of technology from Europe to America and its diffusion within the United States, the rise of professionalism in general during the early nineteenth century, the relationship between private interest and governmental policy particularly as manifested in internal improvements, and the clash between differing races and national cultures evoked so strikingly by Latrobe in his descriptions of New Orleans. His sketchbooks, maps, and other drawings are among the finest existing pictorial representations of early American towns, landscapes, and everyday life. Our selection is based on their uniqueness as social and historical documents and in acknowledgment of their merit as works of art.

Series I contains all the Latrobe journals, or memorandum books, and will be published in three volumes. The journals themselves are supplemented with relevant sketchbook materials, literary and visual, and occasionally with individual letters which strengthen the sense of chronology. The first two volumes contain journals for the period 1795 to 1798; the third volume of the series comprises journals written sporadically between 1799 and 1818 and those Latrobe wrote regularly during the last two years of his life.

Series II will be devoted to those architectural and engineering drawings executed by Latrobe or under his direction. The format of these two volumes will be similar in that each will contain an introductory essay followed by a critical catalog of Latrobe's extant drawings organized by categories. However, each will receive a different emphasis from its editor. The engineering drawings volume opens with a major study of Latrobe the engineer, then turns to the historical study and annotation of the Susquehanna River Survey Map, and concludes with the critical description of about eighty technological drawings and plans. On the other hand, the introductory essay of the architectural drawings volume is shorter and more limited whereas the descriptive catalog is much longer, treating almost 200 perspective drawings, elevations, sections, and plans. Also included are chronologies and bibliographies of Latrobe's major structures, among them the Virginia State Penitentiary, the Bank of Pennsylvania, the Baltimore Roman Catholic Cathedral, and the U. S. Capitol.

Series III will consist of a single folio volume containing selected examples from Latrobe's sketchbooks. It will also include Latrobe's accompanying text to his sketches and watercolors. The format of this volume will conform as closely as possible to that of the original manuscripts. A full catalog of the complete series of sketchbooks will be included as an appendix; the accompanying commentary will be limited to a brief biographical sketch and an essay evaluating Latrobe as a watercolorist.

Series IV will consist of four to six volumes of correspondence and miscellaneous papers. It is premature to lay down any definitive principles of selection, but the nature of extant material dictates that letters written by Latrobe will be more numerous than those addressed to him. Doubtless Latrobe's career as surveyor of the public buildings and architect of the U. S. Capitol, his relationship with Jefferson, and his role in the creation of the American technological community will be illuminated in these volumes. The editors will include annotated examples of Latrobe's scientific papers, technical reports, newspaper and journal articles, and essays that significantly enlarge our comprehension of his intellectual and professional achievements.

3. The Virginia Journals

RATIONALE AND STRUCTURE

On first surveying Latrobe's papers, the editors were struck by the close interrelationship between the early journals, or as they were inscribed, memorandum books, and other contemporary elements of the collection. Indeed, the journals and sketchbooks are extensions of each other, containing numerous cross-references and indicating in various ways that Latrobe himself conceived of the latter as illustrating the former.[1] The "Essay on Landscape" is tied to both; it supplements the journal description of Virginia life, expands topographical knowledge, and as an elementary guide to watercolor painting provides special insights into those techniques Latrobe so skillfully exercised in the sketchbooks themselves. We have entitled these volumes *The Virginia Journals of Benjamin Henry Latrobe* because journal materials—the account of the Atlantic voyage, nine memorandum books, and one appendix—account for more than four-fifths of all Latrobe's text in the volumes. Related literary categories, the "Essay on Landscape," sketchbook commentary or descriptions, and nonjournal correspondence comprise the remainder and have been set off from the journal texts by ornaments and a descriptive heading. We have also included reproductions of Latrobe's visual commentary from the journals, sketchbooks, and the "Essay on Landscape": seventy-five pen-and-ink journal and "Essay" drawings, fifty-eight black-and-white illustrations of relevant sketchbook and "Essay" drawings and watercolors, and twenty-five colorplates of watercolors. A determined effort has been made to integrate the text and illustrations so that most black-and-white illustrations appear near the passages they elucidate or which describe them.

From his departure from England in 1795 to his arrival in Philadelphia in 1798, Latrobe apparently completed sixteen journals and two journal appendixes. Unfortunately only ten of these survive in manuscript form; one—the account of the Atlantic voyage—has been reconstituted from typed transcriptions which were based on the original manuscript, now lost or destroyed. In three of the ten manuscript journals comprising the Virginia journals Latrobe provided an index, either of a few major categories or a more comprehensive alphabetical listing. We have elected not to publish these, as the volumes will carry our own complete index of the entire contents. As Latrobe numbered his Virginia journals sequentially, it is possible to reconstruct the series, noting which journals are missing. References in extant journals confirm the previous existence of the missing journals, and in some cases the partial contents as well. The following chart attempts such a reconstruction; the dates of the missing journals are approximations.

---

1. The ten manuscript journals were composed in writing books which range in size from $7\frac{7}{8}$ x $5\frac{1}{4}$ in. (19.9 x 13.3 cm.) to 9 x $7\frac{3}{8}$ in. (22.8 x 18.6 cm.), with $7\frac{3}{4}$ x $6\frac{3}{8}$ in. (19.8 x 16.3 cm.) being the most common size. Eight of the ten surviving manuscripts have covers of marbled paper, and vary in length from twenty-seven to ninety-one pages. The two other journals have nonmarbled paper covers and are seventy-five and eighty-two pages long.

The four sketchbooks have cover sizes which vary from $7\frac{3}{16}$ x $10\frac{7}{16}$ in. (18.3 x 26.6 cm.) to $9\frac{5}{16}$ x 7 in. (23.7 x 17.8 cm.). Page size is slightly smaller. All the sketchbooks have paper boards covered with marbled paper, and are bound in three-quarter leather.

LATROBE'S JOURNALS, 1795–1798

BHL's Volumes	Chapter in these volumes	Dates	Subject
[I]	1 [exists only in transcription]	25 Nov 1795–8 Mar 1796	Atlantic Voyage
II	2	23 Mar–31 May 1796	Norfolk and Richmond
III	2–3	10 June–24 July 1796	Virginia
IV	4	3 Aug–26 Aug 1796	Virginia
[V]	Missing		
[VI]	Missing	27 Aug 1796–12 Apr 1797	[blue wasps and geology]
[VII]	Missing		
VIII	5–6	13 Apr–6 Aug 1797	Virginia
VIII (Appendix)	5	10 June–28 June 1797	Dismal Swamp
IX	6	6 Aug–5 Sept 1797	Virginia
X	7	20 Sept–19 Oct 1797	Virginia
XI	8–9	9 Nov 1797–26 Feb 1798 and draft of letter to Ferdinando Fairfax, 28 May 1798	Virginia
[XII]	Missing		[geology, Washington, D.C., and Philadelphia]
[XIII]	Missing	27 Feb–18 Apr 1798	
XIV	9	19 Apr–4 May 1798	Virginia
[XIV Appendix]	Missing	c. 4 May 1798	[geology]
[XV]	Missing	5 May–23 Sept 1798	
XVI	10	24 Sept–29 Nov 1798	Richmond

The "Essay on Landscape," composed for Latrobe's friend Susan Catharine Spotswood (1774–1854) of Virginia, while not a journal in the usual sense, contained important literary impressions of Virginia, some of which were expansions or replications of earlier journal comments. Latrobe wrote the greater part of the "Essay" in Virginia, but circumstances caused him to delay its completion until his arrival in Philadelphia.

Another type of literary material that has been included is Latrobe's sketchbook commentary or descriptions. These generally were written on the verso of a sketch or watercolor and refer to the drawing on the opposite recto. When a pertinent description exists for an illustration appearing in these volumes, it either is inserted at an appropriate place in the text or accompanies the illustration as part of the caption, in both cases preceded by the heading "From the Sketchbooks."

The final literary genre incorporated into *The Virginia Journals of Benjamin Henry Latrobe* is correspondence. Three types of letters are included: drafts or copies of letters which Latrobe wrote in the journals, letters referred to by Latrobe in the journals, and those inserted by the editors to enhance the sense of continuity, particularly for periods where journals are missing. In the first category are letters written to Colonel Thomas Blackburn in April 1796 which Latrobe copied into a journal when he visited Rippon Lodge, Blackburn's home, three months later. Next are letters merely referred to in the journals. On 26 January and 24 February 1798 he noted: "wrote to Dr. [Giambattista] Scandella." Both letters to the famed Italian *philosophe*, whose friendship Latrobe valued so highly, have been printed immediately following those journal entries. A letter from Latrobe to Governor James Wood regarding the Richmond Penitentiary was added by the editors to narrow the gap created by missing journals between August 1796 and April 1797. Similarly, several letters appear when the journals fail to illuminate certain significant events in Latrobe's Virginia career. For example, between the entries of 2 October and 30 October 1798, the editors have placed another letter to Governor Wood describing a minor labor riot at the penitentiary which sheds light on Virginia artisans and the architect's relations with his employees.

The following principles apply to our selection of Latrobe's sketches and watercolors in these volumes. With a few minor exceptions, every journal and "Essay on Landscape" drawing appears as a black-and-white illustration. Each sketchbook item that is directly referred to in the journals has been included, as well as a number of sketches and watercolors that provide a significant background to the text. Certain watercolors of unusual beauty or historical importance have been reproduced in separate color signatures and are tied to their related text by appropriate cross-references.

The editors' principal textual challenge was the reconstitution of the account of Latrobe's Atlantic voyage, which was closely related to the extant sketchbooks for the corresponding time span, November 1795 to March 1796. We have come to believe that the missing journal was still in the possession of the family in the 1890s and shortly thereafter was either destroyed or lost. This theory, which will be developed below, contradicts Talbot Hamlin's earlier assumption concerning the document's fate. In a footnote he speculated that:

> Latrobe's journal of his voyage to America exists in transcript only, in two versions, one slightly more extensive than the other. These two transcripts were in the hands of Gamble and Osmun Latrobe when they were collated and re-transcribed by Ferdinand C. Latrobe II. . . . It is my surmise that the original

was brought to this country by Charles Joseph Latrobe, Christian's son, the famous traveler and author; that it was transcribed during his visit here in 1832 and was taken back with him when he left the country. If the original still exists, it very probably is in Australia, where Charles spent many years; he was Lieutenant Governor of the state of Victoria from 1851 to 1854.[2]

The first two typed transcriptions were located and used in editing our account of Latrobe's Atlantic voyage; however, Ferdinand C. Latrobe II's version has not been found. Doubtlessly, Hamlin believed that Latrobe, on his arrival in Virginia, sent the manuscript journal to his elder brother in England, basing his assumption on three factors: the epistolary nature of the early portion of the journal, an editorial comment by John H. B. Latrobe at the conclusion of the transcriptions ("This letter was written to my father's eldest brother"), and the fact that the first Virginia memorandum book commenced with the salutation "My dear Brother." But no mention of either Benjamin's voyage or the journal is to be found in Christian Ignatius Latrobe's surviving letters to his younger brother, John Frederick, although there are numerous other references to the architect and his family. Of greater significance is the fact that Charles Joseph Latrobe became fast friends with Latrobe's widow and children during his American sojourn, and for over a decade conducted an extensive and at times intimate correspondence with his Baltimore relations that touched on a wide range of family matters in addition to his travels and his literary aspirations and achievements. Charles Joseph's letters concerning his Baltimore experiences are detailed and nostalgic, but never once does he allude to the journal, its transcription, or to its author, his uncle Benjamin Henry Latrobe. Nor has an extensive search produced the purported manuscript transcription from which the two typed transcriptions might have been made. The editors made a line-by-line comparative analysis of the two transcriptions formerly in the possession of Osmun and Gamble Latrobe, compared each of these with the corresponding sketchbooks and the succeeding manuscript journals as to style, form, and content, reviewed relevant correspondence for hints concerning the provenance of these transcriptions, and searched the transcriptions themselves for significant internal evidence. Our considered opinion is that the history of Latrobe's Atlantic voyage journal runs along the following lines.

John H. B. Latrobe was well acquainted with his father's journals, on occasion copying accurately long passages and reading lengthy selections from them to the members of the Maryland Historical Society.[3] Sometime in the 1880s he began copy-

2. Hamlin, *Latrobe*, p. 54n. Ferdinand C. Latrobe II probably helped shape Hamlin's speculation.

3. Maryland Historical Society Minutes, 1 June 1871, 8 December 1873, 14 June 1875, and 13 April 1891, MS 2008, MdHS.

ing the Atlantic voyage journal in longhand perhaps because, unlike those that survived, it was in fragile condition. As he transcribed, he edited the manuscript—spelling out dates and months, inverting word order and attempting in other ways to modernize passages, excluding several statements he judged bawdy or irreverent, and inserting the editorial comment mentioned above. In 1889 John H. B. Latrobe concluded the transcription of the journal proper with the following notation:

> The diary ends here and the only evidence I have of the termination of the voyage is that afforded by the indorsement of the manuscript book, that this is the "Journal of a voyage from London to Virginia from November 25th 1795 to March 20th 1796." Of the events of the days between March 9th and March 20th I have no record.
>
> At page 27 of the sketch book there is a drawing of the condition of the table equipage on board the Eliza with a description that seems so germane to the history of the voyage, that I copy both; and if the drawing wants the skill of the original, it must be remembered that the copiest is in his 86th year, when he makes it.[4]

A typewritten copy of the transcription was then prepared that contained a number of errors resulting from the typist's unfamiliarity with nautical terminology and inability to decipher certain words in John H. B. Latrobe's difficult hand. We have designated this version as AJT 1 (Atlantic Journal Transcription One). Nothing more is known of its provenance until it was borrowed by Ferdinand C. Latrobe II from his cousin Osmun in 1932.

The manuscript journal itself evidently was still in existence in 1893, for in April of that year Charles H. Latrobe wrote:

> My Grandfather was four months in crossing the Ocean in an American Sailing Vessel, the voyage was tempestuous, the vessel ill supplied with comforts, and the Captain a brute; all of which, is admirably set forth in the journal now in the possession of Uncle John's family.[5]

Sometime during the 1890s, Charles H. Latrobe decided he wanted a copy for his

---

4. See PLATE 7 in this book for BHL's watercolor. John H. B. Latrobe's copy is lost, but his exact transcription of the sketchbook description brings the manuscript to an end.

5. Charles H. Latrobe, "Sketch of the Latrobe Family," April 1893, Richard Onderdonk Collection, Malvern, Pa.

personal enjoyment, borrowed the original manuscript, and engaged a professional typist who produced a skillful transcription marred only by a few misspelled personal and place names. AJT 2 conformed far more closely to the 1796 Virginia journals' date entries, style, spelling, and use of eighteenth-century language than did its predecessor, AJT 1. Also, it was slightly longer than the earlier version and contained more exact sketchbook page references and Latrobe's previously deleted earthy statements. Following modern editorial practice, the transcriber left a square space in the typescript of the 5 February 1796 entry for a drawing of a Portuguese man-of-war described in the text. This is further evidence that the typist worked from the original journal; interestingly, there is no such corresponding space in AJT 1. Evidently Charles thought there existed a separate portion of the journal recording the last difficult days of the voyage from the final entry, of 8 March 1796, until the safe arrival of the Eliza at Norfolk. AJT 2 ended abruptly merely with the date 9 March 1796, below which the following handwritten inscription was later added:

> I have been unable to find the conclusion of this interesting and graphic journal. He landed however at Norfolk I think about March 15?, 1796. C. H. Latrobe 189[..].

We do not believe the final date with the absent last figure refers to the inscription itself, for surely Charles H. Latrobe knew the year in which he wrote it. A better guess is that just prior to his death, while reading through AJT 2, he entered the partial date to record when the transcription was completed or when the unsuccessful search was undertaken. Not recalling the exact year but intending to verify it from another source, he left the space blank. Thus we believe that AJT 2 was transcribed sometime between 1893 and 1899.

By the turn of the century Benjamin Henry Latrobe's Atlantic voyage journal had vanished and even the two transcriptions faded from view for over thirty years. It is inconceivable that the anonymous editor who in 1905 produced *The Journal of Latrobe* would not have included some account of the voyage if either the manuscript or a transcription had been among the major cache of journals, letterbooks, and sketchbooks he consulted at Mayor Ferdinand C. Latrobe's home. It was the poor quality of this work which helped to foster Ferdinand C. Latrobe II's determination to preserve and ultimately publish the family's papers. Ferdinand borrowed AJT 1 on 3 March 1932 from Osmun Latrobe, who knew nothing of its provenance.[6] Ferdinand

6. Typed notation at the top of AJT 1: "A Typewritten copy of [the?] journal was loaned to me by Osmun. March 3, 1932. He had no idea where he obtained it."

made his own copy, designated AJT 3, eliminating only *st*, *d*, and *th* after numerals in dates. In due course, AJT 1 and other of Osmun's documents were given to the Library of Congress, where we discovered them during our collection phase. Meanwhile Gamble Latrobe, a grandson of Charles H. Latrobe, had inherited AJT 2 and made it available to Ferdinand about 1938, so that he could produce his now missing collated transcription.

For the reasons advanced above, the editors believe that AJT 2 was nearly an exact reproduction of the manuscript journal itself. Thus when it came to preparing our own version of Latrobe's account of his Atlantic voyage we employed AJT 2 as our basic document. We carefully compared both AJT 1 and AJT 3 with Charles H. Latrobe's transcription, making those few silent changes that afforded a more plausible reading.

To avoid burdening Latrobe's engaging narrative with additional annotation elucidating these textual alternations, we have written this lengthy commentary. All of our working notes and the various transcriptions mentioned are available at *The Papers of Benjamin Henry Latrobe* for inspection by those who might care to inquire further into our editorial procedures.

4. General Editorial Method

Realizing that each of the four series of volumes which constitute *The Papers of Benjamin Henry Latrobe* demands its own specific set of editorial rules and that it would be impossible to foresee every textual problem that may arise, we have chosen not to set forth here comprehensive rules to be applied to all volumes. Rather, we present the general editorial principles of the project and the specific textual rules that apply to these two volumes of the Latrobe Papers.

The purpose of this edition is to place before the general reader and scholar selected works of Benjamin Henry Latrobe in a clear and comprehensive fashion so that both may study and enjoy the genius of his artistic, literary, and technological achievements. Like the editors of those esteemed editorial projects which have preceded ours—*The Papers of Benjamin Franklin*, *The Papers of Thomas Jefferson*, and *The Adams Papers*—we have attempted to follow a "middle course" in presenting a printed text that stands between a type facsimile of the manuscript itself and a modernized version. The objective is to produce a text that conveys the *meaning* of the original (even though it may not be in the precise *form* of the original), while at the same time is free from the peculiarities of eighteenth-century orthography (and the editorial explanations that must accompany them). Happily, this was not a difficult task in our case, as Latrobe possessed a hand of admirable clarity and definition, wrote, spelled, and punctuated in a nearly modern manner, and did not employ unusual signs or abbreviations. His expository and narrative styles, while graceful, are straightforward and clear, rarely requiring explanation. Latrobe's journals, letterbooks, sketchbooks, and other manuscript materials are generally free from unusual chronological or textual problems. Nearly everything he wrote therefore can be accommodated by modern typography, and his numerous illustrative textual drawings can be reproduced readily by photo offset.

The rendering of an accurate and complete text has been the purpose of documentary editing from the Renaissance to the present; with a minimum of change, we were able to reach that goal and also to capture visually much of Latrobe's élan. All textual materials are presented chronologically, except when Latrobe himself suggested a sequential change, and these and other textual alterations made by the editors are so indicated in footnotes. Documents selected for publication will be presented in their entirety. The captions to the illustrations were composed by the editors, but are based on Latrobe's titles or descriptions of his drawings.

While our general practice is to adhere as closely as possible to the original manuscript, textual alterations were sometimes necessary for the sake of clarity and comprehensibility. In some instances punctuation has been silently added or deleted. For example, commas have been added between components of series where missing; periods have been supplied after abbreviations where missing; quotation marks have been added in dialogues and quoted material when an ambiguity or confusion arose without them; appropriate terminal punctuation has been added where missing; dashes used in place of commas, semicolons, colons, or periods have been replaced by the appropriate mark where necessary; and superfluous dashes have been eliminated, although dashes used to set off parenthetical expressions have been retained.

The original capitalization has been retained, except that all sentences begin with a capital letter. If it cannot be determined whether Latrobe intended a capital or lowercase letter, modern usage is followed.

The original spelling and syntax have been retained, except that obvious errors, such as the repetition of words and slips of the pen, have been silently corrected.

Ampersands have been changed to "and" except in the names of business firms and in the abbreviation "&c."

Superscript letters have been lowered to the line of type, and the resulting abbreviation silently expanded if it is not easily recognizable.

The thorn symbol (y) has been rendered as "th" and the tailed p (ꝓ) has been rendered as either "pre", "pro", or "per" depending on its usage. The tilde (∼) has been silently omitted and the word expanded.

Latrobe's own cross-references to extant pages in his journals or sketchbooks which appear in these two volumes have been replaced with bracketed cross-references to the appropriate pages in our printed text. His cross-references to material now missing carry footnotes to that effect. And Latrobe's cross-references to extant material not printed in these two volumes carry footnotes referring the reader to the documents in the microfiche edition.

We have used square brackets to enclose, in italics, editorial insertions such as [*torn*] and [*illegible*], and to enclose, in roman, editorial expansions, equivalents, or conjectural readings for Latrobe's text. Square brackets also enclose the editors' cross-references to illustrations. A double ellipsis within brackets [. .] indicates a blank space in Latrobe's text. Angle brackets enclose, in italics, material canceled in the manuscript but restored in our text.

We have not used [*sic*] to indicate peculiarities of spelling, grammar, or syntax, except in transcriptions from printed sources, which are not altered according to our editorial procedures. Thus, barring human error, the reader must assume that supposed errors encountered are a faithful transcription of Latrobe's words.

The texts of the letters included in these volumes have been transcribed in the same manner as have the other manuscript materials. However, certain editorial principles apply only to letters. The complimentary closes have been run together, with only the signature being assigned a separate line. All the letters included in these volumes are autograph letters signed (abbreviated as ALS in the text).

In the annotation of these initial volumes, the editors have attempted to explain that which was necessary to clarify the immediate text or to place larger passages or events in historical perspective. There has been a conscious effort to avoid clutter and pedantry while retaining flexible judgment as to the nature and length of individual editorial notes and footnotes. Aside from Benjamin Franklin and Thomas Jefferson, Benjamin Henry Latrobe had a wider range of interests and skills than other leaders of the early republic whose papers have been edited for publication. This fact has proved to be both the editors' joy and frustration. We have grappled with our avowed dedication to moderate annotation and our natural inclination to explain fully the idiosyncrasies and nuances of Latrobe's words and drawings. The following types of annotation also reflect the editors' preferences in this matter:

Editorial Notes. This generally precedes a passage that requires commentary or explanation. Editorial notes vary in length, depending on the nature of the material under discussion. Latrobe's observations on Virginia geology and his most important "Essay on Landscape" merit lengthy commentary, as do his mathematical notes, formulas, and diagrams on Hadley's Quadrant, which form a separate entity within the journal. On the other hand, Latrobe's transcription of his letters to Thomas Blackburn requires an editorial note of only a few lines.

Footnotes. The editors generally have used footnotes, numbered consecutively within each chapter, to explain their textual changes, identify persons and places, give scientific and bibliographical citations, translate foreign phrases, gloss eighteenth-century terms, and clarify events that have not been touched upon in editorial notes. On occasion, Latrobe himself annotated his text by means of traditional footnotes or marginal commentary keyed to the manuscript by "NB," an asterisk, or some other sign. Whether these have been set in the text or transposed into footnotes carrying numbers or symbols, Latrobe's authorship is noted in all cases. We have identified individuals who can be located in standard reference works such as the *DAB*. Many of our readers will not have such aids at hand, others will prefer to read Latrobe's words without interruption; therefore, we have provided short biographical notes on all identifiable figures mentioned, except for those Virginians included in the biographical appendix.

Biographical Appendix. Latrobe encountered literally scores of Virginians whose names, personalities, and activities are recorded in the pages that follow. Again, we decided to break step with our colleagues and place our Virginia biographies alphabetically in an appendix rather than in the traditional location at the foot of the page of reference. If we judged the subject's reputation to be local rather than national or international in nature, his or her name is marked with an asterisk to indicate inclusion in the appendix. We hope modern Virginians will weigh our decisions on the scales of generosity. The advantages of this mode of annotation are many. The general reader may avoid or utilize this information according to taste or disposition. The specialist will discover a series of detailed biographical sketches, each with ample bibliographical support, that illuminates Virginia society of the 1790s. The appendix elevates many tertiary and even some secondary figures to a level of historical exposure previously not enjoyed by them. Indeed, the collegial nature of the appendix renders the biographies a most important scholarly resource. We can present them here in a more expanded form than if they appeared as footnotes, and gathered together they constitute a handy reference tool and a significant source for historians of collective biography and social stratification as well as for genealogists.

Baltimore, March 1977   EDWARD C. CARTER II

Acknowledgments

More than any other area of humanistic scholarship, historical editing is a collaborative affair. If the scholarly, technical, and financial requirements of *The Papers of Benjamin Henry Latrobe* have been considerable and complex, the assistance we have received from all quarters in meeting these needs has been both gratifying and impressive. Not only have we drawn on the resources of the traditional "community of scholars," but we have also enjoyed the sympathetic support of the architectural, engineering, and photographic professions, and numerous foundations and public agencies. Similarly, hundreds of individuals have given generously of their knowledge, time, and money so that the staff of *The Papers of Benjamin Henry Latrobe* could proceed toward its goals without delay or inconvenience.

Recognizing the impossibility of acknowledging all these debts, we wish to thank a number of persons, groups, and institutions that have assisted in the general collection and editing phases of our project as of this date and also to record our gratitude for the invaluable support we have received in the preparation of these particular volumes.

This edition of Benjamin Henry Latrobe's works has been cosponsored by the Maryland Historical Society, the National Endowment for the Humanities, and the National Historical Publications and Records Commission. The officers and staffs of these three organizations have supplied us with much valuable information and advice on how best to address the wide array of problems we have confronted. The Society's former director, Harold R. Manakee, who like his predecessor, James W. Foster, was determined that this project should become a reality, also was unstinting in his efforts to give us the best possible environment in which to work. P. William Filby, the present director, has continued this tradition of friendly cooperation by providing us with larger quarters as our staff increased, joining in the search for Latrobe documents, and placing his unique bibliographical skills at our disposal. At the NEH, we are greatly indebted to William E. Emerson, former director of its Research Division, whose enthusiasm for the project has remained unflagging and who assisted in the search for matching funds. Simone Reagor, initially our grant officer and now director of the division, has responded to every one of our various requests promptly and effectively despite the ever-increasing press of NEH business. At the NHPRC, we wish to thank the chairman, James B. Rhoads, archivist of the United States, who has shown a continuing and informed interest in our enterprise; three executive directors, Oliver W. Holmes, E. Berkeley Tompkins, and Frank G. Burke; and most especially Fred Shelley, former deputy director, who has advised us wisely on the collection of documents, the writing of grant proposals, the structure of budgets, the merits of various modes of microform publication, and the selection of personnel.

The American Philosophical Society generously underwrote our first year of work and the cost of much of our photography. Direct grants from the Rockefeller Foundation and the United States Capitol Historical Society allowed us to produce the microfiche edition and to appoint an assistant editor for technology, who is now funded by the National Science Foundation. A significant contribution has been made by the Eleutherian Mills Historical Library of Greenville, Wilmington, Delaware, which has provided our historian of technology with office space, secretarial help, and access to its outstanding research facilities. Gifts from an anonymous donor and D. Luke Hopkins permitted flexibility in our budget at a critical moment, allowing us to undertake vital bibliographical research. The Catholic University of America has made a major contribution to the project by reducing the teaching responsibilities of the editor in chief.

We are indebted to the following private citizens, foundations, and institutions for matching grants made in our favor to the NEH:

A. S. Abell Company Foundation, American Institute of Architects, American Society of Civil Engineers, Margot Schutt Backas, Historical Society of Delaware, Fenner Family Fund, D. M. Ferry, Jr. Trustee Corporation of Detroit, C. A. Porter Hopkins, Frederic B. Ingram, The Kiplinger Foundation, Legg & Company Foundation, John A. Luetkemeyer, The Andrew W. Mellon Foundation, Municipal Arts Society of Baltimore, Historical Society of Pennsylvania, Queene Ferry Coonley Foundation, The RosaMary Foundation, Mrs. Edgar B. Stern, and the United States Capitol Historical Society.

These indispensable funds could not have been secured without the help of Josephine Cobb, Mr. and Mrs. Waldon Faulkner, Mr. and Mrs. Winthrop W. Faulkner, and Mr. and Mrs. Arthur V. Hooper. Special thanks is reserved for Frederic B. Ingram, who was instrumental in raising a major portion of the required matching gifts for our second NEH grant.

Acknowledgments

To the members of the Latrobe family the editors are especially indebted. Aileen Ford Latrobe, widow of Ferdinand Claiborne Latrobe II, was both our staunch friend and invaluable source of information concerning the history of the architect's papers. She determined that her Latrobe holdings would be transferred as a single unit to the Maryland Historical Society because she understood that such an action would not only encourage but also greatly facilitate publication. Elizabeth Reese Latrobe likewise patiently explained the provenance of her Latrobe manuscripts and made additional papers available for study. Both ladies graciously granted permission to publish their portraits of Latrobe—one by Charles Willson Peale, the other by Rembrandt Peale. Samuel and Elizabeth Latrobe Wilson, Jr., made our search of New Orleans archives not only productive but, because of their unmatched hospitality, a very pleasurable experience. John Henry de La Trobe of Hamburg, a descendant of Latrobe's younger brother John Frederick, has clarified the family's European genealogy and provided us with an informative collection of letters. This correspondence, written by Latrobe's elder brother, Christian Ignatius, and his sister, Mary Agnes Latrobe Bateman, to John Frederick, throws additional light on Benjamin Henry Latrobe's aspirations, views on American society and government, and activities during his final days of life.

All the members of the Editorial Board whose names appear at the head of this volume have made significant contributions by first setting the editor in chief correctly on course and then responding promptly and generously to every request for information and support. To Lyman H. Butterfield, editor in chief emeritus of *The Adams Papers*, go our special thanks. He urged complete publication and suggested integrated microfiche and printed editions, placed his project's organizational and editorial directives at our disposal, assisted in our early search for funding, and read critically the draft of the composite account of Latrobe's Atlantic voyage. Whitfield J. Bell, Jr., has rendered valuable technical advice relative to editing and has helped in selecting the project's consultants whose work has been supported by NEH funds. Rhoda M. Dorsey was a prime mover in establishing the project, first as a member and then as chairman of the Maryland Historical Society's Publications Committee. Alan Gowans played a major role in the search for and selection of our assistant for architectural history. The editor in chief was drawn initially into this grand design by Jack P. Greene. Walter Muir Whitehill has, as always, been our wise and valuable counselor on publication matters. Samuel Wilson, Jr.'s own considerable contributions have been mentioned previously.

We wish to acknowledge our gratitude to the editors and staffs of those documentary editing projects who have allowed us to draw upon their professional experience and who also searched their files for Latrobe materials. The dean of American editors, Julian P. Boyd of *The Papers of Thomas Jefferson*, made available his project's calendar of Jefferson-Latrobe correspondence and was instrumental in securing our initial funding. Charles M. Wiltse, editor in chief, *The Papers of Daniel Webster*, permitted the use of that project's microfilm edition copyright statement in our microfiche edition. We also have received information or copies of documents from the following: *The Adams Papers, The Papers of John C. Calhoun, The Papers of Henry Clay, The Papers of Andrew Jackson, The Papers of James Madison, The Papers of John Marshall,* and *The Papers of Jonathan Trumbull, Sr.*

Copies of almost 2,200 documents from outside the Maryland Historical Society have been generously provided by individuals and institutions here and abroad. The major repositories which assisted us are noted below, but the large number of persons and institutions supplying single items or small collections of documents precludes individual acknowledgment here. To all those who rendered this valuable service, we offer our special thanks. Those who have permitted photocopying of documents are credited on the appropriate microfiche entry and in the printed edition if their material appears there. The editors also thank the many librarians, manuscript custodians, and historical society officers who responded to our letters of inquiry requesting Latrobe materials. Of special assistance in the collecting process have been Whitfield J. Bell, Jr., and Murphy D. Smith, American Philosophical Society; the Reverend John J. Tierney, Archives of the Roman Catholic Archdiocese of Baltimore; Peter J. Parker, Historical Society of Pennsylvania; Virginia Daiker of the Prints and Photographs Division and Carolyn Sung of the Manuscript Division, Library of Congress; Roger Bruns, Col. H. B. Fant, Mary Guinta, Richard N. Sheldon, and Fred Shelley, NHPRC; Howard Wiseman, The New Jersey Historical Society; John W. Dudley of the Archives Branch and Katherine M. Smith of the Picture Collection, Virginia State Library; Louise W. Carter, Washington, D.C.; and Mr. and Mrs. Nicholas Philip, New York City.

The Library and Manuscript Divisions of the Maryland Historical Society have responded cheerfully and with great exactitude to our numerous requests for assistance. We are also indebted to Alice Kriete for clarifying the history of the acquisition of Latrobe collections, and to two of the Society's members: William Cogswell, who made available for study his firm's blueprints of its 1944–47 renovation of the Baltimore Cathedral, and H. H. Walker Lewis, who arranged and analyzed Latrobe's legal papers. Lacking the bibliographical and research resources of the Milton S. Eisenhower Library of Johns Hopkins University, the Peabody Library, and the Enoch Pratt Free Library, our work would have been impeded significantly; we thank these Baltimore institutions for the important contribution each has made.

To the director and staff of the Yale University Press go both our admiration and gratitude. Chester Kerr's enthusiasm for our project has been translated into the fullest range of editorial, design, and production support imaginable. Both he and

Acknowledgments

John McCrillis, our designer, determined that the Yale edition of *The Papers of Benjamin Henry Latrobe* was to match the artistic and technical standards of excellence established by Latrobe himself in so many fields of endeavor. We have been guided through the editorial process by three talented, sympathetic, but firm editors; we have learned from each and are grateful to all. Robin Bledsoe helped establish our editorial procedure, Anne Wilde moved these volumes through the initial copyediting stage, and Judy Metro has seen them through the press with unusual skill.

The Virginia journals were greatly enhanced by the inclusion of Latrobe's illustrated "Essay on Landscape" in its entirety; the editors are grateful to the Library Board of the Virginia State Library for making these materials available for publication. Louis H. Manarin, Virginia State Archivist, not only presented our request to the Library Board and aided us in study of the "Essay" but also worked closely with us in securing the best possible reproduction of Latrobe's subtle sketches and watercolors. For these and many other courtesies, we thank him.

The great variety of subjects which Latrobe discussed in his journals included a number which required the specialized knowledge of outside consultants. Some consultants produced editorial notes or the data from which such commentary was crafted; others annotated portions of Latrobe's writings and drawings. The editors wish to thank and recognize each for his or her valuable contribution to these volumes: Robert Barnes of the Maryland Historical Society for assistance in the preparation of the Latrobe family genealogy and the Pocahontas-Rolfe-Bolling pedigree editorial note; Lewis A. Beck, Jr., and Ferdinand E. Chatard of the Radcliffe Maritime Museum, Maryland Historical Society for charting Latrobe's Atlantic voyage and reading the account of that passage; Edmund and Dorothy S. Berkeley of Charlottesville, Virginia, for their annotation of the zoological material and their consideration of Latrobe as a natural scientist, which has been incorporated into the introductory biographical essay; Edward L. Boggs of the department of romance languages, Connecticut College, for his translation of certain German and Italian passages and bibliographical work on Italian opera; Joseph and Nesta Ewan of the department of biology, Tulane University, for their annotation of Latrobe's botanical observations; Thomas Fulton of the department of physics, Johns Hopkins University, for reviewing Latrobe's mathematical computations and providing much information contained in the Pico and Hadley's Quadrant editorial notes; Charles B. Hunt, formerly of the department of geography and environmental engineering, Johns Hopkins University, for writing the editorial note on Virginia geology and annotating all related materials; Michael J. Marcuse of the department of English, Catholic University of America, for placing Osbert's Tale in literary and historical perspective; James W. Poultney of the department of classics, Johns Hopkins University, for revealing and evaluating

Latrobe's classical knowledge and translating passages in classical languages; William M. E. Rachal of the Virginia Historical Society for reviewing everything touching on Virginia figures and place names; and Mary P. Winsor of the Institute for the History and Philosophy of Science and Technology, University of Toronto, for her annotation of Latrobe's observations on marine biology. Finally, we would like to thank two of our staff, Charles E. Brownell, assistant editor for architectural history, who though deeply involved in preparing *The Architectural Drawings of Benjamin Henry Latrobe* for publication, supplied ample annotation for the "Essay on Lanscape" and wrote the editorial note that serves as an admirable introduction to that document, and Lee W. Formwalt, editorial assistant, who skillfully compiled the valuable Biographical Appendix.

We extend our appreciation to the following who have answered specific questions germane to these volumes: Silvio A. Bedini, National Museum of History and Technology, Smithsonian Institution; Maxwell H. Bloomfield III, department of history, Catholic University of America; John Henry de La Trobe, Hamburg, West Germany; Thomas Dunn, school of music, Catholic University of America; the Reverend John E. Lynch, C.S.P., department of history, Catholic University of America; the Reverend W. J. Mortimore, Pudsey, England; Paul F. Norton, department of art, University of Massachusetts, Amherst; Ronald Paulson, department of English, Yale University; Edgar P. Richardson, Philadelphia; F. Garner Ranney, historiographer, Episcopal Diocese of Maryland; Eduardo Saccone, department of romance languages, Johns Hopkins University; and Richard B. Stone, Columbia University School of Law.

Those of us whose names appear on the title page represent many devoted staff members of *The Papers of Benjamin Henry Latrobe*, past and present, without whose efforts and myriad talents neither the project as a whole nor these volumes in particular would have advanced to their present state. The editors wish to recognize the unusual contribution of Geraldine S. Vickers, secretary-transcriber, who has typed our correspondence, search letters, grant applications, the catalog of Latrobe's sketchbooks, uncounted drafts of editorial notes and footnotes, and much of the final version of this manuscript with skill and good humor—complaining only when these many tasks kept her too long from her primary joy, the transcription of Benjamin Henry Latrobe's journals and letters. Thomas E. Jeffrey, microfiche editor, assisted in preparing the Latrobe genealogy. To those colleagues listed below, some of whom worked with us for a brief period, others for a longer duration, the editors of *The Papers of Benjamin Henry Latrobe* extend their grateful thanks:

Margot Schutt Backas, Charlotte Bucknell, Kathleen Dalton, Ruth E. Friedman, Susanne Moore, John C. Poppeliers, Nigel A. Redden, Darwin H. Stapleton, Doris Stude, and David V. Trotman.

Short Titles and Abbreviations

Alumni Oxonienses
Joseph Foster, *Alumni Oxonienses: The Members of the University of Oxford, 1715–1886: Their Parentage, Birthplace, and Year of Birth, with a Record of Their Degrees*, 4 vols. (Oxford, 1887–88).

Appletons' Cyclopedia
James G. Wilson and John Fiske, eds., *Appletons' Cyclopedia of American Biography*, 6 vols. (New York, 1888–89).

BDAC
Biographical Directory of the American Congress, 1774–1961 (Washington, D.C.: Government Printing Office, 1961).

Beeman, *Old Dominion*
Richard R. Beeman, *The Old Dominion and the New Nation, 1788–1801* (Lexington, Ky.: University of Kentucky Press, 1972).

BHL
Benjamin Henry Latrobe.

Bondurant, *Poe's Richmond*
Agnes M. Bondurant, *Poe's Richmond* (Richmond, Va.: Garrett & Massie, 1942).

Bradshaw, *Hist. Pr. Ed. Co.*
Herbert C. Bradshaw, *History of Prince Edward County, Virginia, from Its Earliest Settlements Through Its Establishment in 1754 to Its Bicentennial Year* (Richmond, Va.: Dietz Press, 1955).

Burke's Landed Gentry
John Burke and John B. Burke, *A Genealogical and Heraldic Dictionary of the Landed Gentry of Great Britain and Ireland*, 3 vols. (London, 1846–48).

Burke's Landed Gentry, 11th ed.
Sir Bernard Burke and Ashworth P. Burke, *A Genealogical and Heraldic History of the Landed Gentry of Great Britain*, 11th ed., 2 vols. (London: Harrison & Sons, 1906).

Burke's Landed Gentry, 18th ed.

Burke's Genealogical and Heraldic History of the Landed Gentry, 18th ed., 3 vols. (London: Burke's Peerage Ltd., 1965–72).

Christian, *Richmond*

William A. Christian, *Richmond, Her Past and Present* (Richmond, Va.: L. H. Jenkins, 1912).

Commager, ed., *Atlas to Official Records*

Henry Steele Commager, ed., *Atlas to Accompany the Official Records of the Union and Confederate Armies* (New York: Thomas Yoseloff, 1958).

Cummings et al., *Romantic Art in Britain*

Frederick Cummings, Allen Staley, and Robert Rosenblum, *Romantic Art in Britain: Paintings and Drawings, 1760–1860* (Philadelphia, Pa.: Philadelphia Museum of Art, 1968).

CVSP

William P. Palmer, Sherwin McRae, and H. W. Flournoy, eds., *Calendar of Virginia State Papers and Other Manuscripts . . . Preserved in the Capitol at Richmond*, 11 vols. (Richmond, Va., 1875–93).

DAB

Allen Johnson and Dumas Malone, eds., *Dictionary of American Biography*, 20 vols. plus index and supplements (New York: Charles Scribner's Sons, 1928–36).

Daniels, *Randolphs of Va.*

Jonathan Daniels, *The Randolphs of Virginia* (New York: Doubleday & Co., 1972).

Darwin, *Botanic Garden*

Erasmus Darwin, *The Botanic Garden; a Poem in Two Parts* (Part 1, *The Economy of Vegetation* [London, 1791]; Part 2, *The Loves of the Plants* [London, 1789]).

DNB

Leslie Stephen and Sidney Lee, eds., *The Dictionary of National Biography*, 21 vols. plus supplements (New York and London, 1885–1912).

Dunn, *Hist. of Nansemond Co.*

Joseph B. Dunn, *The History of Nansemond County, Virginia* (n.p., 1907).

Eavenson, *Coal*

Howard N. Eavenson, *The First Century and a Quarter of American Coal Industry* (Pittsburgh, Pa.: privately printed, 1942).

Evans

Charles Evans et al., comps., *American Bibliography: A Chronological Dictionary of All Books, Pamphlets and Periodical Publications Printed in the United States of America from the Genesis of Printing in 1639 Down to and Including the Year 1820*, 14 vols. (Chicago, Ill.: Blakely Press and Columbia Press, 1903–34 [vols. 1–12]; Worcester, Mass.: American Antiquarian Society, 1955–59 [vols. 13–14]).

Fischer, *Revolution of American Conservatism*
　　David Hackett Fischer, *The Revolution of American Conservatism: The Federalist Party in the Era of Jeffersonian Democracy* (New York: Harper & Row, 1965).

Forrest, *Norfolk*
　　William S. Forrest, *Historical and Descriptive Sketches of Norfolk and Vicinity, Including Portsmouth and the Adjacent Counties, During a Period of Two Hundred Years. Also, Sketches of Williamsburg, Hampton, Suffolk, Smithfield, and Other Places* (Philadelphia, Pa., 1853).

Friis, *Guidebook*
　　Herman R. Friis, *Guidebook: Geological Reconnaissance of the Potomac River Tidewater Fringe of Virginia from Arlington Memorial Bridge to Mount Vernon* (Washington, D.C.: Association of American Geographers, 1968).

Fry & Jefferson Map
　　The Fry & Jefferson Map of Virginia and Maryland: Facsimiles of the 1754 and 1794 Printings, with an Index (Charlottesville, Va.: University Press of Virginia, 1966).

Hamlin, *Latrobe*
　　Talbot Hamlin, *Benjamin Henry Latrobe* (New York: Oxford University Press, 1955).

Hardie, *Water-colour Painting*
　　Martin Hardie, *Water-colour Painting in Britain*, ed. Dudley Snelgrove with Jonathan Mayne and Basil Taylor, 3 vols. (London: B. T. Batsford, 1966–68.)

Hening, *Statutes*
　　William Waller Hening, *The Statutes at Large: Being a Collection of All the Laws of Virginia from the First Session of the Legislature in the Year 1619*, 13 vols. (Richmond, Philadelphia, and New York, 1809–23).

James, *Norfolk Antiquary*
　　Edward W. James, *The Lower Norfolk County Virginia Antiquary*, 5 vols. (Baltimore, Md., 1897–1906).

Jefferson, *Notes on Virginia*
　　Thomas Jefferson, *Notes on the State of Virginia*, ed. William Peden (Chapel Hill, N.C.: University of North Carolina Press, 1955/1787).

Latrobe Letterbooks
　　Letterbooks of Benjamin Henry Latrobe, Papers of Benjamin Henry Latrobe, Maryland Historical Society, Baltimore.

Lutz, *Chesterfield Co.*
　　Earle Lutz, *Chesterfield, an Old Virginia County* (Richmond, Va.: William Byrd Press, 1954).

Martin's Gazetteer
　　Joseph Martin, *A New and Comprehensive Gazetteer of Virginia, and the District of*

Columbia. To Which is Added a History of Virginia from Its First Settlement to the Year 1754: With an Abstract of the Principal Events from that Period to the Independence of Virginia (Charlottesville, Va., 1835).

MdHS

Maryland Historical Society, Baltimore.

Meade, *Old Churches*

William Meade, *Old Churches, Ministers, and Families of Virginia*, 2 vols. (Baltimore, Md., 1966/1857).

Mordecai, *Richmond*

Samuel Mordecai, *Virginia, Especially Richmond, in By-Gone Days; With a Glance at the Present: Being Reminiscences and Last Words of an Old Citizen* (Richmond, Va., 1860).

OED

The Oxford English Dictionary, 12 vols. plus supplement (Oxford: Clarendon Press, 1933).

PBHL, microfiche ed.

Thomas E. Jeffrey, ed., *The Microfiche Edition of The Papers of Benjamin Henry Latrobe* (Clifton, N.J.: James T. White & Co., 1976).

Quinn, *History of Fredericksburg*

Silvanus J. Quinn, *The History of the City of Fredericksburg, Virginia* (Richmond, Va.: Hermitage Press, 1908).

Reynolds, *Discourses*

Sir Joshua Reynolds, *Discourses on Art*, ed. Robert R. Wark (San Marino, Cal.: Henry E. Huntington Library and Art Gallery, 1959).

Richmond Portraits

Richmond Portraits in an Exhibition of Makers of Richmond, 1737–1860 (Richmond, Va.: The Valentine Museum, 1949).

Rutland, *Mason*

Robert A. Rutland, ed., *The Papers of George Mason, 1725–1792*, 3 vols. (Chapel Hill, N.C.: University of North Carolina Press, 1970).

Senate Executive Journal

Journal of the Executive Proceedings of the Senate of the United States of America: From the Commencement of the First, to the Termination of the Nineteenth Congress, vol. 1 (Washington, D.C., 1828).

Shepherd, *Statutes*

Samuel Shepherd, *The Statutes at Large of Virginia, from October Session 1792, to December Session 1806, Inclusive, in Three Volumes (New Series), Being a Continuation of Hening*, 3 vols. (New York: AMS Press, 1970/1835).

Sherman, "West"
    Susanne K. Sherman, "Thomas Wade West, Theatrical Impressario, 1790–1799," *William and Mary Quarterly*, 3d ser. 9 (1952): 10–28.
Stanard, *Richmond*
    Mary Newton Stanard, *Richmond, Its People and Its Story* (Philadelphia, Pa.: J. B. Lippincott Co., 1923).
Swem and Williams, *Reg. Va. Assembly*
    Earl G. Swem and John W. Williams, *A Register of the General Assembly of Virginia, 1776–1918 and of the Constitutional Conventions* (Richmond, Va.: Davis Bottom, 1918).
Thieme-Becker
    Ulrich Thieme and Felix Becker, eds., *Allgemeines Lexikon der bildenden Künstler*, 37 vols. (Leipzig: E. A. Seeman, 1908–50).
Tyler, *Encycl. Va. Biog.*
    Lyon Gardiner Tyler, ed., *Encyclopedia of Virginia Biography*, 5 vols. (New York: Lewis Historical Publishing Co., 1915).
Tyler's Quarterly
    Tyler's Quarterly Historical and Genealogical Magazine.
Vestry Book of Upper Parish Nansemond
    Wilmer L. Hall, ed., *The Vestry Book of the Upper Parish, Nansemond County, Virginia, 1743–1793* (Richmond, Va.: Virginia State Library, 1949).
VMHB
    Virginia Magazine of History and Biography.
Wertenbaker, *Norfolk*
    Thomas J. Wertenbaker, *Norfolk: Historic Southern Port*, 2d ed. (Durham, N.C.: Duke University Press, 1962).
Williams, *Amelia Marriages*
    Kathleen Booth Williams, *Marriages of Amelia County, Virginia, 1735–1815* (n.p., 1961).
WMQ
    William and Mary Quarterly.
Wollock, "Latrobe . . . American Theatre"
    Abe Wollock, "Benjamin Henry Latrobe's Activities in the American Theatre (1797–1808)," (Ph.D. dissertation, University of Illinois, 1962).
WPA, *Dinwiddie County*
    Dinwiddie County, "The Countrey of the Apamatica," compiled by the workers of the Writer's Program of the Works Projects Administration (Richmond, Va.: Whittet & Shepperson, 1942).

Genealogy

Until relatively recently, American historians believed that the Latrobe family descended from Count Henri Bonneval, a Huguenot nobleman whose third son, Jean Henri Bonneval de la Trobe, fled to Ireland after the revocation of the Edict of Nantes. Christian Ignatius Latrobe discussed this theory in detail in a letter of 1820 written to his younger brother, John Frederick, in Livonia. Although acknowledging that he possessed no documentation to prove the noble origin of their family, Christian Ignatius put forward his father's claim that "his great grandfather was a French Nobleman, generally called a Marquis. That the family was Bonne*val* or *vaux* . . . and Latrobe a name derived from some event in the family."[1]

Previously he had transmitted the same account to Benjamin Henry Latrobe, which was later copied into a large family record book. Thus the legend of the Bonneval family was perpetuated, appearing in the genealogy appended to John E. Semmes, *John H. B. Latrobe and His Times, 1803–1891* (Baltimore: Norman, Remington Co., 1917). Talbot Hamlin did not seriously question this tradition in his biography of Latrobe.

However, as early as 1822 Joachim Latrobe, a French cousin of Benjamin Henry Latrobe, compiled a "Livre de Raison" which correctly set forth the family's origins. His account, which can be confirmed from church registers and other primary sources, demonstrated that the Latrobe family originated in the province of Guienne, where its members lived as simple tradesmen and merchants in the early seventeenth century. A genealogical history of the Baltic Knights, based in part on the "Livre de Raison," confirmed that the Bonnevals, who were always Catholics, lived in a different part of France and were in no way related to the Latrobes.

The Latrobe family genealogy is presented below both in narrative and in two charts. The first chart begins with Bertrand Latrobe, the earliest known ancestor,

1. Christian Ignatius Latrobe to John Frederick Latrobe, 1 February 1820, John Henry de La Trobe Collection, Hamburg. For variant spellings of the name "Latrobe" see p. xvii, n. 12 above.

and traces the line through the children, nephews, and nieces of Benjamin Henry Latrobe. This chart is preceded by a detailed narrative account of these generations; the numbers assigned to individuals on the chart correspond to the numbers used in the narrative. The second chart is a selective genealogy of Benjamin Henry Latrobe's descendants who figure prominently in the history and provenance of the Latrobe collection. A more detailed account of Latrobe's descendants, as well as collateral branches of the family, appeared in the December 1975 issue of *The Genealogist*, the official journal of the Australian Institute of Genealogical Studies.

1. BERTRAND LATROBE, earliest known progenitor of the family, was living in 1621 in Montauban, France. He married Gaillarde Benetz, by whom he had at least three children:[2]

> 2. PIERRE LATROBE. See below.
>
> 3. JEAN LATROBE, living in 1612, married Antoinette Davens.
>
> 4. PIERRE-JEAN LATROBE.

2. PIERRE LATROBE, son of Bertrand and Gaillarde, was living as early as 1628 in Montauban. He was twice married: to Marguerite Vidal, by whom he had two children; and to Jeanne Dalard (or Alard), by whom he also had two children. Pierre, a mason and property owner, was the father of:[3]

> 5. JEAN LATROBE (by Marguerite), married Paule de Carrel, died September 1646.
>
> 6. PAULE LATROBE (by Marguerite), married Antoine le Little on 25 April 1661.
>
> 7. MICHEL LATROBE (by Jeanne). See below.
>
> 8. THÉZARE LATROBE (by Jeanne), married Barthe (de Villemur).

7. MICHEL LATROBE, son of Pierre and Jeanne, was born on 26 April 1640 at Montauban and died in 1705. A merchant at Villemur, he married Maffre Raimond (or Marthe Ramond) on 29 July 1663. She was born in Montauban, the daughter of Alexis Raimond and Marie de Limosy. Michel and Maffre were the parents of:[4]

> 9. PIERRE LATROBE, born at Villemur on 9 April 1665, married Anne Mariette on 15 October 1722 and died at Varennes on 16 July 1767.[5]

---

2. "Généalogie des Latrobe" (unpublished manuscript in the possession of John Henry de La Trobe, Hamburg, Germany); *Genealogisches Handbuch der baltischen Ritterschaften* . . . Teil: Livland, Band II, Lieferung 10 (Görlitz i. Schlesien: C. A. Starke Verlag, n.d.), p. 794.

3. Ibid.

4. Ibid.

5. *Genealogisches Handbuch* lists Pierre's wife as Anne Mariette Rabot.

Pierre and Anne were the ancestors of Joachim Latrobe, compiler of the "Livre de Raison." The scope of this genealogy does not permit the listing of their descendants, but a chart of the French branch of the Latrobe Family was graciously given to *The Papers of Benjamin Henry Latrobe* by Dr. John Henry de La Trobe of Hamburg, Germany.

10. JEAN LATROBE. See below.
11. JEAN-MARC LATROBE, died unmarried at Varennes on 27 November 1744.
12. JOACHIM LATROBE, married and had a daughter.
13. MARTHE LATROBE, died unmarried.

10. JEAN LATROBE, son of Michel and Maffre, was born on 26 September 1670 at Villemur. He was a member of the Company of the Chevalier de Cominges for two months and then left the company and the country, severing his connections with his family in France. He is probably the same Jean, or John, Latrobe who was a compatriot of Louis Crommelin, a Huguenot leader, and the founder of the Irish linen industry.[6]

John Latrobe is said to have left France after the Revocation of the Edict of Nantes and to have fought under William III at the Battle of the Boyne in 1690. He is known to have been a linen manufacturer at Waterford, Ireland, between 1715 and 1730. He died at an advanced age in Dublin.[7] John Latrobe was the father of:

14. JAMES LATROBE. See below.
15. HENRY LATROBE, born in 1711 or 1712, died on 27 September 1781. He married Allinor Coates on 21 February 1731.[8] Another source gives his birth date as 19 March 1715 and his wife's name as Anne Edwards.[9] They had no children. They lived for a while with their nephew James Gottlieb Latrobe (#20 below) and left their estate in Dublin to their nephew Benjamin Latrobe (#17 below).
16. (Possibly) THOMAS LATROBE, who was the father of a child buried in 1739.[10]

14. JAMES LATROBE, son of John, was born in 1700 at Waterford, Ireland, and died in 1752 at Dublin. He was a linen manufacturer and merchant in Dublin. He married Elizabeth Thornton on 21 January 1720 in Dublin, and after her

6. Ibid., pp. 793–94.
7. Ibid., pp. 793, 795.
8. Ibid., p. 799.
9. Genealogical papers of Mrs. Fan La Trobe Chapman, Waterford, Ireland.
10. *Genealogisches Handbuch*, p. 799.

death on 19 March 1744, married Rebecca Adams in 1745. Rebecca (Adams) Latrobe died in 1769.[11]

James Latrobe was raised as a Baptist, but later became a churchwarden of St. Mark's in Dublin.[12] He had one son by his first wife and three sons by his second wife. His children were:[13]

> 17. BENJAMIN LATROBE (by Elizabeth). See below.
>
> 18. HENRY LATROBE (by Rebecca), born on 30 March 1746, died in 1776 without issue.[14]
>
> 19. JOHN LATROBE (by Rebecca), born on 24 July 1747, died in March 1771.[15]
>
> 20. JAMES GOTTLIEB LATROBE (by Rebecca). See below.

17. BENJAMIN LATROBE, son of James and Elizabeth, was born on 10 April 1728 in Dublin and died on 29 November 1786 in London. He married Anna Margaretta Antes on 25 April 1756. Anna Margaretta, daughter of Henry Antes, was born on 9 September 1728 at Hanover, Pennsylvania, and died on 17 March 1794 at Fulneck, England.[16]

Benjamin Latrobe was a leading minister of the Moravian Church. He and Anna were the parents of:[17]

> 21. CHRISTIAN IGNATIUS LATROBE. See below.
>
> 22. ANNA LOUISA ELEANORA LATROBE. See below.
>
> 23. BENJAMIN HENRY LATROBE. See below.
>
> 24. JOHN FREDERICK LATROBE. See below.
>
> 25. MARY AGNES LATROBE. See below.
>
> 26. JUSTINA LATROBE, died in infancy.

20. JAMES GOTTLIEB LATROBE, son of James and Rebecca, was born on 19 June 1750 and died on 30 January 1836 at Fulneck, England. He married Mary Watson on 16 June 1788 and had at least one child:[18]

> 27. JAMES LATROBE. See below.

21. CHRISTIAN IGNATIUS LATROBE, son of Benjamin and Anna Margaretta, was

---

11. Ibid., p. 798.

12. Fan La Trobe Chapman Papers. This source lists James Latrobe's birth date as 1702.

13. *Genealogisches Handbuch*, p. 798; Fan La Trobe Chapman Papers.

14. Fan La Trobe Chapman Papers.

15. Ibid.

16. *Genealogisches Handbuch*, p. 798; "Extract from the Church Record of the three High Dutch Reformed Churches . . . in Pennsylvania," 10 January 1736, Latrobe–Cogswell Papers, MdHS. *Genealogisches Handbuch* lists Anna Margaretta's birth date as 20 September 1728.

17. "Latrobe Family Journal" (unpublished manuscript in the possession of the Latrobe family, Baltimore, Md.); *Genealogisches Handbuch*, p. 798.

18. *Genealogisches Handbuch*, p. 798; Fan La Trobe Chapman Papers. The Chapman Papers lists James Gottlieb

born on 12 February 1758 and died on 6 May 1836. He married Anna B. Syms, who died in 1824. Christian Ignatius became a bishop of the Moravian Church. He and Anna were the parents of:[19]

28. CHARLOTTE LOUISA LATROBE, born 1793, died 1878; unmarried.

29. PETER LATROBE, born in 1795, married his first cousin Mary Louisa Foster (#38 below), died in 1863. He was a bishop of the Moravian Church.

30. ANNA AGNES LATROBE, born 1797, died 1827; unmarried.

31. JOHN ANTES LATROBE, born 1799, died 1878.

32. CHARLES JOSEPH LATROBE, born on 20 March 1801, died on 4 December 1875. His first wife, whom he married on 16 September 1835, was Sophie de Montmollin (1809–1854). In 1855 he married Rose (de Montmollin) de Meuron, the widowed sister of his first wife. Rose (de Meuron) Latrobe died in 1883. Charles Joseph Latrobe was the first lieutenant governor of the Colony of Victoria and the founder of the Australian branch of the Latrobe family.

33. FREDERICK BENJAMIN LATROBE, born 1803, died 1841; married Elizabeth Scott.

22. ANNA LOUISA ELEANORA LATROBE, daughter of Benjamin and Anna Margaretta, was born in 1761 and died on 24 July 1824. She married Frederic William Foster on 15 May 1791. Foster, the son of William and Dorothy (Gale) Foster, was born on 1 August 1760 and died on 12 April 1835. He was a bishop of the Moravian Church and owned the Bogue estate in Jamaica. Frederic William and Anna Louisa (Latrobe) Foster were the parents of:[20]

34. JOHN FREDERIC FOSTER, born on 18 June 1795 and died on 9 April 1858. He resided on the Bogue estate, Jamaica, and at Kempstone, Bedfordshire, where he was a barrister and justice of the peace. He married Caroline, eldest daughter of Sir William Chambers Bagshawe, on 13 May 1817.

35. WILLIAM FOSTER, born on 20 January 1797 and died in 1829. In 1817 he married Marianne, daughter of Sir William Chambers Bagshawe.

Latrobe's wife as Anna Elizabeth Watson, born September 1760. According to this source, Latrobe married again in 1806. His second wife was Sarah Rouse, born September 1762.

19. Genealogical chart compiled by Agnes Louisa La Trobe (unpublished manuscript in the possession of the Latrobe family, Baltimore, Md.); *Genealogisches Handbuch*, p. 798; *The Genealogist* (official journal of the Australian Institute of Genealogical Studies) 1 (1975): 188.

20. Agnes Louisa La Trobe Genealogy; *Burke's Landed Gentry*, 11th ed., pp. 618–19.

36. ISAAC HENRY FOSTER, born 1800, died on 11 September 1827; unmarried.

37. ANNA DOROTHY FOSTER, married John Amery, a banker from Stourbridge, England, in 1824; died in 1857.

38. MARY LOUISA FOSTER, married her cousin, Rev. Peter Latrobe (#29 above); died in June 1839.

39. MARGARET ELEANORA FOSTER, died in 1833; unmarried.

23. BENJAMIN HENRY LATROBE, son of Benjamin and Anna Margaretta, was born on 1 May 1764 at Fulneck, England, and died on 3 September 1820 at New Orleans, Louisiana. He married Lydia Sellon (c. 1761–1793) in 1790. His second wife, whom he married on 1 May 1800, was Mary Elizabeth Hazlehurst, who was born on 1 January 1771 in Philadelphia and died on 16 October 1841 at Clover Hill, New Jersey.[21]

Benjamin Henry Latrobe had three children by his first wife and six by his second. He was the father of:

40. LYDIA LATROBE (by Lydia), born on 23 March 1791, died on 2 March 1878; married Nicholas J. Roosevelt of New York on 15 November 1808. Nicholas, son of Jacobus and Annetje (Bogard) Roosevelt, was born on 27 December 1767 in New York and died on 30 July 1854. An inventor and engineer, Roosevelt was associated with Latrobe in the production of steam engines for the Philadelphia Waterworks and in several other business ventures. He and his wife had nine children.[22]

41. HENRY SELLON BONEVAL LATROBE (by Lydia), born on 19 July 1792, died on 3 September 1817 at New Orleans. During the latter part of his life, he was actively engaged in New Orleans as an engineer.[23]

42. Child (by Lydia), unnamed, died at birth November 1793.[24]

43. JULIANA LATROBE (by Mary Elizabeth), born on 29 June 1801, died on 7 August 1801.[25]

44. JOHN HAZLEHURST BONEVAL LATROBE (by Mary Elizabeth), born on 4 May 1803, died on 11 September 1891. He married Margaret Steuart of Baltimore on 29 November 1828. After her death in 1831, he married

---

21. Hamlin, *Latrobe*, pp. 7, 29–30, 32, 142, 528; G. B. Hazlehurst, "Chart of Descent from Mary Elizabeth Hazlehurst . . ." (unpublished manuscript, 1916, copy at MdHS).

22. Benjamin Henry Latrobe, Jr., Diary, 2 March 1878, MdHS; Hamlin, *Latrobe*, pp. 32, 230; *DAB*, s.v. Nicholas J. Roosevelt.

23. *National Intelligencer* (Washington, D.C.), 1 October 1817; Hamlin, *Latrobe*, pp. 32, 473.

24. Hamlin, *Latrobe*, p. 32.

25. Hazlehurst Genealogy; Hamlin, *Latrobe*, p. 181. Hamlin gives Juliana's birth date as 9 June 1801.

Charlotte Virginia Claiborne (1815–1903) of Mississippi. John H. B. Latrobe was a lawyer and inventor. As attorney for the Baltimore & Ohio Railroad, he received wide recognition as a railroad lawyer. He was a founder of the Maryland State Colonization Society and became president of the national society in 1853. He was also the inventor of the Latrobe Stove, and a founder and president of the Maryland Historical Society. John H. B. Latrobe had one child by his first wife and seven children by his second wife. His son, Ferdinand Claiborne Latrobe (1833–1911), was seven times mayor of Baltimore.[26]

45. JULIA LATROBE (by Mary Elizabeth), born on 17 July 1804, died on 3 March 1890; unmarried.[27]

46. MARY AGNES LATROBE (by Mary Elizabeth), born on 5 November 1805, died on 19 March 1806.[28]

47. BENJAMIN HENRY LATROBE (by Mary Elizabeth), born on 19 December 1806, died on 19 October 1878. On 12 March 1833, he married his cousin, Maria Eleanor Hazlehurst (1806–1872). Benjamin Henry Latrobe became chief engineer for the Baltimore & Ohio Railroad in 1842 and in this capacity supervised the construction of the western extension to Wheeling, West Virginia. Benjamin and Maria Eleanor Latrobe were the parents of five children, one of whom, Charles Hazlehurst Latrobe (1834–1902), attained distinction in his father's profession.[29]

48. LOUISA LATROBE (by Mary Elizabeth), died at birth, 1808.[30]

24. JOHN FREDERICK LATROBE, son of Benjamin and Anna Margaretta, was born on 10 June 1769 at Chelsea, England, and died on 19 December 1845 at Dorpat, Livonia. He married Alwine Marie, Baroness von Stackelberg, on 29 March 1820. John Frederick, a landowner and composer, was the founder of the Livonian branch of the Latrobe family. He was the father of:[31]

49. EDWARD (DE) LATROBE, born on 3 March 1825 at Woiseck and died on 2 September 1879. He married Alexandra Elizabeth von Wahl, born 24 July 1836 and died 15 May 1914. Edward took Livonian citizenship in 1864.

26. Hazlehurst Genealogy; *DAB*.

27. Hazlehurst Genealogy.

28. BHL to John Lenthall, 21 March 1806, Latrobe Letterbooks, *PBHL*, *microfiche ed.*, 48/A12; Hamlin, *Latrobe*, p. 181.

29. Hazlehurst Genealogy; *DAB*.

30. "Latrobe Family Journal."

31. *Genealogisches Handbuch*, pp. 799–800; Semmes, *John H. B. Latrobe*, p. 576.

50. SOPHIA LATROBE, married Waldemar von Bock.

51. ALVINA LATROBE, married Leo Manteuffel.

52. JOHN HENRY LATROBE, was living as late as 1857 in Poll, Weissenberg.

53. Child, unnamed.

54. Child, unnamed.

25. MARY AGNES LATROBE, daughter of Benjamin and Anna Margaretta, was born in 1772 and died in 1848. She married John Bateman of Wyke, and later of Ockbrook, Derbyshire, England. Bateman, the son of Jonas and Sarah (Foster) Bateman, was born in 1772 and died on 20 November 1851. John and Mary Agnes (Latrobe) Bateman were the parents of:[32]

55. SARAH LOUISA BATEMAN, born in 1806, died in 1869; married Rev. Robert Sproull.

56. ANNA JUSTINA BATEMAN, born in 1808, died in 1829, unmarried.

57. JOHN FREDERIC LATROBE-BATEMAN, born on 30 May 1810 and died in June 1889. He assumed the "Prefix, Surname, and Arms" of Latrobe by Royal License in 1883. He married Anne, only daughter of Sir William Fairbairn, Bart., on 1 September 1841.

58. CHRISTIAN HENRY BATEMAN, born in 1813, married Margaret Fleming, daughter of J. Browne, of Esk Vale, Pennycuik, New Brunswick.

59. EDWARD BATEMAN, born in 1816.

60. CHARLES BENJAMIN BATEMAN, born in 1819, settled in America.

27. JAMES LATROBE, son of James Gottlieb and Mary (Watson) Latrobe, was born in 1802 at Tytherton, England, and died in 1897. He was twice married and had at least one son by his second wife, Mary Grimes:[33]

61. BENJAMIN LATROBE, born on 29 June 1847, died on 4 October 1917. He married Emily Louisa Harding on 10 November 1881 at Bath, England.

---

32. *Burke's Landed Gentry*, 11th ed., p. 92; Agnes Louisa La Trobe Genealogy.

33. *Genealogisches Handbuch*, p. 798.

Chart A. Line of Descent from Bertrand Latrobe to the Generation of Benjamin Henry Latrobe's Children*

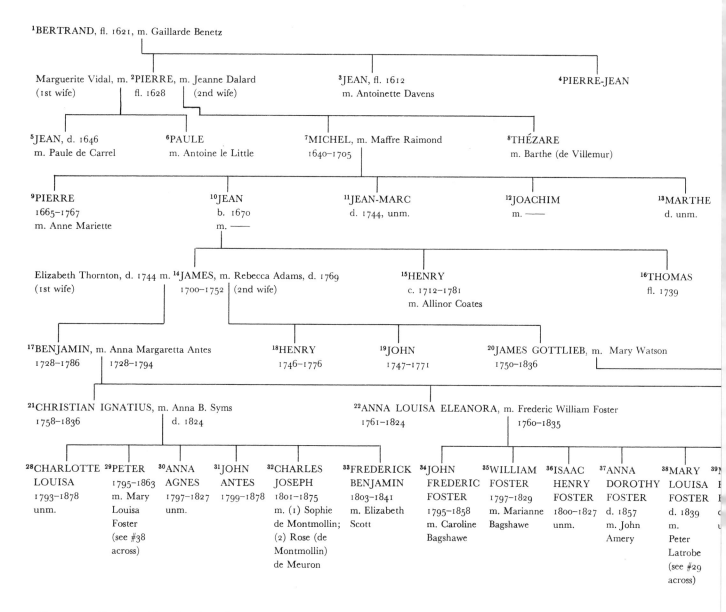

¹BERTRAND, fl. 1621, m. Gaillarde Benetz

Marguerite Vidal, m. **²PIERRE**, m. Jeanne Dalard
(1st wife)   fl. 1628   (2nd wife)

³JEAN, fl. 1612
m. Antoinette Davens

⁴PIERRE-JEAN

⁵JEAN, d. 1646
m. Paule de Carrel

⁶PAULE
m. Antoine le Little

⁷MICHEL, m. Maffre Raimond
1640–1705

⁸THÉZARE
m. Barthe (de Villemur)

⁹PIERRE
1665–1767
m. Anne Mariette

¹⁰JEAN
b. 1670
m. ——

¹¹JEAN-MARC
d. 1744, unm.

¹²JOACHIM
m. ——

¹³MARTHE
d. unm.

Elizabeth Thornton, d. 1744 m. **¹⁴JAMES**, m. Rebecca Adams, d. 1769
(1st wife)   1700–1752   (2nd wife)

¹⁵HENRY
c. 1712–1781
m. Allinor Coates

¹⁶THOMAS
fl. 1739

¹⁷BENJAMIN, m. Anna Margaretta Antes
1728–1786   1728–1794

¹⁸HENRY
1746–1776

¹⁹JOHN
1747–1771

²⁰JAMES GOTTLIEB, m. Mary Watson
1750–1836

²¹CHRISTIAN IGNATIUS, m. Anna B. Syms
1758–1836   d. 1824

²²ANNA LOUISA ELEANORA, m. Frederic William Foster
1761–1824   1760–1835

²⁸CHARLOTTE LOUISA
1793–1878
unm.

²⁹PETER
1795–1863
m. Mary Louisa Foster
(see #38 across)

³⁰ANNA AGNES
1797–1827
unm.

³¹JOHN ANTES
1799–1878

³²CHARLES JOSEPH
1801–1875
m. (1) Sophie de Montmollin;
(2) Rose (de Montmollin) de Meuron

³³FREDERICK BENJAMIN
1803–1841
m. Elizabeth Scott

³⁴JOHN FREDERIC FOSTER
1795–1858
m. Caroline Bagshawe

³⁵WILLIAM FOSTER
1797–1829
m. Marianne Bagshawe

³⁶ISAAC HENRY FOSTER
1800–1827
unm.

³⁷ANNA DOROTHY FOSTER
d. 1857
m. John Amery

³⁸MARY LOUISA FOSTER
d. 1839
m. Peter Latrobe
(see #29 across)

³⁹

* All persons on Charts A and B are Latrobes unless otherwise stated.

Chart B. Selected Descendants of Benjamin Henry Latrobe

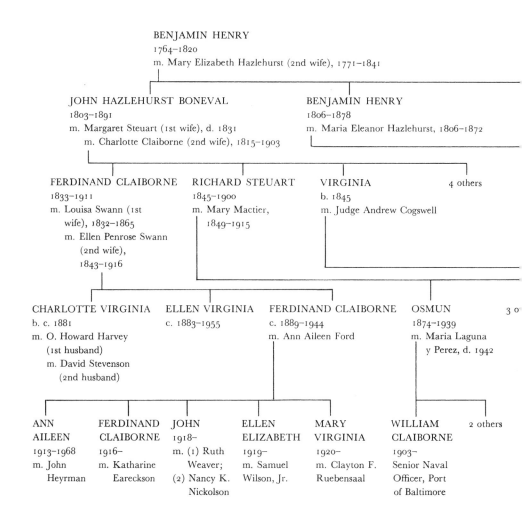

BENJAMIN HENRY
1764–1820
m. Mary Elizabeth Hazlehurst (2nd wife), 1771–1841

JOHN HAZLEHURST BONEVAL
1803–1891
m. Margaret Steuart (1st wife), d. 1831
  m. Charlotte Claiborne (2nd wife), 1815–1903

BENJAMIN HENRY
1806–1878
m. Maria Eleanor Hazlehurst, 1806–1872

FERDINAND CLAIBORNE
1833–1911
m. Louisa Swann (1st
  wife), 1832–1865
  m. Ellen Penrose Swann
    (2nd wife),
    1843–1916

RICHARD STEUART
1845–1900
m. Mary Mactier,
  1849–1915

VIRGINIA
b. 1845
m. Judge Andrew Cogswell

4 others

CHARLOTTE VIRGINIA
b. c. 1881
m. O. Howard Harvey
  (1st husband)
m. David Stevenson
  (2nd husband)

ELLEN VIRGINIA
c. 1883–1955

FERDINAND CLAIBORNE
c. 1889–1944
m. Ann Aileen Ford

OSMUN
1874–1939
m. Maria Laguna
  y Perez, d. 1942

3 o

ANN
AILEEN
1913–1968
m. John
  Heyrman

FERDINAND
CLAIBORNE
1916–
m. Katharine
  Eareckson

JOHN
1918–
m. (1) Ruth
  Weaver;
(2) Nancy K.
  Nickolson

ELLEN
ELIZABETH
1919–
m. Samuel
  Wilson, Jr.

MARY
VIRGINIA
1920–
m. Clayton F.
  Ruebensaal

WILLIAM
CLAIBORNE
1903–
Senior Naval
Officer, Port
of Baltimore

2 others

CHRONOLOGY

1764	*May 1*	BHL born in Fulneck, Yorkshire, England, son of the Rev. Benjamin and Anna Margaretta (Antes) Latrobe
1767	*June 13*	Enters Fulneck School in Yorkshire
1776	*October*	Leaves England to study in Europe
1784	*Summer*	Returns to England and works in the Stamp Office, London
c. 1787–1788		Works under John Smeaton
1788	*May–June*	Assists in writing Volume I of James Bruce's *Travels to Discover the Source of the Nile*
1788		Publishes annotated translation of *Characteristic Anecdotes . . . to Illustrate the Character of Frederic II*
1789		Publishes annotated translation of *Authentic Elucidation of the History of Counts Struensee and Brandt, and of the Revolution in Denmark in the Year 1772*
c. 1789–1792		Works in offices of Samuel Pepys Cockerell
1790	*February 27*	Marries Lydia Sellon
1791	*March 23*	Birth of first child, Lydia Sellon Latrobe
1792	*July 19*	Birth of second child, Henry Sellon Latrobe
1792		Designs and builds Hammerwood Lodge in Sussex
c. 1792		Opens his own architectural office in London
c. 1792		Appointed surveyor of the police offices in London
1793	*October 25*	Begins survey for Chelmer and Blackwater Navigation improvement
1793	*November*	Lydia Latrobe dies in childbirth
1793		Designs and builds Ashdown House in Berkshire
1795	*May 12*	Chelmer and Blackwater improvement scheme fails in Parliament
1795	*November 25*	Sails for America on the *Eliza*
1796	*mid-March*	Arrives in Norfolk, Virginia
1796	*March*	Designs the William Pennock House, Norfolk, his first American house design
1796	*April 3*	Arrives in Richmond

1796	*June 7–17*	Makes trip down Appomattox River as engineering consultant to the Upper Appomattox Navigation Company
1797	*June 6–27*	Makes excursion into the Dismal Swamp as engineering consultant to the Dismal Swamp Land Company
1797	*June 22*	Appointed by Governor James Wood to build the Virginia State Penitentiary, Richmond
1798	*January 6*	Completes design for the Richmond theater, assembly rooms, and hotel complex
1798	*January 20*	Opening night of BHL's play, *The Apology*, in Richmond
1798	*March 26*	Arrives in Philadelphia to examine Walnut Street Jail
1798	*April 16*	Returns to Richmond
1798	*July*	Draws plans for Fort Nelson, Norfolk
1798	*September 1*	Completes "Essay on Landscape," Volume I
1798	*November*	Appointed architect of the Bank of Pennsylvania
1798	*December 1*	Leaves Richmond for Philadelphia

Illustrations

FIGURES

MAPS

The Virginia Journals of

Benjamin Henry Latrobe

1795–1798

I

Journal of the Voyage from London, England,

to Norfolk, Virginia, in 1795/96

WEDNESDAY NOV. 25TH, 1795. About 9 o'clock everything being packed and adjusted, one boat carried Mr. Califf, Mr. Brewster, myself and most of our luggage on board the *Elisa*.[1] To our utter astonishment the first object on deck was a decent, rosey looking woman with a child of 3 months old. A pleasant prospect of nocturnal howlings intermixed with soporific lullabies. Nothing at present presents itself but dirt and disappointment. Mr. Califf, Mr. B. and I, clubbed a guinea to provide an additional allowance of vegetables of which but a small stock seems to have been laid in. We have plenty of fowls, but they being in a starving condition. The poor goat is fallen off terribly. The cabin is one mass of dirt and confusion. The Captain seems to have no habit or idea of cleanliness, or the accommodations expected by gentlemen. We gave up all hopes therefore at once. Mr. C. who had been on shore, returned with a load of cabbages, parsnips and some other comforts. We got our anchor up about 12. The Pilot who is a very old Captain is a very good sort of a civil man, with more than common information. The Wind easterly. In the evening after a miserably dirty dinner, we attempted some arrangement of the Cabin. A canvass screen put up before the berth of Mrs. Taylor, hid the source of perpetual crying and singing. A busy little good natured man appeared who seemed to act the part of her Cicisbeo and nurserymaid. In the midst of our arrangement, Mr. Martin discovered his error in not having provided himself a bed. A violent quarrel between him and the Captain was managed with so much apparent good temper on his part as to engage the party more on his side; though the Captain's object seemed to be and was to drive him back to Gravesend. We clubbed a kind of makeshift bed for him, when he had the art to wheedle me out of my berth on the Larboard side of the Cabin, and I took ignorantly, one of the cross berths. We cast anchor off Southend of the Nore.[2] All the night we were serenaded with the wails of the child. And the lugubrious nursing of Mr. Tenny. The mother provided an interlude of seasickness at proper intervals.

THURSDAY, NOV. 26TH. Very early we weighed anchor and with a NE Wind proceeded close to the Narrows. A very cold frosty morning, some of our fowls dead. Made great exertions and got them fed at last, and committed to the care of a

1. BHL mentioned thirteen passengers and sixteen crew members of the *Eliza*. *Passengers:* BHL, Mr. Califf, Mr. Brewster, Mr. and Mrs. Taylor and their baby, Mr. Martin, Rev. Mr. Young. *Steerage passengers:* Mr. Tenny, Mr. Cotton, Mr. Christie, Mr. Young's two sons. *Crew:* Captain Noble, Mr. Shaw—1st mate, Mr. Frost—2d mate, Mr. William Newman Hog—groom, black cook, Dick—cabin boy, Peter—black sailor, Figuero—Portuguese sailor, Antony—Portuguese sailor, Joseph—French sailor, carpenter, helmsman, and four other sailors.

2. The Nore is a sand bank in the center of the Thames River estuary. It is usually considered the dividing point between the river and its wide estuary.

groom who looks after some horses in the hold. The Captain has now dressed himself completely in character and is bustling among the trunks and packages in the Cabin, of which we have a superabundance. The beautiful view of the Coast of Kent and the delightful weather afforded an entertainment, which was much dampened by the miserable prospect of personal comfort which pressed upon us in the necessary arrangements that occupied us all. About five o'clock in the evening we cast anchor off Deal, and our pilot left us. Here the Captain expected to take up Mr. Taylor the husband of the lady who is on board; Mr. Tenny went on shore in search of him. From the information of the Pilot, I understood our situation as to real necessary articles to be almost desperate. We have two boats, no sails to either of them, only three oars, one of them broken, but then we have a paddle about six feet long. Our stock of brooms and dirt are by no means well proportioned, two only of the former and ten cart loads of the latter, but then we have an old mop and in calm weather we can employ the men to make swabs. As a proof however, of the Captain's provident care, six new hand spikes were sent on board from Gravesend, one of them indeed was broken as soon as tried, but as the rest are evidently too weak, they will last the longer. During Mr. Tennys absence, it became necessary to light a candle. Now the fact is, that we really have two candle sticks on board, one contains a tinder box in its belly, which merit must atone for its shaky dwarfed appearance, the other is lacquered, and though the snuffers are lost, an extinguisher accompanies it, as a badge of its original distinction in the service of a lady's bed chamber. It would have been folly in our Captain to have laid in a stock of mould candles. Their height would have overturned and their thickness have refused to enter our candle sticks. With curious prudence he has therefore provided a box of what are called *long tens*, which do not require much paper to keep them steady. In looking back I am ashamed of the length of my account of this day, but like the description of the reign of the founder of a new state, it must necessarily occupy more room than that of any of its successors. Part of our Captain's time this morning was employed in making a table cloth of some fine duck (canvass), which was so exactly fitted to the size of our table, that to shrink and to be extended would have equally injured its perfection. Upon this table cloth our dinner was served in square tin dishes, fitted to our Caboose. I thought them very dirty, but as I have since frequently seen them washed, without their changing color, I must have been mistaken. Pewter spoons, dirty knives, soup plates for fowls, and pudding plates for boiled beef. Potatoes boiled in their skins without washing, out[3] not to have appeared under the regular management of polite precision. The Captain therefore consistently enough hacked up the hens, slashed the beef, and then pushed the dishes about. But the beef was excellent, the bottled porter delightful, the wine not at all bad, and though the chickens were perfectly

3. Obsolete form of ought. *OED.*

4

ossified, and could not be eaten by the united strength of the whole party, no one left the table hungry. This may serve as a general description of all our future dinners, till the apprehension of want, and our lengthened passage begin to vary them. We were waited upon by a short, thick, lame boy, whose hat the color of his hair and face, never quitted his head, and who seemed either to have assisted at the fire or to have kept the chimney clean during the cooking of our repast. After dinner he sat down upon the ground at the Cabin door and finished what we had left. Good humor was the order of the day, and when novelty ceases to keep it up, habit may perhaps have thrown a veil over that which now offends.

In the evening Mr. Tenny returned bringing a supply of fresh beef. He had heard of Mr. Taylor, but feared he was returned to London, and we began seriously to consult about sending Mrs. Taylor ashore again. Very late at night he again went to Deal with a commission to buy snuffers &c. Soap was also an article of which we had not an atom.

NOVEMBER 27TH, FRIDAY. The night was still and only interrupted by the squalling of the child, and the seasickness of the mother. The wind in the morning blew from the South West and we laid patiently at anchor. Mr. Tenny returned about 10 o'clock with a pair of snuffers and a tin tureen. Now this said pair of snuffers, and tin tureen are not of so little consequence as land lubbers may suppose. For I solemnly declare that their appearance occasioned more joy and the occasional loss of the snuffers only afterwards more sorrow, than a very serious circumstance might have created in the City of London. Mr. Tenny brought also with him a dreadful wound in his hand, which much interfered with his office as nurseryman, and of which for want of a better, I undertook to cure as surgeon. The day was beautiful, and in the evening Mr. Taylor came on board. From the moment of his arrival, he was taken violently seasick. He had scarce got on board when the wind rose and the night threatened to be stormy. The dauntless activity of the Deal watermen and their expert management of their slight boats is almost proverbial. Whether tossing in the waves or riding athwart our cable they seemed equally at their ease. As the Captain had never before been in Europe, he agreed with the men who brought Mr. Taylor on board to pilot him into Ramsgate Pier in case of very blowing weather. The signal of danger proposed by the Deal men was two lights at the Mizenpeak, but alas we have but one Lanthorn on board. "*Damn your eyes you must find another,*" said the pilot and leapt into his boat, which was immediately out of sight. My observation to-day agreed exactly with Hamilton Moores Lat. of Deal.[4]

4. John Hamilton Moore (d. 1807), *The Practical Navigator and Seaman's new daily assistant: being a complete system of practical navigation* (London, 1772); and *The New Practical Navigator, being an epitome of navigation rendered easy* (London, 1793). *BMC.*

NOVEMBER 28TH, SATURDAY. The wind blew a violent storm last night, and the ship was very uneasy on account of her being much too light. We rode it out however very well at a single anchor. We are surrounded by a squadron of Russian vessels. A number of English Line of Battle Ships and Frigates are also in the Downs, and about 50 or 60 Merchant men. The Coast between the north and south Foreland has a character of beauty peculiar to England. A deep Bay skirted by lowland which rises into a mild amphitheatre of cultivation and is bounded at each end by bold and abrupt chalk cliffs. The hills were this morning covered with snow. Deal has not even the merit of most dirty towns, to afford a good prospect from a distance. It lies upon the edge of the Sea like a black heap of rubbish. Sanddown Castle is a bold object. The wind changed early to the NE. We immediately weighed anchor, and stood round the Foreland. A large Convoy weighed at the same time. We had the start of most of them, but a brig or two which were luckily a head of us piloted us along. The coast of England, which cannot have varied much since the days of Caesar in its appearance, has sufficient beauty to have tempted a less ambitious conqueror, than he was. It is not probable that the bleak Chalk Downs were ever covered with wood. They are now, I should suppose, no more, nor less the smooth undulation of hills variegated only by the mixture of clear turf and purple heath, and the occasional breaks of light and shade, which they presented to his eye. If, as some antiquarians suppose, he landed in Pevensey bay, the beautiful woody country breaking into the cold extent of Chalk Cliffs between Folkestone and Romney and again between Fairlight and Bexhill to Beacheyhead must have formed a landscape of the most romantic contrast. We sailed along the charming coast with a fair brisk wind till the evening haze hid the yellow cliffs of Hastings from us. Every spot of the coast was so well known to me, that I had a superior pleasure in seeing and recognized the different towns and eminences. We had the advantage of a delightful moon, by the assistance of which, we could just discover Beacheyhead about 9 o'clock upon our starboard beam. The wind hauling more to the Northward we took in our studding sails. [See PLATE I.]

We have scarce had time to know one another—Mr. B. and C. may remain agreeable long enough without personal intimacy. This is an advantage which good sense and good breeding insures. If however I mistake not, our Captain will not be behind hand in forwarding personal knowledge, if he should fail of producing personal respect among us. The private history of Mr. Martin is already detailed. All that I need repeat is that he has been *rich* and is unfortunate. But we have had him long enough among us to find him very troublesome. There is a total want of common sense, and one degree less of conduct must have stamped him an idiot. The vacuum however is sufficiently filled with conceit. Mr. Young is a Clergyman whose private history has also been enlarged upon from the same quarter. He has two sons on board, both steerage passengers. The eldest is an acknowledged fool, the youngest is a fine smart boy of 6 years old. He [Mr. Young] sleeps only in the cabin, finding his own provisions, which he eats in the steerage. Mr. Taylor is at present incog. No poor devil was ever more tormented than he by seasickness. He neither eats nor drinks, but performs day and night the probationary libations especially afforded to Neptune. By the bye, I wonder the Ancients did not improve upon this circumstance in their ceremonies and offerings to the God of the Ocean. I was somewhat seasick to-day, but less than I expected.

NOVEMBER 29TH, SUNDAY. A beautiful morning without a breath of air, shewed us the high land of the East end of the Isle of Wight bearing N by E about 3 leagues distant. But the wind soon hauled round to the NW and increased to a gale. We got a reef in our top sails, took several trips across Channel and in the afternoon were obliged to lay to under reefed courses. Our ship has got a most unlucky knack of missing stays since the pilot left her, but as she does not refuse to wear, our Captain only swears that she has a Mast too many. I have discovered a most arrogant and mutinous spirit in our Mate, Mr. Shaw, for in spite of the superfluous mast, he has stayed the ship twice to-day. Our fowls, among whom there is a kind of murrain, were this day after much entreaty and exertion, put out of the way of the weather, between decks. In my opinion they had better be thrown overboard for to eat them is out of the power of a jaw, which is inferior to a shark's. As to our cooking in general, which is performed by a miserable negro, who is at the same time dying of disease, it is so filthy, that much better meat would be spoiled by it. I was very sick to-day. Our vessel is very light, and what cargo and ballast she has on board is all in the hold. Between decks we have nothing but the seamen and passengers chests. She labors therefore intolerably. While we lay too, we began to clear the decks. The capstan was unshipped and got below, and the Anchor got upon the Bow, and unbent. Many of our crew are very ill yet, and this weather does not favor their recovery. The night was to me dreadful. My folly in taking a cross berth was sufficiently apparent. Indeed I could not lay down at all, but was obliged to catch, when I could, a few moments of sleep sitting upon my bed, and I lay my head upon the transom. To mend my situation, one of the squares of the window above my head was broken, through which a plentiful stream of cold air flowed upon me. I found however, an old flock pillow which being firmly stuffed into the opening promises to be a durable cure, though not a very ornamental one. These were my private calamities, but we all suffered from the total neglect of our Captain to fix any thing to its place. Before the cabin door 3 casks of bread were dancing backwards and forwards; a cupboard of crockery in the cabin, was every moment clattering with the ruins of our plates and dishes, and at every *Weather roll and lee lurch*, all the trunks, chairs, and chests in the cabin, travelled from one side to the other. The Captain seemed to reign in his glory during this confusion. Hallooing every moment—"a Mistress, how do you carry sail?" "Damn her, she rolls on her own bottom." "Brewster how do you go?" "Keep her along, she goes dry yet." "Never mind her she [is] young and skittish"—&c. &c. Mrs. Taylor's child was sufficiently troublesome to her and to us all, squalling most unmercifully, and as she herself was extremely sick, she may perhaps be excused if her passion prompted her to bestow both threats and blows not exactly suited to the age of an infant of 4 months old. The broadest and most barbarous Scotch dialect, I ever heard, did not soften such expressions as, "*Cum, cum, ye muckle fashous brat, tak yere suke, yere enow to mak un take the knife tull ye, ye muckle calf, I'll scalp ye, if ye wunna haud yere tongue.*" Better than this was even the good tempered Mr. Tenny's nursing, accompanied with a monotonous hum, more like the drone of a bag pipe than any thing else. The only happy man in the party was Mr. Martin, to whom, on account of his plea of delicate habits of life I had given up my berth. He slept sound, and snored tremendously, the whole night. Miserable prospects for a long voyage! Mr. Taylor continued so terribly ill, that we began to be seriously uneasy about him.

MONDAY, NOVEMBER 30TH.   Early in the morning we hailed a Brig. Found the Isle of Wight to bear N and by W. The gale rather fresher than yesterday and the motion of the ship so violent, as to astonish even the seamen on board. About 11 spoke a frigate, who did not detain us. Took all day trips of 4 hours each across the Channel, under close reefed top sails and reefed courses. I lay as well as I could in bed all day and eat [*pronounced* "et"] nothing. Not very seasick. All the passengers down in the mouth. The storm encreasing. Lay to all night under reefed courses. The infernal music of the last night was encreased by the addition of the capstan and three or four tar barrels rolling violently about between decks, no measures having yet been taken to secure anything. We find already a great deficiency of plates and glasses.

TUESDAY, DECEMBER 1ST.   In the morning the wind had abated and the weather was much milder. The Frigate had got much to windward of us. Some thought was now bestowed on the cabin, and our trunks fixed to the floor. As I found it utterly impossible to sleep in the cross berth, I resolved to get my bed clothes on to the floor and sleep there. But though so ill with want of rest and food that I could scarce stand, this liberty and privilege of a dog was granted with the ill humour, which the Captain has now adopted to every one of us. Indeed the scene is much altered, and suspicion and moroseness has succeeded to the cheerfulness and civility of the first two or three days of our passage. Dirt and filth gain ground every day. The knives and forks come to table wiped only, as laid down, by a dirty cloth, the glasses are never washed, and the table never wiped. The table cloth is filthy beyond description, and the grease it contains qualifies it for a Tarpaulin. We have however no other. The Captain is extremely uneasy about his situation in the Channel of which he is wholly ignorant, as no sort of account is kept of the ship's way. In the night a most singular conversation took place between him, Mr. Young and myself, which opened his character much more than he intended. He began by expressing his extreme uneasiness, and the possibility of his being obliged to run into Havre de Grace. "Well," said I, "if that should be the case, the neutrality of your Vessel would sufficiently protect us and our property, and I confess it would be more pleasant to me to take a peep into a French Port, than to be a tossing about in the Channel without gaining a single league upon our voyage." "Why," says the Captain, "I could make my fortune by going to Havre and giving up the ship and cargo as English property. I don't say I should do so, but no man can answer for himself when a strong temptation comes in his way." "If you will excuse my opinion, Captain," said I, "I believe you incapable of the idea you suggest, and that you only play with our feelings, but if you could for a moment entertain it, I think you would deserve to swing at your own yard arm." "Why," replied he, "I know that such things have happened, and I can't say but that I should be sorry to have any such temptation, especially as some of you have left families in England, and therefore I would rather not go to Havre, but I do not think any man ought answer for himself, why now even the passengers goods are worth something." It is almost impossible to believe that all this and much more to the same effect can have been seriously meant, but I am convinced it was. After much conversation, Mr. Young, who is extremely timid, and has been much used to the sea (having been, I believe, Chaplain to some man of war), persuaded him to stand over for the English coast, till he could get sight of land and ascertain exactly his situation.[5]

5. While BHL's view of America's neutral rights was perhaps somewhat ingenuous, the captain's was more pragmatic. After war broke out between Britain and France in 1793, the United States issued a Proclamation of Neutrality. Americans sailing under their neutral flag grew rich transporting vital produce and goods to and from the French West Indies. Indeed, America's carrying trade during the decade after 1793 accounted for the republic's first large-scale accumulation of capital to fuel domestic agricultural and commercial growth. Great Britain struck back, issuing an Order in Council, dated 6 November 1793, that instructed the Royal Navy and British privateers to seize all ships engaged in the "illicit" French West Indies trade. The American envoy to Great Britain was notified of the Order too late to issue a warning before British cruisers had captured 250 American vessels, of which 150 were condemned. After the outcry for war and congressional schemes for commercial

WEDNESDAY, DECEMBER 2ND. The wind still violent and contrary being WSW. As the weather was hazy we stood off and on all day. Towards evening, thinking, or hoping ourselves well over to the French coast resolved to make stretch all night to the Northward. But whether our light vessel has been driven back to the neighborhood of the Goodwin sands,[6] or whether we have got to windward of the Isle of Wight, the last land we have seen, not a soul on board can tell. Several casks having broke from their moorings, the night was unusually noisy. The squalling of the child is now a thing of course, it is perpetual and most distressing. When we first got on board, the Captain very civilly granted us perfect liberty of action in the cabin, merely prohibiting the use of cards and tobacco. However at 4 o'clock in the morning we were awakened by the fumes of a pipe of wretched tobacco, begged of one of the sailors (for he has none of his own) which he was smoking in the midst of us.

THURSDAY, DECEMBER 3RD. At day light we discovered land bearing N by E and soon after descried two Dutch-looking Vessels, one sloop rigged, the other

---

retaliation receded, President Washington sent John Jay to England in an attempt to reduce tensions and to settle the outstanding issues between the two nations. The Jay Treaty, signed 19 November 1794, while partially satisfying certain American demands (the British were to evacuate the frontier posts held in violation of the Treaty of Paris of 1783 and allow American shipping into the British West Indies on a limited basis), failed to consider the termination of British impressment or to accept the broad definition of neutral rights favored by the United States. A copy of the treaty was carried across the Atlantic to Norfolk exactly a year previous to BHL's passage. The treaty inflamed domestic politics and angered the French, who already felt that America's Neutrality Proclamation had violated the spirit, if not the letter, of the Franco-American treaties of 1778. France encouraged its privateers to attack its former ally's shipping, especially in the Caribbean; in 1795 alone, 316 American ships were captured.

American vessels feared a threat from yet another potential foe, the Algerians, who worried the *Eliza*'s captain until he had safely passed well beyond the Azores. In 1793 British diplomacy effected a year's truce between her ally Portugal and the Dey of Algiers. Previously, the Portuguese navy had kept Algerian corsairs out of the Atlantic and provided escort for American ships through the dangerous waters north of Algiers. Britain's main purpose was to free Portugal's navy for action against France; however, in the United States the move was seen as a further attempt to destroy the American merchant marine. BHL might ridicule the captain's "Algerine" phobia (see pp. 14–15, 21, 26), but it was not without foundation, for the United States alone among Atlantic powers lacked a protective treaty with the Dey. Early in October 1793, an Algerian fleet had passed through the Straits of Gibraltar, and by December 119 American seamen from thirteen vessels were in captivity in Algiers, along with the remainder of two crews seized in 1785. After much delay and negotiation, a peace treaty between the United States and Algiers was signed in September 1795 and ratified by the Senate in March 1796. However, difficulties in raising the gold bullion in Europe necessary to secure the captives' release prevented their departure from Algiers as free men until 12 July 1796. For further information see Bradford Perkins, *The First Rapprochement: England and the United States, 1795–1805* (Philadelphia: University of Pennsylvania Press, 1955); Charles R. Ritcheson, *Aftermath of Revolution: British Policy Toward the United States, 1783–1795* (Dallas: Southern Methodist University Press, 1969); and Henry G. Barnby, *The Prisoners of Algiers: An Account of the Forgotten American-Algerian War, 1785–1797* (London: Oxford University Press, 1966).

6. The dangerous shoals ten miles long in the North Strait of Dover approximately seven miles east of Deal; they enclose the Downs, the famous roadstead where the English defeated the Dutch fleet in the first Anglo-Dutch War (1652). *Webster's Geographical Dictionary*.

carrying only a large Sprit-sail and fore-sail. We hailed them, but could not under-stand what they said. They seemed excellent seaboats. The sea ran mountains high, but they turned so well to the wind, and steered so well, as to sail round our ship with ease. We stood in for the shore till we were within a league of it. It proved to be the Cliffs to the West of Beacheyhead. The wind having hauled to the Northward we shaped a westerly course, and had some hopes of getting out of the Channel should it continue in the same quarter. At 4 we descried a fleet of 7 very large ships standing for the Downs, supposed Indiamen under Convoy. At 11 o'clock at night it blew a terrible gale. Lay to under reefed top sails with her head to the NE. Wore at 6 in the morning and stood to the SW. Every night has been so equally noisy, troublesome, and to me devoid of sleep, and every meal such a scene of nastiness, that till they change, the worse description I have given may do for all. Mr. Brewster is grown entirely silent, and the loss of his conversation is the loss of one of the few comforts on board.

FRIDAY, DECEMBER 4TH. The wind being N and by W we again made a due westerly course, and our spirits somewhat revived. The weather was fine, and we got up on deck. Not a razor has passed over any of our chins since we left the Downs, nor has a shirt been changed. A more miserable dirty looking crew never assembled under the name of gentlemen. Some small approach however, towards a return to decency was made in towing the table cloth alongside by way of washing it. For these several days passed its smell has been as disgusting as its appearance. It was laid down again wet, but the better weather, clean knives and forks, and a good dish of beef put us in better humor than I could have supposed any of us susceptible of. In the evening we got a sight of the French Coast bearing SW. Wore immediately and stood NE. The Captain again agitated about his situation in the Channel. Several ships were in sight all day. Taking trips of 4 hours each all night.

SATURDAY, DECEMBER 5TH. Fresh gales from the WSW all day. A most unpleasant and dismal sensation of uncertainty and apprehension occupied us all. In the afternoon the weather became more moderate, and we descried very high land on our larboard bow, the ship lying NW. It seemed impossible that this land could be any part of the Isle of Wight from the course we had held for some days passed, and as the only similar land is Fairlight, the Captain condescended to call a general council in which it was seriously debated whether we should not return to the Downs, as the perpetual gales, have considerably strained the ship and impaired our rigging and sails. Mr. Califf's opinion however, carried it, to stand off and on all night, and to endeavor to run in close in the morning, and then to decide. The wind blew very fresh all night.

SUNDAY, DECEMBER 6TH.   Daylight again discovered the same land exactly in the same situation. We had the good fortune to fall in with 3 Cutters about 9 o'clock, one of which carried a Pennant. We hailed her, and she very *politely* informed us that the land in sight was the East end of the Isle of Wight, Dunnose bearing WSW southerly. We must therefore have been in a situation all night rather dangerous, off the entrance of Portsmouth harbour, surrounded by shoals and sunken rocks. Our joy was great, though the wind continued contrary. Tacked, and stood S by W and in the evening took a trip to the Northward. At 12, tacked and stood SW the remainder of the night; the wind continuing at W and WNW.

MONDAY, DECEMBER 7TH.   Early in the morning made land bearing S by W supposed to be the Island of Alderney. Wore ship and stood again to the Northward. Our total ignorance of the tides and currents of the Channel must necessarily be most injurious to us. With an obstinacy equal to that of the wind we have now been beating about in the Channel for nine days as close hauled as the vessel would lay, but without the most distant plan as to our situation, the Captain having determined, as he says, *"to beat her bottom out before he gives in."* To remedy this evil, if possible, I to-day made a complete tide-table of the Channel from Dover to the Landsend [Lands End], to last for 10 days to come. I hope it will be unnecessary before half that time is expired. In the evening the wind became very variable and almost died away towards night; about 12 shifted to the NE. Our spirits were revived.

TUESDAY, DECEMBER 8TH.   The pleasure we felt in the idea that we should at last get out of the channel where we have suffered so much inconvenience and misery, was suddenly blasted about 5 o'clock this morning by a hoarse voice which through a speaking trumpet ordered the mate to haul up his mainsail and to stand up channel. The rage of the Captain burst forth into a thousand execrations, part of which fell upon the second mate who had already obeyed the order, and the rest were profusely scattered over the Tyrants of the Ocean, the English. We were all soon upon deck and found ourselves between two ships of war, it was too dark to see their force. After a few questions from the Commodore, who demanded the ships and Captain's name, her destination, and whether we had met with any cruisers, we were permitted to proceed. The behaviour of the Officer who hailed us was polite, but as soon as we were released by him, we were hailed from the other frigate, who would not suffer us to proceed till her consort was out of hearing. With petty insolence we were then asked several captious questions relative to France which seemed dictated by disappointment for the loss of a prize, and when she had done, we were ordered to put up our helm and to pass under her stern, when with less inconvenience to her and ourselves the ceremony might have been dispensed with. With a fresh and fair breeze we now stood down the channel. The Islands of Alderney and Guernsey towering over the sea to the South. The day was warm and mild, and the spirits of every soul on board elevated. But we are a set whose characters seem not well to coincide and the general dislike to the Captain, his total carelessness about our comfort and accommodation, and his most incautious or malicious exposure of every circumstance he knows respecting the character and fortunes of his passengers, destroys every prospect for the future.

It is impossible to enumerate all the petty grievances, under which we labor; and which to us are of great importance, who have nothing to balance them. We are most shamefully short of water, and the crew are already on allowance of half a gallon a day. We are not allowed a drop to wash our hands and faces. (For the commonest calls of nature) in illness no provision is made. The cabin which is only 22 feet wide by 14 is occupied by two sleeping places on each side and two others across over the lockers. A stove in which we seldom dared to make a fire, on account of the insufferable smoke, and a filthy table occupy the remaining space. The floor is the receptacle of every species of filth, and the violent agitation of the ship so frequently overturns dishes, cups and glasses, that indifference about it is almost necessary. In regard to our meals, I have already mentioned how they are conducted. We have one tin Coffee pot and a tin kettle. In the tea kettle, Dick, our cabin boy, makes coffee for breakfast, and in the coffee pot, water is boiled for tea. The coffee is not by any means bad. But the tea is the coarsest bohea. We have a few pewter teaspoons which are never cleaned, and their deficiency is made up by pewter tablespoons still blacker than the others. Our biscuits are good, and the butter tolerable, but put upon the table in the nastiest manner imaginable. Every one helps himself to sugar as he can. Our dinners I have described. At tea the water is boiled in the kettle that contained the coffee for breakfast and of course its taste is, if possible, worse than naturally it would be. For supper we eat up the remains of dinner, if any cold cabbage, cold beef, all mixed up in the square tin pans in which they were chopped. We have not a sufficient number of wine glasses to serve all, we therefore assist one another. All our tumblers are broken but 3, and the glass passes from the hand of the grog drinker to that of the porter drinker, contains brown sugar at tea and serves for a slop basin at breakfast. If in the course of these several offices it gets one washing, we are more than unusually happy. Mr. Brewster has a collection of books of the best sorts, which with great liberality he has given to the general use of us, and Mr. Taylor has many

Volumes of Novels. We are extremely unsociable. General conversation exists not among us. The evenings are necessarily employed in reading, in which we all crowd round a farthing candle swinging by a rope yarn in a lacquered chamber candlestick upon a nail in the midst of a dining table. Every other day the snuffers are lost. The violent agitation of the ship renders sitting at the table at any rate a most severe exercise. But to sit and read by a movable candle, holding fast by a ricketty table, and to remember what is read requires more genius than is usually granted to mortals. Poor Martin alone finds comfort in listening to his own harangues upon Law, Religion, the prolifixity (a noun derived from prolific) of rabbits and scotch-women, the inspiration of Milton and Mr. Newton the rector of Woolchurch,[7] the bundling of American inamorati, and the prophecies of Jeremiah. With most sublime and unintelligible elequence he descants upon obscene and holy subjects, settles the difficult points of cards and duelling and of the doctrine of the Trinity. If Grammar, history, geography and common sense are sacrificed in his abstracted discussions, it is impossible to feel disappointment or regret. The Captain with a degree of brutality which Mrs. Taylor's situation cannot check, halloos his rude enquiries, how each of us *"carry sail"* or *"go,"* whenever he wakes. The ship is wholly navigated by the Mate, and well it is for our lives and safety that he is unlike his Captain. This is the true picture of our life, in which though you may suspect that pen whose wild sallies your kind prudence has so often checked, "nothing is set down in malice, nor aught extenuated."[8] Latitude by observation 50°3'.

WEDNESDAY, DEC. 9TH. Our NE Wind continued fresh through the night and this morning we were out of sight of land on Deck. From the Main topmast head Scilly was descried bearing N by E. The mate took his departure and commenced his journal. We got up our top gallant mast, let out all our reefs and set fore Top mast Steering sail.[9] The Cabin was also washed and cleaned out. But what improvement in its appearance was occasioned by the operation, I declare I could not discern. Having now at last quitted the channel, we are promised a great variety of conveniences which the constant and necessary attention to the ship in the narrow seas rendered impracticable; I confess I have no very fond expectations in that respect. But a sudden panic which has this morning seized the Captain, makes me seriously uneasy. He has taken it into his head, that should he go to the Southward, East of

7. John Newton (1725–1807), an evangelical Anglican clergyman, wrote *An Authentic Narrative of some . . . Particulars in the Life of . . . John Newton* (London, 1764), an account of his early life at sea and of his religious conversion and experiences. *DNB.*

8. "Speak of me as I am; nothing extenuate,/Nor set down aught in malice." Shakespeare, *Othello,* act 5, sc. 2, lines 341–42.

9. Steering sail: an obsolete term for studding sail.

the Azores, he will inevitably fall into the hands of the Algerines. Now by the best accounts peace has subsisted between the Algerines and America these 18 months, nor has a single vessel been captured during that time. Upon Mr. M's wise suggestion concerning the straight road to America, the Captain has always declared that it was a sacred thing with him to go into the trade winds as soon as he could get clear of the Channel. Indeed common sense at this time of the Year points out that, as the only rational means of a tolerable passage.

We are now approaching the solstice, and though our present wind is very flattering, we can hardly expect its continuance for many days. Instead therefore of improving the breeze to cross the Bay of Biscay, we are steering W by S so that the first SW or West wind will undoubtedly send us immediately into it.

The beauty of the afternoon and a good glass of wine has drawn us a little more together again. The evening is mild and the wind dies, a bad presage of a change. Lat. by Observation 47.47.

THURSDAY, DECEMBER 10TH. A perfect calm accompanied with a tremendous swell. To mend the matter, as if she were not sufficiently uneasy already, all the cables were this day stowed in the hold under the forehatch. She was already too much (to use the sailors' phrase), "by the head." But ignorance and obstinacy always go together. In the evening a light westerly wind sprung up, which before 12 increased to a gale and brought us under close reefed top-sails. Lat. by Obs. 46°0′.

FRIDAY, DECEMBER 11TH. Moderate breezes with a heavy sea. Ill humour and disappointment in every body's countenance. The wind high towards night. We are all in indifferent health, but none very sick expect poor Mr. Taylor, who is now moved into Mr. Tenny's cot in the steerage.

SATURDAY, DECEMBER 12TH. The wind still at WSW and fresh. In the afternoon very moderate, steering as close to the wind as we could lay. The Captain who is not often upon deck excepting to look after the dinner, has become a great reader; about 8 in the evening he had just finished the *Vicar of Wakefield*, and was enquiring of me "whether I recollected how Goldsmith had disposed of Burchell," when I observed to him that I thought the vessel began to pitch more than usually. "I suppose," said he, "the gib is set, I will order it down presently." Mr. Califf however, whose intrepidity saved the ship, ran upon deck, and before the Captain could follow him, the wind blew a hurricane. The Mate had turned in, the second mate was frightened out of his wits, and the Captain knew not what to do. Mr. Califf, however, got the ship before the wind, but every sail was shivered. All hands were soon upon deck, and the Mate got up. For a considerable time it was doubtful whether we could save our Masts. The Ship was with difficulty kept large. The sea was mountainous, and the danger, I believe equal to our fears. With much exertion in the course of an hour, we got our courses, the Main, and Mizentop sail[s] as well handed as the violence of the storm would permit, and scudded under our foretop sail, which threatened every moment to go. The foremast bent like a cane. In two or three hours the gale somewhat moderated. At ten the Captain went to bed, nor did he rise till the next morning after 9 o'clock. The Mates and crew were up all night wet to the skin, and hard at work. Towards morning the wind died. Though the danger existed more in the total unskillfulness of the Captain, his entire neglect of precaution, and his miserable laziness, than in the violence of the storm, we for an hour had in the Captain's opinion, no chance of saving the Mast. To the exertions of Mr. Califf and of the Mate, we owed our escape.

SUNDAY, DECEMBER 13TH. The Deck was a miserable scene this morning, the wind was quite down, and the ship rolled at the mercy of a mountainous swell. The deck was covered with tattered rigging, and the poor sailors crawled about as wet as drowned rats. The ship still lay to, and as soon as the Captain came upon deck, he for the first time began to exert himself with great vociferation to get the sails and rigging repaired. But we are miserably provided against such accidents. The only spare sail we have is a new foretop sail. This was bent. Every other sail was more or less shivered, all hands therefore went to work to mend them. But not a yard of canvas is there on board. All the old canvas bags in the ship were therefore collected and supplied the place of new cloth. The fine duck of which Royal Sails are usually made, was employed, when the odds and ends failed. Another fresh gale would leave us a perfect wreck without the means of refitting. After such a night of fatigue, the crew deserved some extraordinary good treatment. But for want of proper discipline on board, the two blacks, who should provide the mens' and our dinner, do just as they please, and the men seldom can get any regular dinner cooked. The coach which should defend their caboose from the spray of the sea covers the cabin caboose which is fixed on the larboard quarter, and the sea perpetually breaking in at the fore chains puts out their fire. This day the men could get no dinner at all. The cabin passengers took the matter up, but the Captain damned their souls and wished they might go without dinner till they could contrive to get it without plaguing him about it. The Mate however, exerted himself and though the men went without food for this day, a different arrangement for the future was the consequence. Our cabin boy, Dick, was taken very ill, the Captain suddenly became active, and attended him with an incredible degree of tenderness and assiduity. Latitude by observation 44°53'.

MONDAY, DECEMBER 14TH. We had a fresh breeze from the NW all night which continued through the day. As our Beef becomes unpleasantly salt, we this day killed one of our sheep. The live stock we took on board, was four sheep, four pigs, and some dozen of fowls. The sheep have done very well, and seem in as good case as when they came on board. The pigs are miserably poor and two of them not likely to live. Of the fowls we have lost one-half, and the others are not likely to be eaten, so wretchedly old and tough are they. Besides these live provisions we have a cask or two of Beef salted in London, five or six hams, and a barrel or two of potatoes. This is all we have to look to, for subsistance on a voyage, one-tenth part of which is not yet finished, and which from the obstinate panic which has seized the Captain is so conducted, that our provisions may be at an end before we pass the Azores. Very fresh gales during the night, and a dreadful sea. Latitude 44°21′.

TUESDAY, DECEMBER 15TH. A dreadful gale, which sprung up at 6 in the morning and lasted till 12, from the NW brought us under our forecourse. We scudded all the morning and lay to in the afternoon; the wind died in the evening. We are all very unwell, Mr. Taylor somewhat better. For my part, though not seasick, I can neither eat, drink nor sleep, and have lost all strength. My bed on the ground is rendered extremely unpleasant by the filth of the cabin. Wind died in the evening.

WEDNESDAY, DECEMBER 16TH. It was perfectly calm this morning, with a dreadful swell. We began to have serious apprehensions about shifting of the cargo, and some steps were taken to prevent it. One of the mares we have on board lost her foal this morning, and the other who is also in foal will most likely follow her example. The groom is in deep mourning for the infant. We have daily consultations in the cabin about the Algerines, and if the Captain's panic should increase there is much reason to fear that he may die of a dysentery. The fresh mutton upon which we have dined these few days past has done somewhat towards producing better humour among us. Latitude 44.24. In the evening the wind arose again from the old quarter NW.

THURSDAY, DECEMBER 17TH. Another very heavy gale from the WSW. Lay to all day. I was very seriously ill. The Captain has shown uncommon affection for the cabin boy Dick who continues very sick, and is more likely to die than live. Half the attention bestowed upon his passengers would make their lives easy if not comfortable. One very great nuisance is a circular orifice in the transom, the frequent visits to which, by one or two of the gentlemen who have not courage to mount the mizen chains, and among whom the Captain is the most assiduous, have rendered the cabin equal in strength of odor to the private cells of a college. We put up our quarter dead lights to-day. Shipped several very heavy seas. Mr. Taylor is so far recovered as to read *Tom Jones* aloud to his wife behind the canvas screen that protects her berth, in the persevering monotany of a school boy. Mr. Tenny (who is a steerage passenger), being necessary in the cabin, as the substitute of a nursery maid, is now perfectly domiciliated among us. He lately kept an alamode beef shop in Seven Dials,[10] was formerly cook on board a Hudson bay vessel, and once clerk to Mr. Taylor. His manners are what may be expected from these habits, but he deserves the praise of extreme good humour, and willingness to assist every body. His ignorance however, renders him troublesome, and the noise he makes in order to quiet his baby, and his soporific tunes from which we have no escape but into the pelting of the pitiless storm upon us require an uncommon portion of Christian fortitude to bear.

FRIDAY, DECEMBER 18TH. A damp and rainy morning, wind at WNW. A sudden whim to scour out the cabin, notwithstanding the rain, having seized the Captain, we, for the first time, ventured to oppose him. He became rude and abusive, but desisted. Mr. Taylor continued his lectures[11] all the evening. My illness continues. A fresh gale at night from the W by S stood to the Northward Latitude 43°17'.

SATURDAY, DECEMBER 19TH. Mild pleasant morning. Got the cabin most completely wetted, but the pretense even of cleanliness is vanished. The conversation at dinner is never interesting, to-day however, it was extraordinary at least. Our Captain advanced an opinion which he thought fit to state as probable, and to defend—that General Washington's birth and parentage is wholly unknown, but that he is most probably a bastard of George the II, and that, during the tumult of the well known action on the Ohio, General Braddock fell by his hand!! In the evening we had a very heavy gale from the NNW. Stood to the Southward. Latitude at noon 44°28.

SUNDAY, DECEMBER 20TH. The Wind changed in the night to the SW and continued with extreme violence all day. At night it blew a storm. The ship was too much agitated to permit me to lay down all night. We lay to till midnight,

10. Located in the parish of St. Giles in the Fields, London, where a huge seven-sided column with a sun dial on each face marked the meeting point of seven streets. The column was removed in 1773 and the area later became "notorious as the refuge and residence of criminals." H. B. Wheatley, *London Past and Present: Its History, Associations and Traditions* (London, 1877), pp. 234–35; Sir Walter Besant, *London in the Eighteenth Century* (London: Adam and Charles Black, 1902), p. 529.

11. Used in the eighteenth-century sense, meaning "readings." *OED*.

scudded till morning. Latitude at noon 44.47. We have had but little rain with all this bad weather. A pig which was half dead was to-day killed, but the meat was so bad that the men though half starving could not eat it and it was thrown overboard.

MONDAY, DECEMBER 21ST. Poor Mrs. Taylor's child seems to be very ill, for its squalling is the order of the day. The mother has continued so seasick, that I have not seen her since she first retired behind her screen. The Captain has contrived to baffle all the attempts of the passengers to get her into the state room, although he professed to wish it. The gale continued with encreased violence all this morning and a most serious dispute between the Captain and first Mate added to its unpleasantness. Mr. Shaw, is a young man not above 21. He has a good natural understanding, and is a good seaman. We have to thank him for many little accommodations, he behaves with prudence to the Captain, and with good temper to us all. He has won our good opinions, though his character and history has received some of the dirt which the Captain indiscriminately scatters over us all. The management of the vessel entirely depends upon him under the general restriction to pass the Azores to the Northward, and not to go nearer to them than 2 Degrees of Latitude. We are thus at the mercy of the Westerly winds which seem set in for the winter.

Fig. 1. The *Eliza* in a heavy gale, 21 December 1795.

19

In the afternoon with a very clear sky, the gale blew with astonishing violence. About 6 a very heavy cloud collected towards the West, from which issued frequent flashes of lightning but without thunder. By degrees the whole horizon was encircled with low heavy clouds, the lightning was frequent, and notwithstanding, the moon shone most brilliantly. Its effect was strong and awful. The wind blew with the greatest force about 9 o'clock and the jar was tremendous. Our situation, as scudding before the Wind under our foresail, I have attempted to represent in the Drawing [FIG. 1]. A more sublime scene it is almost impossible to imagine, than the united effect of the dark Ocean agitated into mountainous waves, the broad shadows of which were contrasted by their white foaming summits; the horizon covered with heavy clouds from which perpetually flashes of red lightning issued; and the Moon breaking through the gloom and beaming a silver light upon the whole scene from a sky of the clearest blue. There was no thunder. At ten the ship was laid to under her forecourses. We were well prepared for the storm and received no injury. (45°25'.)

TUESDAY, DECEMBER 22ND. The wind was something more moderate, and having got much to the north in the night, we stood to the southward all day. In the evening it again blew a gale as usual. We lay to all night, the storm continued till the morning. (Lat. 45.52'.)

WEDNESDAY, DECEMBER 23RD. When we made a little sail standing to the northward. We had much rain, and no observation, to-day.

THURSDAY, DECEMBER 24TH. The wind is usually more moderate in the morning, and we have regularly a gale in the evening, which in the course of the night increases to a storm and begins to abate about 3 or 4 o'clock in the morning. I am so perfectly tired of recording the misery of heavy gales from the westward and dull conversation, and filthy dinners in the cabin, that a plate of pan cakes which Mr. Shaw has cooked for our tea comes in as a most seasonable relief, and I could willingly write a dissertation upon Pancakes, which, reminding me of Shrove Tuesday, might lead me into the thick of ecclesiastic controversy about the true time of keeping Easter, the cruel diversion of throwing at cocks, and the life of St. Dunstan.[12] But as it would all end in unavailing, though very moral lamentation over the folly and weakness of man, and perhaps in a most just, though immoral (as divines tell us) contempt and hatred of my own species, I will return to the Pancakes, which spread satisfaction over our whole party, and distinguished Christmas eve from the rest of our stormy days. In order that due honour might not be wanting to the celebration

12. Throwing at cocks: cock-throwing, the sport of throwing sticks at a cock tied to a post, formerly an ordinary Shrove-tide pastime. *OED*. St. Dunstan (c. 910–988), archbishop of Canterbury.

of Xmas (to-morrow) we also killed a sheep. But to moderate our joy, one of our three remaining pigs, who have a miserably wet lodging in the long boat, was this day squeezed to death by the small boat, and his body committed to the mighty deep. The two survivors are as lean and miserable as they could wish to be in order to escape the knife of our carpenter, for he is our butcher. Our latitude was 47°57′ at noon.

FRIDAY, DECEMBER 25TH. Neither fresh mutton nor wine, nor Christmas day could render us less shy and unsociable than we have tacitly agreed to be. The violent agitation of the ship, which to-day was unusually bad, and which jumbles everything else together, has no effect on our minds and sentiments. Mr. Brewster having exchanged with Mr. Califf and retired into the State room, seems banished. I mention this as one of the most unpleasant circumstances that attend us. Mrs. Taylor came from behind her screen to dinner, as rosy and fat as ever. Commend me to such a constitution. The wind dying in the evening and the Moon shining pleasantly, the hopes of seeing the wind change, kept me on deck till midnight. In the course of the day a brig appeared upon the horizon. The Captain begins at last to lean to the opinion of those who wish to go more to the Southward.

SATURDAY, DECEMBER 26TH. The weather continued mild and the wind moderate. We held a southwardly course all day with the wind at WNW. A very thick fog, at noon, suddenly persuaded half of us, that we have reached the Newfoundland banks. But by what means we should have reached them, the wisest of us cannot conjecture, unless our having had sufficient length of time, and a plentiful stock of desire, has effected it. Mr. Young was taken so ill, and continued so bad all night, that we gave him over for lost, and the Captain began most seriously to lament the expense his two children might occasion him, and that his goods on board would scarcely reimburse on half of what he might lay out.

SUNDAY, DECEMBER 27TH. Mr. Young being a little better, moved into his boys cot in the steerage, and sent his eldest son to sleep in the cabin. A schooner which appeared all day about a league to windward of us, revived the idea of the Banks of Newfoundland. She was undoubtedly (we agreed) an American fisherman, whom the Westerly wind had driven off the Banks, and was beating to regain her station; she had a quantity of fresh fish on board, and could supply us with water, rum and sugar, all articles of which we are likely to be in want, before the end of our voyage. It was therefore very unfortunate that the Captain's head was full of Algerine corsairs, and that this said schooner, could not in his opinion be anything else. He kept therefore out of her way, and she was so obliging as not to carry us into captivity,

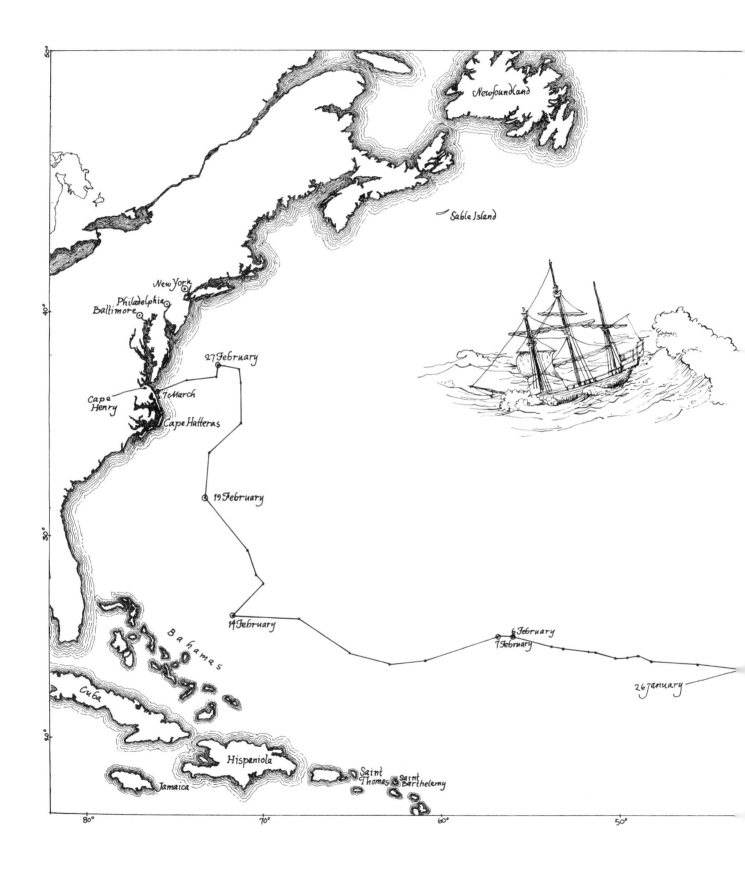

Newfoundland

Sable Island

New York

Philadelphia
Baltimore

27 February

7 March

Cape
Henry

Cape Hatteras

19 February

B a h a m a s

Cuba

14 February

6 February

7 February

26 January

Hispaniola

Jamaica

Saint
Thomas

Saint
Barthelemy

80°

70°

60°

50°

50°

40°

30°

20°

The Atlantic Voyage
25 November 1795 - mid March 1796

English Channel

France

24 December

Bay of Biscay

13 December 1795

27 December

18 December

Portugal

Spain

4 January 1796

Azores

Pico

6 January

13 January

Canary Islands

22 January

5 January

Africa

40°   30°   20°   10°

notwithstanding our noble Captain's family have £4,000. ready to ransom him. Lat. at noon 44°23′. Supposed longitude the Banks of Newfoundland—I think, the bay of Biscay.

MONDAY, DECEMBER 28TH. A very pleasant day. The wind continues fair, and all the usual prognostics fail. A very little sense is required in the trade of prophecy. Mr. M. has therefore undertaken that office, and a large Shoal of Porpoises, which, at some distance from the ship, took their course to the North East, are without fail to bring us a breeze from that quarter. But we have long given over belief in the unusually successful predictions of this sort. The sea has been fussing and the scud flying merely to mock us for this fortnight past. The moon, who in inconstancy has always been allowed to give way to the Wind, has this time been the more constant of the two. We this day began to scrape and scour the decks, which have hitherto remained in a very filthy and slippery condition. It is not easy to tell how long this fit of cleanliness may last, it seems a preternatural effort.

The sailors were this afternoon extremely dissatisfied and almost ready to mutiny on account of the wretched bread with which they are supplied. Indeed their condition is extremely wretched. Mr. Young's illness carried me on a visit between decks, and a more dirty and unwholesome hole I never saw. Many of the crew are now sick, and none of them perfectly well. We have been a month at sea, the pigs, the sheep, the fowls, the goat and kid, and two filthy negroes have accumulated manure sufficient for a small farm, without one attempt to remove any part of it. Notwithstanding the Value of our Cargo there is not one Tarpaulin on board, and the constant sprays and seas that break in upon us, and find their way down into the steerage keep the mass in a moderately fluid state. In order to accommodate the Cabin, the Caboose was lately fixed just under the Booby hatch. The bad weather rendered it necessary that the Hatch should in general be down and an intolerable smoke is added to every other Evil. But the worst of all is, that the Biscuits, with which the sailors and steerage Passengers are favored, is mouldy, and magotty. There is better bread on board, but it is reserved for the time when an Allowance of bread may become necessary. The Captain persisted and the bad bread was continued for the present.

There are two evils of an apparently incompatable nature in the government of this vessel. The most absolute and unreasonable tyranny, and the laxest discipline. In the case of the bread, a positive command, and a volley of oaths and imprecations, succeeded in forcing the men to do what the laws of their country would have entitled them to have resisted. All hands were one day called (by the Captain) at six in the morning (when one Watch was asleep) to take the grease out of the binnacle. Oaths and imprecations produced obedience and scarce a day passes without some unreasonable command being enforced by the same means. But if in a sudden squall, or when the ship is to be stayed or wore, all hands are ordered on deck, it appears as if every man were perfectly at liberty either to obey or refuse.

There are two passengers in the steerage. The one, Cotton, is a journeyman Painter and Glazier, the other, Christie, a Scotch farmer, both of whom mean to try what they can do at their trades in America. They live as the sailors do and are at present in a most mutinous humor, having paid twelve guineas a piece for their passage. Their diet is salt beef (much of which is horse flesh, as the round ribs and the form of many of the bones prove), about once a week a mess of fat pork, beans and water. The men, have been allowed about six drams a piece since leaving the Downs. Our rum runs now very short so that let the weather and the work be ever so hard, any further indulgence of this sort is out of the question. Latitude 43°30.

TUESDAY, DECEMBER 29TH. The Deck cleaning rage operated powerfully this morning, and the men finished scraping the whole of it. The weather was very mild and pleasant and the sea more easy than we have yet seen it. At night the luminous appearance of the sea where agitated by the passage of the ship, was very considerable. This phenomenon, will most likely forever baffle inquiry. In order to try whether the same effect would be produced, I requested Frost, our Second Mate, to draw some water in the bucket and to throw it with violence on the deck. I was satisfied by the experiment that the sparkling of the water was occasioned by its agitation, but my philosophical curiosity proved unfortunate to Mr. Young who had some salt provisions in the bucket soaking, which owing to the darkness of the night were thrown overboard. We have made chiefly a westerly course today. Our Lat. at noon was 42°11′.

WEDNESDAY, DECEMBER 30TH. We were roused this morning by a most violent wordy war between Mr. Young and Mr. Frost, the Second Mate, concerning the beef lost by my experiment. The two combatants, one of whom forgot, and the other perhaps disregarded, the precepts of Christian patience and resignation, vented and, I hope, worked off their feelings in the violence of the debate, and left me, the innocent cause of the misfortune, all the punishment of unavailing regret. Something however, of the ridiculous in the transaction assisted to comfort me. Our evenings have for some time been sulky and silent. To-night it particularly struck me. Those that do not read, suck their teeth in silence. We had some rain at night. The floor is now so nasty, that in spite of the abominable sensation the ship's motion creates, I moved into the cross berth again. The Captain much inclined to venture to the south, but still fluctuating. The Algerine corsairs were again conjured up to keep him in countenance. Latitude 41°3′.

THURSDAY, DECEMBER 31ST. The morning was the calmest and most pleasant we have yet experienced, and we got up our Main top gallant sails. The wind still at W by S. We stood to the Northward the greatest part of the day; having for a week past made more southing than our reckoning gave, we suppose ourselves in a current. The Captain was unusually at a loss, and unintelligible upon the subject of his operations. To assist him in the perturbed state of his mind, it was this day discovered that of the two minute glasses which have hitherto settled our reckoning, one runs 10 seconds longer than the other. They were both tried, and both found wrong, the average error, being nearly 1/4 of our course too much. The Captain thought proper to be insolent to me on account of the conversation which induced Mr. Shaw to make the examination, which was nothing more than a common place enquiry into the usual mode of marking the log line. We had intended to close the year with a social glass of Punch, but the Captain continued to put it off so long that it could not be made; and it was as well, for we had a heavy gale in the evening which lasted part of the night. The men renewed this day their complaints and procured better bread. Latitude at noon 40°16′.

1796. JANUARY 1ST. After a night of misery in the cross berth the early news of a fair wind from the NE was extremely agreeable. At all hazards, I however, determined no longer to sacrifice my health with my sleep, to any consideration, and having procured two sacks of the groom, I got Antoni, one of our Portugese sailors, to make me a hammock which I got strung in the steerage between the Main and Forehatch. Though the Captain could not either absolutely oppose or prevent my removal, he threw every difficulty in my way, and though he had formerly proposed that my pianoforte should be put up in the Cabin and on account of the dryness of the situation I much wished it, he now opposed that measure. As I was however determined to claim the situation in the cabin for which I had paid, an altercation took place—the first since we left England, the natural effect of the extreme illblood which has long brooded, between him and every other passenger. His violation of the confidence placed in him by every individual, was by this time the topic of private conversation, and it was known to each of us, that independent of the disclosure of what was true, his own malignity had added falsehood of the most infamous nature. As not one of us escaped, mutual good opinion was in some measure restored by the explanations which took place, but the reserve which is grown habitual among us will scarcely be rubbed off, during the continuance of our voyage. In the afternoon the wind shifted to the South and we stood to the West again.

JANUARY 2ND, 1796. SATURDAY. For the first time, I slept well in my hammock, and felt myself better this morning than I have done for a month past. The wind having shifted to the WNW, we stood all day to the South. At noon our Latitude was 40°19′.

SUNDAY, JANUARY 3RD. Mr. Tenney who has occupied the other cross berth encouraged by my example, had a hammock made, and having resumed his cot in the steerage, Mr. Taylor removed into it, so that two of the cabin passengers have now been driven by necessity to run the risk of peopling their clothes and persons with the vermin of which the sailors are said to entertain a considerable quantity. We have however taken every possible precaution, and swing at a distance from any other hammocks. My pianoforte was this day moved into the cabin, not without murmurs. It is too much out of tune to afford amusement. Latitude at noon 39°40′.

MONDAY, JANUARY 4TH. We are by some means all persuaded that though by our reckoning we are now in the meridian of Corvo, the most northerly and westerly of the Azores, we must be considerably to the westward of them. The wind being N and by E we kept a westerly course, and a good lookout for land all night. Corvo lies in Latitude 39°41′ and in the 31st degree of West Longitude from London.[13] We this day killed a sheep, a circumstance which never failed to produce pleasant faces and some good humour, and if philosophic ideas were ever the subject of discussion among us, I believe the doctrine of Epicurus, who has placed the seat of the soul in the stomach would not be without its advocates. Latitude 39°38′.

TUESDAY, JANUARY 5TH. This was a remarkably fine day. We made a most voracious dinner of excellent mutton, and for the first time pushed about a social bottle with so much briskness, that the Captain and some others were more than *half seas* over. We were sure we had passed the Azores and scarce kept a look out at night, though we are now exactly in their Latitude. Wind still fair at NE. Latitude 38°52′.

WEDNESDAY, JANUARY 6TH. Soon after six we were all called upon deck by the cry of land to the NNW of us. Surprise and vexation took possession of all our

13. Corvo's latitude is 39°40′7″N; its longitude is 31°8′W.

seafolks from the Captain to the cabin boy.[14] For my own part, I confess that the beauty of the morning, and the grandeur of the scene exhibiting three or four Islands covered with clouds that were gilded by the rising Sun, gave me much more pleasure, than I felt disappointment from the certainty of our being most considerably behind our hopes and our reckoning. By degrees the Sun dispelling the clouds, showed the majesty of Pico di Azores, half covered with snow, the brilliant whiteness of which, was equal to polished silver. It was a view that cannot be described. With the encreased elevation of the Sun it became a more distinct, and splendid object. The wind was light, and we seemed during the whole day scarcely to change our distance or our position respecting it. Fayal and Tercera appeared one on each side of Pico, more distant but clear. My ideas upon the height of the mountain I have put together in the sketch book [see below]; and [PLATE 2] is a very imperfect, but as to lines and color, an exact drawing of the Island. The mountains on the East end of the Island appear of very considerable height; I could not discover any snow upon them. The snowy region of the Pic[15] seemed level with their tops excepting where two or three arms of snow extended lower down. Those seemed to fill some valleys or ravines as seen through a small acromatic glass belonging to my sextant. The snow upon the tops of the Mountain was broken through in every few places by the appearance of black rock. The Depressed parts of its surface were very visible by the shadows upon the snow, and they appeared to consist of ravines radiating towards the point. The Crater seemed to be elevated upon two bases or offsets near the top of the mountain, perhaps the vestiges of very old eruptions. The Crater itself is a beautiful conic mountain, appearing at the extreme eastern end of the Pic, and sparkling in the Sun like a Diamond, especially when backed by a cloud. Below the Crater is a black spot, some of the Portugese sailors who have been at Fayal said that a pond of water is on that place. Perhaps some remaining volcanic heat may keep snow melted in a reservoir which happens to have no vent. The surface of the snow below it seemed not to be interrupted by any stream which might issue from this supposed piece of water. I do not recollect ever to have heard or read of an irruption of this volcano. Not the smallest appearance of vapor was about its head. The day was so perfectly clear that it could not escape observation had their been any such thing. Might not

14. Although BHL and the crew believed they had already passed the westernmost Azores, they had unknowingly sailed through the dangerous eastern channel between Terceira and São Miguel on the night of the fifth. The *Eliza*'s east-west position was continually miscalculated throughout the voyage because the ship lacked a chronometer, a marine timekeeper used for determining longitude at sea. The instrument, invented sixty years earlier and proven accurate in four decades of sea trials, was still very expensive. BHL felt the *Eliza* made little progress on 6 January, but if his sketchbook information of that date is accurate, a plot of the course between 8 A.M. and noon indicates that the ship covered twenty-six nautical miles.

15. Obsolete word meaning "peak." *OED.*

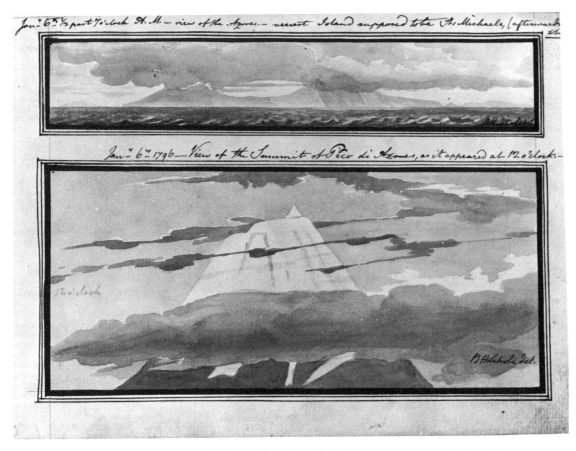

Fig. 2. Two views of the Azores, 7:30 A.M. and Noon, 6 January 1796.

this mountain be the Atlas of the Ancients as well as Teneriffe, as Gibbon suggests?[16] Was it not equally accessible to them? Though the other is nearer Africa, it is more distant from Greece.

About noon a girdle of heavy clouds collected just above the commencement of the snowy region [FIG. 2]. By degrees they fell below it, and detached the snowy top from the blue tint of the Island below. Before sunset the whole mountain was enveloped in clouds, the wind changed to the SW and blew hard with a short unpleasant sea. We stood to the NNW and I was in hopes that we should be in the morning so near some of the Islands as to obtain refreshments and supplies, of which we stand much in need. Our Latitude at noon was 37°[3]4', Longitude W of L[ondon] 28°20'.

One of our Luxuries, has been for some time past, what we call nuts, being in fact nothing but flour and water, made into dough, cut into pieces about 2 inches

16. According to Gibbon "the long range, moderate height, and gentle declivity of mount Atlas . . . are very unlike a solitary mountain which rears its head into the clouds, and seems to support the heavens. The peak of Teneriffe, on the contrary, rises a league and a half above the surface of the sea, and as it was frequently visited by the Phoenecians, might engage the notice of the Greek poets." Edward Gibbon, *The History of the Decline and Fall of the Roman Empire*, 8 vols. (Philadelphia, 1804), 1:30n.

square, and fried in pork fat, in a great iron pot. To-day Mr. Tenny by the addition of a little butter to the dough very much improved this article of indulgence, and made us more than unusually happy. I mention this as an event of consequence to us, though of none to any one else. As however human felicity is a precarious treasure, the discovery of two or three fat maggots in a biscuit I was eating kept my raptures within bounds. We have been for three weeks past under the necessity of eating the sailors biscuits of the better sort. Of these we have but a few casks on board, and they both magotty and mouldy and much below the ordinary standard of sailor's bread in quality. However, we shall not complain, provided they do not grow worse, and our other provisions last. Our prospects are now a little better decided though not so flattering as they were a few days ago.

⧉ ⧉ ⧉

FROM THE SKETCHBOOKS

[1]   *Remarks on the Altitude of Pico di Azores.*
[2]   The angle of Altitude of Pico measured by my Sextant is 1°9′30″.
[3]   Pico, according to Mr. Hamilton Moore is situated in 38°.29′ N Latitude
[4]   By a very accurate Observation at noon⎰

                                                              ⎱ 37°.34′
[5]   Pico bearing due N, we were in N Lat.⎰   ───────
[6]   Distance from Pico, ----------------- .55 Geographical Miles.
[7]   now as the Cosine of 1°.29′ to its sine—so its the distance, to the heigh above the Horizon
[8]   99.979 --------- 2007. --------- 55. miles --------- 1 Mile 549 feet, or 5.829 feet
[9]   Supposing therefore the distance correct, which is given by the difference of
[10]   Latitude, adding nothing for the semidiameter of the mountain (as I have
[11]   supposed the Latitude given by Hamilton Moore to be the Latitude of the
[12]   *Pic* itself and have therefore added nothing to the distance of 55 nor abated
[13]   for the heigh of the Ship, which rolled from 12 feet to 5 without making any
[14]   sensible difference in the measurement of the angle) there must be added for
[15]   the heigh of an Object which at 55 Miles distance appears level with the
[16]   Horizon, according to Hamilton Moore, the only book I have to refer to—   2.050 feet
[17]   7.879, or
[18]   One Mile, and 2.050 feet.

Mr. Brydone in his travels through Sicily supposes the heigh of Aetna to be 12,000 feet or something above two miles. This supposition seems to be the result of barometrical experiment, for (as he says) the Italians have made the heigh of Aetna from eight to three miles high. Kircher (see Brydone) who has a sufficient tendency in all cases to believe the marvellous, makes Aetna 4,000 toises or about 50,000 English feet. Brydone remarks upon the improbability of this supposed measurement, and from the tremendous *apparent* heigh of Pico it seems (if there is any accuracy in

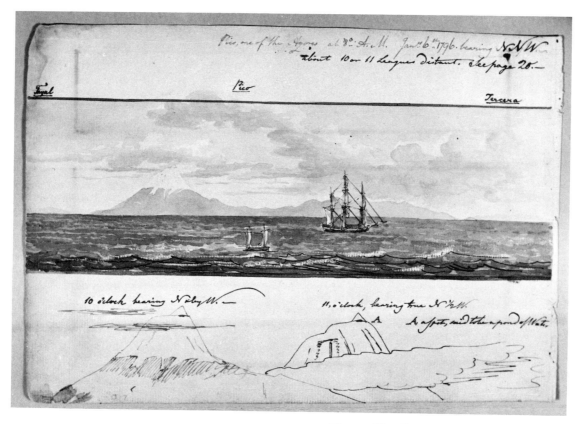

Fig. 3. Pico di Azores, 8 A.M., 6 January 1796.

my supposed heigth of about 8,000 feet) that Aetna cannot possibly be more than six times the heigth without having excited still greater astonishment than it has already done.[17]

Latrobe's Estimate of Pico's Altitude

EDITORIAL NOTE

During the day of 6 January the *Eliza* passed below the island of Pico and its snow-covered summit on a southwesterly course at approximately six knots an hour. Latrobe's drawing of the scene indicated how the peak's profile, as viewed from the ship, changed during the morning run. At noon he established the *Eliza's* latitude using his sextant and the tables in John Hamilton Moore's (d. 1807) *The New Practical Navigator*, an all-purpose handbook on navigation and seamanship.[18] He then wrote the above

17. Patrick Brydone, *A Tour Through Sicily and Malta, in a Series of Letters to William Beckford, Esq., of Somerly in Suffolk*, 2 vols. (London, 1773). Athanasius Kircher (1602–80) was a German Jesuit priest, mathematician, physicist, and chemist.

18. The first American edition, printed from the thirteenth English edition, was *The New Practical Navigator* (Newburyport, [1799]). This edition was partially edited by the American mathematican and astronomer Na-

"Remarks on the Altitude of Pico di Azores." Latrobe calculated the height of the mountain to be 7,879 feet, rather close to the actual height of 7,673 feet.[19] This agreement is fortuitous, however, as Latrobe made a number of errors in obtaining his results.

The three essential elements of Latrobe's calculations were:

(a) The conversion of a latitude difference to a horizontal distance d.
(b) Use of triangulation to determine height h above the horizon, i.e. taking

$$h = d \tan \theta$$

where θ is the angle of altitude.

(c) Adding a correction term l to h. This is the height by which ground level is below the horizon for a given great circle distance. The term l can be read from Table XVII in Hamilton Moore's book.

In the following detailed discussion of the sketchbook entry Latrobe's entries are converted to modern decimal notation. *Lines 1–5* will be accepted as given.

Line 6. This is Latrobe's major source of error. He correctly established the base line as 55 nautical miles but proceeded to treat them as statute miles in his computations. One minute ($1'$) of latitude equals one nautical or geographical mile (Hamilton Moore employs the phrase "sea mile," which is a third alternative usage) and is longer than a statute mile by a factor of 1.15157, or approximately 15 percent. Calculating from Latrobe's latitude data, the distance is 63.3, rather than 55, statute miles.

Line 7. The angle given in line 2 is copied incorrectly.

Line 8. The cosine of the angle in line 2 is almost correctly given, i.e. cos $1°9'30'' = 0.99980$ but the next number is not the correct number for either the sine or the tangent, which are equal to the given accuracy for such a small angle:

$$\tan 1°9'30'' = 0.02022,$$

and not 0.02007. This leads to a negligible error of .5 percent. However, since the base line is 63.3 (not 55) miles, the height above the horizon is 6,762 (instead of 5,829) feet.

Line 16. This is the correction for the curvature of the earth, discussed in (c) above. The height is 2,675 feet, but because of his nautical / statute mile confusion, Latrobe erroneously calculated 2,050 feet.

Line 17. With all preceding corrections, the number on this line should be 6,762 + 2,675, or 9,437 feet.

Line 18. There is an error in converting from the (incorrect) result of line 17.

$$7,879 \text{ feet} = 1 \text{ mile and } 2,599 \text{ feet.}$$

The discrepancy between the height of Pico as correctly calculated from Latrobe's data and the actual height is 23 percent. This can be considered a good result, given the errors inherent in his data. For instance, it is difficult to believe his remark that the rolling of the ship did not noticeably affect his observations.

---

thaniel Bowditch (1773–1838), who revised and corrected a number of tables; an expanded version, *The New American Practical Navigator* (1802), was the first of more than sixty editions of Bowditch's famed book. Moore's standard work passed through twenty editions and three title variations between 1772 and 1829. *The New Practical Navigator* contained useful mathematical tables and formulae, rules for ascertaining a ship's tonnage, an introduction to the art of navigation, tables of the latitudes, longitudes, and times of high water for Europe and the Western Isles, formulae for finding the height and distances of objects at sea, and information concerning the use of Hadley's Quadrant, the antecedent of the seaman's sextant.

19. As given in *The Times Atlas of the World* (Boston: Houghton Mifflin, 1971), pl. 88. In estimating this height, BHL assumed "the Latitude given by Hamilton Moore [Table IV] to be the Latitude of the *Pic* itself." Moore located the island at lat. 38°29'N, long. 28°20'W; the mountain's summit is at lat. 38°28'N, long. 28°25'W.

Plate 1. Dover as seen from the *Eliza*, 28 November 1795.

Plate 2. Pico di Azores with one of the boats used among the Western Isles, 13 February 1796.

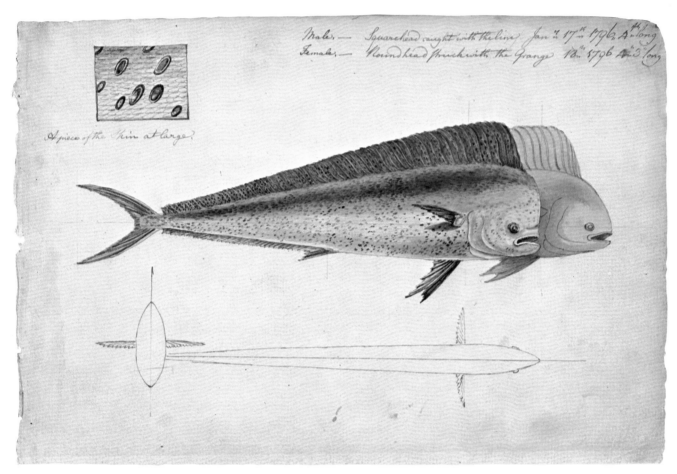

Plate 3. Male and female dolphins, 17 and 18 January 1796.

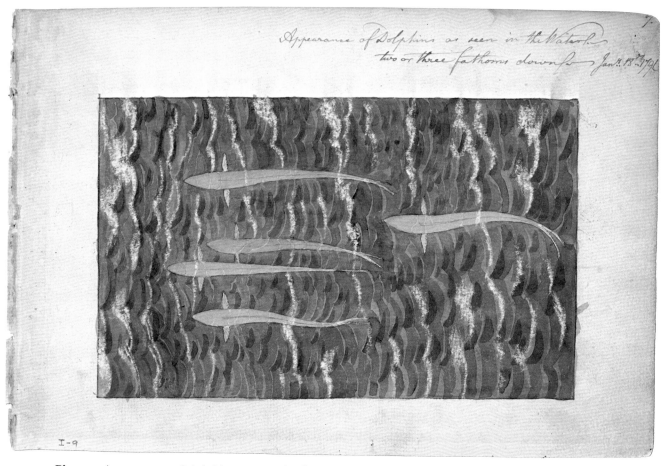

Plate 4. Appearance of dolphins as seen in the water two or three fathoms down, 18 January 1796.

FROM THE SKETCHBOOKS

Barnacles.

These Barnacles were taken from the Rudder and are drawn the real size. Their original mode of Generation, I mean *that* by which they are lodged in an infant state upon the bottoms of Ships will, I presume always be a secret.[1] But after they once get hold of a ship they seem to vegetate, and to form one of the many links that connect the animal with the vegetable world, though they may be a link near the animal end of the Chain.[2] The young ones seem to grow like scions from the root of the old stem, and contain a little active animal when no larger than they are drawn on the next page.[3] The stem is tough and pliable and seems organized like a common Grub. The animal opens that part of the Shell which resembles an S, and plays out his fibres, of which those which I dissected had 16 on each side, fixed in pairs to 8 short stems (see fig. *b* and *c*) the 16 fibres have a vermicular appearance the others are smooth and plain. The flesh of the Animal adheres to the blue spot (see the figure). He possesses the faculty of shutting his Valves with some power against a forcible attempt to open them. All three shells are internally united by a tough Skin being open only at the top and curved Side. There seems no cohesion of the *shell itself* at the Crossline, but the lower one is lapped over the upper one a little. These Barnacles seem to have grown in the course of a Month.

NB. I observe that the round Edge of the Barnacle which is fortified by the Shell (*a*), is always opposed to the stream of the Water, and that they seem to croud round the Water's edge, so as to be alternately wet and dry. Their position in the drawing is therefore incorrect.

1. Their mode of generation, by microscopic free-swimming larvae, was not discovered until 1834. See M. P. Winsor, "Barnacle larvae in the nineteenth century," *Journal of the History of Medicine and Allied Sciences* 24 (1969): 300.

2. At this time it was still widely believed that all natural productions could be arranged in a continuous series, with no definite demarcation between plants and animals. See Arthur O. Lovejoy, *The Great Chain of Being* (Cambridge, Mass.: Harvard University Press, 1936). Along the middle portion of the chain were the sensitive plant *Mimosa*, and "zoophytes" such as *Hydra*, sponges, and corals.

3. Some of the "zoophytes" do arise by budding, but in fact barnacles do not. Each young larva swims independently in search of a place to settle. They grow in clumps, even on top of one another, because the larvae are attracted by the smell of other barnacles. The lively motion of the creature within the protective shell indicated to BHL that barnacles should be placed at the animal end of the zoophyte segment of the chain of being.

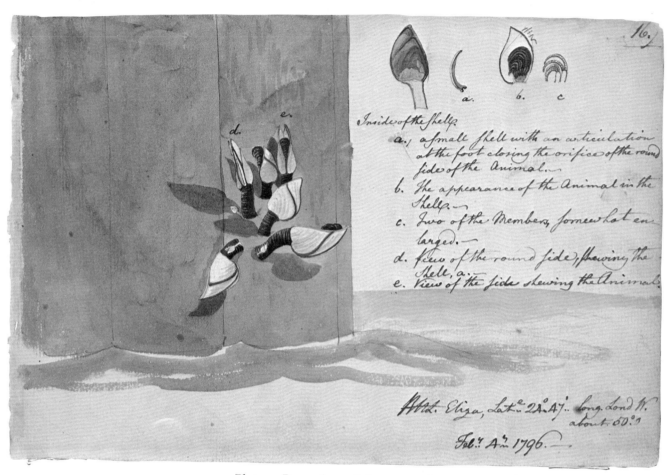

16.

Inside of the Shell.

a., a small Shell with an articulation
at the foot closing the orifice of the round
side of the Animal.

b. the appearance of the Animal in the
Shell.

c. two of the Members, somewhat en
larged.

d. View of the round side, shewing the
Shell, a.

e. View of the side shewing the Animal.

Attd. Eliza, Latd. 22°.47'. Long. Lond W.
about 60°.?

Febr. Ano 1796.

Plate 5. Barnacles, 4 February 1796.

THURSDAY, JANUARY 7TH. The morning was so hazy that no land could be seen, though by our reckoning we could not be much distant from Fayal and Pico. Some of our people thought they saw the latter through the fog, but I was not so fortunate. The wind was again in the old quarter, the SW, and we now seriously put about for the Trade Winds. This gave real pleasure to us all, not that we had any confidence in the Captain's declaration to that effect, but that the obstinacy of the wind has induced us to believe that we shall be forced into easier weather, where we and the poor fatigued and half starved men may recover strength and spirit in spite of his ignorance and whims. About 2 we descried a sail to the W[estward]. She bore away for us, and the Captain's Algerine panic returned. We upon this occasion heard so many professions, assertions, and offers in which truth had no share, that I am sickened in writing of it. Having approached us within musket shot, she steered again her own course, and passed us. She appeared to be a large Portugese Brazil vessel. Immediately after she had passed us, Antony, who is a knowing hand threw out a line and caught a fish of about 3 foot long, which he called an Albacore, and our Americans a Cavalli Mackerel. It was much the color of a Mackerel, had a very large head and two very long narrow fins projecting at right angles from each side. Its form was most beautiful, but before I could take a drawing of it, it was already cut into twenty pieces. All our attempts to catch more were fruitless. I understood these fish follow the Portugese ships in great numbers from the Brazils, where they are indigenous.

Our meat at dinner was found to be tainted. The cask therefore was overhauled and all the rest of it found to be in the same condition. I am sorry to fill up so many lines of this tedious description of a miserable voyage with the gross misconduct of the most despicable wretch on board. He on this occasion refused to take or to suffer the mate to take the necessary measures to save what Beef might have been preserved, and endeavor to recover the rest. That which we could not eat for dinner, he gave to Antony for his fresh fish, a bargain which the poor fellow durst not refuse. Our objections to this injustice availed nothing. Latitude 37°20′.

FRIDAY, JANUARY 8TH. Mr. Shaw undertook the office of cook to-day and made an excellent chowder of our Albacore. Chowder would be no very palatable dish but in such a case as ours, who have to choose between that, and tainted beef, and to eat both out of a square tin dish as black and dirty as the back of the chimney. It consisted of Pork, pieces of biscuit, onions, chopped potatoes, and the fish cut in slices, stewed together till the different ingredients were not easily to be distinguished from one another. It was however the most delicious morsel we had tasted, since our last banquet of baked mutton. Our amusement to-day, which we most eagerly followed was, to make fishing lines, and luckily Mr. Taylor had plenty of very excellent hooks, which he most good humoredly supplied us with. Latitude 35°9′.

SATURDAY, JANUARY 9TH. The wind still continues SW and though our course is somewhat reluctantly directed to the South, the Captain has not obliged the mate to take trips to the Northward since we left the Azores. The weather is become warm and easy, and our spirits I think improved. We for the first time to-day met with the species of Sea Weed called Gulphweed, in considerable quantities. I have put all my thoughts upon that subject together in the sketch book [see pp. 43–47 and FIG. 5]. The evening was squally.

Among our innumerable wants, the want of candles is one of the most serious. We are already so short that we cannot afford to burn one in the binnacle, and a substitute for a candle, being a piece of pork fat, with a stick twisted through it, throws a dismal gleam upon our compass. In this way a pound and a half of pork is consumed every night, value in America 1s.0d. A candle worth a penny would go as far. Thus avarice disappoints itself. The 3 gentlemen who sleep in the steerage grope their way every night in the dark to their hammocks at the risk of their necks, as the main hatch, along the brink of which they must pass, is always open, on account of the horses that inhabit the hold. One of them has received a few days ago much ill language on account of a small stump consumed in such an expedition. Latitude 33°23′.

SUNDAY, JANUARY 10TH. Since the weather has proved milder and the sea easier, we are become more attentive to cleanliness, and Sunday in general produces beardless faces and clean hands, though it is with difficulty we procure fresh water to wash them. This day was one of the most pleasant we have yet seen in every respect, excepting that it finished the last joint of our fresh mutton. Our fowls, of which half a dozen are protected by their age, are given over as uneatable. We have two half starved pigs left, and these are now to be better fed and rendered fit for our table. Mr. Martin, who has been lately employed in reading Young's *Night thoughts* with the assistance of the second volume of Johnson's *Dictionary*[20] has kindly undertaken the care of them. Latitude 33°16′.

20. Edward Young, *The Complaint; or Night-Thoughts on Life, Death, and Immortality* (London, 1742–45). Young belonged to the "Graveyard School" of English poetry. Samuel Johnson, *A Dictionary of the English Language, in which the words are deduced from their originals, and illustrated in their different significations by examples from the best writers. To which are prefixed, a History of the Language and an English Grammar*, 2 vols. (London, 1755).

MONDAY, JANUARY IITH. The warmth of the weather has produced a general disposition to sauntering and idleness. I have read through since we left the Downs, Hume's *History of England*, all Smollett's and Fielding's Novels which Mr. Taylor has, some parts of Voltaire's Works, and several other small volumes. I have now undertaken Gibbon's *History of the Decline and Fall of the Roman empire*. But I am either worn out of my intention, or debilitated by the warmth of the air, and cannot now attend to any pursuit of exertion. Mr. Shaw, the mate, gave up to-day his State Room to Mrs. Taylor, an accommodation which is as acceptable to us all, as to her. We likewise got the stove moved away, and the cabin now assumes a more decent and roomy appearance. In the evening we had several trifling squalls attended with rain. Latitude 33°40′.

TUESDAY, JANUARY 12TH. A very squally day, the wind from SW. A single Dolphin accompanied us all the afternoon. Our attempts to strike him were vain, and he refused to bite. No observation.

WEDNESDAY, JANUARY 13TH. A high unpleasant sea with very frequent and heavy squalls. For these three days past our Captain has taken frequent trips to the North and Northwest, for which no one on board can account. I believe them to be the working off of the Algerine disease. He seems to be afraid of the Barbary Coast, and therefore runs about a league a day from it, and 5 leagues towards it. The sky, at the setting of the sun, has every evening uncommon beauty, and the new moon is in our dearth of comforts a great acquisition. Latitude 31°49′.

THURSDAY, JANUARY 14TH. Though the squally weather continues we had upon the whole a pleasant and easy day. The squalls precede each other at the distance of about 2 hours and are but of short duration. They have never commenced before 10 in the morning. The general wind is between SW and West. Every squall occasions a variation of 3 or 4 points, but the wind returns, when they are over, to the old quarter. Latitude 30°23′. We have made much headway to the East since we left Pico. I think our Longitude must be about 24° West of London.

FRIDAY, JANUARY 15TH. About one o'clock in the morning we had a very heavy squall which called up all hands. The rain was very violent indeed. There were several others equally severe during the morning, and at half past eight a very heavy shower of rain fell. At nine without the smallest appearance in the heavens, a gust of wind attacked us with the impetuosity and suddenness of a battering-ram, and in a moment sprung our foremast, shivered our main and mizen topsails to rags, and injured every other sail. It was accompanied with a deluge of rain, but lasted only a few minutes. A squall of a different kind quite as unexpected as it was undeserved fell from the Captain upon the mate, to whom all the blame was attributed. Part of his vexation was scattered profusely upon every one on board. We had several more heavy squalls in the course of the forenoon. The weather was mild and clear in the afternoon and all hands employed in mending rigging and sails. The sea ran tremendously high and the ship rolled as bad as in the bay of Biscay. We got up our foretop gallant sail for a mizen top sail, and our spare foretopsail (the only spare sail in the ship) for a maintopsail, carrying no sail upon the foretopmast. The deck presented a miserably wrecked appearance. We made but little southing the last 24 hours, the Captain having taken trips to all points of the compass, and lain to part of the morning. Latitude 30°12′.

SATURDAY, JANUARY 16TH. After a few slight squalls in the morning, we had a delightful day. Several Dolphins were playing about the ship, and exhibiting their incomparable form and color. We got our foremast fixed, and made as strong as ever. The men were employed in mending the sails. We stood to the southward all the last 24 hours and were at noon in Latitude 29°3′.

SUNDAY, JANUARY 17TH. The Dolphins that amused us yesterday were still about the ship. There were either 9 or 10 of them. The Captain had the good fortune to take one with my line; another bit, but broke the line and got off. All my ideas upon the subject of Dolphins I have put together [in] the sketch book [see below and PLATES 3 and 4]. We made a chowder of our prisoner. It was not so good as the former, I think the Dolphin as indifferent a fish upon the table as he is beautiful in the water. Seamen have a notion that his flesh is frequently poisonous, from his feeding upon copperas banks and therefore use the precaution of cooking a piece of silver with it, which, if it turns black, is supposed to decide the noxious quality. This fact experience only can decide, and as there was a doubt about it, with some of our seamen, it may be false. Should it however be true, and the reason assigned be good, it would prove that shellfish forms an essential part of the Dolphins' food, as little as the construction of his mouth and head seems adapted to procure it. The flying fish is certainly his favorite sustinence. The day was pleasant, and warm, with a light SW breeze. In the evening it was calm. At noon our Latitude was 28°9′. A very heavy swell hove to the SE.

FROM THE SKETCHBOOKS

Remarks on *Dolphins*. (French, *Dorade*)

The first Dolphin we saw was on the 12th of Jany. in Lat. 31°30′. The Wind blew then from the SW a very fresh breeze, the Ship closehauled going at the rate of 4 Knots an hour. He seemed to be solitary, though some of us *thought* they saw another. He would not bite, perhaps the extreme roughness of the sea prevented him, as the bait was suspended from the Spritsail yard, and the ship pitched much. He kept close to the Ship all the evening, but was not to be seen in the morning. Though they are certainly a gregarious fish, they are sometimes seen alone. Our mate struck a single one between *Fayal* and *Pico* Lat. 38°40′. The chief food of the Dolphins is I believe the flying fish, that fish being most frequently found in their maw when opened, but they must have other inducement to hover about a vessel in flocks as they do, than to prey upon fish, or indeed than the hope of food at all. They do not bite eagerly in general, and as to the Barnacles or other Shell fish which may adhere to the Bottom of the Ship, their Mouth seems not in the least adapted to the business of breaking, or drawing them from their strong holds; so that I doubt whether they attempt it. Besides as inhabitants of *deep* water, nature would scarcely give them an appetite for a Species of food, not generally to be procured by them. How far *curiosity* may be attributable to Dolphins, Metaphysicians may determine, but if they possess it, it is in a most insuperable degree. One of the Dolphins who took a strong hook on the 16th of Jany. broke the line, and though his jaws were extremely lacerated, he continued with the flock dragging a fathom or two of line after him the whole day. He contrived to disengage himself however from the line, but still was one of the five that remained with the Ship, till they all left us on the 18th meeting perhaps with some food to divert their attention, for with us they would have starved. I perceived that they permitted all the Offall that fell overboard to pass them unheeded. The flock that came to us on the 16th consisted either of 9 or 10. I never saw more than 9. Two were caught. One was struck in the side with the Grange[21] which tore out his bowels and quitted him. Another received the Grange in his back, was drawn about 10 feet out of the water and then fell back and escaped. He was seen to drop astern. The remaining five (one of whom was the fish with the lacerated jaw) seem not to have grown wise by the experience of their own or their fellows misfortunes, but like most others who have a *redundance* of *curiosity*, to have had a great *deficiency of prudence*.

21. BHL probably meant to use the word "grains," a fish-spear or harpoon with two or more grains or prongs. *OED.*

Colour. Nothing can exceed the beauty and gaiety of the colours of the dolphins. When at a very great depth, so that their form cannot be distinctly seen, the curled surface of the waters above them, sparkles with the beauty of a labrador stone,[22] and indeed their is nothing, to which the effect can be more properly compared, unless (if the comparison be not too humble) to the beautifull colors that are often seen swimming on the surface of stagnate water. When they rise nearer to the surface, they appear of a light blue, as lively and transparent, as that of the neck of a peacock. Their side fins appear of a pale gold and green color, and their tails of the most brilliant gold. When drawn up out of the water, their whole bodies play with blue purple pale green and gold colors, which by degrees approach to a warm brown, but almost vanish as the fish dies, which is in about a quarter of an hour. They are however not wholly lost even when he is dead. The Gold predominates on the belly part, and the purple and blue on the back and back fin. Besides these general colors, the whole body and head is covered with small spots, each of which is equal in beauty and color to the eye of a peacock's feather, changing in the same manner with every inclination of light.

The color of the water however evidently adds to the beauty of the dolphin while he remains in it, notwithstanding that imagination cannot exceed his appearance, even without its assistance. The Dolphin may properly be called the *Peacock* of the Ocean.

In Oldendorp's *History of the Danish Islands, St. Thomas, St. Croix, and St. Jan,* which I have not read for many years, I recollect a description of the *Dorade* (dolphin) (*NB. The book is written in German*) the pompous coloring of which still dwells upon my mind.[23] Oldendorp was a *Clergyman,* and I believe a Dane, and I am ashamed to say that nothing in his book has left so strong an impression upon my memory, as the warmth with which he speaks of the complicated luxury of the taste of the *Pineapple* (*Ananas*) and of the beauty of the *Dorade,* which (if I remember right) he also praises as an excellent Dish.[24]

22. Labradorite, a kind of feldspar, flashes with blues and greens.

23. What had so stuck in BHL's memory was a brief unexaggerated description of a splendid fish: "The *Dorade* or Goldfisch, which the English call dolphin, gets its Portuguese and German names because its scales often shine just as if they were of pure gold. They shine thus when they swim at the surface of the ocean; deeper down, they shine green or blue, or shimmer with all the colors of the rainbow. . . ." Christian Georg Andreas Oldendorp, *Geschichte der Mission der Evangelischen Brüder auf den Caraibischen Inselm S. Thomas, D. Croix und S. Jan* (herausgegeben durch Johann Jacob Bossart, Barby, 1777), 1:59–60.

24. Oldendorp (1721–87) was in fact a German; the islands he wrote about belonged to Denmark. He was a poet and an avid observer of nature; the first 230 pages of his *Geschichte* are devoted solely to natural history, in orderly arrangement and with Linnean names given in the footnotes. His careful appreciation of the pineapple is worth recalling: "The excellent *Ananas* is native to these islands, and often grows in abundance in wholly wild

MONDAY, JANUARY 18TH. Early in the morning Antony struck two Dolphins with the grains. One of them he lost, the other he secured. It proved a female, and was full of roe. Its stomach contained 3 articulations of the back bone of a fish, and a small flyfish an inch and a half long—see the Sketch Book. The instrument called grains,[25] by the seamen, (in the plural number) is certainly two or three thousand years old, and, with submission to his Godship, I cannot see any difference between our three pronged grains in the rough hand of Antony, and the Trident of Neptune sculptured by Phidias on the Frieze of the Parthenon at Athens. In fact, every representation of Neptune with his trident that I have seen might pass for a good jolly fisherman going to catch Eels or strike Dolphins, and indeed this is a considerable merit, as few of the Gods of Mythology are half so well equipped for the business assigned to them.

A long altercation or explanation between Mr. Martin and the Captain produced to-day fresh uneasiness among the passengers, and encouraged the mutual distrust which poisons our society. But the perpetual repetition of his misconduct is so disgusting and distressing, that I must beg you to suppose that whenever there may seem a chasm in my narrative, it ought to have been filled up with some recital of his meanness, ignorance, insolence, or folly.

A more serious evil, perhaps because it is a new one, is the quantity of vermin, which either former or present neglect has bred and multiplied in Mr. Young's family, and which we find it difficult to keep perfectly clear of. As a part of our sufferings, this mention belongs to my narrative, but there is no occasion to dwell upon it. Latitude at noon 27°57'.

TUESDAY, JANUARY 19TH. A very calm day, with a perfectly smooth sea. All our Dolphins have disappeared. We may perhaps hang in these calm latitudes for some time. No hint of a trade wind has yet appeared. Every air comes from the Westward. Several of the birds called by the sailors, Mother Cary's chicken,[26] hovered

---

places between large rocks. Their ripe fruits, which are surrounded by long narrow leaves and embellished with green crowns, have a golden yellow color which gives them a very beautiful appearance. . . . The fruit is six to nine inches high, up to the crown. Their aroma and flavor give them superiority over all other fruit. The flavor is sweet, with the tartness of wine, and spicy; it has something of nutmeg, of peaches, of rennets [a kind of apple], and of nearly ripe wild strawberries prepared with sugar and wine, and still over all of these, an inexpressible charm of its own. They are as wholesome as they are delicious. They fortify the stomach, awaken the appetite, refresh the blood, and make you cheery." If this seems an extravagant description, remember that Oldendorp tasted them fresh-picked and sun-ripened.

BHL's recollection was correct; Oldendorp did say that dolphins "are also a savoury dish" (*Geschichte*, p. 60), though, like BHL, he thought the tuna family tastier.

25. See n. 21 above.

26. A name given by sailors to the stormy petrel (*Procellaria pelagica*). *OED*.

about, but not near enough for distinct examination. Our bread grows very maggotty and mouldy, and our salt meat is quite useless. We have plenty of Potatoes and upon these I live. Latitude at noon 27°15′.

WEDNESDAY, JANUARY 20TH.   Finding my clothes in one of my trunks damp and somewhat mouldy, I procured a variety of occupation, from the business of spreading them out upon the Quarterdeck in the sun. A keg of Codsounds²⁷ made a variety at dinner, but it was a wretched one. A young whale rose very near the ship and blew. Latitude 27°1′, very calm weather.

THURSDAY, JANUARY 21ST.   The morning was damp, and it rained a little. Immediately after, the first breath of the Trade Wind blew from the NE and in-spired us with new hopes. We immediately hoisted the starboard and larboard top masts steering sails upon our main mast, and a lower steering sail forward, and ran before it. A very heavy swell from the North made the ship roll exceedingly, and our rigging tumbling down about our ears, rendered the deck dangerous. Latitude at noon 26°11′.

FRIDAY, JANUARY 22ND.   The rolling of the ship and the failure of the rigging continued through the day and our hands were employed in repairs. As our porter is upon the decline, we agreed to take a bottle per man a day, and to restrict ourselves to the use of three bottles of wine a day for the cabin. Our water having been in-sufficient for the service of the day for sometime past, Mr. Taylor agreed to take upon himself the management of it for one week. I am to succeed him. Latitude 24°2′.

SATURDAY, JANUARY 23RD.   Got up our M[ain] T[op] G[allant] Royal in the morning. We do not venture to carry more sail than a single reefed Foretop-sail on our damaged Foremast. As the Captain does not mean to go further to the South-ward, in order to encourage the usual merriment of the seamen in passing the tropics, he gave out the observation to-day instead of 24°7′ (which it was) as 23°43′ and stood southward for a few hours. Antony personates Neptune, and Joseph (a French sailor on board) transformed himself into a species of Priest with a rosary of blocks, a cross of hoops, and a beard of Rope yarn. How Neptune came to be transformed into an old Portugese sailor and to be attended by a French Priest, cannot easily be explained, but it would be still more difficult to account for his occupation as barber to the green

27. The air-bladders of the cod fish. *OED*.

sailors on board. An opportunity was taken when all the men and steerage passengers were at dinner, to fasten down the hatches. Unluckily Mr. Young was among the number, and his Christian resignation having forsaken him, he made a forcible escape from his confinement, and by words and actions not altogether classically religious, disturbed the sport. His example was followed by Mr. Christie, a Scotch farmer, six foot high who with a hand spike forced open the fore scuttle, and obtained his liberty. Both Neptune and his Priest were a little disconcerted by this rebellion against their authority, and they were obliged to content themselves by lathering with slush and tar and shaving with an Harpoon, our miserable negro Peter. All the rest escaped, and the elegant amusement which was to have rewarded Antony and Joseph's ingenuity at least with a gallon of grog, ended in disappointment and ill humor. We had several young whales blowing about us in the afternoon. One of our pigs though most wretchedly lean, was killed to save his allowance of water.

SUNDAY, JANUARY 24TH. After a squally night which raised an unpleasant sea, we had a very brisk breeze at ENE and made 6 knots. There was an uncommon quantity of Gulphweed in sight. The day was warm and pleasant with short and frequent showers of rain. Our Pork was very bad at dinner and so underdone, as to require a second baking and it came down burnt for supper. Latitude 23°48′.

MONDAY, JANUARY 25TH. Squally weather, a high sea, much seaweed, the last of our Pork, and our rigging tumbling to the deck, include all the transactions of this day. Latitude 23°54′. A fine ENE breeze carried us at the rate of 7 knots.

TUESDAY, JANUARY 26. A very squally day with frequent rain. This kind of weather is very common upon the edge of the Trade Winds, upon which the Captain very imprudently hangs, as the same situation is also subject to frequent calms. Flying fish have been very frequently seen by several on board. I did not see any till this day. They flew low and dropped after having flown about 100 yards. The ship in its progress through the water seems to start them.[28]

Mr. Tenny, whose former modes of life have qualified him to be very useful in superintending our table, and whose good temper makes him anxious to be so, has so many difficulties thrown in the way of his endeavors by the Captain, as to disappoint us and him, and to produce much ill blood. As we have nothing but maggoty biscuits on board, Mr. Tenny proposed making bread daily of the flour which remains. The Captain would not permit him, but made himself to-day some cakes for tea, which

---

28. These were presumably the common *Cypselurus heterurus*. See n. 36 below.

Fig. 4. Figuero, a Portuguese sailor on the *Eliza*, 25 January 1796.

Figuero, a Sailor on board the Eliza. Jan.y 25.th
A very steady honest fellow, born at Macoa in the East In-
dies. — He is one of our best seamen, and has much ingenuity
of various kinds. —

were such wretched things, that they were not eaten, and we must now be content to live upon maggoty bread for a week, and then descend to a few casks of completely rotten biscuit, which is all that remains to us. Our state is miserable as to food, but our apprehensions are worse. The sailors have already refused, and indeed are unable to do anything but the commonest work of the ship and famine must attack us in a fortnight, unless we are relieved, or resolve to eat up the horses. They even, are upon very short allowance and would furnish but a lean supply of beef. Latitude 23°27'.

Rate of going eight or nine knots.

WEDNESDAY, JANUARY 27TH. The weather was much more moderate and
pleasant with a fine 5 knot breeze. We are very unfortunate in not meeting with
any sort of fish either for our table or amusement. The flying fish are uncomeatable.
Even a waterspout or two would be something new, and create a moment's ripple
upon our stagnating ideas. But we are condemned to irremediable ennui. Latitude
23°43'.

THURSDAY, JANUARY 28TH. A very pleasant day, as to wind, weather, and a
social glass of wine, which made us all merry and if we went further and got to
bed late, the loss of time was not aggravated by the violation of good manners. Mr.
Taylor had an accidental fall by which he received a very severe hurt on his right
hand, which appears at present serious. Latitude 23°49'.

FRIDAY, JANUARY 29TH. Headaches, silence and clouds in the atmosphere with
very little wind. Latitude 24°5'.

SATURDAY, JANUARY 30TH. A sprig of seaweed, which I drew and to which I
added my idea upon the Gulphstream amused me for this day [see FIG. 5 and
below]. The evening was muggy and perfectly calm. Latitude at noon 24°0'.

FROM THE SKETCHBOOKS

Eliza, January 30th, 1796. *The Seaweed*, commonly called *Gulph Weed*.[29]

The first appearance of this Weed was on the 9th of Jany. 1796 about N Lat.
34°0' the Azores bearing N by E. We were then evidently in a strong current setting
to the South. For though our course was never more southerly than SW by S, and
we tacked and stood N and by W, 12 out of the 24 hours, we regularly made near a
degree southing for four days running, part of which, however may have been leeway
made when upon the Starboard tack, the Ship being very light. On the 18th being in
Lat. 27°.57', we entirely lost the Weed. The Wind had been obstinately W, W and
by N, WSW, and SW, and my *own* opinion is that we were then much nearer the
Coast of Africa than our reckoning, perhaps 24° or 25° West Longitude from the
Meridian of London. We had also no reason to suppose ourselves in any Current.
On the 22d. of Jany. we met the Trade Wind Lat. 25°9', and immediately also the
Gulph Weed in small Quantities, and the next day, having gone about 1–1/2 degree

---

29. A species of *Sargassum*.

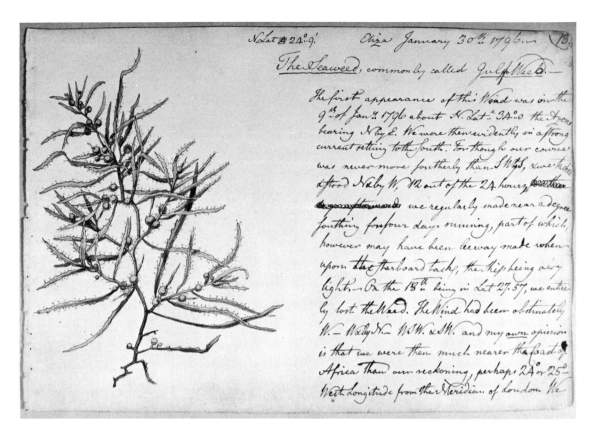

Fig. 5.　Seaweed, 30 January 1796.

to the Westwd. there seemed to be about the same proportion of it, which we had left on the 18th. Since then it has daily encreased, and we have seen some large patches of it, perhaps 20 or 30 feet in length and width. It has appeared these two days floating in long lines which extend as far as the Eye can reach in the direction of the Wind, ENE and NE at the distance of 6 or 7 Ship lengths from one another (600 or 700 feet). The intermediate spaces seem quite clear of it. As we keep the Wind upon our Quarter, and cross these lines, I have been able to observe and examine this circumstance for an hour together, and it has not varied. I cannot well account for it. (See remarks further on.)

From these data, I have been led to amuse myself with an Hypotheses respecting the *Gulph stream*, which, *if true*, has no doubt been a thousand times anticipated, and established upon much better grounds and information than I can furnish myself with at present. But in a situation where time cannot be *wasted* the paper is of no consequence.

The incessant stream of Air impelling the Waters of the Atlantic to the Westward, produces, as is well known, an accumulation in the Gulph of Mexico, which finds Vent through the Gulph of Florida, and produces what is called the Gulph stream. It

44

is about 20 or 30 leagues broad, runs in close with Cape Hattaras and Nantucket, and is very perceptible off Sable Island where it turns to the Eastward.[30] From Cape Sable, a direct line will carry you by the Southernmost point of the Great bank of Newfoundland to the Azores. I will therefore suppose that the *Gulph stream* continues its course in that direction, and that the current we so decidedly met with to the South of the Western Islands was a continuation of the same stream, whose Waters, a few more degrees to the South, meet again with the trade Wind which returns them into the Gulph of Mexico, from whence they once more commence their *eternal round*.[31] Might we not at the same time suppose that the Shoals about Cape Sable, and even the Great Bank of Newfoundland has been thrown up by the perpetual heaving of this Current? Now all this conjecture is founded upon the circumstance of the Gulph-weed. Every plant is furnished with a root which evidently appears to have adhered to some hard substance, and I am informed that the rocks in the Gulph of Mexico are covered with it. It also brings with it innumerable small Crabs. I am not aware of their breeding any where but upon Soundings. Should it be ascertained that this Weed is really and *only* the production of the Gulph, the influence of the Gulphstream might be pretty exactly confined to its presence. We were beating about for near 6 Weeks to the Northward and NW of the Azores without seeing any of it. Has any-body ever observed it in the latitudes of the Great Bank? Is it ever observed in the Longitude of Madeira, or two or three degrees to the Westward of it?

I recollect that Columbus (see Robertson's *History* or Russells, *of America*, I forget which) saw such quantities *as to impede his Vessel*, and was disappointed in not meeting with Land immediately.[32] Was this said merely to astonish and amuse the Spanish Court?

30. Largely as a result of the efforts of Benjamin Franklin, the course of the Gulf Stream and the idea that it was caused by the trade winds were well known in the 1790s. Margaret Deacon, *Scientists and the Sea 1650–1900: A Study of Marine Science* (London and N.Y.: Academic Press, 1971), pp. 201–03, shows that it was not until the 1870s that the Gulf Stream began to be understood as part of a great circulation of the entire ocean, caused largely by differences in temperature, rather than as an anomalous river of water caused by winds.

31. When Thomas Pownall proposed this same circular current in 1787, he too had used the pattern of gulf-weed as part of his evidence, and considered it an unproven but exciting idea. See Pownall, *Hydraulic and Nautical Observations on the Currents in the Atlantic Ocean, forming an hypothetical theorem for investigation* (London, 1787).

32. Robertson's story was very well known. "He [Columbus] found the sea so covered with weeds, that it resembled a meadow of vast extent; and in some places they were so thick, as to retard the motion of the vessels. This strange appearance occasioned new alarm and disquiet. The sailors imagined that they were now arrived at the utmost boundary of the navigable ocean; that these floating weeds would obstruct their farther progress, and concealed dangerous rocks, or some large tract of land, which had sunk, they knew not how, in that place. Columbus endeavoured to persuade them, that what had alarmed, ought rather to have encouraged them, and was to be considered as a sign of approaching land." Russell gives the same story, in almost the same words. William Robertson, *The History of America*, 2 vols. (London, 1783; 1st ed. 1777), 1:106; William Russell, *The History of America, from its discovery by Columbus to the Conclusion of the late war*, 2 vols. (London, 1778), 1:19. Columbus's

The drawing describes the Plant pretty exactly. It seems, when taken out of the Sea to be perfectly healthy and fresh, though disengaged from the place where it grew; but it very soon withers in the Air. The leaves are full of the volucra[33] of small shellfish, and are frequently covered with a beautiful minute network the work of some small animal: also with a viscous substance full of very small red eggs like spawn. The berries are hollow, and, I think, empty.[34] They, as well as the stem and leaves are covered with what I should call *tentacula* in an animal, very small hairs spreading into a ball at the end. Perhaps the plant absorbs nutriment by their means. They seem to possess a small degree of the power of Suction.[35] The leaves are very irregularly *serrated*. The berries, if they are *the fruit*, seem not to be preceeded by any flower. A leaf grows out of many of them opposite to the stalk.

The luminous Quality of Seawater when agitated, belongs to this Plant while wet, and nothing can appear more beautifull than a handfull of it when shaken in the dark, every berry assuming the appearance of an illuminated Pearl.

Feby. 4th, 1796. In examining several very large bunches of Gulphweed growing from the same stalk, I have not found one berry *with a leaf proceeding from it*, as above mentioned. In another Bunch the contrary exactly was the case. This can hardly be the effect of accident.

Yesterday (the 5th Feby.) very large lines of Weed were floating in the direction of the Wind (SW and NE) not more than 50 or 60 feet distant from each other, for several hours. The spaces between them were clear of Weed. They suddenly ceased, and we saw only straggling pieces the rest of the day in very small Quantities.

Feby. 11th. The Weed floated in lines still nearer to one another, connecting large Masses or Islands. It seems to serve as an harbor for a variety of sea animals. An *Eel*, and several Crabs were seen by me in some of it, when in the boat a few days ago.

---

ships were not in fact impeded, as no ship is by gulfweed, but the sailors were afraid they might become entrapped; see Samuel Eliot Morison, *Admiral of the Ocean Sea: A Life of Christopher Columbus* (Boston: Little, Brown & Co., 1946), p. 202. Morison points out that Columbus's theory that gulfweed had been torn from the American shore was not corrected until this century. Although similar seaweeds are coastal, *Sargassum* lives and reproduces afloat.

33. This is possibly a reference to the winglike shells of small molluscs, often called "wing-shells," which may accumulate on the surface of large marine algae. (From the Latin *volucris*, winged.)

34. The hollow "berries" enable the gulfweed to float, as BHL's contemporaries had correctly guessed. A brief treatise was devoted to this plant in 1798 (Hippolito Ruiz, *De Vero Fuci Natantis Fructificatione Commentarius*) and reported upon by Dawson Turner (*Fuci: Sive Plantarum Fucorum Generi*, 2 vols. [London, 1801]): "to satisfy himself that they were designed by nature to assist the plant in swimming, [Ruiz] cut them off from some individuals, which, upon being again thrown into the sea, immediately sank to the bottom" (1:107, from Ruiz, pp. 22–23).

35. These "hairs," which are so clear in BHL's drawing, fooled Ruiz too (see n. 34 above); he thought they were organs of reproduction. But Dawson Turner correctly said that these were sertularians and other zoophytes growing on the gulfweed.

Fig. 6.   Goat and kid under the *Eliza*'s longboat, 27 January 1796.

Upon attempting to take them they dived with instantaneous velocity. We are now in Longitude 67°0′ West of London, and of course near the Bahama Islands. Its quantity has wonderfully increased. Perhaps it is *brought up* by the Islands.

SUNDAY, JANUARY 31ST.   We had plenty of flying fish about the ship to-day, the day was very warm, with very little wind. The thermometer stood at 76°. I think it was the hottest day we have yet had, but Mr. Taylor's thermometer is fixed to a barometer and is not easily accessible, so that I cannot keep the account I could otherwise have wished.

Our poor little kid [see FIG. 6], the entertainment of the crew and passengers by her tameness and activity was to-day sacrificed to our hunger, and afforded us one meal. We have still one pig left who is too lean to kill, and whom we keep upon our rotten bread. The goat is expected to give milk enough for our tea and coffee in future, but I fear her scanty food will not afford her much spare subsistence. Latitude at noon 23°58′.

MONDAY, FEBRUARY 1ST. We were disappointed in our expectation of milk this morning. There is an order of men who, if they can insure eternal life by the doctrines they are educated to teach, might perhaps be permitted to render the present less pleasant to their disciples than it would be, were they to remain ignorant, and be damned. It is impossible to ascertain whether the soul of many a good Christian has not suffered from the abatement of the Parson's marriage fee from the first [. .] to the first kiss. I hope we shall all profit, and in default of our profit that our old goat will profit from the clerical appropriation of her first milk, and that the wicked person who affixed to her neck a label requesting "That you would not trespass upon these premises" may be forgiven. A good plain pudding for dinner to-day is an important event worthy of notice. Be it therefore mentioned with due respect to Dick the cabin boy.

The wind at noon hauled to the South, and in the evening to the West of South. This is a most uncommon circumstance in this Trade-wind latitude. Our Captain whose assertions ought to be believed in an inverse proportion to the degree of positiveness with which they are made, has frequently told me, that within these 7 or 8 years the trade-winds have retired considerable within their former extent. He gives this intelligence upon his own experience, and that of all the Captains of his acquaintance who trade to the West Indies from North America. Philosophers might find amusement in an enquiry into this circumstance, if it be a fact, though that may most probably be of no consequence to the amusement of the said Philosopher. No observation to-day.

TUESDAY, FEBRUARY 2ND. The wind still continues SSW with frequent rain.

An uncommon number of flying fish rose before the ship. I have now observed near an hundred of them. They regularly have taken their flight against the wind, and if upon rising from the water when started by the ship, they were obliged to fly before the wind to clear the bows, they immediately turned round and continued their flight against the wind, or in a diagonal direction.[36] They look extremely well and have something elegant in their color and motion, but their square head gives

36. Innumerable travelers have stared long and hard at flying fish, trying to understand the laws of their motion. Linnaeus's student Pehr Kalm, crossing the Atlantic in 1748, also thought they always fly against the wind, ". . . and though I was contradicted by the sailors, who affirmed that they went at any direction, I nevertheless was confirmed in my opinion by a careful observation during the whole voyage, according to which they fly constantly either directly against the wind, or somewhat in an oblique direction" (*Travels into North America*, trans. J. R. Forster, 2d ed. [London, 1772], 1:16–17). Louis Agassiz was also engrossed in watching these fish and insisted that they could change the direction of their flight at will (Louis and Elizabeth Agassiz, *A Journey in Brazil* [Boston, 1868], pp. 522–24). Modern observers tend to think that they take flight in any direction, but faster when headed into the wind, and that they cannot much alter their direction of flight.

them the air of a fish whose head has been cut off. We had a heavy swell from the North. Latitude 24°11′.

WEDNESDAY, FEBRUARY 3RD. A very heavy swell and perfect calm excepting when interrupted by short but heavy squalls from the SW. Latitude as yesterday 24°11.

THURSDAY, FEBRUARY 4TH. At six o'clock in the morning we had a slight squall with a deluge of rain and immediately after a steady Trade-wind which continued all day at the rate of 4 knots. More Gulphweed this morning, earlier than ever before, but not a sprig from 12 o'clock till night. Latitude at noon 24°27′.

FRIDAY, FEBRUARY 5TH. The wind was again this morning variable from WSW to WNW and about 10 o'clock died entirely and left only a heavy swell. We persuaded our Captain to order the small boat out, and Mr. Taylor and myself with two of the sailors rowed into a large Island of seaweed about a mile from the ship. We saw a small Eel and some crabs harboring in it, but they dived when attempted to be caught. The exercise of rowing improved my health and spirits extremely and though it was very hot, I felt no inconvenience. I got some barnacles from the bottom of the ship upon our return, which I have drawn and described [see PLATE 5]. Our ship has at a distance a most dismally black and dirty appearance, and towers preposterously above the water. After dinner the surface of the sea was without a ripple, litterally as smooth as glass, but not without swells. Several Bonnetas were playing about but did not approach near enough to be taken. A shark also came near us, but before I could take a good view of him he and his half dozen Pilot fish were out of sight. A Barracooter (Bollock biter as the sailors call him)[37] continued a considerable time about the ship. He was beautifully formed, but kept clear of all our fishing tackle. A young whale was more complaisant. He amused himself till quite dark with swimming slowly round our ship, rose now and then for breath, turned himself on his back, and might have been struck and taken had we been provided with proper lines and harpoons. [See FIG. 7 and below.] A singular animal, called a Portuguese Man-of-War was taken by some of the sailors in the boat. It has been frequently described. Its body about 3 inches long has the appearance of a bag filled with air, thicker at one end than at the other, with a ridge not unlike a puckered seam upon the top of it. Upon running a pin into this bag or bladder, it did not however discharge any air or diminish in size as I expected. At the side of this bladder, at the thickest end, a cluster of short fibres like a tassel of the most

---

37. Ballock is an obsolete word meaning testicle. *OED.*

beautiful pale blue seemed to compose the mouth or head of the animal, and from these short fibres issued a great many others three feet in length of the finest texture which it moved about at pleasure. Having been exposed to the sun for some minutes out of the water when in the boat, it seemed to be in pain, and turned, alternately so as to carry the ridge of its body upwards, or to lay it on the edge of the water. This action was performed by drawing the two ends of its body towards one another, in form of a crescent. This animal has a caustic quality when handled and leaves a painful sensation which lasts for some time upon the skin. If crushed, its juice will take off the skin. The sailors play tricks with the green lads, by telling them that it answers the purpose of soap for washing and one or two of our people were taken in. By this means I lost the opportunity of as close an examination of this singular animal as I wished. When shone upon by the sun, its body was of a most delightful pink color.[38]

This is a representation of it from memory.[39] All those that I have seen from the ship swimming in the sea carry the red ridge uppermost. I have never seen the animal called a Nautilus, and have no book to refer to, but as far as I recollect, from the reading of some years back the Nautilus is a shell fish who hoists a sail consisting of a skin, with which he sails before the wind. The body of the Portugese Man-of-War seems ill adapted for the action of the wind.[40] These amusements which were crowded into this calm day, entertained us till the most beautiful setting sun, called us to the consideration of bread and water and the loss of time, and of course the nearer approach of famine only occurred to us when the last 10 buscuits per man were delivered. The same quantity is reserved for us in the cabin and when they are consumed nothing remains but 10 or 12 casks which are absolutely rotten. Our Latitude at noon was 24°31′. A very gentle breeze at South sprung up at 10.

FROM THE SKETCHBOOKS

On board the *Eliza* Feby. 5th, 1796. *Whales*.

A small Whale, apparently about 20 feet long, amused himself for some hours in swimming round the ship and passing under her. He sometimes turned himself on

38. This is a fine description of a species of *Physalia*, probably *P. arethusa*.

39. This is a reference to a drawing in the original manuscript, now lost.

40. This story of the Nautilus, *Argonauta argo*, is still current, but false. *Physalia* seemed ill-adapted for sailing because it is thick, not thin like the sail of a boat. Yet it is a true sailor, holding to a tack which keeps it from drifting out to the open sea.

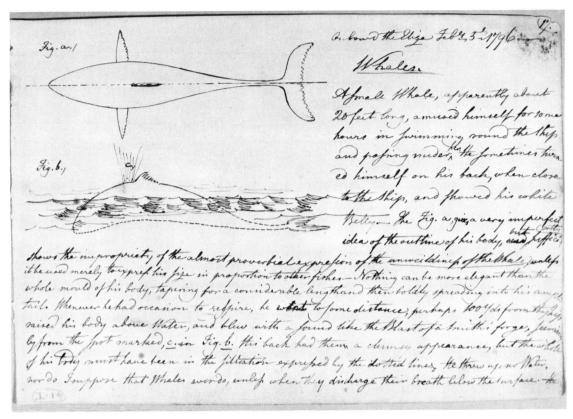

Fig. 7.   Whales, 5 February 1796.

his back, when close to the Ship, and showed his white Belly. The Fig. *a*, gives a very imperfect idea of the outline of his body, but sufficiently shows the impropriety of the almost proverbial expression of the *unweildiness of the Whale*, unless it be used merely to express his size in proportion to other fishes. Nothing can be more elegant than the whole mould of his body, tapering for a considerable length and then boldly spreading into his ample tail. Whenever he had occasion to respire, he went to some distance, perhaps 100 Yds. from the ship, raised his body above Water, and blew with a sound like the Blast of a Smith's forge, seemingly from the spot marked, *c*. in Fig. *b*. His back had then a clumsy appearance, but the whole of his body must have been in the situation expressed by the dotted lines. He threw up no Water, nor do I suppose that Whales ever do, unless when they discharge their breath below the Surface. He seemed perfectly at his leisure, and to be as much amused with the Vessell as we were with him. It was most perfectly calm, and we had severall other fish about us at the same time; among others, a Shark accompanied by 7 or 8 Pilot fish made his appearance.

Several Gentlemen on board, who are not such strangers at sea, as myself, informed me, that the discharged breath of the Whale is sometimes horridly offensive, especially, when they are engaged in their *unweildy loves*, as Thompson calls a passion which they perhaps think *mighty* sentimental.[41]

Our whale was of the species called *Grampus*, its back was of a dingy dark color, its belly white. The Remark I have made respecting dolphins, I find corroborated in this instance, for when a few fathoms down, the *whale* even assumed a most beautifully cerulean blue appearance.

On the 10th of Feby. I saw another Whale close aboard. His action in blowing agreed exactly with what I said above.

SATURDAY, FEBRUARY 6TH. We had all day a tolerable breeze at SSW. Mr. Taylor took such excellent care of the water a fortnight ago, that instead of a deficiency some quarts were saved. The Captain succeeded him last week, and I am to undertake the general care of our few remaining provisions for the ensuing. Our last pig being now in tolerable case, but consuming much more water than we can spare, I ordered him to be killed, in hopes of relief before we shall eat him all up. Latitude 25°3'.

SUNDAY, FEBRUARY 7TH. A pleasant day with moderate wind at WNW tacked and stood to the Southward. Our pork was excellent, but we eat up the last of our potatoes. Latitude at noon again 25°3'. Had gone to the Northward the night before.

MONDAY, FEBRUARY 8TH. We had all day a moderate breeze from the North-ward. The weather was rather damp and chilly. Towards evening we descried, with a degree of pleasure which can only be purchased by enduring the apprehensions of a famine, a sail to the windward. Notwithstanding the evening proved squally we hoisted our Ensign at the M[ain] T[op] G[allant] Mast head, and got out our boat. She however kept her course and it grew dark. Our lantern was therefore hoisted at the Mizenmast and rope yarn burnt over the stern as a signal for the boat to return, which she did in half an hour, having got within 3 miles of the strange ship. We have to-day eaten our second dinner of pork. To-morrow we shall put the last joint of fresh meat into the pot, excepting one old hen, and the old she goat who is the very picture of famine. We have candles only for 8 days on board, flour for 6, somewhat damaged, and bread for four. There is about as much Pork on board as might last

41. James Thompson (1700–48), British poet, was known for his fondness of rustic scenes and nature.

us and the crew a fortnight, it is not very bad, though rusty and almost entirely fat. The salt beef of the sailors, is salt itself, and much of it is horseflesh. The men cannot eat it with their present allowance of water, on account of the thirst it occasions. Besides this, we have as many peas and beans, as would, if distributed throughout the ship, support us and the crew 3 days. A few trifling articles, as half a ham, a small quantity of cheese and some portable soup belonging to Mr. Brewster make up the whole catalogue of the stores of 29 persons. Sugar and spirits we have none. Porter will hold out perhaps a fortnight, and wine three weeks.

Should we, however, not meet with relief for three days, we must then live upon the rotten bread to which the crew are already reduced, and which they bake in the oven to kill the vermin; for animal food we must choose between the old junk of the steerage, and our own tainted beef (which is almost as salt); for six days we may distinguish our table by a pudding or a dumpling, and as a rarity, we may treat ourselves with pea soup, or baked beans. But this cannot last above a week. We may be becalmed, or we may not fall in with a vessel even then. No observation this day.

TUESDAY, FEBRUARY 9TH. About 8 o'clock we descried a sloop to windward of us. We immediately hoisted our ensign at the Mizen peak and she bore away for us. She was about 2 leagues distant. She would have spoke us sooner had our wise Captain not immediately upon her hoisting her colours at her top-mast head backed his Main and Mizen Topsails and lain to for her, so that she was obliged to keep close to the wind to fetch us. Mr. Shaw left the ship with Mr. Califf in the small boat and reached her about half a league from the ship. She seemed loaded on purpose for us, and when she came within hail we found that she could supply us with every article in the list sent on board. She came from Stonington in the state of Connecticut, was called the *Olive branch*, commanded, and as it seemed owned by [Captain] Stanton. He sailed round our unmanageable vessel several times, and was under the disgraceful necessity of requesting in the politest manner that our Captain would make such sail, as not to distress him in the management of his sloop, and as every common sailor on board could have directed. The articles with which he supplied us were: 4 dozen fowls, 2 turkeys, 1 barrel of Captain's biscuit, 1/2 barrel of excellent beef, 1 barrel of butter, a cask of potatoes, 6 lbs. of sugar (all he could spare), 6 gallons of rum, a bag of white beans, 2 hams, a box of mould candles, and a quantity of Tobacco. He offered to break his cargo in order to supply us with common biscuits, but Mr. Shaw very properly would not suffer it. Besides this, he sent as a present to the cabin passengers two case bottles of Brandy, and to Mrs. Taylor whom he accidentally saw upon deck a cheese. His bill, which he offered to reduce if thought unreasonable,

Fig. 8.   The *Olive Branch* of Stonington, Connecticut, 9 February 1796.

amounted only to 79 1/2 dollars or £17.17s.9d. sterling, being the market price in America, without taking the smallest advantage of our distress, or considering the advance of price he would have charged at the Swedish Island of St. Bartholomew[42] whither he was bound. Such liberal disinterested conduct wants no great commendation, than a plain statement of the fact. The contrast of the two American Captains which was before our eyes, was infinitely advantageous to Captain Stanton. Upon his departure we gave him three hearty cheers, and our half starved sailors reminded me of the scene in *The Surrender of Calais*[43] in which Coleman has thought proper to exhibit human misery as an object of merriment in the feeble acclamation of the famished inhabitants of a beseiged town. We eat our last joint of pork with some of Captain Stanton's potatoes, and with heart and stomachfelt satisfaction poured out copious libations to his health and success. His sloop was a beautiful little vessel of 60 tons, I have sketched it [in] the Sketch Book [FIG. 8]. Latitude 23°24′.[44] We had 7 Dolphins about in the morning, they were shy and very soon left us.

42. Known today as St. Barthélemy. In 1878 Sweden ceded the island to France.

43. A musical drama in three acts, written by George Coleman, the younger (1762–1836), English dramatist, theatrical manager, and "miscellaneous writer." It was first performed on 30 July 1791. *DNB*.

44. In his sketchbook BHL noted that the vessel was "a beautiful sloop of 50 Tons" and that the *Eliza* "fell in with her, Lat. 24°3′, W. Long. of London 62°8′." See *PBHL, microfiche ed.*, 245/E13, F1.

54

WEDNESDAY, FEBRUARY 10TH. A very strong gale from the NNE with more sea than we have had for some time past. A whale accompanied us a little way and blew close aboard. The quantity of seaweed has much increased this day or two. Latitude 23°48′.

THURSDAY, FEBRUARY 11TH. A pleasant breeze carried us on at the rate of 5 knots. We had a very great number of flying fish about. The men have already eaten up all the bread we gave up to them upon receiving a supply, but as they have all the flour, beans and peas at their command they do pretty well, and I think look better, and are in better spirits. Latitude 24°29′.

FRIDAY, FEBRUARY 12TH. On this day I did not forget the birthday of my brother C[hristian] I[gnatius] L[atrobe]. It has always been one of my most ardent wishes and sanguine hopes, to be placed in a situation in which a constant intercourse might give me a full opportunity of receiving all the pleasure, happiness, and instruction which the goodness of his heart, and the brilliancy of his genius, render inseparable from his society and conversation. The winter of 1788, during which we lived together will be ever memorable to me as almost the happiest of my life. Time, then marriage and business have separated us, and whenever I have met him, the regret arising from the rarity of our interviews has almost always overbalanced the pleasure they gave. We are now perhaps forever divided.

A South East wind which blew fresh all this day tempted the Captain to haul to the Northward and to leave the trade. Our Longitude by reckoning is 68° West of London. Latitude by observation at noon 25°52′.

SATURDAY, FEBRUARY 13TH. The wind has changed to the NW; we stood again to the SSW. There was very little of it. In the afternoon we had a kind of shooting match. Having fixed a target upon the windlass, we fired from the after hencoops. Mr. Califf put in the nearest bullet. It was an awkward kind of undertaking as the rolling of the ship was considerable. The spirit of gambling got among us and spoiled our good humour. The Rev. Mr. Young furnished powder and gun, the Captain not having on board an ounce of ammunition nor even a pocket pistol. Surely in cases of distress a small swivel would be necessary on board the most peaceful ship, and in the most peaceful time. Mr. Martin has brought forward some capital Madeira which tempted us to sit up late, and be very merry. What else have we to do? No observation.

SUNDAY, FEBRUARY 14TH. Though we have a Clergyman on board, so much has been discovered by the Captain of his private character, and the causes of his leaving England that we have not wished for his assistance in distinguishing Sunday from any other day of the week, and indeed no further deference has been paid to it than the ceremony of beardless faces, clean shirts, and idle sailors. But this morning our Chaplain was engaged not in saying prayers publicly, but in regulating a cock-fight in the steerage in which the favorite killed two of his antagonists. Mr. Califf and myself have the demerit of interrupting this cruel diversion to which all our cocks would have been sacrificed, so strongly were all the seamen on board engaged in it. We had for dinner a most excellent turkey of Captain Stanton's supply, which we washed down with copious draughts of Mr. Martin's Madeira, whose liberality in this instance has every character of gentlemanly ideas and gentlemanly habits. We had all day and throughout the night a fresh breeze from the South East which carried us on a NW course at the rate of 7 to 9 knots. At noon Latitude 26°8′.

MONDAY, FEBRUARY 15TH. Early in the morning a squall with the heaviest shower I think I ever saw shifted the wind to the NW and we stood NE. The cables were this day got out of the hold and stowed between decks ready to bend. The wind got more to the southward in the afternoon and died away. About 2, we descried a brig to windward of us, and hoisted our ensign. She bore down upon us, and proved to be the Hermaphrodite Brig *Sally* of New York, Captain Match, bound to Jamaica. She was in every respect the ugliest machine I ever saw, and though there was very little wind and scarce any swell, she rolled her chains in on each side, and appeared at a distance as she bore down upon us, most ridiculously drunk. Mr. Shaw and Taylor went on board and found her Captain in liquor, but sufficiently sober to sell us two barrels of seamen's biscuit at 7 dollars, a very high price. He had nothing else that we wanted, and was uncivil. She therefore reeled off without receiving the usual compliment of three cheers. Latitude at noon 27°50′.

TUESDAY, FEBRUARY 16TH. Remarkable fine cool weather with light winds. About 9 we saw a sloop to leeward who immediately put about, and at 12 o'clock was in our wake, when she again tacked and followed us. She gained upon us considerably before evening, and we all determined her to be a Bermudan or French privateer. The Captain assumed an air of infinite importance, as to his influence with the former, who would make a prize of us, and his courage against the latter who would rob us. The discussion provoked by the assistance offered to all, reluctantly accepted by some, and declined by others was highly unpleasant, and renewed some of those insults from which our systematic indifference towards him has lately guarded us. As it could be of no consequence to me how I lost my property, I made it over to him at once in case of the event we dreaded, and avoided by that means everything unpleasant. As long as the moon shone, the sloop remained in sight and gained upon us. The evening was almost calm. Latitude 28°20′. Standing NW.

WEDNESDAY, FEBRUARY 17TH. At daylight, our sloop was visible only from the mast head upon our starboard beam to windward of us. She came in sight about 10 o'clock, but seemed perfectly indifferent about us. The day was almost calm, and we eat up our last turkey. We had no observation to-day. We continue to meet great quantities of Gulphweed.

My rest last night was disturbed by two circumstances, the lamentation of Mr. William Newman Hog over his sick mare, and the crowing of the victorious fighting cock, who fixed his stand upon a chest close to the head of my hammock. Indeed, though the felicity of sleeping in a hammock in the steerage, compared with a cross berth in the cabin is transcendent, it is not without its constant alloy, nor its occasional interruptions. In the first place, the two sacks of which my hammock is composed are of different textures, and as that to the righthand is the most elastic, it permits the weight of my body to descend most on that side which has produced two ruptures of the hammock, and one fall of its owner. A third is now threatened, and will probably take place in the course of a week, and occasion a new repair. In the second place, the music of the back and breast back stay blocks, accompanied by that of the main top sail halliard-block, beating against the ship's side is not at all of a lulling nature, nor does the creaking of the masts much improve it, nor yet the clatter of the pumps every four hours, nor the vociferation of Lar or Star bawling "a_____hoy &c. Do you hear the news there," 3 times every night. To all this however I am now tolerably deaf, unless upon extraordinary occasions when the ship rolls more than usually, or the addition of *"All hands reef sails,"* or *"All hands take in sail,"* or *"haul the Mainsail,"* keeps me upon the alert. The snorting and other sounds that proceeds from the horses close under my head pass also unnoticed, with the snoring of the sailors (some of whom excel in the first, others in the latter accomplishment). Whenever the weather is easy, the Mainhatch and forescuttle being kept open, my nose has few observations to make, but the case is often otherwise. Whenever we ship a sea, the greatest part of it is received through the Mainhatch (for we have not a tarpaulin on board) in trickling streams, which in a warm imagination might produce the recollection of more agreeable scenes. These are the permanent evils of the night, but there are others of an occasional and transitory nature. When I first took up my residence in the steerage, it was also inhabited by the old goat and her kid, two pigs and a sheep. Of the pigs I very soon got rid, by insisting upon their being turned upon deck, but they very frequently tumbled into the steerage through the hatchways, and were commonly indulged with one nights lodging in consequence, as I found by experience that the screams attending their forcible removal, were more injurious to the nerves, than a whole night's moderate grunting. Against the bleating of the sheep there was no remedy, but death, and after having borne it a fortnight, I one morning saw the poor beast hanging at the foot of my hammock with his throat cut, and Mr. Christie engaged in skinning him. The dialogues of the kid and her mother continued till we got into warm weather about the end of January, when they were also sent upon deck and kept the pigs company. But the greatest of my plagues are the two sons of our reverend Divine, whose understandings are infinitely more upon a par than their strength, the youngest is 7 and the eldest 17. Their nocturnal feuds were so violent when I first came into the steerage, that very coercive language and measures were necessary on my part to quell them. I have now at last made them afraid of me, and my nights are peaceable; though at the occasional inconvenience of a lump of tar spread upon my pillow, a stolen nightcap, or a lost pair of trowsers or waistcoat. But with this I have learnt to put up philosophically enough. (Another grievance of a more troublesome cast, I have also made great progress in curing. The steerage deck is not thought by either of these gentlemen too clean, to suffer their depositing that upon it, which at sea is usually cast over the bows or the mizen chains; nor their father's breakfast utensils too sacred to receive a fluid from which Vespasian collected a revenue untainted by its smell. Our poor negroes upon whom they at first laid the blame, have been flogged and their noses have performed the office of shovels more than once for their offences. An actual discovery however, though it saved the blacks from future persecution, has scarcely cured the evil. What a corporeal chastisement inflicted this morning upon the eldest offender, who was taken in the fact, may do, I cannot tell.) The fodder of the horses runs so short, that unless 10 days carry us to Norfolk they must most probably be thrown overboard. They are thin and weak, and should they once be unable to stand in their stalls, it will be impossible to raise them up again. They have no litter having eaten up all the straw, and they stand upon the ballast. The groom who attends them deserves more than usual praise for his great and indefatigable attention. He daily washes them all over with salt water by which means a less portion of fresh water is required for their support. At every hour in the night if any extraordinary noise is heard in the hold he rises and attends them and his anxiety about his sick mare, who in a fit of the gripes had fallen down, would not have been greater had he lost a favorite child. To his attention in providing an extraordinary quantity of fresh water for the horses we owe the circumstance of our not being at present in extreme distress for want of that necessary article. When the Captain arrived at Gravesend, he brought with him for the supply of 29 persons, only 19 Puncheons of fresh Water, each containing at the utmost 115 gallons upon an average. The groom laid in for his 3 horses 10 Puncheons of nearly the same size. On the 13th or 16th of December the whole ship's company, passengers included, were put upon an allowance of 2 quarts a day. We had then not been out more than 3 weeks. The allowance of the horses was stinted, I believe to a bucket a day. The Captain upon this occasion exerted a power over the groom's supply of water, which though beneficial to the ship's company, was injurious, and unjust towards him. However, he submitted. Quaere—might not the groom by saving his water and retaining a surplus after our supply was expended, have made a fair advantage of it by supplying the ship, of which he has now been forcibly deprived? By a law of the United States every Master of a Vessel who crosses the Atlantic ought under a heavy penalty to take on board water at the rate of 160 gallons per man. Without taking the water provided by the groom into account, there is a deficiency of 90 gallons nearly per man, or near two wine hogsheads, and in all of 23 casks of the size of those on board containing 115 gallons. Taking the groom's water into account, and allowing, 2 men to a horse, the deficiency per man will be more than 65 gallons, and the whole deficiency nearly 20 casks of 115 gallons each. But of his misconduct there is so much to be said, that I sicken at the idea of dwelling upon it. No observation to-day.

THURSDAY, FEBRUARY 18TH. There were to-day sail in sight all round the horizon. We steered our course with a very pleasant and gentle breeze with an intention of speaking two or three of them, but they all got the wind of us at too great a distance, till a Brig hove to upon our signal and waited for us. The Captain took the command on deck, and swore he would shave her, and so he did, but so clumsy a barber is he, that he nearly cut her throat in the operation. In fact he run foul of her, and had she not been commanded by a skillful seaman, he would inevitably have sunk her, and perhaps gone to the bottom himself. Captain Audlin as soon as he saw the danger, called out to our helmsman to put up the helm, by which means we just cleared the forechains of the brig, who having luffed up, came along side, and carried away our lower steering sail boom, and some of her own rigging forward. This saved us both, and the ships came gently together. The Brig was a beautiful vessel, the *Sally* of Philadelphia, bound from New York to the Havannah.[45] The Philadelphians

---

45. BHL sketched the *Sally* in his sketchbook. See *PBHL, microfiche ed.*, 245/F11.

have the knack of giving their vessels an air of light elegance, which I observe nowhere but in the English and French ships of War. This little Brig of 100 tons, had a well carved and well turned head, and was altogether moulded in a manner that would have done credit to a Royal Yard. I went on board the Brig with Mr. Shaw, the passengers having subscribed a few guineas for luxuries in case we should meet with them, and made me their agent. We however, got only some sugar, of which we had none on board, two kegs of small American biscuits called crackers, a few apples, but the Captain did not give us directions to get any bread for the men. Captain Audlin refused to receive any recompense whatever for this supply, and behaved with the utmost good humour notwithstanding the danger into which we had led him. A very acceptable part of his presents were the latest New York papers, by which we saw that no account has been received in America from Europe later than the date of our departure, when the last paper was published Feb. 11th. A very fresh breeze has sprung up while we were on board the Brig, and our little boat, had become a dangerous vehicle across the breaking waves. We arrived safe at the ship, which was fallen much to leeward, but it was not an easy matter to get in on account of the high sea running. Our latitude at noon was 29°17′. Captain Audlin's longitude, who had been out only 6 days, 71° West of London, our reckoning is 73°.

FRIDAY, FEBRUARY 19TH. We had still a fresh and favorable breeze from the south and setting every sail the ship would bear, we hoped to be in Norfolk on Sunday. The Gulph Stream, which we plainly perceived in the evening by the appearance of the waves and warmth of the water, was also in our favor. Latitude 31°46′.

SATURDAY, FEBRUARY 20TH. A NW wind which sprung up this morning and raised a tremendous sea in the Gulph Stream in which we now are, blasted all our fair hopes. The ship was excessively uneasy, and the weather very cold with frequent squalls attended with hail. Latitude at noon 33°40′.

SUNDAY, FEBRUARY 21ST. An exact counterpart of yesterday. If possible more cold and unpleasant. This is a second edition of the Bay of Biscay, and we seem to have got the old westerly winds that persecuted us there. We fear that we are driven much to the eastward. No observation.

MONDAY, FEBRUARY 22ND. The same wind, terrible sea, rolling of the ship, and absence of comfort and good humour. Mr. Washington's birthday, to which we had proposed doing some honor, and had hoped to celebrate at Norfolk passed unnoticed but by a solitary bumper to his health. In the evening a very dreadful storm of thunder and lightning informed us that we were off Cape Hattaras. It is singular that at this point, at which the Gulph Stream breaks and takes an easterly direction, there should be perpetual thunder and lightnings. We have not a seaman on board who ever crossed this latitude within 30 leagues of the Cape, that met easy weather. On shore, I am told, the weather is not more disturbed than in other parts of the coast. Latitude 35°2′.

TUESDAY, FEBRUARY 23RD. Another day of dreadful gales and sea, the weather became rather more moderate at night, but the ship rolled worse than ever before, and just as I had turned into my hammock about 10 o'clock, a dreadful sea laid her on her beam ends, and started everything in the steerage that was but moderately secured. Half the night was spent in knocking up stancheons in the hold and fixing steadily the old ones. We tried for soundings but without success. No observation.

WEDNESDAY, FEBRUARY 24TH. Moderate weather in the morning. We suppose ourselves carried far to the eastward by the Gulph Stream, and contrary winds. A tremendous gale at NW obliged us to lay to under our foresail from the afternoon till early the next morning. Latitude 37°10′, being North of the Capes of the Chesapeake.

THURSDAY, FEBRUARY 25TH. The wind extremely variable but chiefly at NW. We lay to the whole day under our foresails. Early in the morning we descried a schooner to Windward and made a signal to speak her. But she either from fear or unwillingness to go to Leeward disregarded it. She remained in sight all day, also lying to under her foresails. In the night it became perfectly calm. We this day drank our last bottle of Porter, and have now only a few bottles of white and red wine on board, besides water. No observation.

FRIDAY, FEBRUARY 26TH. Towards morning a gentle South Wind enabled us to make a Westerly course. About eight it encreased with the most violent rain we have yet had and before noon it blew a hurricane. The ship was hove to under her foresail all day. In the evening it became perfectly calm with a very high swell. As soon as the wind subsided we got down our Top Gallant Mast, which has weathered it since we left the channel. A momentary glimpse of the sun at noon gave us our Latitude 37°38′ (but not with certainty), or one degree past our Port, and God knows how much to the Eastward. The water however has changed its color from the deep blue of the unfathomable Ocean to the Sea green of shallow water. We got however no bottom with 80 fathoms of line. About 11 at night a favorable NE breeze sprung up and cleared the sky, but it continued only 2 hours, and then died again into a calm.

SATURDAY, FEBRUARY 27TH. The morning was perfectly calm but a gentle SW breeze which increasing hauled to the South enabled us once more to steer a right course, S by W. The day was favorable and mild, and nothing but a more imminent prospect of famine than we have yet had interrupted the pleasure of our new hopes. We have no good bread now on board, only 3 fowls and 2 pieces of beef. We have a few beans and peas, a small quantity of flour and one ham. The whole ship's company dined to-day on a mess of boiled beans, cabin and all. Latitude by observation 37°46′, still a degree too much to the North.

SUNDAY, FEBRUARY 28TH. We had for the first time a mess of the bad bread for breakfast, and the bottoms and scraps of the last good cask were scrambled for. The same schooner that was to windward of us on Thursday the 25th was again on our weather beam, standing in for the Chesapeake. We hoisted our Burgee at the foretop mast head, and our Jack wiffed or tied in a knot at the mizen peak. But she was blind to these signals of extreme distress. Perhaps she took us for a privateer. We then backed our main and mizen top sails to wait for her. She certainly saw this signal, but answered it by luffing up and going from us, as she could lay two points nearer the wind than we did. At last however she suddenly altered her mind and at 2 o'clock bore down upon us at once. She was commanded by Captain Hovey, was of Baltimore last from Cayenne, an Island close to the continent of South America, returning with a cargo of coffee, and cotton. She had been out from Cayenne 40 days, her Captain and men were all laid up with a fever and ague, she had no firing on board, her sails were worn out and we should have given her our Royal Sails had she had a yard of twine to adapt them to her use, and of this article we were also entirely destitute. She could only supply us with two casks of bread, not much better than our own miserable stuff. One of the sailors gave Mr. Shaw a dozen oranges. They were tasteless. It was a misfortune to us to meet her for we should otherwise have spoken to one of two Brigs seemingly bound to the West Indies, which passed soon afterwards under our stern and could not have left the coast many days. Finished our last bottle of port. Latitude by observation 37°27′. The whole day we kept a S by W course with a pleasant breeze from the Northward, the sky was perfectly free from clouds and the weather delightful. We can now keep soul and body together a little longer, and but a little. Our last ham, half of which we dressed for dinner is unfortunately tainted, but we contrived to eat heartily of it. We have allowed ourselves no bread for dinner for sometime past. Our potatoes which we got from Captain Stanton are a very indifferent substitute. They are of a bad sort, and many of them rotten and frostbitten into the bargain.

MONDAY, FEBRUARY 29TH. The wind was very light and hauling to the NE carried us about 3 knots steering sails set. About 10, Antony caught an Albacore, which I have drawn and described [see FIGS. 9 and 10 and below]. It came exactly in time and made the whole crew an excellent chowder, leaving a dozen pounds for the cabin to be dressed to-morrow. We this day eat up our last fowls. They had been entirely without food for three days and were lean and bad. The wind freshened in the afternoon at NE. We have still no bottom, though by our reckoning we are two degrees beyond our Port. The Gulph Stream must have set us amazingly to the eastward.

FROM THE SKETCHBOOKS

Feby. 29th, 1796. Latitude 37°11′. Long. 73°.
Albacore, called by *Joe* a French Sailor, *Le Ton*.

On the 7th of Jany. Antoni caught a small fish in form and the arangement of fins as nearly as possible like the drawing on the next Leaf [FIG. 9]. But it was not above 1/4 of the Size of the Albacore caught today, nor had it any colour but a silvery and brown hue upon its body. Nor could it lay back its side fins, which were apparently fixed at right angles with its body, and its head was larger in Prop[ortion].[46] The fish caught this morning from which the drawing is made was about 3 ft. 6″ long; it was taken with a line. They are common in the more southern Latitudes, and the Portuguese Ships going to the Brazils reckon upon them for a Supply of provisions, together with the Bonetas, and Dolphins which abound near, and South of, the Line. (Information of Antoni the Portuguese Sailor.)

Every fin of this fish excepting the back and belly fins at the end of the Body and the small fins on the tail, had a space sunk into its body which exactly contained it, and

46. The fish caught on 29 February, which BHL called albacore and sketched in FIGS. 9 and 10, is a species of *Thunnus*. Regarding the smaller fish caught on 7 January BHL wrote this footnote: "This small fish was caught immediately after passing a Portuguese Brazil Ship, which it most probably had followed from a warm latitude. It might be a very young Albacore, though I think, upon *recollection only* of its peculiarities, it was materially different in several essential particulars. It was caught nearly in the same latitude 37°20′. Long. 25° or 26°. I recollect also that the small fins of this fish were in Pairs; in the Albacore they were single." See p. 33.

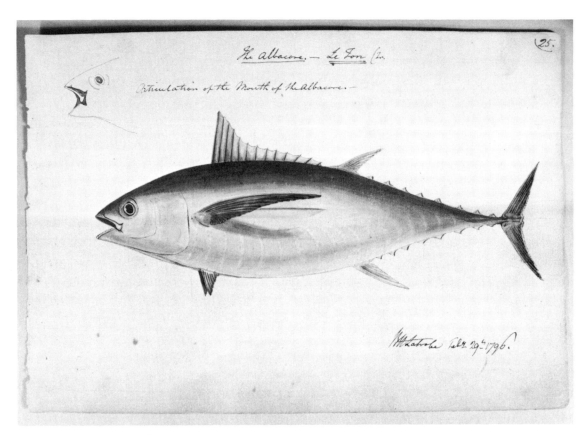

Fig. 9.   The albacore, 29 February 1796.

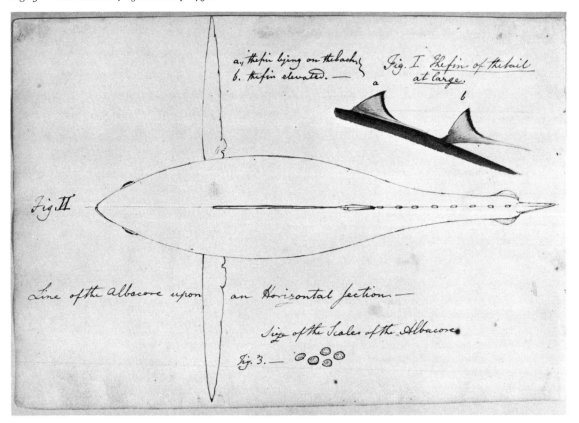

Fig. 10.   The albacore, drawing and details.

the back fin sunk intirely into a *Case* (to use the expression) in his back which was two inches deep, so that, after he was dead, it was drawn out with some difficulty. The back fin consisted of very strong pointed spines, connected by an extremely fine pellucid membrane, and was unlike every other, which were composed of the usual fibres. The bowels occupied a very small portion of its body, for it was the fleshiest fish I ever saw. They contained a great number of very small fish, and in its Mouth was an eight rayed star fish (Echinus).[47] The Stomach was long and narrow, and very much like that of a Dolphin. Its jaws were furnished with a row of very small teeth. On each side of the Tail a semicircular substance of a horny appearance projected horizontally. (See figure 2 [of FIG. 10].)

The under jaw of the Albacore, like that of the *Male* dolphin, projects somewhat before the upper when *shut*. I thought I observed a great similarity between the whole construction of the Gills of the Albacore and those of the Dolphin, but he had not those hard and prickly Knobs which seem to serve the latter for the mastication of its food, but a sort of *Cheval de frize* of Bone, that was moveable and very rough, and which, when the Mouth was shut lay along perfectly flat and even. His body is covered with small Scales (see Fig. 3 [of FIG. 10]) that come off with the slightest touch. The particular construction of the Back-fin, the strength and sharpness of its Rays, and the extreme Weakness of the Membrane connecting them induce me to think that it is intended more as an offensive or defensive Weapon than for its use in swimming. Upon cutting off the back and tail fins much clear *Oil* was discharged.

TUESDAY, MARCH 1ST. Our favorable breeze still continues but to our great disappointment we still find no bottom with 100 fathoms of line. Our Albacore furnished us with an excellent chowder, and what remained for supper was a luxury indeed eaten with a little vinegar. We had neither wine nor porter nor grog, but Mr. Brewster's discovery of a bottle of brandy cherries was inestimable, and had we had bottom we might have been quite happy.[48] The sea was uncommonly luminous, and had the appearance of being agitated by a shoal of small fish. No observation. Cold, damp weather.

47. Echinus is from the Greek *echinos*, meaning a hedgehog or a sea urchin. The "spiny-skinned" marine animals, including the starfishes, sea stars, brittle stars, sand dollars, sea lilies, and sea cucumbers, as well as the sea urchins, are today placed in the phylum Echinodermata. The starfishes may have from five to fifty arms.

48. In addition to its meaning of ocean floor, "bottom" also meant the dregs, or sediment, of liquors; the last portion of the wine in a cask. *OED*.

WEDNESDAY, MARCH 2ND. The wind still continued favorable and was very fresh. We have now run 300 miles since our reckoning was up, and have still no bottom. About noon we spoke a Marblehead fishing Schooner. He informed us that Cape Henry bore WSW 30 leagues distant, and a very imperfect observation of the sun seemed to confirm his idea. There is here a very strong current setting to the south which may still carry us astray. But the Captain is very confident, and allows nothing for its effect. The mate occasionally steers to the Northward in the night; but that is *sub rosa*.

THURSDAY, MARCH 3RD. The morning was extremely cold and hazy. Indeed for this week past, it has been most miserably cold and damp with frequent sleet. As soon as the mist rose, we saw the tops of trees ahead, and soon after a long range of very low land ending in a low point at Cape Henry. In the Southward was the peninsula of Currituck somewhat more elevated, upon a range of sand hills. [See PLATE 6.] Our joy was damped by the impossibility of weathering the Cape with the wind we had, and at noon we found ourselves by observation in Latitude 36°38′, 20 miles to the south of it. The coast was entirely woody. The wind died away and it became perfectly calm. At 10 at night we spoke a sloop which had drifted down upon us. It was so dark, and the Master of her appeared so surly, that we did not send a board to try to obtain some relief. We could put up with the want of everything else, as we have good water and plenty of Captain Stanton's excellent butter; had we only good bread. But that with which Captain Hovey supplied us is worse than our own. We have had no firing on board, but our spare spars, for a fortnight and sit shivering in the Cabin in our great coats for want of it. We hoisted a signal for a Pilot, but they were too wise to come to us in a situation from which we could not be extricated but by a change of wind.

FRIDAY, MARCH 4TH. We found ourselves this morning abreast of Currituck, still 10 miles further to the South. A large ship which appeared yesterday on the horizon to leeward was close aboard of us. We spoke her but found her in greater distress than ourselves. She was the *Birmingham* of Baltimore, Captain Briggs, left from Liverpool. She left Liverpool on the 9th of October and in the next night met with a gale in which she broke her rudder, and received such other damage, that she was obliged to put back into Kinsale[49] where her repairs cost her £400. She left Kinsale

49. Market town and seaport of County Cork in the Republic of Ireland.

the 9th or 10 of December, tried to effect a Northern course and when all her sails were shivered to pieces, she ran down into the trade winds. For the last 40 days each man on board had been served a single biscuit, and a very small quantity of beef and they had nothing but water to drink; they all looked half starved. They had plenty of water, and a tolerable stock of Irish Potatoes, which had kept them alive. In return for a boat load of fire wood, and a bushel of potatoes we supplied them with half a dozen pieces of our salt junk and half a barrel of our wretched bread, an exchange advantageous to both. Our cabin stove being put up we have now the additional comfort of a good fire. The wind had sprung up from the north about 10 o'clock and blew fresh. We beat all the day to windward keeping in sight of land, and drifted about twice as much to leeward. A good dinner of Irish potatoes, and a small piece of Stanton's beef, the last on board. We were however not hungry enough to make up the meal with our last scrap of stinking ham we have left. Now, for saltjunk and horseflesh!!! A schooner drove close aboard of us in the night. She was bound to the Northward.

SATURDAY, MARCH 5TH. The wind still in the same quarter with extremely heavy rain, which lasted through the night. We made however a comfortable fire in the cabin and lived upon our Irish potatoes. We have also discovered a cask of better pork than we supposed ourselves in possession of. These are great events on board the *Eliza*.

SUNDAY, MARCH 6TH. At day break it was perfectly calm, and we found ourselves within hail of a beautiful brig. She was the *Two Sisters*, Captain Isaac Phillips, bound from the Danish Island of St. Thomas[50] to Baltimore. We immediately sent Mr. Shaw on board, having among us subscribed a few guineas in hopes of laying them out advantageously. The boat had scarcely reached her when a violent squall from the NNW overtook us and in a moment split our mizen top sail to pieces. It was not of long continuance but brought much rain with it. As soon as it was over the boat returned, bringing us a barrel of bread, 4 gallons of rum, some oranges and limes, a few dozen crackers (biscuits), some rice (a most valuable acquisition), and some pounds of sugar. The bread was worse than any we have yet had, being quite alive and the rum was new and excessively strong. We were in high spirits however with this seasonable relief and resolved to drink Captain Phillip's health in a good bowl of punch after dinner.

50. St. Thomas is now one of the United States Virgin Islands; it was purchased from Denmark in 1917.

— A Conversation. —

Captain Noble. Pray who makes punch? (A pause.)

Mr. Latrobe. If no other gentleman steps forward, I will try if my hand is not yet out. (All agreed.)

Mr. Latrobe. But this swell makes the ship roll so much that I fear some difficulty will attend the task.

Mr. Martin. Mr. Young's berth will be the most convenient place for you. You can settle the things in the bed and thus they will not give way.

Mr. Califf. But keep a good look out for the Fleas, they jump about as big as sparrows, as his reverence informs us.

Mr. Latrobe. True! I will cover the bed with my box great coat; it is heavy and will keep them down. Now, where are my utensils? Here are the limes, and I can squeeze them into this cup, but what shall I mix the punch in?

Captain. Take a couple of soup plates.

Mr. Taylor. Their flatness is an objection, the tureen will do better.

Mr. Brewster. So it will. (Rings the bell, Dick appears.)

Dick. What did you want with me?

Mr. Latrobe. Dick! bring me the mustard pot full of sugar, and the soup dish to make the punch in.

Captain. But wash the tureen well, or it will be very greasy.

Dick. It has not had soup in it very lately.

Mr. Taylor. True, the bread was kept in it till this morning, when it served as a slop dish at breakfast.

Dick. Will it want washing?

Captain. Why yes, you may just give it a rinse.

The punch was made, and the fat swam upon top of it, however, it was approved and we were all merry enough with it. The sailors were also the better for our acquisition, and some of them got merrily drunk. A thick fog came on in the afternoon and hid the brig from us. In the night she came on board us. It was so calm that no mischief was done. Neither vessel had steerage way.

MONDAY, MARCH 7TH. A very light, but fair SW breeze sprung up in the morning. The sea was as smooth as glass, the weather delightfully warm and the coast in sight. The brig had got somewhat ahead of us. We set topmast and lower steering sails and skimmed along without the slightest apparent motion, at the rate of about 2 knots an hour. Our hopes of safe arrival within the capes before the evening,

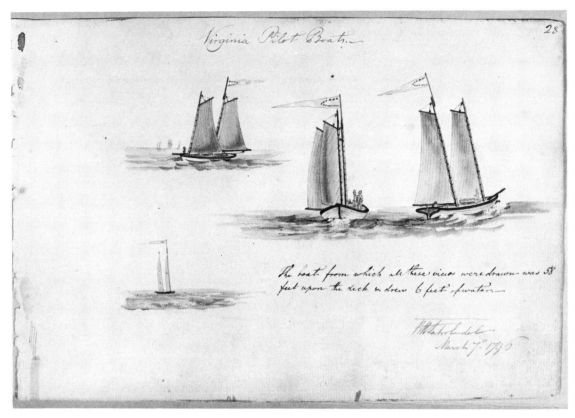

Fig. 11. Virginia pilot boats, 7 March 1796.

the delicious weather, and a good fresh dinner (ducks, rice, soup &c.), after so long a state of almost fasting and despair, raised sensations to which we had long been strangers. Seventeen vessels of different kinds were in sight, steering the same course with ourselves, and every moment brought us nearer to the shore. A whale attended us the whole day, and amused us and apparently himself. A circumstance struck me which our Captain, said he had never before observed. The wake of our ship with all its flexures could be seen from the top mast head, as far as the eye could reach, and another wake exactly similar to it in every bending, diverged from it at a small distance from our stern continually increasing its separation. I am at a loss entirely to account for this double appearance. We were then in a southerly current steering NNW. About 4 a Pilot boat came alongside of us, but she had no Norfolk pilots on Board, and the Patowmack and Baltimore pilots, have no right in the navigation of James River. The boat was a beautiful thing [see FIG. 11]. Its form is not easily described but by a drawing; and I had no time to make a perfect one. It was scooner rigged, its masts very strong and beautifully tapering, and its deck without waist, the gunnel being raised only about four inches. The masts were perfectly free from stays and shrouds, secured only in the step and wedged on the deck. A single halliard raised the gaff (throat and peak) at once. The foresail sheet was without a boom, the sheet blocks being fixed to the clue and leading on to the deck. The mainsail had a long boom. The gaffs were very short in proportion. The Master of her said that he would take any bet to sail her at the rate of 12 knots close hauled upon the wind. They are excellent sea boats and peculiar to Virginia, very few of them being used even in other parts of America.[51] The deck is so perfectly free from any thing to support the seaman when the vessel is in motion; that it appears a dangerous surface to tread, and yet no man was ever known to be lost from it. Security in more cases begets incaution and consequently danger. The sun set with uncommon beauty, the wind fell, it was perfectly calm and we prepared to cast anchor about 4 leagues from the light house upon Cape Henry which could plainly be descerned with the naked eye. About 7, another pilot boat of the same construction came along side, but she had no Norfolk pilot. It is astonishing with how little wind these boats steer along. At a time when our vessel had not sufficient motion to obey her helm, both these boats approached and left us at pleasure, steering within 3 1/2 points of the wind. About 8 o'clock we sat down to supper, and had scarcely finished when a brisk breeze from the ESE sprung up without giving a moments notice, started everything from the table and sent all upon deck. The ship was going at the rate of 7 knots directly for the mouth of the Chesapeake with the most favorable wind at ESE we could possibly wish, the light house bearing NW by N upon our Larboard bow. Our joy was such as the deliverance from a fifteen weeks voyage, in which everything that deserves the name of anxiety had been experienced, could only occasion, the man in the chains sung quarter less six, and the Lighthouse was only one mile distant, when in a moment —all our prospects vanished, the wind chopped round to the NE by N and began to blow a gale. No time was to be lost, we put about and at 5 the light was discerned no more. It then began to snow and grew excessively cold. Our mainsail was shivered and we were glad to come under close reefed main top sails and our forecourse. I had been up the greatest part of the night, and was perfectly seasick in the morning so violently was the ship agitated.

TUESDAY, MARCH 8TH. The most dismal day we had yet experienced. The weather was so cold that the ropes were frozen in the blocks, the snow lay thick on

51. BHL was describing a vessel similar to the Virginia pilot schooner *Swift*, which had been built at Norfolk before 1794 and crossed the Atlantic to become a model for a class of Royal Navy dispatch boats. Length on deck: 49 feet; beam: 15 feet, 7 inches; draft: 6 feet, 3 inches. *Sailing Vessels of the Chesapeake: Nine original lithographed prints from the International and Historical Watercraft Collection by Melbourne Smith* (Annapolis: Admiralty Publishing House, 1973), pl. 1. For other plans and later views (1815 and 1825) of the Virginia pilot boat, see Howard Irving Chapelle, *The Baltimore Clipper: Its Origin and Development* (Hatboro, Pa.: Tradition Press, 1965), pp. 28, 64–65.

the yard and the deck was covered with a sheet of ice. The gale continued with immense violence and we shipped many heavy seas. The agitation of the vessel would not permit us to light a fire in the cabin, we sat shivering though covered with great coats. Our meals were eaten upon the floor (for the bars which had secured our plates and dishes on the table were destroyed on the day of our hopes [see PLATE 7]). I was so ill that I neither eat nor drank the whole day. A beautiful mare in foal, belonging to Colonel Home,[52] fell down through weakness for want of food, and could not rise. Our poor sailors were miserably cold and wet and quite dispirited. I went to bed at 9, put all the clothes I could get over me, and slept tolerably, but was frequently awakened by the convulsive kicking of the mare in the hold, who died about 4 o'clock.

WEDNESDAY, MARCH 9TH, 1796. [*This handwritten inscription follows the date.*]
I have been unable to find the conclusion of this interesting and graphic journal. He landed however at Norfolk I think about March 15?, 1796. C. H. Latrobe 189[··].

[*These two paragraphs follow the John H. B. Latrobe transcription of the Atlantic Journal.*]

The diary ends here and the only evidence I have of the termination of the voyage is that afforded by the indorsement of the manuscript book, that is the "Journal of a voyage from London to Virginia from November 25th 1795 to March 20th 1796." Of the events of the days between March 9th and March 20th I have no record.

At page 27 of the sketch book there is a drawing of the condition of the table equipage on board the *Eliza* with a description that seems so germane to the history of the voyage, that I copy both; and if the drawing wants the skill of of the original, it must be remembered that the copiest is in his 86th year, when he makes it.[53]

---

52. This was Colonel John Hoomes, race-horse breeder and owner of a stagecoach line monopoly in Virginia. See the Biographical Appendix.

53. The copyist, John Hazlehurst Boneval Latrobe, drew his version of the sketch in 1889, two years before his death. For BHL's sketch, see PLATE 7. The whereabouts of John H. B.'s copy is unknown.

2

Norfolk and Richmond, Virginia

23 March–31 May 1796

NORFOLK, VIRGINIA, MARCH 23D, 1796.

My dear Brother,[1]

Cooper thought 5 or 6 months a sufficient length of time to collect decissive information, information which might lead to the disposal of an immense mass of emigrant property, upon a country extending 1000 miles every way. His book is well written, and contains truth enough to make it a usefull companion in a jaunt of speculation from Virginia to New Hampshire; but I find it is not entirely approved here either by the Federalist or Antifederalist parties, whose combined judgement, as they look at their Country in different lights ought to be decissive.[2] I cannot make up my mind so rapidly, and in a fortnight have got no further in settling an opinion of Virginia and Virginians, than to lay down a few principles, all of them perceived by the senses. The first is, that Norfolk is [I.] an illbuilt, [and] II. [an] unhealthy town. I. The streets are *irregular, unpaved, dusty* or *dirty* according to the weather, crooked [and] *too narrow* where they should be widest, near the river, and accompanied by an innumerable retinue of narrow and filthy lanes and alleys. The ruins of the old houses in this town (which was burnt down in 1776) are almost as numerous as the inhabited houses. [They] are intermixed in every street, and the former give way very [slow]ly to the latter. One cause of this is the difficulty found in pulling down the old walls, cemented together by Shell lime [*torn page*] a strong mortar [*torn page*]. The public Buildings are, *the Church, the Courthouse,* and the *Playhouse.* The first is uncieled, unplaistered and unpewed. Half the squares of Glass in the Windows are broken, and the miserable fourlegged turret is tumbling down. The Courthouse is a plain mean building, with a meaner spire. The playhouse is decent and better than either of the former. I had almost forgotten the Market house, the irregular position of which is in harmoney with its filth and deformity.[3] The stile of the houses of private Gentlemen is plain and decent, but of the fashion of 30 Years ago. They are kept very clean and

1. Christian Ignatius Latrobe.

2. Thomas Cooper (1759–1839), publicist, lawyer, physician, and scientist, visited the United States for several months in 1793–94. Upon his return to England, he published *Some Information respecting America* (London, 1794). He moved to America permanently later in 1794, where he pursued his various interests. Cooper served as a state judge in Pennsylvania (1804–11) and professor of chemistry at Carlisle (now Dickinson) College (1811–15), at the University of Pennsylvania (1816–19), and at South Carolina College (1820–34), where he also worked on a revision of the South Carolina statutes. Cooper became a close friend of BHL's and published several of the architect's pieces in the *Emporium of Arts and Sciences* (1813–14), which he edited. *DAB; DNB.*

3. The Borough Church for Elizabeth River Parish, renamed St. Paul's in 1832, was constructed in 1739. It was the only building to survive the British bombardment and burning of Norfolk on 1 January 1776. The Church "was cruciform in shape, with arched windows and doors. The walls were of unusual thickness, and ornamented with glazed bricks placed at regular intervals." *St. Paul's Church 1832 Originally the Borough Church 1739 Elizabeth River Parish Norfolk, Virginia* (Norfolk: The Altar Guild of St. Paul's Church, 1934), pp. 23, 25–26.

The Norfolk County Courthouse, built on Main St. east of Church St., was completed in 1789 by the builders Lemuel Carter and William Hobday. The courthouse was destroyed by fire in February 1824. Forrest, *Norfolk,*

independent of papering, which is not universal, fitted up much in the English style. The inferior houses are chiefly framed and weatherboarded, and the sort of double roof, called by the french *un Mansard* (from the Architect who first employed them in France)[4]—by the English Carpenters, a *Curbroof*, are very common. I suspect that they may have been introduced by German builders, after the fashion of Saxony, and most other parts of Germany. All the buildings are covered with shingles, a light and durable covering, but dangerous in a country where fires are not provided against by any regulations of police, and where *wood* is the most common fuel. The Shingles are plain pieces of board round at the edge, and nailed on in the manner of tiles, not groved into one another like the German shingles. The river is crouded with [*torn page*] and ill looking weatherboarded Warehouses, upon *log Wharfs* turn[ed] into every direction of obliquity. The *said Log wharfs* des[erve] description more than imitation, but they answer the purpose [for] several years, in a country where wood is in greater plenty, than capitals, large enough to spare a sufficiency for a more permanent but more expensive erection. In the first place a number of round logs are lapped together to the length of the wharf on the edge of the Water. The angles are returned by other logs with diagonal pieces; and pieces are dove-tailed into the front logs to serve as land ties. This machine being made, is carried into the river where it floats. Another is then made exactly of the same size and construction and being laid upon it, is fixed with *treenails* (Trunnells). A third and fourth succeeds, and as the Wharf sinks it is pushed further and further from Shore. At last it finds the bottom at the depth intended, and the back is then filled up with Ballast Stones and *Wharf-wood* (that is, young fir trees of about 4 or 6 inches diameter) cut into lengths of 10 or 12 feet and laid parrallel across the ties. The lower logs which are either sunk in the mud or constantly covered with water last a great number of Years without injury, but those that are alternately wet and dry, are devoured by the Worm in the course of 7 or 8 years, and the Work is to be done over again. The Wharf then assumes the most irregular twisted appearance imaginable and the Warehouses erected upon it nod in unison with their support. These wooden Wharfs are said to have been the invention of Mr. Owen, a Welchman. He was a drunk dog, continuing in a state of

pp. 100, 172; Charles B. Cross, Jr., *The County Court, 1637–1904, Norfolk County, Virginia* (Portsmouth, Va.: Printcraft Press, 1964), p. 69.

The Norfolk theater was erected in 1795 on Fenchurch St. between Main and Bermuda. In 1794, Thomas Wade West had engaged William Hobday to construct the theater for £1200. In 1833 the theater, badly in need of repair, was sold to the Methodists for use as a church. The building was destroyed by fire in 1845. Sherman, "West," p. 18; Forrest, *Norfolk*, p. 252n.; Wertenbaker, *Norfolk*, p. 118.

The Market-house, located on Market Square, was rebuilt after the destruction of Norfolk in the Revolution. The building was again destroyed by fire in 1814. Forrest, *Norfolk*, p. 112; Wertenbaker, *Norfolk*, pp. 91, 129.

4. François Mansart (1598–1666), French architect and exponent of the classicism of seventeenth-century architecture, was best known for the two-sloped roof named after him.

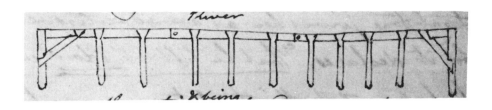

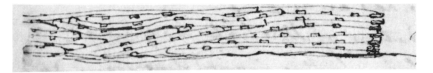

intoxication sometimes a week together, but when moderately sober his ingenuity and industry made up for lost time. The effects of this continual inebriety, and of the means his wife adopted to cure him of it killed him at last. She frequently poisoned his wine with Tartar emetic. She now remains a Widow, who *cries* (weeps) for his loss, although his tombstone serves her as an advertisement for another husband, for it declares *"that he left a **Widow** with an **ample fortune**."* Unfortunately this tombstone was put up by the Mason at the head of the grave of a pauper who left not the means of purchasing one for himself, and it was not till lately that the mistake was discovered. Her affection and at the same time her sagacity appears from other circumstances attending the said monument. When the mason brought in his bill which was 30.00, she was extremely disappointed in its amount. "What!" says she, "you imposing cruel man, to treat a poor widow thus! Three hundred pounds for a tombstone for my poor dear Husband, I should not have grudged 150 or 200 pounds." "Lord bless you," replied the mason, "my bill is only 30 Dollars." To continue *the Gossip* about Mrs. Owen a little longer (for I feel myself interested in a Lady, who is a Widow, has an *ample fortune*, and has the additional recommendation of Martial to a *young* lover— *tussit*),[5] she keeps a shop (a *store* in good American) which she attends herself from morn till night, returns about £80 a day, and in which she receives the courtship of all the old Batchelors and Widowers of the place who have brushed their coats, added ruffles to their Shirts, and bought new Wigs upon the occasion. One of them, an ancient Schoolmaster has even received an inspiration which he has *vented* in a Copy of Verses, ending with, "Then cast off all old men in greasy Flannells And take into your tender arms, Cornelius Daniells." Whether it was really *Owen* or some other drunken sot of this place I cannot tell, but it is said that when he stood at the altar with his bride *ready* to be married, and half tipsy, growing impatient of the length of the ceremony, he called out to the Parson, Rise, *old Gluepot*, and glue us together quickly.

5. Trans.: She has a cough.   BHL alluded to Martial, *Epigrams*, Book I, epigram 10: "Gemellus seeks to marry Maronilla. He desires it, he insists, he pleads, and he gives her presents. Is she so beautiful? No, indeed, there is nothing more repulsive. Then what is attractive and pleasing about her? She has a cough."

But I have strangely wandered—

A very great nuisance in Norfolk, is, that the creeks by which the town is intersected, and which are full only at high water, are suffered to remain open and spreading every way the receptacles of the filth of all privies, and the nurseries of muskitoes. Besides this, they occasion great inconvenience and interruption in going from one part of the town to the other. They might by embankments and bridges become both usefull and ornamental.

II. The boggy creeks, and the narrowness and filth of the lanes and alleys are the cause, at least the principal cause of the unhealthiness of this town. [See PLATE 8.]

MARCH 27TH, 1796. Most of the Journeymen Mechanicks who arrived here last season from England were affected by the Agues and Fevers, and many of them died. I cannot ascertain that the yellow fever of Philadelphia has raged here.[6] Those that recovered were so alarmed that most of them took their course Northward. This has occasioned, with the rapid increase of buildings in Norfolk an extreme scarcity of hands, especially of joiners and carpenters, and other building artisans, and of course an amazing rise in their demands, of wages. But in respect of its *natural* situation, I conceive that the clearing of the Woods, the encreased cultivation and consequent draining of the Neighboring Land, would render Norfolk *sufficiently* healthy, and at all events prevent the epithet of *unhealthy* particularly attaching to the place. The natural elevation of the Land is at the least 10 or 12 Feet higher than the highest tide, it is firm and dry. The bogs are only occasioned by the inundation of the innumerable creeks. Every inch of land which I have seen within 12 miles of the town has a natural though very gentle declivity towards the nearest creek or river.

The creeks which every where branch out from the rivers and are very wide at the mouth, gradually contracting to their head, and spreading again into many subordinate branches, are in general dry at low Water, excepting extremely minute runs of water, meandering through the mud, which seems originally to have created them. Every tree formerly growing around, *distilled* its supply, and the flux and reflux of the tide, in the course of ages converted every rivulet in this loose soil into a capacious creek.

6. A yellow fever epidemic broke out in Norfolk in the summer of 1795 and killed more than five hundred people before it was checked by frost in October. Wertenbaker, *Norfolk*, p. 189. For the Philadelphia epidemic see John. H. Powell, *Bring out Your Dead: The Great Plague of Yellow Fever in Philadelphia in 1793* (Philadelphia: University of Pennsylvania Press, 1949), and Mathew Carey, *A Short account of the malignant fever, lately prevalent in Philadelphia: with a statement of the proceedings that took place on the subject in different parts of the United States* (Philadelphia: printed by the author, 1793).

MARCH 29TH, 1796.

Dear Brother,

It is a great misfortune to me to have begun this Memorandum in a kind of systematic way. Upon opening, it (the book) today . . . I find that I have *taken up* the task of telling the principles I have *laid down*. And so I may as well go on. *One* principal is, that about Norfolk, a joint of salt pork, as a ham, a chine, a piece of bacon, a smoked pigs face, is as necessary at the head of the table as the Lady of the house. I have dined at 10 or 12 different houses, batchelors and married men, and the rule is the same. Even a roast pig at the bottom of the table makes no difference. Surely, if there is a morality in cooking, this must be culinary adultery. *Another* is, that *Hoecake* is a good thing, *Johnny cake* a better, and *Hommany* in my opinion a very bad one. The *Hoecake* is the Meal of Maize or Indian corn, neaded into dough and baked or toasted before the fire upon a hoe till it is brown. *Johnny* cake is the same composition baked upon a piece of board. Both these come warm to table in the bread basket. *Hommany*, is Maize half ground, or broken, boiled into a pulp and eaten with butter and salt. I think it very sickening and insipid, but the natives are very fond of it. *Maize* broken only is in general called Hommaney, and Horses are fed with it.

MARCH 31ST, 1796.   I have been very idly engaged since my arrival. The friends to whom I was recommended have been extremely kind to me, and I have loitered my time away at their Houses, doing odds and ends of little services for them; designing a staircase for Mr. Acheson's* new house, a House and Offices for Captn. Pennock,*[7] tuning a Pianoforte for Mr. Wheeler,* scribbling doggrel for Mrs.

7. In his "Designs of Buildings Erected or Proposed to be Built in Virginia . . . from 1796 to 1799" (Prints and Photographs Division, Library of Congress; *PBHL, microfiche ed.,* 307/A5), BHL described the origins of his Pennock house design:

This design was made in consequence of a trifling Wager laid against me by Captn. Pennock that I could not design a house which should be approved by Mr. Luke Wheeler: which should have only 41 feet front; which should contain on the Ground floor, 3 Rooms, a principal Staircase, and backstairs; and, which was the essential requisite, the front door of which should be in the Center. I won the Wager, and on leaving Norfolk in March 1795, I gave him the drawing, drawn to a very small scale. He had then no idea of executing the plan. About two months afterwards, I dined at the Eagle tavern in Richmond, where accidentally, Colonel Kelly of Norfolk was also present. In the course of general conversation he related, that some time ago, a frenchman was at Norfolk, who had given Captn. Pennock the most preposterous design, which he had ever seen: that Captn. Pennock had been mad enough to attempt to execute it, and that having carried up part of the Walls he was now perfectly at a stand, as none of the Workmen knew how to proceed. From his description, interlarded with many oaths and imprecations against the Frenchman, I learnt that my own design was meant. I wrote immediately to Norfolk, but before my letter could arrive, I received one from thence, soliciting my advice how to proceed with the work. Soon afterwards I went down to view it, and found that it was in the Hands of Mr. Hill, a Ship joiner, and Mr. Gracie an ingenious Scotch joiner, but obstinately wedded to the heavy wooden taste of the last century. It was with much difficulty that I could

Acheson, tragedy for her Mother, and Italian songs for Mrs. Taylor. An excursion into the Dismal Swamp, opened a prospect for professional pursuits of more importance to me. I saw there too much to describe at random, and too little to describe at all without seeing more.[8] In the mean time the management of the James river navigation seems opening for me,[9] and as I am going thither tomorrow, I must leave Norfolk, which I shall soon have an opportunity of knowing better, to make room for my journey to Richmond.

RICHMOND APRIL 4TH, 1796. Two stages set out for Richmond, one goes on the South, the other on the North side of the James river, the former by way of Portsmouth, the latter by Hampton. Hampton lies on the North side of the common Mouth of the James and Elisabeth rivers, and has good Anchorage in its road. It is the rendezvous of all Vessels coming in and going out of the Chesapeak, which have occasion to wait for a fair Wind, and is the station of the cruizers of the English on this coast. Under the English government, Hampton was the place where all vessels going up the contiguous rivers were obliged to make their entries, and became in consequence a place of much business and resort. It is regularly planned, and the innumerable navigable creeks which intersect the town and near neighbourhood have great convenience. Since the removal however of the general ·Custom house, Hampton has declined, its streets are covered with grass, little or no business is done, and many of the houses are uninhabited and are tumbling down.

The Mail boat, a schooner upon the plan of the Virginia pilot boats, carried me and a large party of Gentlemen from Norfolk to Hampton. The distance is about 20

---

repair the mischief already done. No part of the plan had been accurately set out. The front was totally altered: all the sash frames, instead of being in reveals, were solid, and placed on the outside, and no two sides of the bow window were equal, or set out from the same center. The Chimnies occupied double the space requisite for them; and in general it was necessary to accomodate the original plan to the blunders committed by the workmen, to combat their prejudices and obstinacy, and to inform their ignorance as well as I could.

8. During this trip to the Dismal Swamp, BHL apparently consulted for the Dismal Swamp Canal Company. See pp. 147, 238. For his discussion of a later excursion, when he was engaged by the Dismal Swamp Land Company, see pp. 229–39.

9. The General Assembly first passed legislation to open the great falls of James River to navigation in 1765. John Ballendine worked on a canal around the falls in the 1770s, but the project was never completed. "An act for clearing and improving the navigation of James river," passed in 1784, incorporated the James River Company, with a capital limited to $100,000. A year later John Harris, David Ross, William Cabell, and Edmund Randolph were named directors of the Company. A canal was opened from Westham to Broad Rock Landing, a short distance above Richmond, in 1790. The canal entered the city in 1795. BHL apparently believed that there was a prospect of his being put in charge of work on the canal, but evidently he was never appointed to the position. Hening, *Statutes*, 8:148–50, 11:450–62; Mordecai, *Richmond*, pp. 233–34; Kent Druyvestyn, "With Great Vision: The James River and Kanawha Canal," *Virginia Cavalcade* 21 (Winter 1972): 26–29; Hamlin, *Latrobe*, p. 69.

Plate 6. First view of the coast of Virginia, 3 March 1796.

FROM THE SKETCHBOOKS

Breakfast Equipage set out for the Passengers of the Eliza, the Captain and Mate in all 9 Persons, March 4th, 1796, being the compleat set.

1. The table is furnished with Bars and Cross bars, to prevent the Things from rolling down.

2. In the first partition on the left hand are knives and forks for those who love saltbeef for Breakfast: A Plate intended to serve Mr. Shaw for a Saucer, the Vinegar bottle used at Supper the evening before, and a biscuit which has been toasted to kill the Maggots.

3. In the next to the right, is a Cup, for Mrs. Taylor *with a Saucer*, and a Pewter spoon, which the loss of part of its Handle has converted into a Teaspoon. A basket of Biscuit, *all alive-o!* The Slop bason, formerly part of a Gallon keg, and the Salt jar, which once contained candied Ginger. NB. The Slop bason also feeds the Goat, and serves to wash Mrs. Taylor's baby.

4. The right hand partition holds, the tea and sugar Cannister, a saucer with butter, a cup and saucer, a teaspoon as above, a biscuit, and two knives. The Mustard pot serves the Captain in the double capacity of a Coffee cup and tea cup. In the hole of the cross bar is the pepper box.

5. The small partition on the left hand, belongs to Mr. Shaw the Mate who drinks his Coffee out of a Horn Beker (if it does not happen to be employed as a slop bowl). The two others are provided for Passengers, who breakfast as the utensils become vacant.

6. In more prosperous times the cross bars were cut to receive Wineglasses and Tumblers, but these things are now with the dead, with the Wine and Porter that made them usefull.

7. At night the whole table is illumined by a tall brass Candlestick which formerly lighted a Pew in St. John's Church, Wapping.

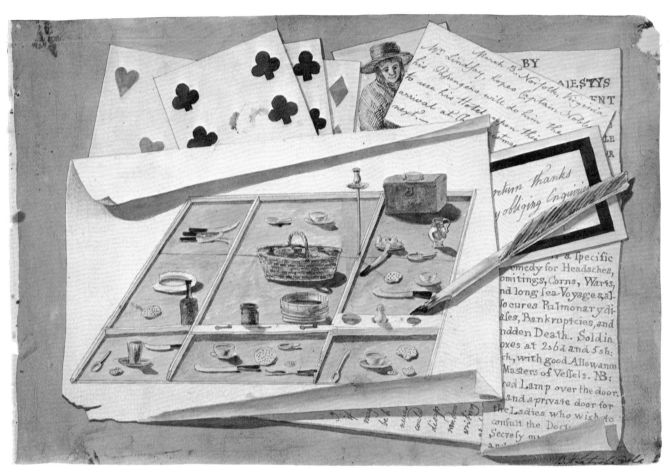

Plate 7. Breakfast table in the cabin of the *Eliza*, 4 March 1796.

Plate 8. View of Norfolk from Town Point.

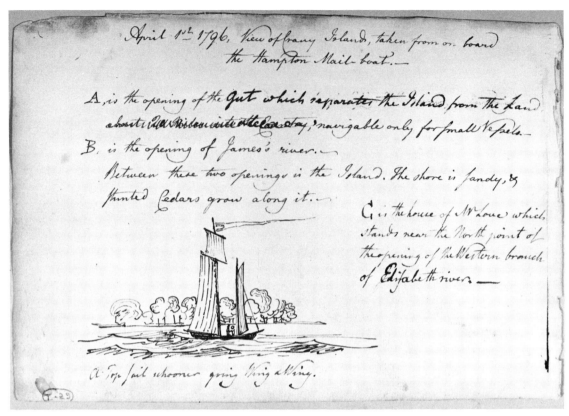

April 1st 1796, View of Craney Island, taken from on board
the Hampton Mail-boat. —

A, is the opening of the Gut which separates the Island from the Land
about *[illegible]* , navigable only for small Vessels. —

B. is the opening of James's river. —

Between these two openings is the Island. The shore is Sandy, &
stunted Cedars grow along it. —

G is the house of Mr Lowe which
stands near the North point of
the opening of the Western branch
of Elizabeth river. —

A Topsail schooner going Wing a Wing.

Fig. 12.   A topsail schooner, 1 April 1796.

View of Craney Island, Elizabeth river, Virginia. —

G   A   B

Fig. 13.   View of Craney Island, Elizabeth River, Virginia, 1 April 1796.

miles. The country on each side of the river, flat and woody, affords many beautifull combinations of Wood and Water, perpetually varying, and enriched by a succession of large and small Vessells differently rigged which are continually moving in the picture. Just below Norfolk are two forts, nearly opposite to one another, called fort Norfolk, and fort Nelson.[10] In the former a very small garrison is kept up. They compleatly command the river, and a good boom defended by them would be impregnable. Nature seems to have narrowed the River and formed the points on which they are built purposely for the defence of one of the best commercial positions in the World.

The Mail boat is the property of Mr. Loyal.* The fare to Hampton is a Dollar. It is navigated by his slaves who make a perquisite of [find]ing the Passengers in a dinner and liquors. We were a large party and got enough to drink, but our victuals were scanty. They however had the impudence to charge half a dollar for two ounces of beefstakes and 1s.6d. for the porter we drank.

The Gentlemen who left Norfolk with me in the boat, were a Magistrate, Mρ. Λεε,* against whom an action had been brought upon a case in which he was said to have acted arbitrarily and illegally in the execution of his duty, and his witnesses. They were all *but one* men of the first respectability at Norfolk, Mρ. Νευ[ι]σον, Βρεντ, Νευσομ, Ὠβδη, Εμερσον, Βεννετ, Θε Ρευδ. Μρ. Ὀυιτεέαδ[11] and his brother. The other was a working man, a tallow chandler. The case, as I understand it, is this. Upon a vacancy in the pulpit of the Episcopal Church, the candidates were one Bland* of Hampton, and the Revd. Mr. Whitehead.* The former is a man of great popular eloquence, but of a violent and extremely immoral character, illiterate and vulgar in his manners and appearance. The latter, with less brilliant ability has the manners and character of a gentleman. The *Vestry*, regularly elected Mr. Whitehead, but a number of the parishioners chose Bland and put him forcibly into possession of the miserable *Cathedral*. An action was brought, and the verdict obtained, as well as the decission of Bishop Maddison* of Williamsburg, gave Mr. Whitehead the possession of the pulpit. The opposite party however obtained a second victory, they broke open the gates of the Churchyard and the doors of the church, and having put on newlocks, retired. Mr. Lee, one of the Magistrates of the Town, upon this occasion granted a warrant to seize the rioters, and to lodge them in jail unless they could give bail. There was an error in this proceeding, for the warrant ought to have directed the

---

10. BHL was commissioned to renovate these forts two years later. See p. 432, n. 3.

11. The first name transcribes as: Mr. [Richard Evers] Lee. The eight names grouped together transcribe as: Messrs. New[i]son, Brent, Newsom, Hobde, Emerson, Bennet, the Revd. Mr. Whitehead.

constable to bring them before him for a hearing, and this was the ground upon which an action was brought.[12]

The party was very agreeable. I have not yet met a Man in America from the Captain of the Pilotboat to the last Stage driver who did not reason justly *from the extent of His information*. They all seem to deserve at least the praise of being men of good common sense. Conversation with such characters is both pleasing and instructive, but many of our party had superior abilities and knowledge. The scenes which we traversed on our Journey reminded those who had carried arms during the American war of the past dangers and labors, and almost every tree and valley had its anecdote. There are few stones in the country or I should have said, *Nullum sine nomine saxum*.[13] Many of them were of a melancholy nature. On passing down Elisabeth river, its eastern shore recalled the shocking remembrance of thousands of miserable negroes who had perished there with hunger and disease. Many Waggon loads of the bones of Men women and Children, stripped of the flesh by Vultures and Hawks which abound here, covered the sand for a most considerable length. Lord Dunmore, soon after the commencement of the War, offered liberty to all the slaves who would rise against, or escape from their *Rebel* masters.[14] The hopes of getting on board the English fleet collected them at the mouth of the Chesapeak bay, they were left behind in thousands and perished. Children died sucking the breasts of their dead mothers, and Women feeding upon the corpses of their starved children. The remnants of decaying rags still point to the skeletons of many of these miserable victims of the *"enormous faith of millions made for one."*

The inn of Hampton lies a little way up a *many-branched* creek, a safe harbor for boats drawing 8 or 9 feet of Water. It is a building like all the rest showing the symptoms of decay. Mr. Kirby the landlord is a good natured man. He has good beds, in bad rooms, bad attendance and bad victuals and drink. Butter is every where wretched. Fresh butter I have very seldom seen in this country.

12. The controversy between Rev. William Bland and Rev. James Whitehead concerned the ministry of Elizabeth River Parish, Norfolk. Whitehead became minister of the parish about 1789, but was challenged for the position by Bland. Each minister had a following in the congregation, and they shared the use of the Borough Church on Sundays, one preaching in the morning, the other in the afternoon. After the Bland faction took control of the church, Whitehead and his followers held services in the courthouse on East Main Street until Christ Church was erected in 1800. Meade, *Old Churches*, 1:273–74.

13. Trans.: No rock without a name.

14. John Murray (1732–1809), fourth earl of Dunmore, served as governor of New York from 1770 to 1771, and as governor of Virginia from 1771 until the Revolution. On 7 November 1775 he declared martial law in Virginia and encouraged slaves to desert to the British. In December of that year his forces were defeated at Great Bridge. After another defeat in July 1776 at Gwynne's Island, Dunmore finally left Virginia for England. *DAB.*

APRIL 5TH, 1796, RICHMOND. Tea and Coffee and *supper* seem at the inns of this part of the world to go together and to form one meal under the general name of supper. This sort of repast we made soon after our arrival. We found a butcher of Richmond, one Mr. White at the inn with his new married wife. He had brought her from Boston in a brig which proceeded up James river, and had landed in hopes of reaching home sooner by land. He had already taken seats in the stage, but it was impossible we should *all* go. Every attempt to deter him by representations of crouded carriage, hot weather, necessary rest, bad roads, and late accidents upon it, was vain, and as the stage put up a distance from the inn the Norfolk passengers with more courage than justice walked up to the Stables and took possession of the Vehicle, which, upon 4 traverse seats, exactly gave room for 12 Persons. The sight of the croud did more than the representation of it the evening before, and the Butcher and his wife *resigned* with the good grace of a Minister of State who can hold *his place* no longer. The majority rules here. Mr. Kirby held the scales with lawyer like exactness.

The Stage was driven by a Black, one of Colonel Holmes's* slaves. The Colonel is proprietor of the stage from Hampton to Georgetown. The Roads are just tolerable. The farms on each side of them were in general badly cultivated, and had a deserted appearance. The soil seems to consist of the same sandy loam as on the other side of the river. For the first 16 miles the country is flat. The woods consist chiefly of the long leaved pine, called feather pine intermixed with Cedars in greater abundance than about Norfolk.[15] The Gulleys formed by small runs of Water grow deeper the further you proceed and begin to contain large Quartzose pebbles at the end of 12 miles from Hampton. There is nothing that has the appearance of a village. We watered our horses at a petty inn called, the halfway house. They were lean and knocked up, but contrived to drag us on at the rate of about 5 miles an hour.

The Sassafras tree just begins now to blossom. It is one of the *filii ante patrem*,[16] and bears a cluster of small yellow flowers of a very aromatic smell and flavor, but unlike the wood, as imported into Europe. There were no large trees of the species near the road, nor were the small ones very common. It is the root that is imported.

At a Mill pond, I saw innumerable Tarapins turtles, of the species called the snapping turtle.[17] They hung to the trees that stood in or near the water, and dropped

15. *Pinus australis* Michx. f., commonly called long-leaf pine; cedars: *Juniperus virginiana* L., or *Chamaecyparis thyoides* (L.) BSP.

16. *Sassafras albidum* (Nutt.) Nees. BHL probably intended *filii ante partem*, "threads before parting," meaning that when the leaf is broken about midway it will show the vascular bundles (*filii*) as bridging the separated halves of the blade. See also p. 97.

17. *Chelydra serpentina* (L.).

into it immediately upon being approached. One of them had strayed into the road, and I picked him up. Had I been a Knight errant he would have made an excellent Dragon with very little alteration of form, and not much of size. A pair of wings would have been all that was wanting. The common representations indeed of dragons are indebted to the snapping turtle at least for head, legs, and tail. It was troublesome to carry the poor devil along and as the sight of him was new *only* to me, my fellow passengers were not very fond of his company, so that I resolved to take another opportunity to examine, describe and draw him.

The country becomes more hilly, as you approach York town. A haze which continued all day rendered it impossible to observe much of its face. Indeed two thirds at least of the road lies in the primeval woods, and much in woods of modern growth. Whenever a field refuses to yield a further crop without manure, it is suffered to lie fallow, and a few years covers it with pine, unmixed with any deciduous trees.[18] By this circumstance the old may be every where distinguished from the modern woods. As the country becomes hilly the *deciduous trees* predominate, in the flats *pine* of the *feather* sort is most frequent. The spruce-pine becomes more common in the hills, and has a picturesque appearance, equal in many instances to a deciduous tree, being void of the formality of most evergreens. The trees new to me, besides the Sassafras, were two species of cedar, the hiccory, the locust, and the wild grapevine.[19] This last is the most impudent of sycophants. He covers and pulls down two or three trees often of a large size that happen to grow in his neighbourhood rambling and twisting about like a snake. I am told that the grape is very palatable after being frost bitten, but sour till then. I have never seen this vine lay hold of a resinous tree. Misseltoe grows in great abundance upon the Oak. In England the apple tree seems to be the chief support of this sycophant; I never saw the Misseltoe upon an Oak but once. The Druids, I believe considered the Oak as sacred that was thus marked.[20] Chesnuts

18. The lying fallow may result in the regrowth of pine in some areas and deciduous trees in others. Indian "fire-hunting" over the centuries also caused some open spaces. See Joseph and Nesta Ewan, *John Banister and His Natural History of Virginia 1678–1692* (Urbana: University of Illinois Press, 1970), pp. 42–43, 385–86.

19. Spruce pine: *Larix laricina* (Du Roi) K. Koch; cedars: *Juniperus virginiana* L. and *Chamaecyparis thyoides* (L.) BSP.; hickory: *Carya* sp.; black locust: *Robinia pseudoacacia* L.; wild grapevine: there are three species of *Vitis* possible for Virginia: *Vitis labrusca* L., *V. vulpina* L., and *V. rotundifolia* Michx.

20. Mistletoe: *Phoradendron flavescens* (Pursh) Nutt. The Druids believed the oak tree to be a symbol of fertility by what has been known as the Doctrine of Signatures, that a plant reveals its uses for man by the shape of some organ. In the oak tree this is the acorn which resembles the *glans penis*. An oak "producing" mistletoe was especially regarded, and worshipped. The acorns were probably a main source of food.

are not uncommon, in these Woods, and Chinkopin is the most frequent under-growth.[21]

A Butterfly very like the *Machaon* of Linnaeus was already very busy. I think he had no spurs, nor was he quite so large as our Europaean *Machaon*.[22] I have no books to refer to.

York town will be known to Posterity as long as the English or American History is read. Here it was that Lord Cornwallis and his army surrendered to the united French and American army. The history of that event it is unnecessary to repeat. The town lies upon an eminence close to the River York. The river is a beautiful stream a mile over, and on the opposite side is a poor village called Gloucester.[23] The York shore is a bold gravelly cliff on a basis of loose shell rock commanding a very extensive view down the river almost as far as the Chesapeak. A haze hung over the Landscape on the other side. The house in which Lord Cornwallis had his head Quarters lies a stone's throw from the East end of the town. It is a large square brick building of tolerable proportions. The remains of very strong works surround it, the house itself is in a most ruinous state, shattered by shells and balls.[24] During the seige he retired under the cliff. Many other houses in the town are nearly as bad, though neither balls nor shells have contributed to their downfall. York like Hampton is half deserted. Trade has almost entirely left this once flourishing place, and none of the ravages of the War have been repaired. During the seige, Lord Cornwallis lived in a Cottage in a deep Gulley safe from annoyance. There are many of them pointing to the river.

We had changed horses at a solitary inn at [. .], four miles from York. We had a good dinner, Madeira for 7s.6d. currency. We were going to drink more wine, but our sly Landlord ordered the Driver to blow his horn by which means he saved the liquor we had paid for. The greatest *fort* of our black Driver seems to be in making a noise. His bawling and whistling to his horses almost stunned me. His whistling especially exceeded the shrillest fife.

21. Chestnuts: *Castanea dentata* (Marsh.) Nutt.; chinquapin: *Castanea pumila* (L.) Mill.

22. BHL probably saw a swallowtail butterfly (*Papilio machaon* [L.]), included by Linnaeus in *Systema Naturae* (Stockholm, 1758), p. 462.

23. Now known as Gloucester Point.

24. Lord Cornwallis's headquarters was the mansion belonging to Secretary Thomas Nelson (1716–82), councillor and secretary of the colony. Nelson remained in the house while it was occupied by the British officers and later was allowed to pass to the American lines. Before its bombardment in 1781, the mansion had been described as a "very handsome house, from which neither European taste nor luxury was excluded." BHL sketched the mansion in his "Essay on Landscape" (see chap. 11, FIG. 52). Randolph W. Church and W. Edwin Hemphill, " 'View at Little York,' " *Virginia Cavalcade* 1 (Autumn 1951): 44; Clyde F. Trudell, *Colonial Yorktown* (Old Greenwich, Conn.: The Chatham Press, 1938/1971), p. 108.

The City of Williamsburg is 12 miles from York town. We arrived there about 5 o'clock having passed through a hilly country pleasantly enough variegated by wood water and open fields, but, upon the whole, of the same cast of the last stage. The principal street of Williamsburg is near a mile in length. At one end of it stands the Capitol, at the other the College. The capitol is a heavy brick pile with a two story-portico towards the street the wooden pillars of which are stripped of their Mouldings, and are twisted and forced out of their places in all directions. They seem to be perfectly rotten, and I am astonished that the pediment and roof still stands. A beautifull Marble statue of Lord Bottetourt, a popular governor of Virginia before the war, is deprived of its head and mutilated in many other respects [see PLATE 9 and FIG. 14].[25] This is not the only proof of the decay of Williamsburg. The Court house, which stands on the North side of the street, has lost all the Columns of its Portico, and the Pediment sticks out like a Penthouse carried only by timbers that bind into the roof.[26] Many ruined and uninhabited houses disgrace the street. But a visit, which I have promised to pay to Mr. Andrews,* the professor of Mathematics in the University will afford better opportunity of viewing this once flourishing city.

Of the poverty of the corporation, I had a curious proof. An old man, the first beggar I have seen in America put into my hand a paper, stating him to be an honest decayed *Barber* and signed by the Revd. John Bracken.* I showed it to a Gentleman, a stranger, who stood near me, and who had entered into conversation with me, and asked him whether that sort of licence to beg were usual and legal. He answered by telling the Man that unless he went about his business he would take care that

---

25. Norborne Berkeley (1718–70), Baron de Botetourt, was governor of Virginia from 1768 to 1770. The statue, now restored, stands in the library of the College of William and Mary. At the end of this journal, BHL made several comments on the Botetourt statue. The page is torn and only part of the remarks survive. They are: "... [outra]ge upon the Statue of Lord Bottetourt was com[mitted by] students of the College whose names deserve recording *infamiae causa* [for infamy's sake], as it was a deliberate act of Barbarism. It was done about the time the *french disease* had its largest scope, and a Lord, a harmless thing in America became the detestation of a few puppies." BHL referred to this incident in a letter to Robert Goodloe Harper written in 1800, explaining why a statue of George Washington might not be the best type of monument: "A very striking proof of the folly of expecting that any Statue will be always respected, exists in Williamsburg, where Lord Botetourt's statue which had remained untouched during the whole war, was mutilated, and decapitated by the young collegians, in the first frenzy of French revolutionary maxims, *because it was the statue of a **Lord**.*" BHL to Harper, post 24 April 1800, Records of Joint Committees of Congress, Record Group 128, National Archives; *PBHL, microfiche ed.*, 162/E10.

26. There is no documentary evidence that columns were ever ordered for the courthouse erected to serve Williamsburg and James City County in 1770. They were added in 1911, when renovations were made following a fire. When the courthouse was restored to its eighteenth-century appearance in 1932, the columns were removed. Research Department, Colonial Williamsburg Foundation.

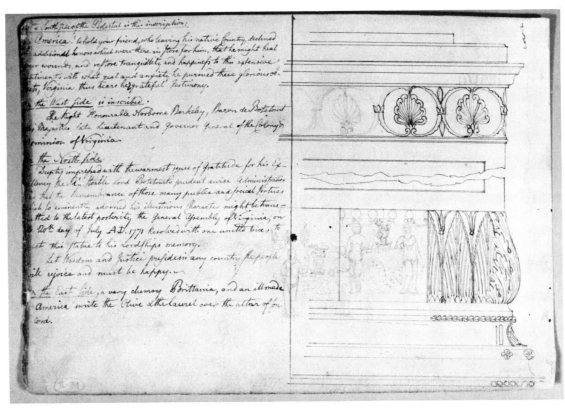

Fig. 14.   Pedestal of statue of Lord Botetourt, Williamsburg.

the maintenance allowed him by the Corporation should be discontinued.[27] The Barber, who appeared by his dialect to be a French man (his name is Lafond,* formerly an usefull man in the [pimping] way)[28] pleaded a bedridden mother, a crazy wife, and half a dozen children dying of the smallpox, and then boldly said, that *"the corporation* was so poor, as to have been unable to pay him and other pensioners, whom he named, their stipend for the last nine *Months.*" This argument dragged a pisterine from each of our pockets, the strange Gentleman told the Beggar *"he was* an impudent fellow to abuse the *Corporation,*" and then whispered [to] me that they had lately pulled down the iron railing around the Capitol and sold it to raise a little money. The Barber's name

27. The courthouse fire of 1911, which destroyed Williamsburg's city ordinances, has made it impossible to document the city's poor relief and begging license systems.

28. BHL wrote this parenthetical remark between the lines in the manuscript.

Plate 9. View of Lord Botetourt's mutilated statue, Williamsburg.

was Lafond and formerly contributed much to the entertainment and scandal of the place, by his buffoonery and news carrying.

We had a tea, coffee, oyster, beef, pickles, and fish supper as usual and good beds. I met here Major Day* who has shown me many civilities and now strengthened Mr. Aitcheson's recommendation to Mr. Andrews.

RICHMOND, APRIL 6TH, 1796. We left Williamsburg at 5 in the morning. It was hazy as yesterday. The country continued gently undulated, with very deep gulleys at every Watercourse. The soil was still a mixture of loamy sand, and clay. In a hollow road, I observed a stratum of shells of different sorts mixed with Gravel and sand, about 3 feet deep, under a superstratum of Clay of about 8 feet. The shells were very perfect and seemed to be chiefly scollops and oysters. Iron ore abounded on the tops of all the hills. The valleys were full of quartz [*illegible*]. We passed many farms in much better order than those nearer Hampton, but there were but few appearances of new Settlers, or newly cleared Grounds. Our driver was a white man, a much more sensible and intelligent fellow than I should have expected upon the box of a Stage Coach. His name is Shaddock. I cannot help observing, that the English language is spoken in more purity, and more grammatically by all ranks of men hereabouts than in any county of England, with which I am acquainted. We breakfasted in the Virginian stile at Allen's ordinary, a good house. Hitherto the civility and attendance at the different inns had been not inferior to what is usually met with in England. We arrived to dinner at New Kent Courthouse.[29] The Courthouse is a mean brick room opposite to the inn. An extremely unpleasant circumstance took place upon the road. Mr. Haycock, the tallow chandler, a vulgar illiterate fellow, went *mad* in the Coach and continued so for two hours. He was half melancholy and half mischeivious, and contrived to give me a grip of the arm which I felt for several days. Formerly he had been sufficiently mad to render it necessary to chain him to the floor. We stopped at a farmer's cottage on the Road. He called for water, and received a Quart of very stiff Grog. Having drank the whole of it, his reason by degrees returned, and he behaved tolerably well during the remainder of the journey. About 5 in the evening we arrived at Richmond. The long dry weather and a very high wind filled the whole atmosphere with dust as we drove up to the inn. It was the most villainous circumstance during the journey and half choaked us all.

RICHMOND APRL. 7TH, 1796. There are I believe few towns, places, or counties in old England that have not a namesake in N. America. In few cases has

29. A small village, the county seat of New Kent County thirty miles east of Richmond. It was situated on the main stage road leading from the capital to Williamsburg. *Martin's Gazetteer.*

similarity of situation had the smallest influence upon the sameness of name. Richmond however is an exception to this remark. The general landscapes from the two Richmond-hills are so similar in their great features, that at first sight the likeness is most striking. The detail of course must be extremely different. But the windings of James river have so much the same *cast* with those of the Thames, the amphitheatre of hills covered partly with wood partly with buildings, and the opposite shore with the town of Manchester[30] in front, and fields and woods in the rear, are so like the range of hills on the south bank of the Thames, and the situation of Twickenham on the north backed by the neighbouring woody parks, that if a man could be imperceptibly and in an instant conveyed from the one side of the Atlantic to the other he might hesitate for some minutes before he could discover the difference.

The want of finish and neatness in the American landscape would first strike his eye, while his ear would be arrested by the roar of the falls of James river below him. He would miss the elegance of Richmond bridge, and find in its place the impatient torrent tumbling over huge masses of granite. To his right he would see the small neat willow Island in the Thames towering into a woody Hill, which seperates the curled stream of James river. Instead of the velvet lawns of Mr. Cambridge's park and the precise arrangement of Twickenham,[31] the wild trees growing among the irregular Islands and the rambling edifices of Manchester would bewilder his attention. The neat walks and iron railings surrounding him there, would here be changed into rough roads and wooden inelegant fences. The perfection of cultivation in the first instance, in the second, the grandeur of Nature, would fill his mind. Other circumstances of important Geographical difference, would pass much longer unnoticed. The Thames flows on the North, James river on the South side of Richmond. The former runs from the left to the right, the latter from the right to the left. When however the whole country was in wood, I am convinced that it was the *general* similarity of the characters of the two situations that impressed upon this spot the name of Richmond. [See PLATE 10.]

RICHMOND APRIL 10TH, 1796. The Falls of James River at this place add much to the beauty of its situation. They extend from about 6 miles above, to the middle of the length of the town. The difference of level from the first fall to the com-

30. A small town in northern Chesterfield County situated on the James River opposite Richmond and connected to that city by Mayo's Bridge. *Martin's Gazetteer.*

31. Richard Owen Cambridge (1717-1802), English poet whose interests included landscape gardening, purchased Cambridge House, a villa in Twickenham, Middlesex, in 1751. He enjoyed decorating and improving his house, where he entertained many notable people. *DNB;* Nikolaus Pevsner, *Middlesex* (Harmondsworth, Eng.: Penguin Books, 1951).

mon surface of high water at this season is about 120 feet, as taken for the purpose of the canal now cutting.[32] There is nothing in that extent that deserves the name of a Cascade. The highest perpendicular fall that I have observed does not exceed 6 feet. The spring has been extremely dry and the river is uncommonly low, so that the breaks of the stream must be at present more abrupt than at any other time. The descent is over an extremely irregular stratum of Granite. In some places the stream is uninterrupted for half a mile together, and in others the rocks are very thickly scattered across the whole river. At the upper and lower ends the water meets with the most frequent interruption. There are many islands over grown with trees in the extent of the falls, of which the principal is a beautiful one, belonging to Mr. Bushrod Washington.* [See PLATE 11.] On the south side of this Island the Channel is filled with immense Masses of Granite, among which the torrent roars with great impetuosity, dividing itself into a thousand separate streams, that wind their way through them tumbling in some places 4 or 5 feet perpendicularly, in others taking a course directly opposite to that of the river till met by some other that rushes again forward. A infinite number of small picturesque groups of rocks, trees and water, present themselves. On the North side several rocky islets, and innumerable broad and bare rocks produce the same effects but in a less degree. The largest Cascade, I have any where observed is at this place. The fall is about 6 feet, it is about 30 feet wide, and the depth at the edge of the fall about 5 feet. The best fishing place in the river is at this fall, which is called *deep skim* (from the manner in which the fish are caught in *skim* or spoon Nets). The proper name of this Island is *Broadrock*. This name is derived from an immense flat rock on the Northern shore extending near 100 feet each way without a fissure. It is covered by a rich carpet of Moss and surrounded on three sides with beautiful Trees. The basis of Washington's Island is an immense Pile of Granite, abrupt and bare at the West end, but gradually sloping and covered in most places with Mould on every other side. Towards the East is a fruitful hanging plain of about 15 Acres; skirted round the edge with trees. The West end appears to have formerly with stood many a tremendous Attack from the Western Waters; huge fragments of rock that seem to have been violently torn from the Cliff cover its foot. At present

32. See n. 9 above.

however a considerable extent of low rocky ground *up the stream* is covered with large trees and under-wood. I am at a loss to account for this, excepting by supposing that the quantity of Water descending in rainy seasons from the Mountains must be much smaller now than formerly. Above this Island the River is confined between steep rocky banks. The Island meets its whole fury. Below, the country opens gradually. Every appearance on the Island, and on the opposite shores speaks the effect of the torrent. But the highest *fresh* in the memory of man, that of last Autumn, did not reach nearly to the very evident marks of its former operations.

JAMES RIVER, CONTINUED. APRL. 12TH, 1796. RICHMOND. Canoes can pass through the *sluices* from the lower to the upper end of the falls when the Water is moderately low. *Sluices* are narrow passages between the rocks where there is a considerable fall, but at the same time a sufficient depth of Water. I have been round Washington's Island in a Canoe, navigated by two Negroes. One stood at each end with a pole about 10 feet long. Their dexterity in making the united operation of their exertions, and of the force and direction of the torrent effect a safe voyage, was admirable.[33] The confidence that was sufficient to make me trust myself with them, failed me at the first sluice we passed, and I have no stomach for such another expedition. The fishermen however make nothing of it. Above the falls, James River is navigated by means of Batteaus. These are very light Boats about 60 feet long and 4 or 5 feet wide. They carry as many as 12 Hogsheads of Tobacco weighing 14 Cwt. each. Three Men are sufficient to manage a Batteau.

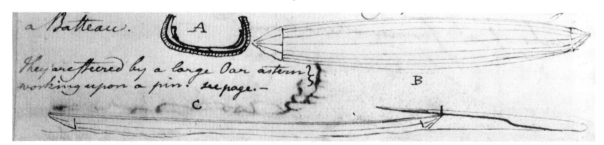

A, is the section, *B* the form on the bottom, *C* the side view of one of these Batteaus, no regard being had to their proportions. With some difficulty and much care and dexterity even a Batteau might be safely carried through the falls, but not in so dry a season as the present. To avoid the delay, danger and inconvenience a canal has been projected and is now nearly completed which runs parrallel with the river, and is intended to discharge the craft at Richmond into the river by means of eight successive locks. A short canal containing 2 locks of about 8 feet each enable boats to

33. See p. 516 for BHL's vignette of the Negro batteaumen in his "Essay on Landscape."

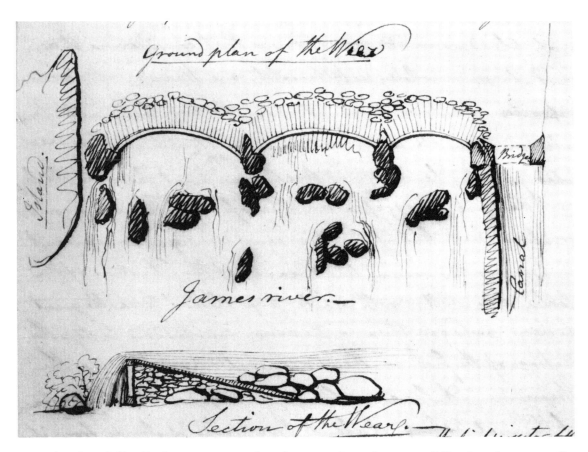

Ground plan of the Wier

James river.

Section of the Wear.

pass the first falls. It then reenters the river, and at the next difficulty about a mile below leaves it, and is continued along the steep bank to Richmond without a lock. The greatest part of it is blown out of the Solid Granite. It is neither judiciously, nor ornamentally managed, and there are several most gross blunders in its execution. But considering it as the Work of a Man wholly self taught, *one Harris*,[34] it deserves great commendation. The two locks at the first falls are very ill contrived and constructed. They are of Granite, hewn, and laid together without Cement. The leakage therefore is excessive. The loss of Water is no consideration, but that of time is considerably inconvenient.

Besides the romantic Beauty of the Situation of the locks, it is well worth while to go thither to see the great fishery carried on there, and the *Wear* constructed to stop the passage of the fish in their annual migration up the stream. A large island lies opposite to the entrance of the Canal at about 300 Yards distance from it. Many very huge masses of Granite lie across the stream 4 of which, at nearly equal distances, have been fixed upon as the Butments of the *Wier*. A strong horizontal Arch of timber is laid between these Butments. The upper side is filled with small stones, over which

34. Probably John Harris, who had been named a director of the James River Company in 1785. See n. 9 above.

thick plank are laid inclined to the bottom of the river. The lower ends, are kept down by large Stones laid upon them; the upper ends are pinned to the front of the Wier. The Water falls over the Edge of it about 3 feet at an average.

This Wear is the Work of Mr. Balandine* the first projector of the Canal. It is boldly conceived and admirably executed. The Wood work being constantly covered with Water, is as perfect as when first erected, and is likely to last for many years, if not for centuries. Independant of the fishery, it also answers the purpose of guiding a full stream of Water into the Mouth of the Canal. The River below the Island is about half a mile over.

RICHMOND APRIL 13TH, 1796. The fisheries carried on upon the rocks that are scattered throughout the falls are the source of wealth to many individuals. Some hundred whites and blacks are employed in them, most of the latter working for the benefit of their owners.

About the 10th of March, the *Chad* arrive, in their annual migration, at the falls of James river. The *Rockfish* migrate at the same time but in smaller number.[35] The Chad come up full roed and fat, and independent of the trouble of picking out their innumerable small bones, are an excellent fish for the table. Several other Species of fish are caught in the *Skim* nets and seines, but the chief dependence both of the fishermen, and of the proprietors of the fisheries who receive the toll is upon the Chad. Just below the Falls they are caught in the Seine. Those that escape fall in numbers a prey to the *skim nets*. The fisherman takes his stand upon a rock close to a *sluice*, or under a Waterfall. The Chad meeting with some difficulty in going up the rapid and strong current at these places remain for a moment stationary, playing their fins and tail, and then at one effort shoot forward against the stream without leaving the Water as the Salmon do. They can mount almost perpendicularly a fall of 4 or 5 feet. Without waiting till he sees the fish, the fisherman is perpetually employed in putting in his net into the highest part of the Sluice, and drawing it down the stream bringing it up at his arm's length. I have seen a haul of 7 Chad each 18 inches long, at once—Gentlemen, upon whom I could depend, have seen as many as 13, 15, and 16 taken up at once. Management is then required to get them ashore. When the Chad run in great abundance, the *Skimmer* is sometimes held fast by a rope round his Waist, by one or more men; the exertions of a large haul of Chad being sufficient to drag him down into the sluice.

The proprietors of the Shores on which the fish are landed or of the Rocks upon

35. Shad: *Alosa sapidissima* (Wilson); rockfish or striped bass: *Roccus lineatus* Bloch.

which they are caught, claim as a toll every 4th Chad. Other fish pay no toll. At the fishery at Rosses Mill [see PLATE 12], a bridge of a single tree is constructed to carry the fishermen to the Rocks. The highest toll ever taken in the beginning of May, by the tollman of whom I enquired, was 250 fish. On the day I made the enquiry Aprl. 8th he had taken 70. In the first instance the fish caught was, of course 1,000, in the latter 280, *average*, 640. At Mr. Washington's Island 800 have been caught in a day. The places however where fish are taken, *paying toll*, are exceedingly numerous, and those where no toll is demanded still more so. It must therefore be impossible to ascertain the number caught, at any time of the Season. The above observations show however that it must be very great indeed. I think 20,000 as an average per day, from the upper to the lower end of the falls must be under the mark, as it is only 200 for each of one hundred *skimming stands*, of which I am sure there must be more. In this *guess* the quantity taken in the Seine is not included.

The Chads continue to mount the river till the 10th or 15th of May. All that go up are fat and full roed. About the 15th the first of them are observed to return. They come back spent, thin, and perfectly lean. No cookery can then make them palatable. A black fisherman expressed his idea upon this subject in these words, "*Masser, I would not give them to eat to a whore's dog, you may stew them in akkerfortiss, and you can't chew them then, Masser.*" Chads are caught at sea in February and March without the Capes of Virginia, and in April and May have been taken at the foot of the Allegany Mountains.

Of the Chads there are two sorts: see the Sketch book page, [. .].[36] Plenty of excellent Perch are taken both with Nets and the Seine among the Rocks of the falls. They are of two or three sorts. The common English perch, and the yellow bellied perch are the most common. Chubs, mullets, hornheads, are innumerable. A fish called a *Carp* sometimes is taken among Chads. I have only seen one *cooked*. It was a much better fish than our Europaean carp, and different entirely in its bones. No Salmon are taken so far to the Southward. Below the falls, excellent, and large Sturgeon are caught in great Plenty.[37]

Prices of fish Aprl. 19th 1796. Richmond. A large sized Chad 9d. or 55[s. per] hundred. Sturgeon, 6d. per Pound; when plenty, as low as $2\frac{1}{2}$ or 3d. Perch, a shilling per dozen, *N.B.* The perch in general are larger than in England, from 9 to 12 inches.

36. This sketch has not been found.

37. Common names of fish are notoriously misleading. There is only one true shad on the Atlantic coast. The tailor herring, or hickory shad, *Pomolobus mediocris* Mitchill is found in the region. Only one perch is recognized, the yellow perch, *Perca flavescens* (Mitchill). The common chub is *Semotilus atromaculatus* Mitchill, the common mullet is *Mugil cephalus* L. and the hornhead is *Hybopsis kentuckiensis* Rafinesque. The Eastern carp sucker is *Carpiodes cyprinus* LeSueur, and the most common sturgeon is *Acipenser sturio* L.

Carp, about 1s. 3d. a pair, about 15 inches long. Of Carps there are two sorts the white and yellow. I have seen neither. The way to know a good Carp is to draw the foot along his side *with* Scales, if Blood immediately appear at the point of every Scale, the carp is good and tender, if not he is as tough as the Negro's Chad.

N.B. The prices above are Virginia currency being to Sterling as 4 to 3.

APRIL 19TH, 1796. For this fortnight past, I have observed in all the low Grounds and on the banks of the river very great numbers of the Papilio [. .] of Linnaeus. The papilio podalirius is also common, and larger than in Europe. Machaon is not yet frequent, but I have seen several individuals. Another *eques* resembling Machaon, I have often seen but not been able to catch. He was less.[38] My disappointments arising from my being entirely without books of Natural history are daily growing more distressing. I have not met with a Single Amateur since my arrival.

I took last week a trip with Mr. John Stewart,* and Mr. Harry Heath* to their Coalpits 12 miles from this place on the South side of the River.

A most wretched bridge leads across the lower end of the falls to Manchester. It is the property of Mr. Mayo,* who levies a toll of 6 Cents upon every foot or horse-passenger that goes over it. Its construction is so various, that to describe it is a task more unpleasant if possible than to pass it. The first part of the bridge which leads to a rocky island consists of piers, or enclosures of timber filled with loose pieces of Granite. The timbers are dovetailed at the angles, exactly upon the system of the Norfolk Wharfs. They are by no means level, and the 3 or 4 first of them incline in an angle of 15 or 16 degrees so that the upstream side of the Bridge is a foot higher than the other. From each pier to the next are four or five long timbers, across which planks are laid traversely, without being in any manner fixed. After passing the sloping part of the bridge, upon which the plank is *somehow or other* kept down, the rattling begins to the consternation of horses and men. Some relief from the noise, but none from the danger are the tops of the piers where large loose stones occupy the place of loose boards. The piers are so distant, that the *rattle trap* between them dances up and down like a slack rope. After passing the first part of this *tripartite* bridge, you land upon a rocky island, as irregular and rough as nature left, or the water wore it. A crooked rutty road over it guides you to the second part of the bridge which exactly resembles the first in every circumstance, but that, along the edges of the boards a heap of stones is piled on each side, which somewhat prevents their restless activity, and gives a slight idea of a parapet, an idea which never occurred to the projector of

38. These are various species of swallowtail butterflies.

Plate 10. View of Richmond from Bushrod Washington's island.

FROM THE SKETCHBOOKS

Mr. Bushrod Washington's Island lies about one Mile above the lower end of the Falls of James's River, and divides the stream.

(35.

Sketch of Washington's Island, James River Virginia. — April. 14.ᵗʰ 96.

Plate 11. Sketch of Washington's Island, James River, Virginia, 14 April 1796.

Sketch of the lower end of the Falls of James River, Virginia

Plate 12. Sketch of the lower end of the Falls of James River, Virginia, 6 April 1796.

the first part. It is the *indegesta moles*, the *discordia semina rerum*.[39] From the bridge you jump up to your ankles into a sandy island of greater extent than the first. Another, part sandy, part rocky, road leads to the Tollhouse, from whence you wade your way onto a bridge of boats. The boats are very low flats, not being more than a foot from the Water's edge. This is the most regular part of the Work, the boards are in part pinned down, and the Swinging exceeds the rattling, the reverse of which is the case at the other end. The ruins of a handrail, the extreme and visible infacillity of which cautions passengers to keep the middle of the bridge, show the maturity of the Architects ideas, upon that subject. From one end to the other, with all its windings, this passage is near a mile in length. Mr. Mortimore* of Fredericksberg was of our party.

Manchester is a small decaying town, irregularly built upon irregular ground. Not a tree exists to enliven the dead appearance of its wooden buildings. From Manchester to the Coalpits is about 10 Miles. The road lies almost entirely through woods in a few places broken by the small opening of a miserably cultivated spot. The woods are enlivened at this season by a thousand busy birds, and beautified by the flowering dogwood trees. The dogwood is a tree of the kind called by Linnaeus, *filius ante patrem*.[40] It bears a fine 4 leaved white flower, see Sketch book p. [. .].[41] I have not yet met with a tree more than 8 inches in diameter. Its wood has this singular Quality, that it makes the best Joiners Mallets from its density, and yet splits into so many and such fine fibres as to be used as the tooth brush, known in England by the name of the *Irish tooth brush*. The *hiccory* just begins to put forth its aromatic leaves. We arrived at the Coal *pits* or rather *Quarries* about 12 o'clock. Such a mine of Wealth, exists I believe nowhere else! A Rock, a *Mountain* of Coal sunk down 30 feet from the Surface, bored 10 feet more, and yet no substratum found! The *open* pit is about 50 Yards square and about 30 feet deep. Many Works or Drifts are from thence carried into the body of the Coal, 5 feet wide. More than half the Coal still remains in Pillars supporting the roof. I hope to have another and better opportunity of examining this wonderful Mass of Coal, till then I postpone further description.

By the bye, I ought to say something in this place of *Jack Stewart*. But as he has a trick of taking up this very book, and reading the loose observations thrown into it, I do not think it perfectly prudent to offend him by praise, however deserved; and I am sure, that to abuse him would tinge the whole substance of my remarks with falsehood.

At a visit to Mr. Wardrup's about 7 miles from hence on the South side of James's river, I saw the most extensive and beautiful scenery which I have yet discovered on

39. *Indigesta moles*: confused (or disordered) mass; *discordia semina rerum*: discord, the seeds of things.

40. *Cornus florida* L. The leaves are bracts, and there are often twenty to thirty flowers in each "flower." See also n.16 above.

41. This sketch has not been found.

May 6. 1796.

A Whig reading a Tory paper.

Fig. 15. Captain William Murray, Amelia County, 6 May 1796.

the banks of this noble stream. The internal hospitality of the house, and a violent thunderstorm interrupted the pleasure I expected out of doors. My attention was particularly drawn to the most rich swarth of white clover that surrounds the house without a blade of grass in it.

AMELIA COUNTY, MAY 7TH, 1796. CAPTN. WM. MURRAY'S.* On the 20th of April I went to Petersburg, 25 miles South East of Richmond. Petersburg is situate on the River Appomattox which falls into the James's river at City point.[42] I expected to stay only one day, but was detained till the first of May. My observations at that place are contained in 3 or 4 letters to Colonel Blackburn* of which I hope to procure Copies.[43] I returned to Richmond on the 1st of May, and on the 4th set out for this place. On the 5th I went to Chinquopin Church[44] to meet the Trustees of the Appomattox navigation,[45] slept that night at Major Eggleston's* and the next morning returned to Captain Murray's hospitable roof.

42. Originally Charles City Point, founded in 1613, City Point is on the south shore of the James River at the confluence of the James and Appomattox rivers. Once a considerable out port to Richmond and Petersburg, it is now part of Hopewell, Virginia.

43. These three letters are printed below, pp. 99–106.

44. The church was built about 1750 in a small village in the northwestern part of Amelia County, now called Paineville, twelve miles from Amelia Court House. Meade, *Old Churches*, 2:21; *Martin's Gazetteer*.

45. The Upper Appomattox Navigation Company was incorporated in 1795 by the Virginia state legislature for the purpose of improving the navigation on the Appomattox River and making it navigable for boats, batteaux, and canoes capable of carrying eight hogsheads of tobacco. Thirty-five trustees were appointed, at least twelve of whom were BHL's acquaintances: Everard Meade, Joseph Eggleston, William Murray, John Wiley, Alexander McRae, Richard N. Venable, John Epperson, Nelson Patterson, Francis Eppes, Henry Skipwith, Joshua Chaffin, and Roger Atkinson, Jr. Shepherd, *Statutes*, 1:390–94.

Letters to Colonel Thomas Blackburn Written at Petersburg

EDITORIAL NOTE

In July 1796 Latrobe visited Colonel Blackburn on his way to and from Mount Vernon. During his first sojourn at Rippon Lodge, 11 to 16 July, Latrobe partially transcribed into his journal several letters he had written to his host from Petersburg in late April 1796. These described the race meeting and rendered some sharp, if not priggish, judgments on the behavior of the Virginia gentry.

RIPPON LODGE JULY 14TH, 1796.[46] COPY OF LETTERS TO COLONEL BLACKBURN, WRITTEN FROM PETERSBURG.

Petersburg April 21st, 1796

My dear Sir,

. . . I travelled hither in company with Col'n. Prior, Mr. Martin (who came with me from England) and a Mr. Thornton.[47] The latter afforded me a good deal of entertainment. He seems to be a professed horsejockey, what at Newmarket[48] you would call, *a knowing one.* . . . Religion and love have old claims to preference in producing that exquisitely delightfull sensation *enthusiasm*, but our friend Thornton in speaking of 50 different coursers proved that horseracing is not behind hand with them. The woods rung to the clattering of Lamplighters hoofs, and the Dogwood shed its flowers to the shrill applauses bestowed on the Haunches of *Daredevil.* It is pleasant to observe the human mind in any state of exertion though it should be stretching itself only from the hind to the forehoofs of a racehorse. In other respects Thornton seemed a good blunt honest kind of a fellow, and had that clear view of matter of fact, and expression of opinion which I have observed in a very great majority of the Americans I have seen.

We dined at Osbornes.[49] A most miserable dinner and six and three pence to pay for it. This is an exception to my general observation of good and plentiful tables and moderate charges in this part of the World. After stopping an hour, and bestowing a few ninepences on a very clumsy slight of hand man we jogged on, and got time enough

46. This journal entry has been brought forward from its original place in the manuscript.

47. According to BHL's index in the manuscript journal, Mr. Thornton was from Hanover, Virginia.

48. Newmarket, a market town and urban district thirteen miles ENE of Cambridge, is the home of the Jockey Club and the headquarters of English racing. Although it has been famous since the time of James I and the first cup race was run there in 1634, its reputation and prominence increased under the patronage of Charles II, who was a regular visitor. Richard Onslow, *The Heath and the Turf: A History of Newmarket* (London: Arthur Barker Ltd., 1971), chaps. 1, 3.

49. On the James River at the mouth of Proctor's Creek in Chesterfield County. The ferry at Osborne's that operated between Henrico and Chesterfield counties was an important link in the most direct overland route between Richmond and Petersburg. Lutz, *Chesterfield Co.*, pp. 31, 94.

to Petersburg for me to find that I might as well have staid at home as to business, and for as all to see the horses entered for the race. The same scenes I find collect in every country the same sort of people and for the same purposes. Here was a *duodecimo* edition of a Newmarket horserace in *folio*. The contents on the first turning over the leaves were the same in every respect. Respectable Gentlemen attending for amusement, young puppies waiting to be pilfered, sharpers ready to do their business, and whores all agog to drain the Sharpers. The *lusus naturae*[50] are in general supposed to be exceptions to her general rules of conduct; for my part, when drought, dust, and disappointment have put me into a philosophic humour, I cannot help thinking that Dame Nature's *freaks* and *fun* are the principal part of her employment, and that if ever *Nature's self shall die*, as some mad poet expresses himself, she will be choaked by a fit of laughter. *Rational beings* indeed! Things in leather breeches with a great four legged irrational being between their two legs jostling, and bustling, and pushing, and grinning and mad to pay the cash which should support their families in order to acquire a supposed interest in the fore and hind quarters of another man's horse. Surely the Maker of these said rational beings must smile most violently at their folly. Just as I was going on in a train of reflections which might have ended in a compleat elucidation of the doctrine of the transmigration of the soul, and the inexhaustible source of fun and frolic which that very rational system must furnish for the amusement of Dame Nature, a glass of punch washed away the whole fabric, and I betted a quarter of a Dollar, or a drink of Grog upon the field against the Carolina horse with Captn. Howel Lewis.*

But the worst is still to come. Having sufficiently gratified my contemplatory powers with the *Lusus naturae*, a *lusus artis*[51] still remained behind more dangerous to the morals and interests of your friend. In company with two Majors, one Colonel, three Captains, a Member of the house of Representatives of the State of Virginia and a rich Merchant, I returned to Mrs. Armstead's lodging house, and when we had dismissed our horses, we just went *to take a touch*. I shall detain you to explain that you may avoid splitting upon the same rock. First then this said touch is a circular affair in the center of which is a Whirligig. You may naturally suppose that the Whirligig whirls round. The etymology of the word signifies as much. I hope you are gaining a clear conception as I go on. Upon the edge of this said Whirligig are 72 Boxes alternately marked with the letters ABC. The Whirligig, which I think you may call the Wheel of Misfortune, being set in Motion, a Ball is thrown into it which naturally must find its way

50. Trans.: Tricks of nature (*lusus* plural here).
51. Trans.: Trick of art.

into one or other of these 72 Boxes. The Ball runs round and round bobbing from box to box, while the anxious spectators hearts bob about in their breasts, and the restless dollars in their pockets till at last it settles in some one of the litterary boxes, and those who have betted on A, B or C pay or receive the stake. As the devil is in perpetual want of Kitchen boys and Turnspits to attend his fire, *Nature* has provided a number of Gentlemen, professed Gamblers, who by providing and attending his business here, qualify themselves for so usefull and necessary a situation hereafter. Messrs. Hayden, Harris, Overton,* and Willis,* the latter of whom may perhaps, from the merit of his size be promoted to be Head cook are at present in due preparation at Petersburg. "But what," you will ask, "puts Latrobe into such a passion?" The loss, my dear Sir, no, I can never acknowledge that the loss of *ten* Dollars has any share in it; it is, to be sure, my zeal for the good of society, and my detestation of the vice of gambling. Ah! had I but my ten dollars back!!! Then might I gain credit for sincerity in deploring that the *youth* of a country which once meant its *virtue*, now means only its *poverty, indolence,* and dissipation. . . .

APRIL 21ST [22] 1796. Petersburg.

Some of the preceding Salmagundi I wrote yesterday morning and the rest of it at night. I am afraid your patience is by this time exhausted, but everybody here is so engaged in talking of *Lamplighter* the Sharkmare, the Carolina horse &c. &c. that I am as much at a loss for conversation as if I were among the Hottentots. There indeed I should be much better off, for I could talk to the Women without knowing their language, but the case is desperate in a house occupied by 70 Men in leatherbreeches. I rode yesterday to see the races, accompanied by Mr. Thomas Shore.* I meant to have taken my quarters with him but he is at present building, and occupies his offices only, which in Virginia seem to follow the dwelling house as a litter of pigs their mother. The accomodations at Mrs. Armsteads are quite as good as you ought to expect at such a time as this: I slept in a Garret with 7 other Gentlemen. Their different merits in snoring I could descant upon at great length, having been a wakefull Listener the greatest part of the Night, and could I have got a previous bett, I should have laid any odds upon my old Shipmate Martin, but he was distanced *hollow* by Mr. Ruffin who snored indeed like a Ruffian. I am however afraid that the Subject might prove more soporific to you than it did to me.

The concourse upon the race ground was very great indeed. Perhaps 1500 persons. It cannot much interest you to know that Lamplighter the favorite of the field upon whom all the odds were laid, was beaten two successive heats and came in only third. A light delicate horse from North Carolina, the property of a Mr. Jones won with ease. I have now got into Mr. Shore's house for the day and feel a little more at home than in the buzz of betting on the course. . . .

Petersburg April 23d, 1796.

Dear Sir,

I have neither books, pencils, brushes nor colors, nor any other drawing materials at this place, and my refuge from ennui drinking and gambling is reduced, as you see, to a sheet of bad paper, and my pen. Having once lived in a Polish Alehouse for four days, during a fair which had collected all the Jews and Gentiles from 50 Miles round under one miserable roof, I cannot say that my residence at Mrs. Armstead's tavern in Blandford affords any scenes that are entirely new to me.[52] The Multitude of Colonels and Majors with which I am surrounded bring back the Nobles of the polish Republic to my recollection, whose power and respectability is much upon the same level. The only difference is, that instead of Count Borolabraski, and Leschinski, and Zetroblastmygutski, and Skratchmypolobramboloboski, and Saradomoschittiguttelkowski, we have here Colonel Tom, and Col. Dick, and Major Billy, and Col'n. Ben, and Captain Titmouse, General Rattlesnake, and Brigadier General Opossum. The Rabble in leatherbreeches which fills up the vacuities of swearing and noise is scarcely distinguishable in the two places; only indeed by this difference, that we are here at a loss for even a Jewish Rabbi to help out the appearance of Religion, and a box of lemons and sealing wax to represent commerce.

I much fear that the peace and happiness of the amiable family that surrounds you has been disturbed by the desire of being in a scene of so much pleasure and gaiety as that in which they know their friend is now revelling. Indeed when I reflect on the deprivation they are under, I feel a sensation so akin to pity that it makes me quite melancholy. I feel as if I could be happier in the dull buzz of the conversation at Belvidere[53] than I am in the lively clamor of the gay society here. Perhaps it may afford them a trifling succedaneous comfort to know some of the particulars of the extatic scenes that keep me in a state of enchantment. In my last letter (the dulness

52. Blandford was on the Appomattox River, separated from Petersburg by a small marsh and rivulet. It was chartered as a town in 1748 and was incorporated into the borough of Petersburg in 1784. In the 1790s it contained 200 houses and three tobacco warehouses. Craig Gilborn, "A Romantic Pilgrimage," *Virginia Cavalcade* 25 (Autumn 1965): 44–47; James G. Scott and Edward A. Wyatt IV, *Petersburg's Story: A History* (Petersburg: Titmus Optical Co., 1960), pp. 45–46.

53. Belvidere was the Richmond home built upon a hill near the lower end of the James River falls by William Byrd III, probably in the early 1750s. It was owned in the 1790s by Bushrod Washington, who sold it to Col. John Harvie in 1798. The building burned down in 1854. For BHL's sketch and watercolor of Belvidere, see *PBHL, microfiche ed.*, 248/D3. Mary Wingfield Scott, *Old Richmond Neighborhoods* (Richmond: Whittet & Shepperson, 1950), pp. 179, 213; Edward L. Ryan, "Note on 'Belvidere,'" *VMHB* 39(1931): 139–45.

of which will be a sufficient proof that at that time I was not yet wound up to a proper pitch of enjoyment) I think I gave you some idea of the glorious 20th of April. One thousd. seven hundd. and ninety six years after the birth of somebody whose name I have forgotten since I came hither, nor can I find anybody here who can recollect it, though they allow they might know by enquiry of their Mothers or Grannys.

On that glorious day the invincible Lamplighter was stripped of his Laurels by the Carolina horse, who also beat the whole field of unbeaten coursers. The melancholy events of the evening I also submitted to your sympathy. The next morning spent in the quiet of Mr. Shore's family deserves no notice. The dull combinations of Water, wood and ground lose their charms when compared to the rapturous view of a racehorse darting through the dust like a Meteor through the reddening Clouds. At 12 anxiety again possessed every breast while three—horses I believe they were, but its so common a sort of thing, as not well to account for the enthusiasm they created, so I'll e'en call them, *coursers or steeds*—darted round their orbit; *orbit*, I think helps out the dignity of the period very well.

I was invited with several other Gentlemen to dine with Dr. Shore.[54] About an hour before dinner I was at his Door. I found there Jack Willis, Harris, and many other Gentlemen, *all honorable men no doubt*, very busy indeed. They were doing no harm, only playing at Loo. A very sumptuous dinner soon made me acquainted with Mrs. Shore, a very pleasant Lady who with great ease and goodness of temper presided over a Company of 28 Men. After dinner, and one bumper to the President's health, the whole party adjourned to the Drawing room. Loo, the most trifling of the ingenious contrivances invented to keep folks from the vile habit of biting their nails made a very large party happy. Whist affording a more sulky delight to a few more. The rattling of Dollars is a very pleasant sound when it is at last smothered by the folds of your own pocket. To me whose pockets and mind remained equally void, it was a great relief to go and chatter to Mrs. Shore and a few ladies who called upon her in the afternoon. Just before a magnificent Supper was compleatly arranged I walked off with Jack Willis, resolved—to go— to bed. I had got a bed in a neighbouring house, where only six Gentlemen slept in the same room. But alas! after knocking and bauling for half an hour at the door of the room in which a light was visible through the cracks, a tremendous yawn, which preceeded the slow drawing of the bolt, ushered me in, to disappointment. A huge Mulatto more than half naked, had been left to guard the room. Overcome with sleep and toddy, he had stretched himself upon my bed, indulging the former and evacuating the latter. It was not to be remedied.

---

54. This was either Dr. John Shore, Sr. (d. 1804) or Dr. John Shore, Jr. (d. 1811), Petersburg physicians.

The effluvia of his performance poisoned the whole chamber, and sent me back to the inn. Here in the interval had Falstaff, with Harris, Hayden and Sam Overton, his Nym, Pistol and Bardolph, established the throne of Pharo and assembled his host around him. However I went up stairs and got into bed in the 8 bedded Barrack, and Thornton, who is here *Colonel Thornton*, followed me. Another sober man or two also lay down but the explosions of joy from below banished sleep till past twelve. I am ashamed of my apathy for I really outslept the remaining raptures of the night, nor should, I believe, even have opened my eyes at six o'clock, had not a heavy mass which then fell upon my bed with eructation, *By your leave*, recalled my senses. The motion by which I freed my legs from the weight which oppressed them, might have been injurious to my eyes had they not been closed, for the *Colonel* (it was a Colonel Porteris you must know), called out "Damn your eyes, lay still." After extorting an apology, and a promise of good behavior, I left him in quiet possession of the ground, and got up. Upon going down stairs, I found my self surrounded by half a dozen Colonels and as many Majors in different States of intoxication and noise. The subalterns were still rattling the dollars below. By 8 o'clock most of them had staggered out of the house or into their beds.

And now, my dear Sir, pray inform me how you came to be called Colonel? What folly did you commit in your youth to deserve a term of reproach of any kind? You would also oblige me by your advise, whether I had better overdo the thing by calling every man I meet Colonel, or, underdo it by giving only one here and there the title, or whether tossing up for it would not be the safest and fairest mode I could adopt. Adieu. . . .

Petersburg April 23d, 1796.

My dear Sir

Close to the river Appomattox is a little house inhabited by a man whose Brother I knew in England. He has a large concern of Distillery Bakehouse and Mills here, and under the idea that I might be usefull to him, Major Murray (a Major de facto) introduced me to him. His house stands upon a very high bank under which the river steals along, and winds away into beautifull woods to the right, and to left washes the town of Petersburg. Mr. Bate* is also proprietor of the race Ground[55] and the buildings belonging to it. He is also one of the Stewards of the course. I rode with him to the field. It was the same thing over again. Upon the whole I think running matches a usefull as well as a very amusing entertainment. It encourages a taste for,

---

55. Poplar Lawn Race Track near Petersburg.

and an inclination to breed, handsome horses. The mischief they do, is, I believe, not peculiar to horseracing, but attendant upon all concourses of men for the purposes of amusement. Betting at a horserace I believe is an English passion. Upon the continent of Europe highplay is carried to its utmost extent, but I do not think from my recollection of manners that horse racing would be considered on the continent as a subject into which gambling could deeply enter. There is a Work written in his own fascinating style by Mercier, author of the *Tableaux de Paris*, entitled *la Quinzaine Anglaise a Paris*, which, I believe has been translated into English. It contains if I recollect right a very excellent chapter on horseracing, and the idea of betting upon running horses is therein assumed to be entirely English.[56] Gibbon has entered deeply into the business of the blue and green factions at the Chariot races of Rome and Constantinople. I entirely have forgotten the merits of the betting question, but *they* cut throats upon these occasions, an *addition* to, if not an *improvement* upon the degree of interest we take in the running of our horses. The Greeks, I think, were entirely ignorant of the pleasures of betting. I have been delving into the metaphysics of this strange passion, and have at last found out that a *bett* is a mental dram. It exhilarates and stimulates the mind, till it has worked off, that is, till it is determined. Its effect is then gone, and is, on the losing side, followed by *sickness* and *qualms*, on the winning by lassitude and debility and a longing for another *Dram*. Intoxication is in both the consequence. The amusements of the theatre would be useful to interrupt the gambling and drunkenness of the evening. But there are no players here at present. . . .[57]

About 9 o'clock in the evening I got back to the Barrack which I found in a dreadfull State of Warfare. *Lieutenant Williams had said that General Bradby* was as great a fool as himself*. It is true that a greater affront could not be offered to any man, but the fury with which this affront was taken up was astonishing even to me, whose motto here had become *Nil admirari*.[58] Six Men, each six feet high, swore, bauled, cursed, damned, blasted, drank punch, for nine hours uninterruptedly without settling the important affair. The most valliant of these Champions was a *Colonel*, and *representative of this county*, one *Curden*,* cidevant sargeant of regulars and Methodist Preacher. The rest were to a man Colonels and Majors whose Stentorian rhetoric stunned me while I remained below, that is, from nine till one o'clock. I then retired

56. Louis Sébastien Mercier, *Le Tableau de Paris*, 12 vols. (Paris, 1782–89). James Rutledge (1743–94) was the author of *La Quinzaine Angloise à Paris, ou l'Art de s'y Ruiner en Peu de Tems . . .* (London, 1776).

57. Construction of the Petersburg theater was begun in April 1796 and finished the following fall. The theater, planned by Thomas Wade West, was "erected in the best section of town and was constructed of brick." Sherman, "West," p. 24. See also pp. 334–36 and nn.

58. Trans.: To be surprised at nothing. Sometimes trans.: to be disturbed by nothing. Horace, *Epistles*, Book I, 6.1.

to the eight bedded barrack, but to sleep before three o'clock was impossible. At eight I rose and found Lieutenant Williams still upon his legs, who upon my appearance, wretcked his half spent vengeance upon my spectacles challenging me to fight for a hat. In the fray the Faro table was overset. The dollars scrambled for, and all the host put to flight. . . .

AMELIA COUNTY CAPTN. MURRAY'S SUNDAY MAY 8TH. Whether the aversion of most people to snakes is natural, or is imbibed by Christians from the History of Adam and Eve is of little consequence. The caution necessary to guard against an enemy so hidden and venemous, accounts sufficiently for it. The adoration of snakes by some nations is perhaps one of the strongest instances of this aversion. I believe (though the remark is perhaps more true, than honorable to human nature) that most public expressions of religion are dictated by fear. The many snakes that are now *sneaking* out of their hiding places, have excited much of my attention, though I have not yet met with any Gentleman who has studied their History. The snakes I have frequently seen, are the Black Snake, a lively green snake, and the Water Mockason. The two former are supposed to be perfectly harmless. The latter is poisonous but not dangerously so. Mockason is an indian name. There is a short snake with a blunt tail and thick body which I have not seen called a Land Mockason, the bite of which is extremely dangerous and often fatal. Rattlesnakes are hardly ever seen in these parts of Virginia. They seem to have disappeared as the Country has become more populous. In a swamp at Petersburg Mr. Θωμασ 'Σωρε[59] saw one about 20 Years ago, since then none has been heard of. General Mead* saw one last Summer near this place.[60]

In one of my Walks on Washington's Island in James river, I observed a Black and a Green snake *seemingly fighting* among the leaves in a ditch. I killed the Greensnake with a Stroke of a switch, and the black snake retired under a fence. Mr. Thomas Keld of Baltimore who was with me, drew him out by the tail, and with a sudden jerk, like that given to a Whip, separated his head from his body. It was the boldest and most expeditious execution I ever saw, and equal in merit to that performed by the Guillotine. I am told that the Indians treat very poisonous snakes in the same way. This snake was about two feet six inches long. Many Gentlemen in this country have

59. Mr. Thomas Shore.
60. Several black snakes are common, especially the black racer, *Coluber constrictor* L., and the pilot blacksnake, *Coluber obsoletus* (Say). The green snake was either *Cyclophis aestivus* (L.) or *Liopeltis vernalis* (DeKay). The water moccasin, *Ancistrodon piscivorus* (Lacépède), is not poisonous but the land moccasin or copperhead, *Ancistrodon contortrix* (L.), is quite poisonous. Both the timber rattlesnake, *Crotalus horridus horridus* (L.), and the canebrake rattlesnake, *Crotalus horridus atricaudatus* Latreille, are found in Virginia and are quite poisonous.

seen large collections of twenty or thirty different sorts of snakes. I recollect an idea prevailing among the common people of Germany of what they call *ein Schlangen Gewül, a Ball of Snakes*, consisting of some hundred. Matter of fact may no doubt be at the bottom of this story, but I have never heard any probable reason assigned for *these congregations*. Most people that have spoken to me of them seem to think that the business of copulation brings them together. But if that be the case, how come these meetings to consist of snakes of different species? I never heard that any *mule* or *intermediate* species of snake has been observed. A story however told by *Captain Williamson**who keeps the inn at *Jeneto*[61] is so extraordinary, and yet so well authenticated, that *if true* (and the character of *Captain Williamson* and of Mr. Crump* who was an eye witness with him precludes doubt), one might expect some such phaenomenon. At all events it seems certain that the morality of snakes is very lax. The story is this.

Captn. Williamson riding in Powatan county through an estate of *Mr. Brett Randolph,** with Mr. Crump observed by the road side a large *land Mockason*. He alighted, killed him, and left him in the road. He continued then his ride and some hours after returning by this same spot, he perceived a large *Black snake* coiled round the dead *mockason*. He killed then the *black snake*, and endeavored to separate them, but found them *firmly embraced*, the black snake being a male, *adea ut pudenda serpentis nigri, quae sunt brevia sed satis crassa, essent, usque ad corpus suum, inserta in vulvam anguis mortuae.*[62] Such depravity scarcely exists even among the Yahoos.[63]

The bite of snakes and its deadly consequences must have engaged the attention of the Indians from time immemorial, and they are without doubt in possession of many remedies which it would be well worth while particularly to enquire after and to transplant into our medical practice. The *swamp plantain*[64] as it is here called, is used by the Negro Woodmen to rub the wound immediately after it is given. They have mentioned to me many instances of its efficacy, and I have no doubt but they are right. But as remedy against venemous bites, better authenticated, and *undoubtedly* of Indian discovery is the *blood Wort*.[65] About six Years ago, *Mr. Wm. Murray* met accidentally a

61. Genito: a small village in southeast Powhatan County on the Appomattox River, twenty-nine miles from Richmond and thirty-six miles from Petersburg.

62. Trans.: So that the penis of the black snake, which is short but quite thick, was inserted, all the way up to his own body, into the womb of the dead snake.

63. The Yahoos were an imaginary race of brutes in the form of men described by Jonathan Swift in *Gulliver's Travels*.

64. *Alisma plantago-aquatica* L., also called "mad-dog weed."

65. BHL's sketch (PLATE 13) is of *Heiracium venosum* L., hawkweed or bloodwort. *Lachnanthes tinctoria* (Walt.) Ellis of the *Haemadoraceae*, redroot of swamps and bogs, is now commonly called bloodwort. *Sanguisorba canadensis* L., "blood staunching," is also called bloodwort.

party of *Creek* Indians with their well known Chief, Colonel MacGillvray,[66] and brought them to his house. They were going upon some embassy to New York. MacGillvray among many cures performed by this plant, mentioned this instance. His horse was bit in the nose when feeding by a very venemous snake. The animal immediately swelled all over his body, and was in terrible torment. He took a large parcel of the Blood wort, root, leaves, and flower, and having made it *Blood warm* in Milk, he gave it to the Horse as a drench. In a few hours the horse was grazing as before.

Sometime after a negro woman belonging to Captain Murray was bit by a snake in the foot. The part was excessively swelled and the woman in great agony. It had been done the evening before the day on which Captn. M. heard of it. He immediately ordered her *a drench*, such as the Indian had given to his horse. Upon his return from a short ride the woman was entirely well. It had produced a strong inclination to sleep and a copious perspiration during sleep.

Captain Murray who neglects no opportunity of acquiring and disseminating usefull Knowledge, communicated this remedy to Doctor Judge Flemming.*[67] Sometime after, the doctor informed him that a Waggoner had been bit by *a Spider* (so that it seems there are poisonous Spiders in this country)[68] and was so swelled and felt such agony, that he could not proceed but lay at a house upon the road. The Doctor saw him there and gave him *MacGillvray's drench*. He was soon entirely cured. Quaere, might not the Virginia jig, which, as a piece of Music is the excess of detestability, be as good a cure for the bite of a Virginia spider, as the Neapolitan jig for that of a Tarantula? *Fiat experimentum.*[69]

(*N.B.* Mr. Flemming who is still alive is one of the Judges of the Court of Appeals of this State. He was brought up to the profession of the Law. The wants of his own family, of his negroes and of his neighbours induced him to study medecine. He at

---

66. Alexander McGillivray (c. 1759–93) was a prominent trader and Georgia politician. During the Revolution he was a Loyalist, acting as a British agent among the Southern Indians. When Spain signed a treaty with the Creeks in 1784, McGillivray was appointed Spanish commissary to enforce the Spanish monopoly of trade with the Creeks. McGillivray began a war in 1786 against American frontiersmen in order to end American competition in the Southern Indian trade and to drive back the American frontier line to its 1773 position. In 1790 McGillivray and a delegation of Creeks journeyed to New York to sign a treaty of amity, for which McGillivray received a pension of $1,200. *DAB.*

67. BHL wrote a footnote on William Fleming, which is printed below as the next paragraph.

68. The only spider in Virginia dangerous to man is the common black widow, *Lactrodectus mactans* (Fabricius).

69. Trans.: Let the experiment be tried. What BHL calls the Neapolitan jig is the tarantella, a rapid whirling Italian dance popular since the fifteenth century, when it was supposed to be the remedy for tarantism, a hysterical malady characterized by an extreme impulse to dance and believed to be caused by the sting of a tarantula.

Fig. 16. The horse runner, the swiftest snake, 2 June 1796. Probably the horse racer, *Lampropeltis getulus getulus* (L.).

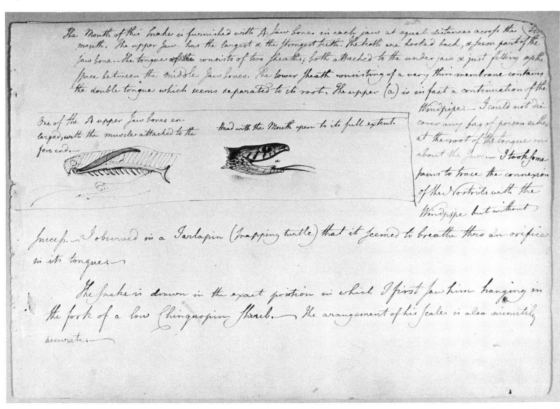

Fig. 17. Details and description of snake's head.

last acquired without seeking a reputation so high as a medical practitioner that he was consulted by persons at a considerable distance, and being of a benevolent disposition he found not only his time much engrossed by medical practice, but his expences for drugs increased. Sometimes to 10 and 15 pounds a Year. He then determined, in order to shake off as much as possible of this accidental profession, to take the usual fees. It was however in vain: the public continued to employ him, and had dubbed him Doctor, a little more honorable to him than if it had been conferred by the concurrence of all the Europaean Universities. Thus while Judge Tyler* breeds race horses, and figures upon the turf, Judge Flemming heals the diseases, when he retires from healing the disensions of the good citizens of Chesterfield county, and of Virginia in general.)

Captain Murray, who does not profess jig playing, though he can make a noise upon the fiddle that sounds not unlike a *jig*, is not very well pleased at my want of taste in this line of Music. Upon starting to him the quaere respecting its effect in the case of the bite of a venemous spider, I find that he has heard of the trial and success of the experiment in more instances than one. Having an opportunity of obtaining information respecting the fact from persons who are said to have been present I shall postpone the recital till I have made further enquiry.

A cause is assigned for the almost total disappearance of Rattlesnakes in the settled parts of Virginia, which compleatly accounts for it. The Hogs it seems are their most inveterate enemies, or in other words, are extremely fond of *eating* them. Whether the fat or the bristles, or the *constitution* of a hog preserve him from the effect of the bite of the Rattlesnake, or whether the mode by which he catches the snake prevents his being bit by him, I cannot ascertain, but I do not find that an instance of a hog poisoned by a snake is known. A great number of Hogs are kept by every farmer, they are turned into the woods where they range in search of Acorns, nuts, roots, and now and then, as a *bonne bouche* they dine upon the delicious morsel, a live Rattlesnake.

AMELIA COUNTY, CAPTN. MURRAY'S MAY 9TH, 1796. Captain Murray is a *matter of fact man*. I feel a great propensity to treat him as Boswell did Dr. Johnson by putting upon paper the conversations with which he instructs and entertains me. Of the latter kind the Subject of which was a *sound* less decent, than it is common, and conducive to the ease of the good citizens; is a story of [a] man well known in this part of the World under the name of *Commodore Mumford*. He was a fat, unweildy, man of enormous dimensions, and of so flatulent a constitution, that it was utterly impossible for him to sneeze without a respondent sound *a posteriore*. After having long contributed to the private entertainment of his friends by this singular accomplishment, he one day attended Church in his neighbourhood, in which in a few minutes he fell fast asleep. Some wicked rogue, "not having the fear of God before his eyes," contrived to give him in this situation a pinch of snuff. Its effects were soon heard in a tremendous sneeze which was immediately followed by a proportionate explosion from the opposite quarter. This was repeated three or four times to the utter consternation of the congregation, and the total discomposure of the parson. It was impossible for the Commodore to preserve common patience, even in a Church. He broke out into the most violent threats and execrations against the author of this mischief interrupted by perpetual repetitions of the loud sneeze and the hollow f____t, while "the *high dome reechoed to his nose and_____.*" At last he left the Church, trumpeting to his own retreat, and continuing the mixture of sneezing swearing and f_____g in the Churchyard.

The Pocahontas–Rolfe–Bolling Pedigree

Editorial Note

While visiting at the home of Captain William and Rebecca (Bolling) Murray in Amelia County in May 1796, Latrobe compiled a pedigree of the descendants of John Rolfe and his wife Pocahontas, through their son, Thomas Rolfe, and his only child Jane, who married Captain Robert Bolling. The pedigree covers eight generations of Virginia Rolfes, Bollings, and related families. The names of each individual descendant and his or her spouse were shown in rectangular boxes with double lines connecting one generation to another, so that later generations could easily be traced back to the first ancestors. Latrobe tried to be thorough. Although he entered only a few birth, death, and marriage dates, he listed the number of children who died young even when he did not always know their names. He also appended biographical notes and humorous comments throughout.

Latrobe's genealogy has been compared to three published accounts of the Bolling descendants of Pocahontas for accuracy and completeness.[70] The first account studied was that of Robert Bolling (1738–69), who wrote a "memoir of a Portion of the Bolling Family . . ." in French shortly before his death. The manuscript, which covered the history of the family to about 1765, probably passed to the author's brother, Thomas Bolling (1735–1804), who gave it to his son-in-law, William Robertson (1760–1829). Robertson was married to Elizabeth Bolling (1758–1830), the elder sister of Rebecca (Bolling) Murray, Latrobe's hostess when he compiled the pedigree. In 1803 the manuscript was given to William Robertson's sixth child John (1787–1873), who translated the work into English and published it in 1868. Latrobe listed seven children of Colonel John and Elizabeth (Blair) Bolling, and noted that eleven others "died at different ages and without issue." The *Memoir* recorded eight, including a son Edward (1746–70), and noted there were other children who died young. There were no other apparent discrepancies, although the *Memoir* did contain fuller biographical information.[71]

70. Robert Bolling, *A Memoir of a Portion of the Bolling Family in England and Virginia*, trans. John Robertson, Jr. (Richmond, 1868); Wyndham Robertson and R. A. Brock, *Pocahontas, alias Matoaka, and her Descendants . . . , with Biographical Sketches . . .* (Richmond, 1887); "The Ancestors and Descendants of John Rolfe with Notices of Some Connected Families: Bolling of Virginia," *VMHB* 22 (1914): 103–07, 215–17, 331–33, 441–46; 23 (1915): 94–96.

71. See pp. 116–17; Bolling, *Memoir*, p. 5. BHL may have excluded Edward purposely, for in this instance he noted only those children who had issue.

The next account considered was by William Robertson's twelfth child, Wyndham (1803–88), who carried the Rolfe-Bolling line through the seventh generation in *Pocahontas and Her Descendants*, published in 1887 and largely based on the *Memoir*. The genealogies of Latrobe and Robertson differ in several respects. In one place Latrobe stated that Thomas Rolfe, son of John Rolfe and Pocahontas, was born in 1617, but elsewhere he noted that Thomas "may have been about three Years old" when his mother died in Gravesend, England in 1617. Robertson gives Thomas's birthdate as 1615.[72] Latrobe stated that John, son of Colonel John and Mary (Bolling) Fleming, married Susanna Skelton and had a son John, who was a "Major in the American Army" and was killed at Princeton. Robertson, however, stated that John was killed at White Plains, and died unmarried, and that his brother Thomas was killed at Princeton.[73] Latrobe listed four children of William and Betty (Champe) Fleming; Robertson said they had six children. Latrobe listed five children of Dr. William and Elizabeth (Bolling) Gay; Robertson listed three.[74] Of the children of Thomas and Martha (Bolling) Eldridge, Latrobe omitted Jenny, Mary (who married Thomas Branch), and Martha (who married John Harris of England), but included Thomas, who married the widow Powell, and John, "the inveterate batchelor," neither of whom was listed by Robertson. Robertson's genealogy does include two names not listed by Latrobe: Leonard Price, first husband of Judith Eldridge; and Thomas, youngest son of James and Ann (Bolling) Murray.[75]

The third account of the Bolling and related families studied was published serially in the *Virginia Magazine of History and Biography* in 1914 and 1915. It showed that Archibald, son of John and Elizabeth (Blair) Bolling, married three times, and not twice, as Latrobe stated. Latrobe listed John, son of Thomas and Elizabeth (Gay) Bolling as dying without issue; John was omitted from the *Virginia Magazine* genealogy.[76] Of the descendants of John and Mary (Jefferson) Bolling, the *Virginia Magazine* stated that their daughter, Martha, married Field Archer, and that their son, John, married Miss Kennon. Latrobe gave the names of the spouses as as Peter Field Archer and Mary Kennon.[77] Finally, it should be noted that Latrobe accurately listed the children of William and Elizabeth (Bolling) Robertson born by 1796 with the exception of Rebecca (1789–91), whom he omitted.[78]

The question naturally arises as to what sources Latrobe drew upon in compiling his extraordinarily accurate and comprehensive pedigree. The heading of the chart indicates that he consulted the appropriate sections of Stith's *History of Virginia* and Jefferson's *Notes on Virginia* concerning establishment of the line.[79] It is likely that Latrobe's primary sources of information were his hosts, the William Murrays, who may have had letters and perhaps a family Bible at their house. William Murray was a grandson, and Rebecca (Bolling) Murray was a great-granddaughter, of Col. John and Mary (Kennon) Bolling.[80] No doubt they knew many of the living descendants of the family personally and were familiar with the earlier generations through oral tradition and the old custom of claiming kin, the practice of recounting and discussing family relationships at weddings, funerals, and other family gatherings. It is also possible that Latrobe consulted the French manuscript of the "Memoir." Certainly the Murrays

72. See pp. 114, 121; Robertson, *Pocahontas*, p. 29.

73. See p. 120; Robertson, *Pocahontas*, p. 33.

74. See pp. 120, 114–15; Robertson, *Pocahontas*, pp. 33–34.

75. See pp. 121, 115; Robertson, *Pocahontas*, pp. 34–35.

76. See pp. 116, 114; *VMHB* 22 (1914): 217.

77. *VMHB* 22 (1914): 332; see p. 116 below.

78. See p. 114; James Samuel Patton, comp., *The Family of William & Elizabeth Bolling Robertson* (n.p., 1975), p. 15.

79. See pp. 114, 115. William Stith, *The History of the First Discovery and Settlement of Virginia: Being an Essay towards a General History of the Colony* (Williamsburg, 1747); Thomas Jefferson, *Notes on the State of Virginia*, ed. William Peden (Chapel Hill: University of North Carolina Press, 1955/1787).

80. See pp. 114–15.

knew of its existence and perhaps had received an additional copy from Mrs. Murrays' father, Thomas Bolling, or made a copy or abstract for themselves when visiting Mrs. Murray's sister and brother-in-law, the William Robertsons, at "Bellefield," below Petersburg in Prince George County.[81]

AMELIA COUNTY, MAY 10TH, 1796. Captn. Murray's.

There are many families in Virginia who derive their origin from the marriage of Mr. John Rolfe with Pocahontas the Daughter of Powhatan, king, or chief of the tribe of Powhatan of the Nation of Powhatans, see Jefferson p. 100 et seq., and Stiths History.

Of some of the youngest branches of this fertile family, I have not yet been able to get exact account, but it will appear from the genealogy [below] that from *Pocahontas* in immediate descent 362 have at least been produced, not reckoning those of whose past or present existence I had not accurate information. Pocahontas died at Gravesend in the beginning of 1617 at which time her son Thomas Rolfe may have been about three Years old, as she was married in 1613 to his father. Of these are now alive, as nearly as I can at present ascertain all arising from the stock of Major John Bolling who was the first of the family who had more children than one:

Coln. Jo. John Bolling	99 members of family,	66 now alive
Coln. Richard Randolph	113	72
Coln. John Flemming	40	28
Dr. William Gay	35	23
Thos. Eldridge	22	20
James Murray	50	30
	359	239 alive

Add 3 between Pocahantas and Major Bolling   3

362

Many of the branches of this family having intermarried, I have arranged the descent according to the accident of the [following] tables, some of the number belonging properly to two or three of them with equal right. In the course of not quite 200 Years, it appears that the family has increased in such a proportion that one third only of the whole number has disappeared. Should the survivors continue to encrease in the same ratio for another century, the proportion of the dead to the living will be still less perhaps one sixth only. A speculation of this sort though not so usefull as mending shoes might keep a philosopher out of mischief for a day or two. Should

81. At the time of his marriage to Rebecca, William Murray was a resident of Prince George County. *Virginia Gazette* (Dixon and Nicolson), 27 November 1779.

48

Amelia County, May 10th 1796. — Captn Murray's.

There are many families in Virginia who derive their origin
from the marriage of ~~Sir Thomas~~ Mr John Rolfe with Pocahontas
see Stith's History of Virginia
daughter

John Rolfe, — Pocahontas

Thomas Rolfe, b 1617. d. marr. unknown.

An only daughter, marr.d Colo. Robt. Bolling

An only Son Major John Bolling, marr.d Miss Kennon

Colonel John Bolling
Marr.d 1st. Miss Lewis
no children
2d. Elisabeth Blair

Jane Bolling
Col. Richd. Randolph

Mary Bolling
Col. Jo. Flemming

Elisth. Bolling
Dr Wm Gay

Carried to ~~the next~~ page 50

carried on p. 52.

carried on p. 54.

1.) Died without issue

2. John, died in the E. Indies no issue

3. Betty Gay Thos. Bolling Son of Col. John B.

4 Mary Gay m Neale Buchan called ugly Neal no issue

1, Elisabeth Bolling Wm Robertson

2. John Bolling died witht. issue

3. Rebecca Bolling married to Capt.n Wm Murray, see his line
N. V

5. Judith Scott
6. Thomas Bolli
7. Francis Gay
3. Neale Buchanan
4.) Mary Buchanan

2 Children dead
~~Carried to the Robertson~~
1, Archibald Robertson
2. Thomas Bolling Do.
3, Elisabeth, ——
4, Mary Buchannan, —
5, William
6, John, —
7, Ann, —
8. Jane Gay

4. Mary Bolling
5 Thomas Bolling
6. William Bolling

Besides five other Children who died without issue

Daughter of Powhatan, king, or chief of the tribe of Powhatan of the Nation of ~~Manacans~~ the Powhatans, see Jefferson p. 100 et seq. and Stith's History

May 10th 1796.

Martha Bolling / Thos. Eldridge

Ann Bolling / James Murray

Married a 2d time to Colo. Wm. Davies

III. IV. V. VI.

Thos. Murray the youngest died no children

James Murray / Martha Ward 1

John Murray / Susanna Yeates 2

Ann Murray / Neale Buchanan called 3 pretty Nan

Marg. Murray / Thos. Gordon 4

Wm. Murray / Rebecca Bolling 5

Mary Murray / Alexr. Gordon 6

married on p. 55.

5. William Gay marrd. to — Francis Bent

Mary Murray / Edmund Harrison

Elisabeth M. / Edd. Randolph Yeates 1.

Ann Bolling M. / Jesse Brown 2.

Susanna Murr / Theodoric Bland Ruffin 3.

James Murray / Jane Doan 4

Wm. Yeates 5. Murray unmarried

Elis.th Gay / Efford Bentley / Wm. Gay

A children, dead, Edmonia Harrison living 15 Months old

1. Jas. Murray Y
2. Mary Deane Y
3. Elisa Caroline Y
4. Jas. Rand. Y

1, Chester Brown
2, Samuel Alfred Brown one dead

Jane Bland
2, Wm. Tickle R one dead

John Murray

6. John Murray
7. Marg. Murray both unmarried

2. the Widow the maiden Egglestone / John Gay

III. Ann Murray pretty / Neale Buchanan

IV. Margaret Murray / Thomas Gordon

V. Wm. Murray, a Rebacca Bolling granddaughter to colonel John Bolling & Elizabeth Blair & also of Elisth. Bolling & Dr. Wm. Gay.

3 Children dead. — Ann Buchannan married in Scotland to Mr. Cross.

Ann Gordon marrd. to Henry Coleman in Halifax County

2 Children dead 1. Ann, 2, Rebacca Bolling, 3, Thomas 4. Mary, 5. Margaret, 6. William

VI. Mary Murray / Alexr. Gordon

Margaret Gordon

three dead young

Colo. Wm. Davies

1, Mary Davies. — 2, Elisabeth Julia Davies

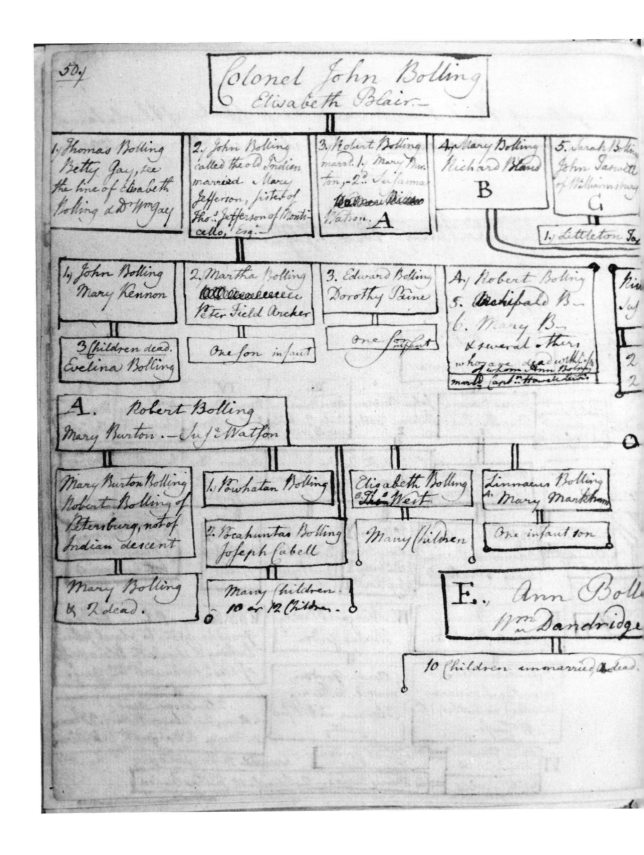

50./

Colonel John Bolling
Elisabeth Blair.—

1./ Thomas Bolling
Betty Gay, see
the line of Elisabeth
Bolling & Dr Wm Gay

2./ John Bolling
called the old Indian
married Mary
Jefferson, sister of
Thos Jefferson of Monti-
cello, Esq.—

3./ Robert Bolling
marrd 1./ Mary Mar-
ton,—2d Susanna
~~Eliza Miss~~
Watson. **A.**

4./ Mary Bolling
Richard Bland
B

5./ Sarah Bolling
John Taswell
of Williamsburg
C

1./ Littleton Ta...

1./ John Bolling
Mary Kennon

2. Martha Bolling
~~illegible~~
Peter Field Archer

3. Edward Bolling
Dorothy Paine

4./ Robert Bolling
5. Archibald B—
6. Mary B—
& several others
who are dead with ...
of whom Ann Bolling
marrd Capt. Hawkletion

Kin...
Su...

2

2

3 Children dead.
Evelina Bolling

One son infant

One son infant

A. Robert Bolling
Mary Burton.—Sus. Watson

Mary Burton Bolling
Robert Bolling of
Petersburg, not of
Indian descent

1./ Powhatan Bolling

2. Pocahuntas Bolling
Joseph Cabell

Elisabeth Bolling
& Thos West

Linnaeus Bolling
& Mary Markham

Mary Bolling
& 2 dead.

Many children
10 or 12 Children.—

Many Children

One infant son

E., Ann Boll...
Wm Dandridge

10 Children unmarried & dead.

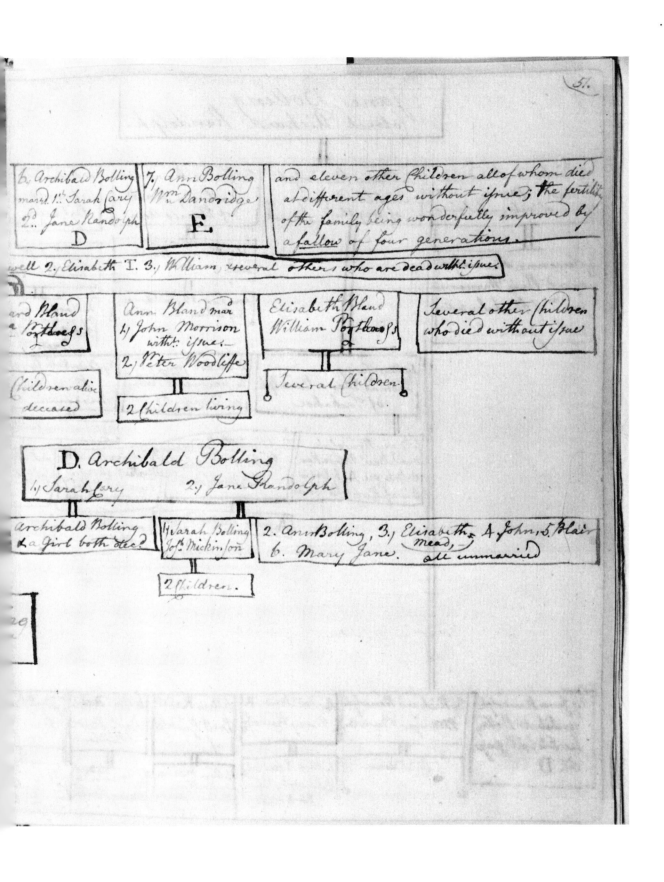

6. Archibald Bolling
mar.d 1.st Sarah Cary
2.d Jane Randolph
D

7. Ann Bolling
Wm. Dandridge
E

and eleven other Children all of whom died at different ages without issue; the fertility of the family being wonderfully improved by a fallow of four generations.

well 2. Elisabeth I. 3. William, & several others who are dead with.t issue

ard Bland
a Portlaoess

Ann Bland mar
1. John Morrison
with.t issue—
2. Peter Woodliffe

Elisabeth Bland
William Portlaoess

Several other Children who died without issue

Children alive
deceased

2 Children living

Several Children

D. Archibald Bolling
1. Sarah Cary   2. Jane Randolph

Archibald Bolling
& a Girl both dec.d

1. Sarah Bolling
Jos.h Mickinson

2. Ann Bolling, 3. Elisabeth
Mead,
6. Mary Jane.

4. John, 5. Blair
all unmarried

2 Children.

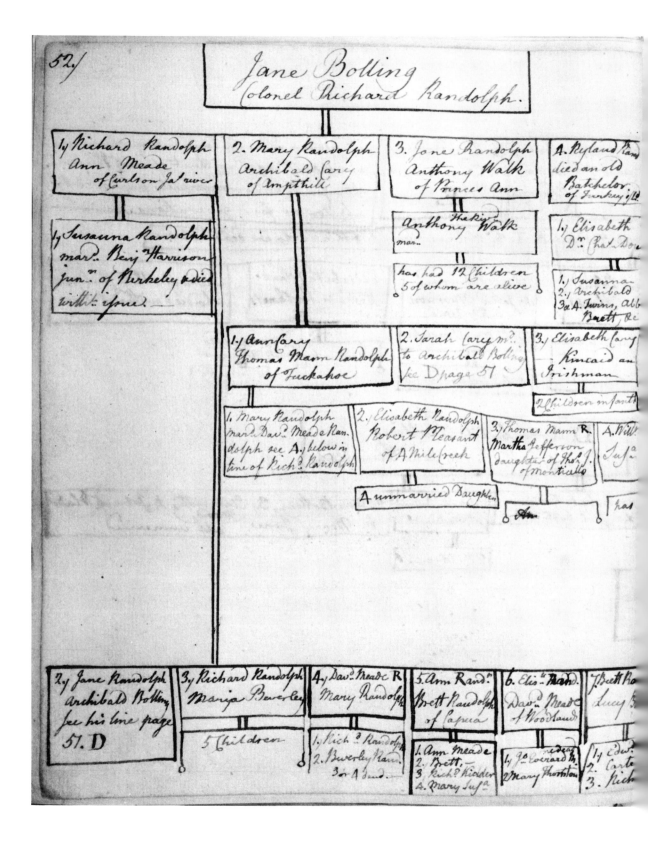

Jane Bolling
Colonel Richard Randolph.

1/ Richard Randolph
Ann Meade
of Curlson fal river

2. Mary Randolph
Archibald Cary
of Ampthill

3. Jone Randolph
Anthony Walk
of Princes Ann

4. Ryland Ran...
died an old
Batchelor
of Turkey isld

1/ Susanna Randolph
mard. Benj Harrison
junr. of Berkeley & died
witht. issue

Anthony Walk the King
mar...

1/ Elisabeth
Dr. Chat Dou...

has had 12 Children
5 of whom are alive

1/ Susanna
2/ Archibald
3 & 4 twins, Abb...
Brett &c

1/ Ann Cary
Thomas Mann Randolph
of Tuckahoe

2. Sarah Cary mard.
to Archibald Bolling
see D page 57

3/ Elisabeth Cary
Kincaid an
Irishman

2 Children infants

---

1. Mary Randolph
mard Davd. Meade Ran-
dolph see A: below in
line of Richd. Randolph

2/ Elisabeth Randolph
Robert Pleasant
of A Mile Creek

3/ Thomas Mann R.
Martha Jefferson
daughter of Thos. J.
of Monticello

4. Will...
Susa...

A unmarried Daughter

Ann

has

2/ Jane Randolph
Archibald Bolling
see his line page
57. D

3/ Richard Randolph
Maria P Beverley

5 Children

4/ Davd. Meade R
Mary Randolph

1/ Richd. Randolph
2. Beverley Rann
3 or 4 daud.

5. Ann Rando.
Brett Randolph
of Capua

1. Ann Meade
2. Brett —
3. Richd Kidder
4. Mary Susa.

6. Elis... Rand.
Davd. Meade
of Woodland

1/ Jo. Everard M...
2 Mary Thornton

7 Brett Ra...
Lucy B...

1/ Edwd.
2. Carter
3. Rich...

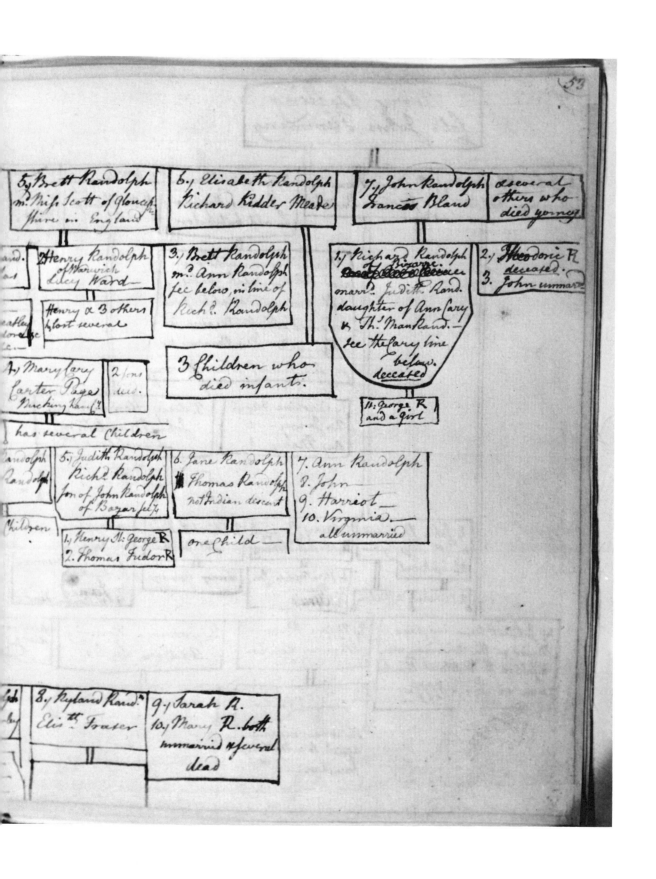

53

5.) Brett Randolph
m. Miss Scott of Glouc.
shire in England

6.) Elisabeth Randolph
Richard Kidder Meade

7.) John Randolph
Frances Bland

& several
others who
died young

Henry Randolph
of Warwick
Lucy Ward

Henry & 3 others
& lost several

3.) Brett Randolph
m. Ann Randolph
see below, in line of
Rich.d Randolph

1.) Richard Randolph
of Bizarre.
marr.d Judith Rand.
daughter of Ann Cary
& Th.s Mankland.
see the Cary line
below.
deceased

2.) Theodoric R
deceased.

3.) John unmarr.d

4.) Mary Cary
Carter Page
Buckingham

2 sons
dec.

3 Children who
died infants.

11. George R
and a girl

has several Children

Randolph
Randolph

5.) Judith Randolph
Rich.d Randolph
son of John Randolph
of Bizarre &c.

6. Jane Randolph
Thomas Randolph
not Indian descent

7. Ann Randolph
8. John
9. Harriot
10. Virginia.
all unmarried

Children

1.) Henry M. George R
2. Thomas Tudor R

one Child

8.) Ryland Rand.n
Elis.th Fraser

9.) Sarah R.
10.) Mary R. both
unmarried & several
dead

54/

```
┌─────────────────────────────┐
│        Mary Bolling         │
│     Colꝉ. John Flemming     │
└─────────────────────────────┘
```

1.) John Flemming	2. Mary Flemming	3. Caroline Flemming	4. Wꟲ Flemming	5. Richard Flemming
Susanna Skelton	William Barnard	James Deanes an old batchelor	Betty Champ	6. Thomas Flemming 7. Charles Flemming died without issue

Mary Deanes who married E₫ Randolph Yeates, left issue one daughter since dead. — E. R. Yeates married afterwards Eliz. Murray see p. 49, line of John Murray

1.) Caroline Flemᵍ.	3. Lucy Flemming
2. Jenny — 1	John Markham
4.) Mary d	of Goochland Cᵗʸ

one Child.

1.) John Barnard m.: 1ˢᵗ. Miss Clopton 2.. Miss Norval	2. Mary Barnard dead Archiᵈ. Brand	3. Elisabeth Barᵈ dead Mr Goodge	4. Robꜩ. deceased 5. Thos. unmarried 6. Richᵈ. 7. Jane 8. William dead
2 Children 2 Children	1.) Christopher Br. 2. Mary — 3. Cyrus	Lucy Goodge	

1.) John Flemming, was Major in the American army & fell in the battle at Princetown in Janʳ. 1777 —	2.) Mary Flemming Warner Lewis.	3.) Susanna Flemming Addison Lewis	several died yo
	several Children	several Children	

She is now married again to a Methodist preacher. Mr Ellis

Martha Bolling
Thos. Eldridge

| 1./ Thomas Eldridge the widow Povall | 2.) Judith Eldridge md. 1st. Leond. Price no issue. 2d. James Ferguson | 3. Rolfe Eldridge Susanna Walker | 4. Jane Eldridge an old maid & 5.) John, an inveterate batchelor |

James Ferguson
unmarried

1.) Susanna Everard Eldridge
2. Mary Meade Eldridge
3. Martha Bolling Eldridge
4. Jane Eldridge
5.) Nancy Eldridge
6.) Courtney Eldridge
7.) Rolfe Eldridge
8. George Walker Eldridge
9. Thomas Eldridge —
10. David Eldridge. —

Of some of the youngest branches of this fertile family, I
have not yet been able to get exact account, but it will appear
from the above genealogy
that from Pocahontas in immediate descent 362 have
at least been produced, not reckoning those of whose
past or present existence I had not accurate information.
Pocahontas died at Gravesend in the beginning of 1617 at which
time her son Thomas Rolfe may have been about three
years old, as she was married in 1613. to his father. —— Of

Monarchy and its concomitant, *Nobility of blood*, ever come again into fashion in this Country, an event which at this moment is most seriously apprehended by, and disturbs the sleep of many of our *good citizens*, I hope the blood of Powhatan will not be neglected, unless the great good sense, and merit of many of his descendants whom I know, should be thought less necessary to a man of title, than to a plain commoner. It is somewhat singular that, though the family are rather proud of their royal Indian blood, not one of them should have preferred the names of their Ancestors in their own family excepting Robert Bolling, son of Colonel John Bolling [see p. 116] who named a son and a daughter Powhatan and Pocahantas. He was a man of great wit and learning.

AMELIA COUNTY, MAY 11TH, 1796. CAPTN. MURRAY'S. The pine which is by the far the most common tree in the woods through which the road hither lies on the South side of James river, gradually give way to the Oak in all its varieties and on this side of the Appomattox, scarce any pines are seen. I have traversed the country 12 or 15 miles each way, and as far as I have seen the observation holds good. The hiccory of three sorts, and the gum are the next in point of frequency. The Persimmon, the Sassafras, and the Shuneck, are frequent on the Skirts of the Woods and along the fences. The wild Grape just now begins to put forth its leaves. Hitherto it has been a dry ill looking contrast to the general verdure. The Sassafras which is a beautiful tree in its appearance does not grow to any considerable size in this neighbourhood. The largest I have seen was not more than 10 inches in diameter. The leaves have an aromatic smell, and a very pleasant taste. The root alone is used in medecine and exported to Europe. The birds, roosting upon the fences drop the seeds by their sides, and by this means most of them are lined with a range of these trees. The Virginian farmers contrary to their former practice, now suffer them to grow, as they have discovered that they make the most durable posts. The leaves of the Shuneck, are used by the Indians, and many white people to mix with their tobacco in smoking. It bears a red berry which remains upon the tree all the winter, and has a pleasant acid taste. The persimmon bears a fruit resembling a plumb, which some people like after it is frostbitten.[82]

82. The gum could be sweet gum or red gum: *Liquidambar styraciflua* L.; or black gum: *Nyssa sylvatica* Marsh. The persimmon is *Diospyros virginiana* L. Thomas Harriot called it Date-plum (*A briefe and true report of the new found land of Virginia* [London, 1588], "Of Fruits"). John Banister said: "a pleasant Fruit enough when rotten" (Joseph and Nesta Ewan, *John Banister and His Natural History of Virginia 1678–1692* [Urbana, Ill.: University of Illinois Press, 1970], p. 44). Shuneck is probably sumac: *Rhus copallina* L.; BHL may have seen smooth sumac: *Rhus glabra* L.; or fragrant sumac: *Rhus aromatica* Ait. Of *Rhus copallina* John Banister wrote: "Possibly this might make some writers affirme that Mastick [*Pistacia lentiscus* L.] grew here. The Berryes of both these kinds [*R. copal-*

The county of Amelia, as far as I have seen is beautifully variegated with considerable hills of gentle forms. The vallies abound in beautiful rivulets, here called *branches*. The Appomattox winds slowly between high banks and is in most places about 40 Yards across. Jeneto bridge is about 40 or 45 paces long. The soil is in general a red loamy clay. The substrata, in all those places where I have seen them pierced, are full of micae (*Glimmer*). I am completely puzzled by the stone which forms the basis of the hills. It seems a species of granite mixed with sparry and quarzose strata and lamina. The surface is covered in many places with large loose stones of a sparry kind. They have nothing calcareous in them upon trial. Chrystals are found in numbers scattered about. Upon General Meade's estate is some of the purest Iron ore I ever saw in immense quantity. He tells me that he has found pieces that were perfectly *malleable*. Very excellent Marle [marl] of a red cast is common. It effervesces easily in common Vinegar.

AMELIA COUNTY, MAY 10TH [11?], 1796. The propagation of Sound in a greater or less degree is known to depend upon the State of the air. Euler's system of vibration is admirably explained in his *Lettres a une jeune dame*. I have not seen them for many years, and am, I believe, not quite correct as to the title.[83] In the manner of Ferguson, he has rendered the subject as entertaining, as he has made it clear. A very strong instance of the difference of the *vibratory state* of the air has been very accurately stated to me by Captain Murray, of whose accuracy of observation I have had innumerable instances in my very pleasant visit to his house.

At the beginning of the siege of Yorktown by the American and french army in the Month of Oct. 1781 Captn. M. was at Petersburg. In a strait line Petersburg must be about 60 Miles distant from York. The firing was distinctly heard there for some days after its commencement. Captain Murray, towards the close of the siege, set off for the scene of action. Upon the road he could hear nothing of the firing. The weather was mild and seasonable. He arrived at the distance of 6 Miles from the lines and still heard nothing. The next night he slept at the distance of 1½ miles from the battery. The report of the Ordnance was then distinctly heard but was not sufficiently loud to disturb his rest. On the night of the [16th] of Oct. Lord Cornwallis

---

lina and *glabra*] are saltish, mixt with that poyant acid which you taste in Tamarinds. . . . Here they are sometimes used to make vinegar" (ibid., p. 241). Mr. John Smart, a surgeon in Maryland, quoted Banister: "The berries are a great Astringent, and the Gum of the Tree eases the pain of Teeth" (James Petiver, *Memoirs for the Curious*, no. 3 [April 1708]: 136 [error for 129]). Perhaps the Indians and whites had learned that smoking the leaves with tobacco eased toothache.

83. Leonard Euler, *Lettres à une Princesse d'Allemagne sur quelques sujets de Physique et de Philosophie*, 3 vols. (St. Petersburg, 1768, 1772).

endeavored to cross York river with his troops and to retire to Gloucester on the opposite side. A dreadfull Storm rendered the attempt abortive. The following day the Weather was cool, and the Wind shifted to the NW. The discharge of the Canon was then not only distinctly heard, but the Whizzing of the Balls, their striking the Walls of the Houses and if they passed through, every opposition they met was clearly perceived by the different strokes. It was impossible to sleep from that time.

AMELIA COUNTY MAY 12TH 1796. The innumerable streams that water this part of Virginia rendered it famous once for its settlements of *Beavers*. The remains of many of the dams are still to be seen, and the names, of *Beaver pond, Beaver creek, Beaver dam, Beaver branch*, prove their residence where every other vestige is lost. Many Mills have been built upon their dams after heightening them, and General Meade informs me that the first Mill built upon *Flat creek*[84] near the spot where his present Mill stands had no other Bay at first but the *Beaver bay*. The remains of this Work are *now* to be seen across the Millpond, but large Trees growing upon it and other obstructions render it impossible to examine it. Indeed I have been unfortunate in my attempts at personal examination of what remains here of the ruins of the Beaver republic, and every year erases some trace or other of their former existence. Now and then a solitary beaver is caught about *Jeneto*. Captain Williamson was formerly a famous beaver hunter. Within his memory they have been at Work in many of the streams in the neighbourhood. But they never compleated any of their undertakings, shifting constantly their residence, and perpetually endeavoring to elude the vigilance of their enemy and rival, Man. The traps of the Americans have been more successful than the Guns of the Indians are, in exterminating them. The trap used is made upon the common principal of the Fox trap, with the difference that it has no teeth. It is set on the Water's edge where the animals usually land. If the Beaver can get sufficient hold of the Bank to draw up the trap, he immediately bites off the foot held by it, and escapes. Captain Williamson mentioned several instances of this circumstance which was also known to a dozen people in the Porch where he related it. The last Beaver he caught had only *one* foot, having *thrice* purchased his liberty by the loss of a limb. The only effectual method is to place the trap at a bank so steep that the Beaver cannot mount it. It is pity that this ingenious and valuable race of beings could not have been kept up as the hares and patridges are in England, by taking only sufficient to supply the market, and leaving the others to propagate the breed. Perhaps great caution, and rigid attention to the regulations which might have conduced to this object, *at first*, would in time have

84. Flows in a northeasterly direction through Amelia County before emptying into the Appomattox River.

reconciled the Beavers to these humiliating terms of existence. As republicans I think they were entitled to the benefits of American laws.

I have formerly observed that better English is spoken by the common people, and even by the Negroes in Virginia than by the lower orders in any county of England with which I am acquainted. The little improprieties and peculiarities that occur seem equally divided among all ranks of Whites. The only singularity of pronunciation which I have noticed is the broad and drawling manner of articulating the Vowel *i*, which is lengthened almost to a distinct *aw*, *e*, or *ai* as every other nation pronounce their Vowels, the English *i* being in fact a *dipthong* though called a Vowel.

A Virginian dialogue.

Tommy. How does your father, *old fellow?*

Billy. He's *right* well, thank you. I *happened* at Manchester yesterday two hours before *sundown*, and saw your brother.

Tommy. Ah! he came from Norfolk *last* evening, and *informs* that the appropriations for carrying the treaty into effect are made.

Billy. So I hear. I am *mighty* glad of it. Our member *Giles*[85] was *mightily opposed to it*, but *Sedgewick*[86] *advocated it* so *mightily*, that it was carried by a majority of *One*.

Tommy. And I am *mightily* sorry for it, but don't let us talk politics. I am afraid we shall *make* but little corn unless we have rain soon. I *made* a good deal of wheat and tobacco last Year or I should be ruined this.

Billy. I *intend* to Mecklenburg county tomorrow to look after *my* crop. I shall call upon *General Billy Booker* on the way.

Tommy. Where was *General Billy Booker* raised?

Billy. He was *raised* in the same county with myself and *Colonel Dicky Jones*.

Tommy. *Booker* and *Jones*. That must be in Amelia county. There you may take whom you please by the hand and ask "How do you, Mr. Jones? If you find yourself wrong, you are sure to get right by saying, *"I beg your pardon Sir, I was mistaken, How do you do Mr. Booker, I'm right heartily glad to see you."*

85. William Branch Giles (1762–1830), Virginia politician, represented his district, including Amelia County, in the U.S. Congress (1790–98), first as an Antifederalist, then as a Jeffersonian Republican. His concern for state politics led him to resign from Congress to serve in the House of Delegates during the critical years when the Virginia Resolutions were under consideration (1798–1800). Giles held numerous other political offices: presidential elector (1800); U.S. congressman (1801–03); U.S. senator (1804–15); member of Virginia House of Delegates (1816–17, 1826–27); governor of Virginia (1827–30); and delegate to the Virginia constitutional convention (1829–30). *BDAC.*

86. Theodore Sedgwick (1746–1813), western Massachusetts Federalist, served at various times as Speaker

> *Billy.* Well, *old fellow*, if you ever *intend* to Mecklenburg, and *happen* in my
> neighbourhood, I hope you will call at my house, where you will find no
> *lack* of *Toddy, hog*, and *hommany*, and you shall have a *mighty hearty welcome.*

N.B. A Virginian *mighty hearty welcome*, must be experienced to be understood. It includes every thing the best heart can prompt, and the most luxuriant country afford. It is that which will oblige a stranger to stop his career to the *cautious prudent* Pennsylvanians, and force him to settle among men whom he experiences to be liberal, friendly, and sensible. *Experto crede Roberto.*[87]

MAY 14TH, 1796. RICHMOND.   Yesterday evening I arrived again at this place, after a hot dusty and solitary ride the greatest part of the way. Hopkins's inn, 20 Miles from Manchester is a tolerable house, where a very decent dinner may be had for 4s. 6d. including Toddy or vilainous Wine. Upon my journey to and from Amelia the dinners were the same—*Hog*, i.e. Ham or Bacon and Greens at one end, and roast Lamb at the other end of the Table; 4 dishes of salted Chads one at each corner, a dish of peas and one of Asparagus on each side, spoiled by wretched stinking butter, and Sallad in the middle. Eggs in plenty were brought for those who had too nice palates. The Wheat bread is bad at all the inns I have seen.

RICHMOND. MAY 16TH, 1796.   I had the misfortune to lose one of the Glasses of my Spectacles in Amelia. I am only half alive without their assistance, having worn them incessantly since my 17th Year. They are concaves No. 6. Upon my first losing one Glass, I felt extremely uneasy in the eye which retained the other, and could not immediately tell the cause. It was some days before I could at all see without shutting my right eye, and though I can now after a weeks practice manage tolerably well to see objects at a distance with one Glass and both eyes open, it in a short time gives me much pain in both eyes. This is the more singular, as I had for about a twelvemonth, a trick of wearing my spectacles awry upon my nose so that while one Glass touched my eyelid the other hung an inch off. But the greatest inconvenience I feel is that when I draw or write without my spectacles, as I am now reduced to do, my pencil or pen appears to touch the paper while it is still about an eighth of an inch distant. For this I cannot on any optical principles account. The concave glasses by diminishing objects certainly carry them apparently to a greater distance but this

---

of the Massachusetts House of Representatives, Speaker of the U.S. House of Representatives, president pro tempore of the U.S. Senate, and Massachusetts Supreme Court Justice. *BDAC.*

87. Trans.: Trust Robert, who knows by experience.

I conceive would have a contrary effect upon leaving them off, and the pen ought to meet the paper before my eye would expect it to do so.

RICHMOND, MAY 17TH, 1796. *Extract of a letter to Colonel Blackburn, Rippon lodge, Dumfries, on the Potowmac.*

..., and in every other aspect my visit to that beautifull part of Virginia (Amelia) was as pleasant, as the hospitality of my host and the kindness of his friends could render it.... In Amelia I could have again fancied myself in a society of English Country Gentlemen (a character to which I attach everything that is desireable as to education, domestic comfort, manners and principles) had not the shabbiness of their mansions undeceived me. Of the latter I do not mean to speak disrespectfully. It is the necessary consequence of the remoteness of the Country from towns where Workmen assemble and can at all times be had. An unlucky boy breaks two or three squares of Glass. The Glazier lives fifty Miles off. An old Newspaper supplies their place in the *mean time*. Before the *mean time* is over the family get used to the Newspaper, and think no more about the Glazier. The same is the case in every other respect, and as all the houses are in the very same state, they keep one another in countenance. In regard to other circumstances also I felt myself almost out of the World. I found it impossible to get a letter to Richmond though only 32 Miles distant. Our latest Newspapers were a fortnight old. A county meeting had been summoned to meet at Stingytown upon the subject of the treaty with Great Britain, on the 12th instant. Only two days before a report was spread that congress had made the appropriations necessary for carrying it into effect; but whether the act containing such modifications as might have rendered it palatable to the Gentlemen who think the treaty a bad and injurious compact, nobody knew. About 50 Gentlemen met. I was there as a visitor, many said as an English spy, and my friends entertained themselves by promoting the idea. But as not a soul knew any thing positive as to the resolutions of Congress, and not [a] Newspaper could be had no one ventured to speak at hazard; the sturgeon was silently eaten, and every one departed to his home.[88]

The frequent intermarriage of near relations, so uncommon in Europe, seemed to me also to result from a great degree of separation from the rest of their fellow citizens. Half the Gentlemen of the county seem to be married at least to second or third cousins. This is not speaking very accurately, to be sure, but of the three Gentlemen

88. On 30 April 1796 the U.S. House of Representatives passed the appropriation bill necessary for carrying the Jay Treaty into effect. It took ten days for the first reports of this action to reach Amelia County, a stronghold of radical Republicanism in Virginia, where BHL attended the county meeting. Noble E. Cunningham, *The Jeffersonian Republicans: The Formation of Party Organization, 1789–1801* (Chapel Hill, N.C.: University of North Carolina Press, 1957), p. 83; Beeman, *Old Dominion*, pp. 131, 141.

who have shown me most civility, Captain Murray is married to a first cousin of his own, the daughter of an own cousin on both sides, and *her* parents were first cousins. Major Eggleston married *first*, a daughter of General Meade, by whom he has three fine Boys. She died, and on Saturday last, he was again married, to his first cousin, Judith Eggleston. During the life time of the first Mrs. Eggleston (General Meade's daughter by a former wife) General Meade married the *Sister* of Major Eggleston by whom he has three Sons and a daughter. Major Eggleston's Children who are thus at the same time the Nephews and the first cousins of the Children of General Meade, are older than their Uncles and aunt. I could give many other instances of this sort which I have heard. For my part I see nothing *morally* wrong in all this, however the old ecclesiastical regulations may have prejudiced the minds of many of us. Nothing seems to me more natural than a sexual affection founded on family inter-course. There is a greater chance of similarity of disposition, among relations in consanguinity. Nature indeed seems to have implanted in us an instinctive abhorrence of connexions between Brothers and Sisters. The idea however is not countenanced by the biblical story of the family of Adam and Eve as it must be *inferred*, although Moses has drawn over it the viel of Silence. But in a political point of view I think it not expedient that relations in a near degree should marry. The arguments res-pecting the utility of crossing the breed have become doubtfull since the famous experiments of Bakewell with his cattle.[89] But there are others of greater force. Society ought to be like a coat of Mail composed of rings, in which none can be strained with-out dividing and communicating the force throughout the whole texture. Its strength, and its pliability depend upon it. I have heard it observed by others, and I think my own observations go to the same point, that of happy marriages few exist between persons of exactly the same disposition and temper. A careless thoughtless husband finds his comfort and interest in a careful notable wife. A choleric man's temper is softened and improved by the yielding pliability of a woman's meekness, and a lazy indolent drone is stimulated to exertion by a rattling bustling housewife. You see how I ramble. But that being the condition of our correspondence, I shall at once jump to the end of my letter and paper by assuring you *&c. &c. &c.*

RICHMOND, MAY 22D, 1796. Every body remarks the uncommon coolness of the present spring. The thermometer has never yet to my knowledge or to my feelings been higher than 76° Farenheit. It reached that degree while I was in Amelia,

89. Robert Bakewell (1725–95) was an English agriculturalist who improved breeds of cattle, sheep, and horses through scientific farm management, culling, and inbreeding. He developed the Dishley cattle, also called the new Leicestershire long-horn. The breed has since disappeared. *DNB*.

on the 8th of May, and on the night of the 10th the Wind at NW, there was so severe a frost that almost all species of trees were affected in their young leaves and shoots. The Persimmon, the Sassafras and the smooth leaved hiccory seemed to me to have suffered most. A Gentleman informed me that the Thermometer was as low as 28°. For a few days afterwards the Weather continued extremely chilly, and there was a slight frost on the 12th again. In my rides about this place, I think I perceive still greater effects from the frosts than took place in Amelia.

Besides the general coolness of the Weather, its dryness till within these 10 days has been remarkable. The Wheat and Barley has in most places suffered considerably to appearance. It is now raining violently as it did the greatest part of yesterday, with the Wind at SE.

RICHMOND, MAY 31ST, 1796. I have had considerable pleasure, since my arrival here, in attending the different courts of Justice held in the Capitol: The foederal court, the district court, the court of Chancery, and the court of Appeals. The first singularity that must immediately impress itself upon the mind of a Europaean, and especially an Englishman, is the plain undecorated appearance of the court. Judges without Wigs or Robes, in the plain dress of farmers, and Council without Wigs or Gowns in the almost *slovenly* dress of a *town*-man of business. A *resuscitated* Grecian would not easily see the connection of Law and Wigs, but an Englishman scarcely conceives their separation to be possible but by the horrors of a divorce. Crombe[90] would here have been sadly at a loss for an abstracted idea of a Judge or a Lord Mayor. About a century ago a full bottomed wig, was in England as necessary to a Beau, as at present a tight pair of Pantaloons are in Virginia. The veneration for wigs was then a passion, a disease of the mind of a most singular nature. Of all the objects that have ever filled the human mind with awe, [a] wig seems to possess the least visible or probable powers. To adore a Rattlesnake as an emblem of a mischievious, or a *bull* of a beneficent, deity, or an Athanasian *trinity* of an incomprehensible deity, seems to be a pardonable folly, quite within the scope of apology or defence; but to adore a Wig, is a *fact* not easily accounted for, upon any of the almost innumerable principles of human folly. A king, a statesman, or a general, a century or two ago could neither have laid claim to power, wisdom or courage without the assistance of a flowing wig. The inconvenience of the wig to the pleasures of the king, the scribbling of the statesmen, or the activity of the motions of a general induced them I believe *first* to discharge the incumbrance. The Cloud hovered longer over

90. John Crome (1768–1821), English landscape painter and founder of the Norwich school of painting, drew his subjects from daily life. His methods were derived from the Dutch masters, especially Hobbema. *DNB.*

the head of foppery, still longer over that of Religion, and still obnubilates that of Law on the other Side of the Atlantic. To the Fop it must soon have become burthensome after the *great* had discarded, and the Spectator ridiculed it. While *Orthodoxy* clouded enquiry in religious matters, the clerical wig was sufficiently emblematic to be retained. The present infidel clergy of England have however found means to preserve or increase the value of their livings without sticking very hard by the good old size of their wigs, or the good old toughness of their doctrines, and even the episcopal wig, has already portentously shrunk to the limits of the faith of the bishops. In a case, in which it is impossible to reason from theory, experience is the only guide. We may therefore, very fairly, I think conclude, that whenever we see wigs decrease or vanish in any profession, bigotry and obscurity will lessen and cease, and good sense and liberal principles gain Ground and become general in the same ratio. I confess that the wigless courts of Virginia have confirmed me in this opinion. From the little I have seen, my opinion of the liberal principles upon which every thing seems to be conducted in them is already made up. No ungentlemanly cross examinations, no quibbling about points of form, no arbitrary dictatings to juries. The pleaders at the bar, whom I have heard have most of them great though various talents.

*Mr. James Innes,** Attorney general of the State (also a *Colonel*), ranks I think, first in genius, in force of thought, in power of expression, in effect of voice and manner. He is, at the same time a man of the most amiable and benevolent disposition, open, generous, and unreserved, more I think of the character of Charles Fox[91] than any

Fig. 18. Sketch of Edmund Randolph and James Innes, Richmond lawyers, 12 April 1796.

91. BHL was personally acquainted with Charles James Fox (1749–1806), the parliamentary leader and advocate of reform measures. See BHL to Christian Ignatius Latrobe, 5 January 1807, and BHL to Henry Sellon Latrobe, 30 January 1814, Latrobe Letterbooks, *PBHL, microfiche ed.*, 54/B2, 114/E9.

Fig. 19. Attempts at the features of Patrick Henry.

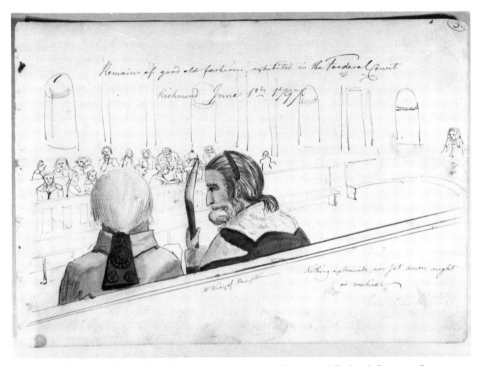

Fig. 20. Remains of good old fashions at Richmond Federal Court, 1 June 1797.

other man I ever knew. His only fault is indolence. He has been known to return a fee of 10 guineas, because he had neglected from mere indolence to give a short opinion, and cared not to leave his bed in which he was reading to consider the case. Speaking of his first rate abilities to *Jack Stewart*, he gave this opinion upon them, which I believe to be founded in truth: "Sir," said he, "you admire Innes with good reason, for you have heard him only speak on the *right* side, your opinion would change were you to hear him defend a bad cause, you would find him so embarrassed, and embroiled with the honesty of his own heart, *as to make no hand at all of it*." A Gentleman who was present, repeated to me the following close of a speech upon liberty of conscience, made some years ago in the Virginia Assembly, which is no bad specimen of his manner. *"May she,"* said he, *"lift her head to the footstool of the Almighty, may the whole earth be covered by her Mantle, and may she embrace all Human nature in her arms!"* Has Demosthenes anything more sublime?

The public opinion gives the next rank as an Orator to Edmund Randolph, çidevant secretary of State.[92] He speaks slowly, smilingly, in a musical voice, a selected phraseology, a polished gentlemanly manner, and with a plentiful flow of words. But his slowness gives his hearer time to anticipate and renders him impatient for the end of his period; his smiles seem to swim only upon the surface of his countenance, the sweetness of his tones do not reconcile to a corrected turn of language, and a selection of words apparently laborious, his manner appears to have been polished in the school of dissimulation, and the Storehouse of his words seems to be his head not his heart. At the instant he labors to persuade the jury, he seems to be unconvinced himself and to be ignorant that *"artis est celare artem."*[93] The coarse praise bestowed by a country man upon honest *Innes* will never be earned by the quondam Secretary, "he has his belly full of words, and they come pouring along like a great fresh." Perhaps he would have said, "Randolph has his head full of words, and there seems to be no end of them." Considering all the circumstances of the political history [of] Edmund Randolph, I cannot help thinking the perpetual political alusions in his speeches upon all sorts of law cases are [*torn page*]ed. In the cause of Tayloe, in which a suit, in Chancery was commenced to divide equally among his sisters upon the principle of a late law, the property bequeathed by his father many years before (1772) he said that (pleading for the equal division) "his cause was the cause of the

92. Edmund Randolph (1753–1813) was appointed U.S. attorney general in 1789 by President Washington and secretary of state upon Thomas Jefferson's resignation in 1794. He resigned in August 1795 when confronted with allegations that he had made indiscreet statements to the French minister, Joseph Fauchet. He then moved to Richmond where he established his law practice and began a brilliant career culminating in his performance as senior counsel for Aaron Burr in the 1807 treason trial. *DAB.*

93. Trans.: It belongs to art to conceal art.

God of nature, against the Daemon of Aristocracy."!!! But the boldness of innocence, if such it be, ought to be respected.

N.B.[94] This opinion was written while I was prejudiced against, before I had any personal acquaintance with Mr. Randolph. It is correct as to the *general* effect of his speaking. But notwithstanding the partial view of his character which, at the time I wrote, was unavoidable, and is here exhibited, I freely acknowledge that my subsequent intimacy with him has shewn him in a light infinitely amiable.

Mr. Randolph. Mr. Randolph is convicted of several political inconsistencies if to change parties, be a political inconsistency; for it will always remain for discussion whether the *party* or the individual have deviated from the original sentiment. In his resignation of his Office as Secretary of State, he appears to me to have been sacrificed to the malignity of a man as detestable in his private character, as Mr. Randolph is amiable.[95] To respect, nay to love Mr. Randolph it is only necessary to see him at his fireside, the father, the husband, and the friend. In a soil which virtues, such as he there exhibits, occupy, there cannot be room for a single depraved intention. And though that suavity of disposition which renders him an object of affection may perhaps give way to the pressure of artifice in others, I should think impossible for him to act wrong, but when he has been deceived.

John Marshall (a general of Militia) is inferior to Ed. Randolph in voice and manner. But for talent he substitutes genius, and instead of talking *about* his subject he talks *upon* it.[96] He possesses neither the energy of expression, nor the sublimity of imagination of Innes, but he is superior to every other orator at the bar of Virginia in closeness of argument, in his most surprising talent of placing his case in that point of view best suited to the purpose he aims at, of throwing a blaze of light upon it, and of keeping the attention of his hearers fixed upon the object to which he originally directed it. He speaks to the man of plain common sense, while he delights and informs the most acute. In a less captivating line of oratory than that which signalizes Innes, he is equally great, and equally successful. The jury obey *Innes* from inclination, and *Marshall* from d[uty?].

Mr. Bushrod Washington is my friend. Could I think impartially of him, I might place some value upon my judgement and commit it to paper. The public voice places him in the triumvirate of eminence, with Innes and Marshall. But if purity and honesty of heart be a disqualification in a Lawyer he cannot deserve that rank.

---

94. BHL inserted the following two paragraphs at a later date.

95. BHL most likely was referring to former Secretary of the Treasury Alexander Hamilton. For BHL's opinion of Hamilton's private character, see p. 333, n. 11.

96. John Marshall (1755–1835) would become chief justice of the United States Supreme Court in 1801.

3

Virginia, 10 June–24 July 1796

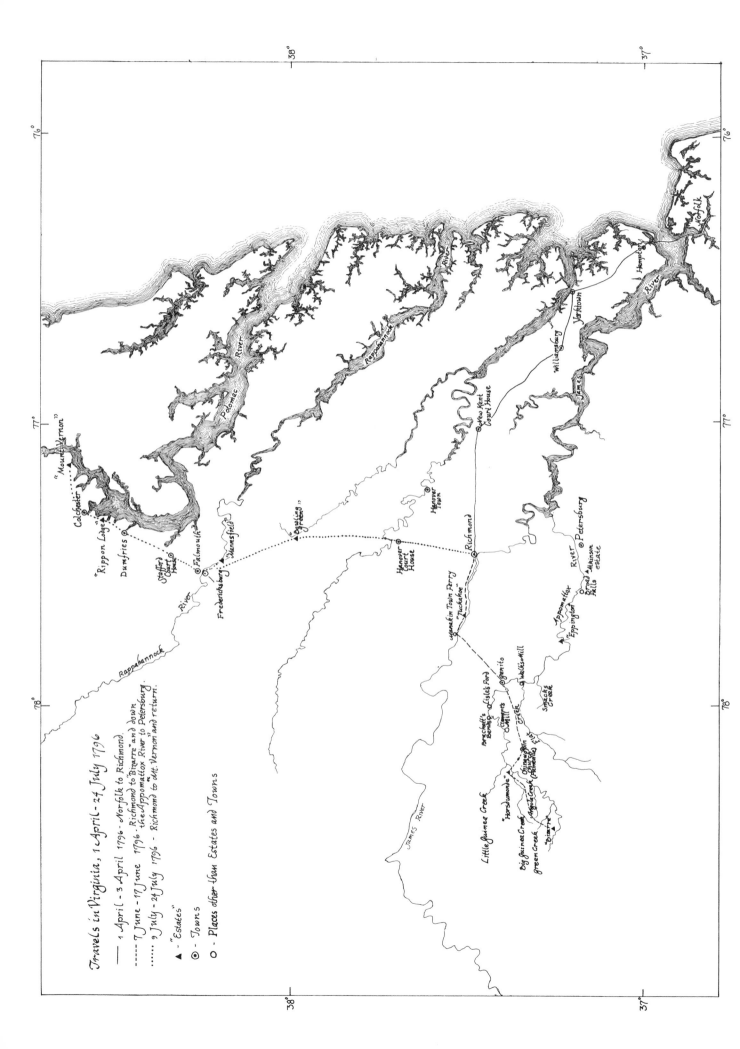

Travels in Virginia, 1 April – 24 July 1796

— 1 April – 3 April 1796 – Norfolk to Richmond.

- - - - 7 June – 17 June 1796 – Richmond to "Bizarre" and down
the Appomattox River to Petersburg.

.... 9 July – 24 July 1796 – Richmond to Mt. Vernon and return.

▲ – "Estates"

⊙ – Towns

O – Places other than Estates and Towns

COLONEL SKIPWITH'S.* CUMBERLAND COUNTY JUNE 10TH 1796. To get my person to this place has been the work of much labor, and some contrivance. I ought to have been 20 miles more to the Westward upon the 7th but that could not be done. The capital of Virginia does not afford a horse for hire. This is not much to be wondered at, nor will the *matter be better*, till *postfeeding* gets out of fashion. The Virginians ride hard, and are into the bargain accused of tying their horses to a Post or tree, when they out[1] to be tied to the manger. My appointment for the 7th was to meet the superintendants of the Apomatox navigation at Mr. Venables* in order to proceed from the head of the river to Petersburg. The weather has been very rainy for this fortnight past, and all my endeavors to hire or beg the use of a horse had been abortive. Mr. Arthur however furnished me at last with a horse, which, having carried me to Tuckaho, I exchanged for another and proceded across the river to Amelia county. Tuckahoe is 16 miles from Richmond on the N side of James river.[2] I shall at a future day have ample opportunity to describe the fertility and the situation of this estate. About 5 miles above Tuckahoe is Manakin town ferry.[3] The river is here about 150 Yards wide and runs in a straight line about 2 Miles. Its scenery of Wood and gentle hills is soft and pleasing. The river is deep at all times at the ferry. The rains had swelled it, and there was about 10 feet of Water nearly across. Fine fertile land lies on the South bank elevated above common freshes but perfectly level. My object was to get to Hopkins tavern. An old talkative Negro, who was ploughing a cornfield directed me. I made him repeat the lesson till I learned it by heart. He happened not to know his right hand from his left but with some trouble I contrived to understand him. This business of enquiring after roads and getting clear directions is a matter that ought to be well understood by a solitary traveller in American Woods. Men that daily traverse the same route, think their road so clear that it cannot possibly be mistaken, and perhaps pass over in their directions most critical points. *My* way is always to hear and if possible to imprint on my memory the direction offered me, and then to make minute enquiry after all the byeroads and

1. Obsolete form of ought. *OED.*

2. The mansion at Tuckahoe plantation had been built between 1712 and 1720 either by or for Thomas Randolph (1683–1729). As his son William (1712–45), who inherited the property, died before his children had reached maturity, William's good friend Peter Jefferson moved to Tuckahoe with his family until William's son, Thomas Mann Randolph (1741–93), came of age. Thomas Jefferson, Peter's son, spent much of his childhood there. After Thomas Mann Randolph's first wife, Anne Cary, died, he married Gabriella Harvie, who controlled the plantation when BHL visited it.

3. On the James River about twenty miles west of Richmond, the ferry provided transportation between Powhatan and Goochland counties. Manakin Town was founded in the early eighteenth century as a refuge for French Huguenots. By 1750 the town had so declined that the site was sold to the Scott family, the only traces of it remaining in the names of the ferry and Manakin Creek. Robert L. Scribner, "Manakintowne in Virginia," *Virginia Cavalcade* 3 (Winter 1953): 38–41; *Martin's Gazetteer.*

turnings which I am to avoid. By this mode of enquiry I in general astonish my directors by discoveries of difficulties they never thought of before. This was the case with my old negroe. After telling me at first that the road was so plain I could not miss it; he then recollected so many devious paths in the first mile, that he turned me over for further guidance to the Overseer, whom, he said, I should meet 1/2 mile off. I met however no Overseer, but continued my ride through the woods following the old mans direction, and steering SW. Having, *by my feelings*, rode about 10 miles without catching a view of any known object, I began to be uneasy, and soon after met a man, who, though himself a stranger, could tell me that Hopkins' tavern lay about 10 miles behind me. He put me into a small path leading into the thickest of the woods which would lead me to a plantation where I could get directions. After following it about 3 miles frequently stopping to chuse among three or four byeways all of which appeared equally likely to be right, I over took another white man who made me turn back about half a mile again, as I unfortunately had pitched upon a wrong one. This path I followed for an hour without seeing an opening in the wood or meeting with any thing that looked like an indication of human habitation. At last I arrived at a fence and saw a small house at a distance. I pulled part of it down got over and rebuilt it. I soon arrived at the house. A man apparently dying of a consumption, sat at the door with his head in the lap of a very beautiful young woman who was crying over him. Her cheeks seemed to flush with a hectic red. There were 3 or four small white children crawling about, attended by as many black ones. Within every thing looked neat and comfortable. I waited for some minutes, and felt a degree of melancholy, that I cannot describe, picturing to myself a long story of distress which I fancied must belong to this unhappy family, of which the poor children might soon perhaps inherit the continuance. Here however there is hospitality and neighbourly feeling to assist and alleviate, in Great Britain the crouded inhabitants are forced to trample on each others sufferings. The man who had fainted soon recovered and I found that the fever and ague, the canker of the plenty and health of this country had harrassed him for a year or two, and he despaired of recovery. He begged me to alight and refresh myself, but the scene was too distressing. I got from him and his wife a clear direction, and in about an hour more escaped from the Woods and arrived at Hopkins's. I was extremely fatigued, got my horse fed and a dish of tea for myself. While I was drinking it the tavern keeper sat in the room, nursing a child, and singing and rattling a table in the most violent manner and exceedingly unpleasantly to a fatigued traveller. There is nothing, thought I, like liberty and equality. I found it impossible to disturb him by the questions I asked with that design, I therefore ordered my horse paid my bill and rode eight miles further to Jeneto. It was dark when

I arrived. It had rained often in the day, and when I alighted I could scarce walk into the house with fatigue having rode about 50 miles in the course of about 9 hours. Extreme fatigue prevented my sleeping much, I got up late, and resolved to go and rest myself for the day at Captain Murray about 4 miles off.

The Apomatox upon which this village lies is subject to sudden freshes that frequently do considerable damage. The country through which it runs is hilly and steep, and the water which falls on the hills find its way rapidly into the Channel. The Water had risen the evening before, six feet in an hour and a half, coming down the river in billows like the surf of the sea. It had beat down great part of Captn. Williamsons milldam which extends across the Stream being a tumbling bay in its whole extent. These bays are erected like the Norfolk wharfs, of logs retained by tie pieces [see p. 76]. The Beavers have taught the Americans how to erect them, but the Beaver dams have still the preference in durability and watertightness. The Mill dams were copied from the Beaver dams, and the Wharfs from the Mill dams. The river was still high and the Cascade would have been beautifull had the Water been less muddy.

I spent all Wednesday at Captain Murray's, and on Thursday morning went to Major Eggleston's. He was out, and I followed him to Mrs. Eggleston's his mother in law's about 2 Miles further. He had also left that place, but I met there his wife and spent a very pleasant day with 3 agreeable Ladies. In the evening he arrived, and I returned to his house joined by Major Scott,* a veteran officer in the American army, and a man of uncommon natural ability, and strength of intellect. About 9 o'clock this morning I pursued my journey up the river hoping in the evening to arrive at Mr. Venables where I proposed staying till the fresh should have subsided, and the superintendants commence their operations.

Major Eggleston favored me with a letter to Colonel Skipwith who has a Mill about 20 Miles higher up upon the Apomatox. The road lay through Stingytown and by Chinquopin Church. The circumstance that gave the name of Stingytown to the small collection of houses round Mr. James Town's tavern is forgotten. The name however is now I dare to say indelibly fixed, and the attempt of the proprietor, to call it by his own name *Jamestown* will scarcely succeed. Nicknames are durable things.

Chinquopin church has a small collection of houses about it, the principal of which is a tavern kept in an indifferent stile by Major Chaffin* who with Major Eggleston is a representative of the County in the State-Legislature. I suppose the quantity of Chinquopin bushes about the Church gave it the name it bears but they are every where so thickly spread that I am at a loss why the preference should be given to this spot. The Church like all the rest is an indifferent wooden building scarcely ever used.

The soil between Major Eggleston's and Chinquopin is so full of mica that after the rain of last night the clear Sun of this morning was reflected from the road in ten thousand spangles as brilliant as Diamonds. It is a circumstance so constantly before the eyes of the inhabitants that nobody remarks it; but a more beautiful and magnificent road for the Chariot of a Mythological deity could not be laid out by the warmest imagination of a poet. Flat Creek winds among these hills to the extent, I am told, of 40 miles above its junction with Appomattox. It deserves the name it bears, and if it were a little straighter, it appears to me that it would be already navigable for Batteaux. The rains of last week had considerably swelled its Water, and General Meades Milldam, situated upon it, was blown up the night before last. The fault was owing in a great measure to its imperfect construction. Indeed the Millers and Millwrights of this country are as remarkably deficient in their knowledge of that part of their business as they are perfect and ingenious in the contrivance of the internal Mill works.

I was in hopes of getting by 12 o'clock to Colonel Skipwiths. At Chinquopin church I struck into the Woods and pursued the *direct road* without suffering any *fork to the right or left to puzzle me*, according to the advise of an old man whom I met *near Chinquopin*. The road indeed was straight enough. I rode without fear till I fancied I must much have exceeded the 7 Miles of distance I had to travell. I then turned into a plantation, the *third* opening only, which I had met with in these eternal woods. A negro man came to the gate, who in a long speech bewailed my having missed the *proper turning to the right* in this infallibly straight road. It was about 4 miles behind me. The day was excessively sultry and my horse appeared as tired as his rider. Nothing however could be done but to go back, and I got nearly the following direction.

"I am right sorry, Masser, you are so far out in this hot day, it is very bad indeed, Masser. You must if you please turn right round to your right hand which was your left hand you see when you were coming here, Masser; I say, you turn right round to your right hand, which was your left hand, and then you go on and go on about 2 mile or 2 miles and a half Masser, its very bad indeed to have so far to ride back again in so hot a day and your horse tired and all, but when you have got back again about 2 miles or 2½ miles you will see a plantation and that plantation is Dicky Hoe's, that's on your right hand now as you're going back but it was on your left hand when you were coming here, you see, Masser. The plantation is Dicky Hoe's on your right hand, right handy to the road, and there is a house with two brick chimnies on it; but it is not one house it only looks like one house with two brick chimnies but it is two houses and is only built like one house, but it is really two houses, you will see it right handy to the road a little way off with two brick chimnies on your right hand which was your left hand when you were coming here, and so you ride by Dicky

Hoe's plantation with the house with two brick chimnies which is two houses you know, and then you ride on and come to another plantation about a mile further which plantation is on your left hand which was your right hand when you came here, right handy to the road . . ."

Well, said I, I know it, and then I get again into the wood, and how then when I am in the wood past the plantation and house?

"Why then, Masser," says the Negro, "when you have passed the plantation on your left hand which was your right when you came here, right handy to the road you go along till you come into the wood and ride about 100 Yards, no Masser, you don't ride 100 Yards, only 50 Yards, but I think Masser you had better ride about 150 Yards and then it will be all plain to you, for you'll see a fork on your right hand which was your left when you came here, turn down there . . . "

Now I know all about it, cried I fatigued, good morning my good fellow and thank you, thank you many times. I rode off in full trot and when he was out of sight he was still called out to me about my right hand which was my left. As soon however as I got out of the wood I saw the house with two brick Chimnies on my left instead of my right, and presently the next house was on my right instead of my left. I therefore tied up my horse got over the fence, and at the house got a direction *in good German* to the Mill from which I was then only two miles distant. The river was very full and I heard the roar of the tumbling bay half a mile off. The Mill and house belonging to it are on the opposite steep bank. Colonel Skipwith had just erected a small mill on the South end of his dam to which I rode and tied my horse to a tree. There was not a human being however to be seen in or near it. I heard voices in the woods and went in search of the women or children from whom they seemed to proceed. But I could not reach them. I then walked down the river, hallooed to the other side but nobody answered. The roaring of the cascade, I presume, drowned my voice, and nobody was in the Mill which was stopped. I therefore undressed and attempted to swim to a canoe which I saw on the other side. The river was very deep at the spot at which I entered it, but I had not swam many yards when my feet, which I dropped to feel for the bottom, were entangled in some bushes and I was glad to get back to the shore again. I then sat down quietly under a tree, dressed, and waited near an hour. At last I saw a negro on the other side. He heard me, and presently a young white man put the canoe across, brought me over and then forded my horse at the ford below the Mill. During this time a dreadful thunderstorm was slowly rising, and before I could get to the Colonels house about a mile above the mill it began to rain. He was gone to another plantation an hour before my arrival. His family however consisting of his lady, two daughters and Miss Johnson, received me with the politeness and hospitality I have every where met with in Virginia, and the terribly stormy wet weather which has set in and continues, renders it extremely necessary as well as pleasant to me.

COLONEL SKIPWITH'S, JUNE 11TH, 1796. This place has a name very appropriate: *Horsdumonde*.[4] No possibility of communication by letter or visit, but by riding half a dozen miles *into* the world. In other respects there is a great deal of wordly beauty and convenience about it. The house is a strange building, but whoever contrived it, and from whatever planet he came he was not a *Lunatic*, for there is much comfort and room in it, though put together very oddly. [See PLATE 14.] Before the South front is a range of hills wooded very much in the Stile of an English park. To the East runs the Apomatox to which a lawn extends. Beyond the hills to the South West the river also winds, and to the Vapours tending Eastward from thence the unhealthiness of the place is ascribed.[5] It is a remark which I have heard from many sensible and examining men that water, even stagnate water, situate to the Eastward of a place, that is, between the place and the rising sun, never affects its health, but that no elevation protects from the noxious evaporation arising from a Western river or pond. The opinion is universally received here, and I dare to say is well founded in fact. The warmth of the rising sun, may expand, and occasion the rise of vapors which have been hovering near the Ground or surface of the Water during the night. But why they should take an Eastern course I cannot guess, as the Wind in warm latitudes in general blows from the Sun, and I should suppose in a *still* morning the tendency of the pressure of the air would be to the westward. Reasoning however against experience is vain work.

Of the unhealthiness of Horsdumonde Mrs. Skipwith is a melancholy instance, having for 5 Years past labored under a fever and ague, which nothing I think can cure but a change of air. All her family have had the same complaint though at present well. They seem to think it a thing of course, and one of them, upon my observing that her looks did not betray an unhealthiness in the situation, answered, "that it was no wonder for she had not had an ague for these *13 Months* past." A miserable existence, this!

BIZARRE. JUNE 12TH 1796. Another french name, but not quite applicable to Mr. Richard Randolph's house at present for there is nothing *bizarre* about it

---

4. *Hors du monde* (Fr.): out of the world.

5. In describing his sketch of Horsdumonde, BHL wrote: "The place is extremely unhealthy, the trees having been cut down to the Water's edge, an operation which admitting the autumnal fogs to creep up the Valleys, has been found to render situations subject to fever and ague which were formerly considered as healthy." *PBHL*, *microfiche ed.*, 247/B9.

that I can see. It was however I am told justly enough applied to the first house built on the Estate. My misfortunes have followed me to this house. It rained violently at Horsdumonde all the night of the 10th and yesterday morning. At eleven I mounted my horse hoping to get to Mr. Venable's last night. I rode gently through the woods following a tolerably good road, and crossing first Guinea creek and then *Green creek,*[6] both of which were so swelled by the rain as to be scarcely fordable. At the distance of 10 Miles I got to Colonel Beverley Randolph's,* who gave me a very distinct direction through the Woods hither. The weather was excessively sultry and a constant peal of thunder from a very black Cloud to the SW hastened my pace. About 1/2 past 2 o'clock I arrived at the last Gate before Mr. Randolph's house, which I found I could not shut without alighting. I then perceived that I had lost my bundle and great coat from behind my saddle containing all my drawing materials besides cloaths of some value. *Heu miserum!*[7] My philosophy was nearly worn out before, but it quite forsook me now, and I stood at the gate absent and uncertain what to do for a quarter of an hour, to the great astonishment of those who observed me from the house, till a heavy shower reminded me of my horse and the neighbouring shelter, and I rode on to the house. I soon forgot my personal loss at finding Mr. Randolph very dangerously ill, of an inflammatory fever. He induced me however to stay and immediately sent a trusty servant to seek my bundle, who in a couple of hours returned with it safe but wet. But this was not all. The Superintendants of the river, of whom I was in quest had passed Bizarre that very morning, and rendered all my journey fruitless. It was no comfort to me that the voyage must be equally so; for the fresh that has

Fig. 21. Nancy Randolph at "Bizarre," drawn from memory, 11 June 1796.

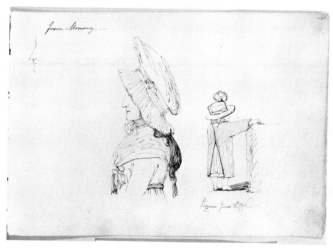

6. Big Guinea Creek, about twenty miles long, and Green Creek, about three miles long, flow east through Cumberland County into the Appomattox.

7. Trans.: O wretched me!

been for a Week in the river must have rendered an examination of it impossible. From the moment of my arrival till 8 this morning it has thundered lightened and rained incessantly. The river however remains just within its banks. Mr. Randolph is much worse. His family however have shown me every attention and kindness in their power. He died the Tuesday following.[8]

PETERSBURG, JUNE 17TH 1796. Mr. Randolph was visited about noon by a medical practitioner in the neighbourhood, Dr. Smith. He appeared a man of good sense. His opinion was against the probability of Mr. Randolphs recovery, though masqued by a long string of hopes and technical phrases. The weather cleared up about noon, I dined with the melancholy family of my host and immediately after, set off for Colonel Skipwiths. My horse was perfectly master of the intricate road and saved me the trouble of much consideration by the quickness with which he turned from broad beaten roads into the narrow paths through which I had to go. Otherwise I have no doubt that I should have, as usual, missed the way. The two Creeks were so swelled by the rain that I had to swim through the middle of their Channels. About 8 o'clock I got back to *Horsdumonde* where I found, Mr. *Venable* and *Epperson** waiting for the fresh to subside.

Colonel Skipwith is related to the Skipwiths of Warwickshire in England. His brother Sir Paton Skipwith* is one of the very few who keep up their title in this country. The title of Baronet is a phantom even *in England*, having no real priviledge annexed to it, here it is the lank Ghost of a phantom, the shadow of a shade. Among the follies of mankind the adoration of this title is one of the most unaccountable. Fifty years hence it will scarcely be credited in this country, that the Baronets of great Britain should have met, appointed a Committee, issued advertisements, held frequent and grave deliberations, and publickly exhibited a pettish kind of anxiety,

8. This last sentence was added sometime later.

BHL appears to be unaware of the history of Bizarre and of the Randolph family. After Richard Randolph married his cousin Judith Randolph, Judith's sister Anne (Nancy) Cary Randolph came to live with them at Bizarre. In 1793 Richard and Nancy were tried and acquitted by the Cumberland County Court for the murder of an illegitimate newborn child, alleged to have been theirs. Nancy later claimed that she had given birth to a stillborn child which she had conceived by Theodorick Randolph, her fiancé and a brother of Richard. Judith, however, never forgave Nancy for what she assumed to have been an illicit relationship between her husband and sister. The circumstances of Richard's death are as curious as those surrounding the earlier scandal. Judith accused Nancy of poisoning Richard, but Judith herself has been suspected of poisoning him out of jealousy. After Richard's death Nancy continued to live at Bizarre totally subject to Judith's will. In 1808, however, she met Gouverneur Morris in New York and married him the following year. Despite the vicious rumors which continually called to mind the past, the Morrises enjoyed a happy marriage. Leonard Baker, "The Scandal of Glenlyvar," *American History Illustrated* 5 (February 1971): 20–29; Francis Biddle, "Scandal at Bizarre," *American Heritage* 12 (August 1961): 10–13, 79–82.

upon the Subject of petitioning the king for leave to wear a *badge of distinction*, to distinguish themselves from the mere Knights dubbed Sir *"right worshipfull on Shoulder blade."* It is impossible to think of it without astonishment and vexation, and indeed a sensation of total despair that the reign of common sense will ever be established in any country. Captains, Majors, Colonels, and Generals elbow a man out of all hopes even of this country.

Colonel Skipwith is a man of strong mental powers. His house is a most pleasant one, though the illness of Mrs. Skipwith operates as a drawback. We were most hospitably entertained, the sense and wit of Mrs. Skipwith and Venables provided also a mental feast.

On Monday morning we took a ride to Colonel Skipwith's Mill consulted about a lock to pass his dam, and then proceeded to examine the river as far as his Estate extends. From every indication I have no doubt of the country abounding, *this far*, in Coal. We discovered a stratum of excellent free stone in the Wood below the Mill, and as I have been fortunate in my conjecture founded upon the analogy of this part of Virginia and many parts of Europe with which I am acquainted I hope I shall be so as to the vehicle of Coal.

The Country on the Banks of Appomattox is undulated in the most pleasant manner. The woods are beautiful, but the mode of cultivation prevents the effect of contrast they might produce, were the ground cleared in smaller patches and the woods separated into bodies of less extent. There are no scenes of abrupt bold rocks breaking through the verdure, and the river glides unseen under the overhanging foliage of its banks.

From the highest hill in the neighbourhood, upon which Colonel Skipwith is erecting a small house for his son-in-law, Mr. Thomas Randolph,* I first saw the Blueridge of Mountains, in a huge round-backed Mass of them of this form:

towering above the Woods distant about 50 Miles. The top of the hill upon which we were is a clean Stratum of round white pebbles evidently rounded by attrition in Water. May not the question: *"How came they there"?* be given up as unanswerable? Mr. deSur would be not a little puzzled in this country of convulsed strata.

In the evening Messrs. Venables, Epperson, and myself rode accompanied by Colonel Skipwith part of the Way, to Captain Patterson's* about 5 miles down the River. Without the polish and refinement, we met here the same hospitality as at

Horsdumonde. The house was small and inconvenient, and Mr. V. and Ep., Mr. Anderson and I, and Mr. Wily* treasurer to The Company of Appomattox slept in one small room upon excellent Beds. Mr. Anderson is a Country gentleman from the neighbourhood of Mr. Venables, who undertook to be captain of our aquatic expedition, being a perfect adept in the management of a boat among rocks, falls and rapids. Captain Patterson furnished us with a roomy boat, we had got a tilt to protect us from the rain or sunbeams and plenty of good ham, bacon Indian bread and spirits. We rose before sunrise; but it was six oclock before we got into the boat ready to *start*, as the Virginians say.

From Mr. Pattersons I returned Mr. Arthur his horse and wrote the following apology to Mrs. [Bushrod] Washington for not dining with her on Sunday according to promise.

Dear Madam,

1. If ever Hommany and Hog
   Stiff Toddy and delightful Grog
   Our Buckskins set a longing;
   If e'er the rattle of the Dice
   Our Men of Council did entice
   To Straas's*a* net to throng in:

2. If ever Billiard ball did roll
   The pride of Legislator's soul
   Slap! into Radford's*b* pocket:
   If e'er to public virtue lost
   Our senate marshall'd Pharaoh's host
   Till candles smok'd in th' socket:

3. If e'er Jack*c* Willis saw a Card
   Or Harry Banks*d* drove Bargains hard,
   Or Edmund*e* took a fee, Ma'am.

---

*a*Straas, is a German who Keeps a Farobank, and presides over the gambling of Richmond. He is in great vogue and countenanced by men of the first character.—BHL

*b*Radford keeps the Eagle tavern, and plays billiards well and successfully at his own table.—BHL

*c*Jack Willis, a man of immense powers and size of body, and equal wit and good sense. The Falstaff of the age. He *professes* Gambling.—BHL

*d*Mr. Henry Banks well known for his wit, and sense, which, contrary to the usual use of those qualities, have contributed extremely to his *wordly* interests. [See the Biographical Appendix.]—BHL

*e*Edmund Randolph, quondam Secretary of state now a successfull Attorney at law.—BHL

If wise Directors*ᶠ* e'er took huff
Or Bishop*ᵍ* lov'd a pinch of Snuff
As well as you do,_____tea Ma'am.

4. Well, well, say you, a little tiff'd
How long am I to be thus iff'd?
By this eternal Scribbler
When Bishop next shall bring a friend
Pray Heav'n in his best mercy send
He be a perfect dribbler.

N.B. The dismal swamp directors were angry, that I did not give a report favorable to the works of Mr. Capern.*⁹

5. Now pray, dear Ma'am, be not so vext
For had you read to Verse the next
You would have seen the end on't;
I only meant to swear it out
That could it have been brought about,
I'had been with you, depend on't.

6. But wind and rain and rivers wide,
Fords, lost beneath th'impetuous tide
Roads zigzag, forked, twisted
The thunder's dread-inspiring sound
The lightning hissing o'er the ground
My wish'd return resisted.

7. Three times where error mark'd the Way
From friendships roof I rode astray
My steps thrice to remeasure
Twice when the long-fought door I'd gained
My host was gone, though wife remain'd
To moderate displeasure.

8. Meanwhile time still stole slyly on
Five long dull tedious days were gone

*ᶠ*Of the Dismal Swamp [Canal Company].—BHL
*ᵍ*A Gentleman who has no faults, unless this be one, which I suppose it must be as Mrs. W. has discontinued the practice.—BHL
  9. For Capron (Capern), see p. 238, n. 54.

And Sunday followed after,
That day to Belvidere due,
To music, friendship, and to *you*,
To Chat and guiltless laughter.

9. How changed the scene!—my friendly host
To health, to sense, to feeling lost.
Death's lingring stroke attended
Around with unavailing woe
See love and friendship's anguish flow
E'en faultring hope suspended.

10. Slow from the house of dumb despair
I turn'd. Before the freshening air
The weeping clouds had vanish'd;
And while your patience I abuse,
In courting my lame doggrell muse,
Dull Melancholy's banish'd.

11. Then brighten up your viel clad face,
And say that, with *a goodish* grace,
I've made excuse so bulky;
And when I next may chance to fail,
Put on a ten times thicker viel,
And,—if you can,—look sulky.

12. While Washington's and virtue's name
Shall in Columbia mean the same,
No,—I'll not swear so strongly
For if I swear I'll near to offend
When bidden at his board to'attend
I fear I might swear wrongly.

Yours &c. B.H. Latrobe

Captain Patterson's house is situate upon a hill rising at the distance of 1/4 of a mile above the low grounds that separate it from the river. He and Mr. Wiley accompanied us as far as Mr. Clemenses* Mill [. .] miles below his house. The river was about a foot higher than in a common winter season. We glided silently down the stream using our oars till we came to a Hammock extending across the stream through which was a narrow and extremely rapid passage. A Hammock, more properly, I suppose, a Hummock is a collection of trees and logs which having once stopped in the river, catches every thing that comes down till its appearance and effect are truly formidable. This Hammock seemed to consist of the timber of many an acre and had two or three Sawyers at work about it. Sawyers are pieces of timber which are constantly alternately depressed by the force of the current and then raised by their elasticity. It would be dangerous to run upon one of them, if of any considerable size. I am informed that in the navigation of the Ohio and Mississippi there are Sawyers of immense size, sometimes playing below the Surface, and capable of Striking a hole into the bottom of a large boat. They are said to constitute the principal danger in the Navigation of these rivers.

The river is too narrow about Clemenses Mill to display in all its beauty the Scenery of its banks. Each side is bordered with trees of a great variety of species and sizes and now and then a bold rock bursts into the river. There is not much large timber near the banks of the river from Captain Pattersons to Jeneto. This is a defect, which deprives the innumerable pleasant groups of that boldness which characterizes them lower down. About 6 we arrived at Clemenses Mill. With the assistance of the people of the Mill we got our Boat unloaded and carried past the mill dam into the Water below. The South shore upon which the Mill stands is a Hard rock of the same species of micous granite which I have observed to extend through Amelia. Much of the interest of a trip of this kind arises from the little difficulties attending it, and we were in a humour to laugh at every seeming inconvenience. Having launched our boat again we went to breakfast as she quietly carried us down the Stream. Mr. V[enable] and myself are Waterdrinkers, the rest drink Grog, and we all live upon Ham and Bacon of which we have great store. The same Cask also contains Cherries, a few Biscuits, and Pones of Indian and Wheat bread. The social manner in which all these Viands inhabit the same dwelling, produces a sympathy of *taste* among them so that with your eyes shut, it would be difficult to decide whether you had a piece of bacon, a Cherry, or biscuit or a slice of bread in your Mouth. Whenever we came to the *rattle* of a Spring from the Bank we recruited our Watercask, and thus kept up a constant supply of cool beverage.

Mr. Wiley and Mr. Patterson having left us at Clemenses Mill, we were perfectly uninformed of the country through which we passed. The various beauties of the Banks of the river employed our admiration sufficiently, and though we saw nothing beyond the immediate verge of the river, the same ingredients of Landscape were thrown into such various composition, as to keep up a constant succession of Novelty. Difficulties of Navigation, the object of our trip, we found none. Had we been furnished with fire arms we might have had plenty of Wild ducks, Indian hens, and kings fishers.[10] The river abounded chiefly with these birds, and innumerable other species rose incessantly among the trees. Having rowed along till we supposed it about 12 o'clock, for we had not a Watch on board, we discovered, through an opening, a house upon a near hill. Anxious to know whereabouts we were, we landed, and marched up in a body to the house. We found nobody at home. Before we discovered the house we had made the banks ring again with singing and hallooing in order to attract some one to the bank and partly to get rid of our superabundant spirits. Mrs. Brackett supposing us drunk had escaped into the kitchen, and Mr. Brackett was gone in search of the Rackett. We sent a message to Mrs. Brackett who then made her appearance and soon afterwards Mr. B. returned, and we were hospitably furnished with as much grog and Buttermilk as we could drink. Mr. Br. accompanied us down the river as far as Lisle's ford, a shallow part of the river which will require some improvement.[11] The river winds amazingly about Mr. Brackett's,[12] but from thence to Jeneto its direction is tolerably straight. We got to Jeneto before 3 o'clock. Mr. Venable and myself walked up to the inn at 1/4 of a miles distance. Captain Williamson returned with us, and furnished us with a number of negroes who soon launched our boat below the dam of his Mill. We have overtaken the fresh, and the Water was very deep and covered all the shallows and falls of which there are a few below this place. Having dined and added some of Captn. Williamson's excellent beer to our Salmagundi, we proceeded down the smooth stream, and arrived about 7 o'clock at the Mouth of Flat creek, a very considerable stream, which with little trouble might be made navigable 40 miles up the Country. The river below Jeneto winds about so much, as to run for a considerable extent in a Northwesterly direction. We found the Stream in Flat creek so rapid and so full of logs that having attempted to get up to the Mill we were obliged to return and land on the shore of the Appomattox. From thence we walked up the hill to Mr. Walk's house, where we were determined to stay all night; no introduction or previous notice being necessary in this hospitable country. Mr. Walk, a sensible, good humored man, made his house so comfortable and pleasant to us, that we were happy to accept of his polite offer to send for Major Eggleston, as a pretence for staying the greatest part of another day with him. We had expected to find Major Eggleston somewhere higher up, but a letter of appointment having missed him we had neither seen nor heard of him.

10. The "wild ducks" were probably the wood duck, *Aix sponsa* L.; the "Indian hens" were the pileated woodpecker, *Dryocopus pileatus* (L.); and the "kings fishers" were the belted kingfisher, *Megaceryle alcyon alcyon* L.

11. That section of the Appomattox River between Amelia and Powhatan counties where the river bends northernmost in its easterly course. *Fry & Jefferson Map.*

12. This part of the river was known as Brackett's Bends. Commager, ed., *Atlas to Official Records*, plate #16.

The morning of June the 15th was chiefly employed in strolling about. I took a view of Mr. Walks mill on Flat creek, a wretched tub mill in a most advantageous situation [see PLATE 15]. Mr. Anderson with, what I considered, a most desperate intrepidity, stripped himself, and furnished only with a pipe of Tobacco, knocked off the head of two bee hives, and robbed them of their contents without being once stung by the thousand bees that were buzzing about him. In this climate very little is necessary to the rearing of large quantities of bees, and I am astonished to find them so little attended to. I conceive that the 4th book of Virgils *Georgics*[13] would contain every possible direction to that end, as it was written in about the same climate. We are here in Late. 38°; Mantua, I believe is in Late. 43° or 44°. The honey was excellent. All the use Mr. Anderson made of his pipe was to drive the bees from the upper to the lower parts of the hive *"least they should get drowned in honey."* In coming down the river we saw many swarms and hives of wild bees. They are not indigenous. Jefferson tells us that they precede the Europaean settlements in propagating themselves to the Westward, and are called by the Indians *the Whiteman's fly.*[14]

Neither the Messenger nor Major Eggleston having returned at 2 o'clock we dined, and immediately afterwards got our things on board and proceeded down the river which had fallen considerably. The Weather had been cloudy since yesterday noon, and it began to thunder soon after our departure. Mr. Walk and his nephew Mr. Fenna accompanied us, and contributed greatly to our mirth and good humor. About 5 o'clock however our tempers were compleatly tried by a most violent Thunder storm and rain which drove us under the lofty trees of the bank at the mouth of Smack creek.[15] Their protection was but of short duration, for the rain which exceeded any that I had yet seen, soon poured in streams from the leaves and we were all wet to the skin. In 3/4 of an hour it was again fair and our good humour was sufficiently elastic to name the spot which failed to shelter us, Pisspot hole. About 7 o'clock we arrived at Watkins mill, and having stowed our goods in it, we proceeded to the house about a mile distant upon the hill on the left bank. Upon approaching the Yard we were attacked by half a dozen dogs. We got however safe to the house. Old Mrs. Watkins sat at the door, apologized for having set the dogs upon us, not knowing who we were, and informed us that her son *Dick* was in bed. Mr. Walk, who is his brother-in-law, undertook to wake him, and in about 10 minutes appeared our

13. Vergil's *Georgics* sought to dignify manual labor, especially that of the farmer. Book IV dealt extensively with bee culture.

14. Jefferson, *Notes on Virginia*, pp. 71–72.

15. Smacks Creek, about seven miles long, rises near Amelia Court House and flows ENE through Amelia County before emptying into the Appomattox River shortly below Goode's Bridge. Commager, ed., *Atlas to Official Records*, plate #16; *Fry & Jefferson Map.*

minute host, a proper study for Lavater.[16] His manner expressed just as much haughtiness and conceit, as it excited contempt. A total want of good breeding might have been forgiven, good sense cannot be acquired, but *civil* hospitality is the spontaneous impulse of the savage. Mr. Venable, with good sense, and mildness of temper which is natural to him, and Mr. Epperson, the best humoured Man in the world stood the brunt of his insolence. Silence protected me in a great measure though not entirely, and Mr. Walk was too much chagrined to say anything. We were wet and hungry, but neither accommodation nor food was offered. Before nine o'clock Mr. Watkins took up a candle and said; Gentlemen I will show you your beds. He led us into a small room containing 2 beds for 4 of us, and putting it down walked away without saying a word. We had asked him to permit some of his Negroes to help us in getting our boat round his mill. His answer was: "If it rains, they may assist you if they like, if *fair, I wish them to be in the Wheat field.*" At six o'clock we escaped from the house and got to our boat, which we contrived to get round by ourselves though with difficulty. Before we were gone, he came down and continued his insulting language. It was met with temper and contempt. The instance of rude inhospitality is so extraordinary, that I take Dick Watkins to be a mere *lusus naturae.*[17] Hogarth somewhere records a singular Caricatura of a very slender Italian singer of which every body discovered the original at first sight. It was nothing but a straight line with a dot over it. Had I the talent of Hogarth, I think I could represent both the body and mind of this animal under the same form.[18]

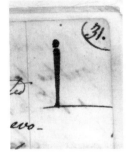

Mr. Walk left us to return home. We parted with extreme regret. His kind benevolent mind must furnish him with as much happiness, as the churlishness of Watkins must lay up of misery. It was a damp chilly morning, but by degrees it grew clear and warm. About a mile below Watkins we took in a white man overseer to an Estate on the left bank. We caught this fish by a hook baited with Grog, and having got out of him all the little intelligence respecting the house of Mr. Eps* which he could furnish us with, for he lives *full 3 miles off,* we sent him with his head and belly full of

---

16. Johann Caspar Lavater (1741–1801), Swiss writer, patriot, Protestant pastor, and founder of physiognomy, the art of discerning temperament and character from facial or body features. BHL may have read Lavater's *Physiognomische Fragmente zur Beförderung der Menschenkenntnis und Menschenliebe*, 4 vols. ([1775–78]; Eng. trans., *Essays on Physiognomy* [1789–98]).

17. Trans.: Trick of nature.

18. BHL mistakenly thought that Hogarth drew the caricature, although Hogarth only mentioned it in a caption to his engraving called "The Bench," published in September 1758. In explaining the difference between Character and Caricatura, Hogarth noted: "Let it be observ'd the more remote in their Nature the greater is the Excellence of these Pieces [i.e. caricatures]; as a proof of this, I remember a famous *Caracatura* of a certain Italian Singer, that Struck at first sight, which consisted only of a Streight perpendicular Stroke with a Dot over it." Ronald Paulson, ed., *Hogarth's Graphic Works: First Complete Edition* (New Haven, Conn.: Yale University Press, 1965), p. 238.

grog ashore again. As his employer must have occasion for every grain of sense he possesses, it would be a pity that he should clog it by a knowledge of the situation of the neighbouring Estate. The river begins to increase in width below Watkins Mill. It is in vain to attempt to describe its scenery. Mrs. Ratcliff[19] herself would be puzzled for words. And after all it is the same thing over and over again. Knight in his *Landscape* quotes some Poetaster who ridiculing the employment of Park making, says something like this:

> Search, as you will the whole creation round
> 'Tis after all but water, trees, and ground
> Vary your spot, seek something new to please,
> What see you? Water, ground, and trees!

The verses are quite different but the idea is the same, and it is fact.[20] But had he been in our boat, had he seen the *dignified playfulness* of nature in the composition of these three ingredients into Landscapes as various as they were harmonious, unless he had recanted he should have received a severe ducking in the Water, have been set a shore on the rocky ground, and then hung upon a tree as a blasphemer.

Mr. Eps has a charming estate about 4 miles below Watkins mill on the North bank. Here we met with a reception different from that of last night, a hearty welcome, an excellent breakfast, and provisions for the day. [See FIG. 22.] We took in Major Eggleston whom we found here, and about 2 o'clock arrived at Moore's Mill, the last we had to pass. With the ready assistance of the owner we soon got our boat past the Milldam. We had met hitherto with no obstruction but Milldams. Robinson's dam between Moores and Watkins gave us no hindrance. The last tremendous fresh opened a channel to the North of the Mill, and has left that and the dam standing. Through this channel which is narrow the river rushes with tremendous fury. It was

19. Ann Radcliffe (1764–1823), English novelist, was the founder of the Gothic school of English literature. Her best known works included *The Romance of the Forest* (1791), *The Mysteries of Udolpho* (1794), and *The Italian* (1797). *DNB.*

20. BHL actually quoted William Mason's *An Heroic Epistle to Sir William Chambers* (London, 1773); see the reprint of the 14th ed. (1777) in *Satirical Poems Published Anonymously by William Mason,* ed. Paget Toynbee (Oxford: Clarendon Press, 1926), lines 45–48:

> For what is Nature? Ring her changes round,
> Her three flat notes are water, plants, and ground;
> Prolong the peal, yet spite of all your clatter,
> The tedious chime is still ground, plants, and water.

Mason's *Epistle* parodied Sir William Chambers's *A Dissertation on Oriental Gardening* (London, 1772); see Eileen Harris in John Harris, *Sir William Chambers, Knight of the Polar Star* (University Park, Pa.: Pennsylvania State University Press, 1970), chap. 10.

Fig. 22. "Eppington," home of Francis Eppes.

a bold experiment to pass it in our little boat. We however effected it in safety, though with an unpleasant rapidity.

We eat our pork-cherry-pone-dinner at a fine spring near Moore's Mill, and then proceeded to the falls which commence about 4 Miles lower down. The river there is divided by numerous rocky Islands covered with beautiful trees. The upper points of these Islands pick up an immense quantity of trees brought down the river by the freshes. They lie in heaps sometimes thirty foot high, and their grey decayed color, forms a picturesque contrast to the verdure of the banks and of the Islands. We passed several small falls without much alarm. Mr. Anderson is compleatly master of his pole, and exerted himself with great skill. Trailors falls however are a most serious obstruction. They are divided by a sheet of water: the upper falls are called Broadfalls.[21] The river tumbles down a ledge of rocks among some Islands which scarce offer any tolerable opening. We were directed entirely by chance in our choice of a passage. We kept the right bank, and by very great exertion arrived in smooth water which continues about 1/4 of a mile, to the second and most dangerous part of Trailors

21. On the Appomattox River ten miles above Petersburg and six miles below the mouth of Namozine Creek. Commager, ed., *Atlas to Official Records*, plate #16.

falls. We were not so fortunate here, for Mr. Anderson's pole breaking we hung upon a rock in the worst part of the cataract, and were all preparing to go overboard, when we got again into a sluice, and soon after were dashed into a tolerably smooth surface. Half a mile lower down the gang of Negroes belonging to the Company were at Work. We took in Mr. Moody their Overseer, who piloted us through the rocky stream into an open sheet of Water of 3/4 of a Mile in length. We landed on the North side, and walked on to Mr. Roger Atkinson's,* about a mile distant. His house stands upon the top of the high bank which overhangs the upper end of the great falls.

A heavy storm of thunder lightning and rain began as soon as we entered the house, and continued all night. On the morning of June 17th we examined the ground below Mr. Atkinson's house, and then went in a Canoe across the river to the land of his two Brothers, and viewed the Mill. Having refreshed ourselves with Grog and Buttermilk at a Cool spring, we proceeded down the river on the South side. The day was excessively hot, but we persevered in forcing our way along the river, through woods and bushes, and deep sand, and swamps for 4 Miles, when our further progress was interrupted by Indian town Creek[22] which tumbles over a rocky precipice into Appomattox. We skirted up the creek to the top of the Cascades and having there built a sort of a bridge of fence rails we crossed over, and from thence took the Shortest cut to Petersburg. We took up our lodging at Dobson's tavern. A pleasant house and a civil Landlord. On Saturday the 18th I dined at Mr. Hayes. On Sunday 19th Mr. Venables and myself rode early to Mr. Campbell's,* where we breakfasted, and then rode with him to Mr. Atkinson's, and surveyed in a cursory manner the difficulties of the river from thence to his Mill on the North side of the stream. Upon our return it began to rain very hard, and before we could get to Mr. Call's to dinner we were nearly wet to the skin.

On Monday the 20th I returned to Richmond in company with Mr. Venables.

On Saturday the 25th Mr. Bishop,[23] Mr. and Mrs. Arthur and Mrs. [Gabriella Harvie] Randolph* and myself went to Tuckahoe. My object was the navigation of Tuckahoe creek, and the coal works.[24] Much time was spent in amusement, and in-

---

22. Indian Town Creek, four miles long, flows into the Appomattox River eight miles below Broad Falls. Commager, ed., *Atlas to Official Records*, plate #16.

23. Identified in BHL's sketchbook index as "Mr. Bishop of Baltimore." This may have been Henry Bishop of Baltimore, with whom BHL corresponded in June 1811.

24. Tuckahoe Creek, about twenty miles long, flows southeasterly in Goochland County before emptying into the James River. Coal mining in the creek area began in 1786. The Tuckahoe Pits were abandoned in 1812, but reopened in 1837. In 1828 the Tuckahoe Canal Company built a five-mile canal north from the James River along Tuckahoe Creek. Though the company made enormous profits, their service was so poor that by 1835 coal operators petitioned the General Assembly for the right to build a railroad to run parallel to the canal. The railroad was completed in 1839. Eavenson, *Coal*, map no. 5, pp. 81, 87–88, 97.

deed the party was so agreeable, that we were all sorry to return on Sunday morning the 3d of July.

Fig. 23. (Henry) Bishop of Baltimore, 16 May 1796.

Jeu d'esprit at Tuckahoe.
Written extempore on Mrs. R[andolph]'s complaining of Mrs. W[ashington]'s avoiding her acquaintance, the same complaint having been also preferred by Mrs. W. against Mrs. R.

> High blew the Wind, clouds dimm'd the lunar Ray
> When two old Hags met in a hollow way:
> Pale, panic-struck, their hair erect by fright
> Each took the other for a ghastly sprite.
> Through the bleak night they shiv'ring stood; till morn
> Smil'd on their folly; then with bitter scorn
> Each curs'd the other, and departing swore
> She ne'er saw such a coward b—ch before.

On Mrs. R's requesting each of the Gentlemen present to mend her a pen.

> 1. To mend a pen
>   Four able men
>   With might and main unite.
>   No wonder why;
>   It was to try
>   To make the Widow write.
> 2. The widow fair
>   With gracious air
>   Smil'd while the pens were making

156

But each poor wight
Till she should write
Was in a desp'rate taking.

3. With fawning look
The pen she took
Which Arthur had made ready.
Alas! how sad
The pen was bad
And never could write steady.

4. That laid aside
The next she tried
Was the pen which Steele*[25] did mend, Sir,
She cried and spoke
At ev'ry stroke,
"Your pen's too soft, and bends, Sir."

5. Latrobe's next came;
To please the Dame
He hop'd with fond reliance
But she took tiff
Call'd it too stiff
And bid his pen defiance

6. The bright'ning face
And jovial grace
Of Bishop soon proclaim'd it
That of four men
His well shap'd pen
Had won the prize they aim'd at.

FREDERICSBERG, JULY 9TH, 1796. Among the many ingenious insects that I have met with in Virginia, the *dirt-daubers*, more decently called Masons, are particularly worth notice. They are a species of Wasp, of a dark blue color. Their cells are built of clay and are in appearance somewhat similar to the nests of the English house martins. These are the nests of the Sphex pensylvanica.[26] I have not

25. BHL's marginal note read "Coln. Steele."
26. The two common species of mud-daubers which BHL studied have different names today. That which he called *Sphex pensylvanica*, the yellow mud-dauber, is now *Sceliphron cementarium* (Drury). The second species, which he called *Sphex caerulea*, the blue mud-dauber, is now *Chalybion californicum* (Saussure). BHL's further observations on these two species of mud-dauber were published in the American Philosophical Society *Transactions* 6 (1809): 73–78, and in the London, Edinburgh & Dublin *Philosophical Magazine* 25 (1806): 236–41. See *PBHL*, *microfiche ed.*, 167/B6.

had an opportunity of examining them, but am told that each cell contains an egg, and a spider. They are now at work, later in the Year I shall break into one of their fortresses, at present I think it a pity to put them out of their way. My attention was this morning drawn to one of them who was walking up and down his mud fort. Near him a very large Spider had extended his net, but had left it to attack a caterpillar about 2 inches long which was crawling up the Wall in order to suspend itself, and retire into the State of Chrysallis. This sketch represents the sizes of the animals pretty exactly. The spider was of a dark purple color with one large and two small white spots on his abdomen and a few slight white marks down the sides. The thorax was almost black. His legs were short and very thick and mottled with white. He had

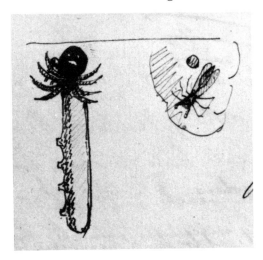

but lately begun his meal, for his body was not much extended. I attacked him with a straw. He immediately ran off sideways with his load, the cubic contents of which were at least 8 or 10 times as large as himself, but upon being closely pursued he dropped it, and suspended himself from my straw by a thread. I wound him up upon it and put him near the *dirt dauber*. The Wasp seemed immediately in great agitation, and ran at him. The spider must have given him a bite for he darted back. He soon however attacked him again, and again retreated. The spider seemed willing to decline the combat, and I had some trouble to keep him near the wasp's fortification. My curiosity was however baulked, for the Dirt dauber got entangled among some neighbouring cobwebs, and the spider took the opportunity of my endeavoring to extricate him, to drop himself by a thread into a crevice beyond my reach. The Wasp cleaned his wings and legs with great address, and then flew off. He soon returned with some dirt held between his legs. The road to his cells was through an abbattis of Cobwebs, and I observed that he took particular Care to clean himself every time he flew off, by running to some clear place and using his legs like a fly.

They are no doubt furnished with means superior to other insects to clear their bodies of the glutinous threads of the Spider, as their subsistence seems to depend upon their engaging among cobwebs. My wasp cleared himself easily of what would have destroyed a large humming bee.

RIPPON LODGE JULY 18TH, 1796. *Sphex caerulea* of Linnaeus *Masons, or Dirtdaubers*, see [PLATE 16]. *See a further account of them* [pp. 239–42].

A whole forenoon has been employed by me in examining the operations of these ingenious Wasps without being yet able to understand completely their domestic Oeconomy. Behind a number of framed prints which hang in the Drawing room here a large colony had established themselves; all of which I destroyed and searched.

Their Cells are of two kinds; but whether two species of the same insects construct them, or whether eggs of different Sexes of the same are deposited in them I have not yet discovered. The first kind consists of a tube which is continued without internal divisions at first for some length, perhaps 4 or 5 inches. The second consists of separate cells joined to one another in a parrallel arrangement, each of which is begun and finished before the next is constructed. The former seem to be executed with more neatness. The latter with more strength, the Dirt being daubed over them in a great number of layers. I have not seen any of the Masons in the act of bringing Dirt to the Cells, but from the Quantity which every Cell requires their Labor must be very great. Internally each species of Cell is finished and filled alike. I think the horizontal Cells however are somewhat less in general.

The inside of the Cells is made perfectly even and smooth. The Mason had fixed his Work to the back of the print frame and made use of the Wood as part of his internal finishing without being at the trouble of carrying his coat of Dirt all round, and I have seen one instance of a pipe being constructed in a hollow moulding of a pannel so as to save nearly half of the Labor which a flat surface would have demanded. The Dirt has the appearance of being platted, the Mason while at work keeping the lowest edge always in an angular form the point of which is upwards, and working first on one and then on the other leg of the angle. The tube being carried to a satisfactory length the Mason collects as many Spiders as will fill about 3/4 of an inch (for the Cells are not exactly equal in length). The poor Devils are crammed in with unrelenting cruelty, as tight as possible. I have counted 27 in two Cells, 12 in *one* frequently, often only 6 or 7 if they happened to be large ones, and once as many as 16 small yellow spiders in one cell. Upon opening many of the Cells these miserable creatures were still alive though so languid that they could but barely move, and soon died when exposed to the Sun. (I have been often shocked and distressed at the Scenes of cruelty and misery that seem to form part of the System of nature; but I scarce ever saw so dreadful a contrivance of torment as appears to be employed by the Masons against the poor Spiders; if we may reason upon their feelings from our own.) The variety of Spiders collected by these industrious Robbers is much greater than my own curiosity ever exhibited to me in my searches after subjects of natural history. They remain in the cells in very good preservation even when dead; not being in the least mutilated till devoured by the grub for whose food they are provided.

Having filled the cell with spiders, the Mason then lays an egg into the lower part of it and closes it up with dirt. Another stop is then put to the head of the next Cell close to the stop of the last and the same provision laid in. The horizontal Cells are managed in the same way. The egg produces as usual a grub. The different appearances of the grub at its different stages are pretty accurately represented in the drawing. The upper most cell produces the first compleat insect.

It is astonishing with what strength and dexterity the Mason attacks conquers and bears off a large Spider much heavier than himself.

In the woods they fix their pipes to the South sides of overhanging rocks.

The young Mason makes a hole in the side of his cell to extricate himself.

RIPPON LODGE JULY 19TH 1796. I had intended to come hither with Mr. Washington's family on the 5th of July. But unfortunately my mare had strayed the day before and I was under the necessity of waiting in Richmond till she could be found. I set out in the stage on Saturday morning at 3 o'clock, crossed in the course of the day the Rivers Chickahomany, Pomunkey and Matapony the two latter forming, after their union, the York river, and arrived in Fredericsberg about six o'clock. The hills gradually grow bolder as you proceed to the North. Fredericsberg lies upon the banks of the Rappahanoc 1/2 mile below the Falls, upon Ground formed by Nature for the site of a town. Three natural terraces rise above one another above the river upon each of which a Street about 3/4 of a mile long is planned. The houses are principally of wood, but the excellent stone quarries in the Neighbourhood already have produced a few stone buildings and promise more.

The Stage does not travel on Sunday. I was astonished to hear the people talk of going to Church, and to see them really go thither, and I understand that more attention is paid in this town to the forms of religion than in the more Southern parts of Virginia.[27] I dined with Mr. Minor* at Mr. Man Page's* at Mansfield where I met several Gentlemen of the town and neighbourhood. Mr. Page's house is built

27. Many of Fredericksburg's leading citizens were Presbyterians who had a much more serious attitude about attending church services than the many Anglicans in the more southern parts of Virginia. Richard Beale Davis, *Intellectual Life in Jefferson's Virginia, 1790–1830* (Chapel Hill: University of North Carolina Press, 1964), p. 132.

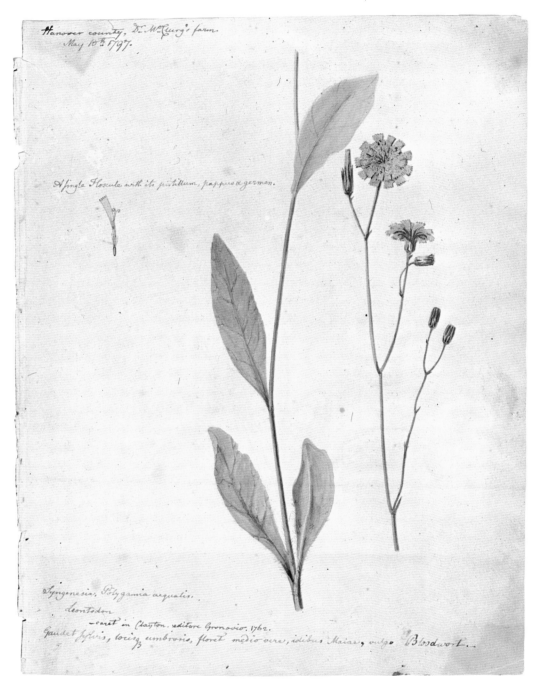

Hanover county, Dr. M.Clurg's farm.
May 10th 1797.

A single Floscule with its pistillum, pappus & germen.

Syngenesia, Polygamia aequalis.
  Leontodon
    —caret in Clayton. editore Gronovio. 1762.
Gaudet sylvis, locis umbrosis, floret medio vere, idibus Maiae, vulgo Bloodwort.

Plate 13. Bloodwort, Hanover County, Dr. McClurg's farm, 10 May 1797.

FROM THE SKETCHBOOKS

Colonel Skipwith's house, lies near the North bank of the Appomattox, which flows on the left hand between the most distant wood and the hill. The place is extremely unhealthy, the trees having been cut down to the Water's edge, an operation which admitting the autumnal fogs to creep up the Valleys, has been found to render situations subject to fever and ague which were formerly considered as healthy.

Horsdumonde, the house of Colonel Skipwith, Cumberland County, Virginia.—

Plate 14. "Hors du monde," Cumberland County, 14 June 1796.

Sketch of Mr. Walk's Mill on Flat Creek, near its junction with Appomattox river.

Plate 15. Sketch of Mr. Walk's Mill on Flat Creek, near its junction with the Appomattox River.

Fig. 1. External appearance of the Cells of *one* species of Masons.

    2. External appearance of the Cells of *another* species of Masons ⎫
    3. Internal appearance of the Cells of the Masons Fig. 2 ⎬ next to the Wall
                                                                          ⎭

    4. Internal appearance of the Cells of the Masons Fig. 1 where attached to the Wall.

      A. Pipe first made without partitions.

      B. A Magazine of spiders containing also an egg or perhaps an infant worm.

      C. A Worm nearer maturity feeding on the Spiders collected for him.

      D. Another Magazine of Spiders: but drawn erroneously, for in this Cell which is the highest and first finished, ought to be a Worm advanced nearly to a Chrysallis, spinning a Web, with only one Spider left.

Fig. 5. The Worm in its last Stage in which it spins its Web, which thinly covers the Cell and Wall.

    6. The Chrysallis, broken across, showing the grub almost transparent and of a bright yellow color.

    7. The Mason newly fledged, building the Cells fig. 1.

    8. The Mason who builds the Cells of Fig. 2.

York River, March 19th, 1797. In reading Derham's *Physico-Theology*, I found the following passage. p. 204 of the Edinburg Edition note *c*. After relating that he had seen a small *Vespa Ichneumon*, lay 2 Eggs into a cell formed in a small hole in his window, and then fetch a Maggot bigger than herself which she disposited with the Eggs, and then close up the cell, Dr. Derham proceeds:

"Of this artifice of these Ichneumons, Aristotle himself takes notice, but I believe he was scarce aware of the Eggs sealed up with the Spiders. *As to the vespae called ichneumones less than others, they kill spiders and carry them to their holes, and having sealed them up with dirt they therein hatch and produce those of the same kind. Hist: Animalium.* L.v.c.20."[1] So that if the Virginian Dirtdauber did not [*torn*] in Greece, his peculiar oeconomy seems to be common to other species of this architectonic Insect.

---

1. William Derham, *Physico-Theology, or a Demonstration of the Being and Attributes of God, from his Works of Creation; Being the substance of 17 Sermons preached at the Hon. Mr. Bayle's Lectures* (London, 1713). BHL used the Edinburgh edition of 1773. The citation from Aristotle is from *Historia Animalium*, or *Inquiry into Animals*.

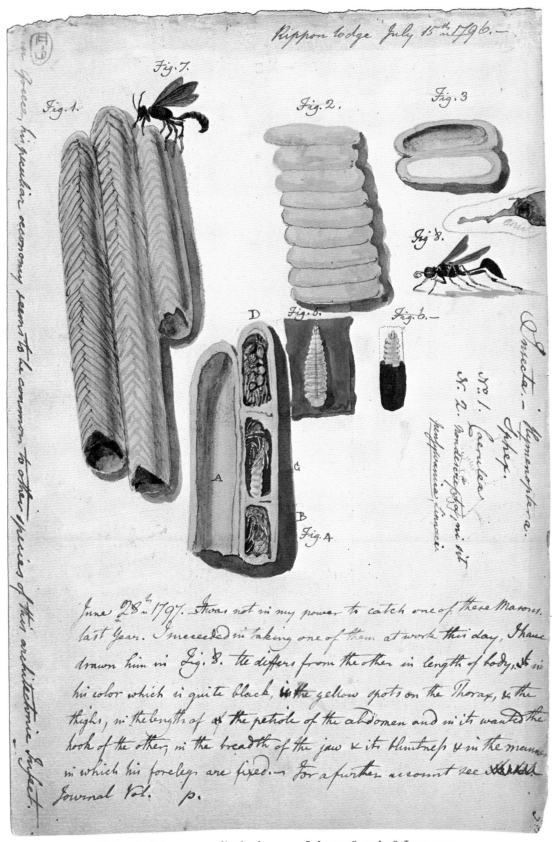

Fig. 7.

Fig. 1.

Fig. 2.

Fig. 3.

Fig. 8.

D Fig. 5. Fig. 6.—

A G

B Fig. 4.

Insecta.— Hymenoptera.
Sphex.
No 1. Caerulea
No 2. Panctica?, or or
hymenium Linnæi.

Green, his peculiar economy seem to be common to other species of this architectonic subject.—

June 28th 1797. It was not in my power to catch one of these Masons last Year. I succeeded in taking one of them at work this day, I have drawn him in Fig. 8. He differs from the other in length of body, & in his color which is quite black, in the yellow spots on the Thorax, & the thighs, in the length of of the petiole of the abdomen and in its wanting the hook of the other; in the breadth of the jaw & its bluntness & in the manner in which his forelegs are fixed.— For a further account see ~~XXXXX~~ Journal Vol.   p.

Plate 16. Masons, or dirtdaubers, 15 July 1796 and 28 June 1797.

FROM THE SKETCHBOOKS

This View shows the Coast of Maryland on the NE side of the Potowmack. Occoquan bay lies between the two Points above *A* and *B* and extends beyond *A* as far as the Occoquan at Colchester. Neabsco creek enters the Potowmack at the Bottom of the bay winding its way through a great extent of Marshy ground to Mr. Tayloe's iron works. The point over *B* is called freestone point. The Ground on the Virginia side of the Potowmack is broken into bold abrupt hills. Rippon lodge is built upon a very magnificent natural level terras, extending in the direction of the large trees in the foreground about ¼ of a mile. The Potowmac flows from the left to the right, and is in this spot about 2½ miles over. Alexandria lies about 22 Miles higher up.

Plate 17. View from the porch of Rippon Lodge, 11 July 1796.

View of Mount Vernon looking to the North. July 17ᵗ 1796. The portico faces to the East.

Plate 18. View of Mount Vernon looking to the north (the portico faces to the east), 17 July 1796.

FROM THE SKETCHBOOKS

This View was taken from under one of the Locust trees extending from the House to the North. The Potowmack takes a short turn round the point over *A* and proceeds to Alexandria and the Foederal City. This turn may be understood by consulting the Map to Jefferson's *Notes* [*on the State of Virginia*], or any good Map of Virginia. From *A* to *B* is the Mouth of the Piskattaway river which appears from Mount Vernon to be a continuation of the Pottowmac, but it extends only a short distance up the country, losing itself behind a bold Headland over *B*. The open Ground on the left is a farm belonging to General Washington containing about 1,300 Acres of cleared Land.

The point *A* is three Miles from Mount Vernon. The river is here about 1½ Miles across.

Plate 19. View to the north from the lawn of Mount Vernon, 17 July 1796.

Plate 20. President Washington and his family on the portico of Mount Vernon.

built 1640.

79

Plate 21. View of "Greenspring," home of William Ludwell Lee.

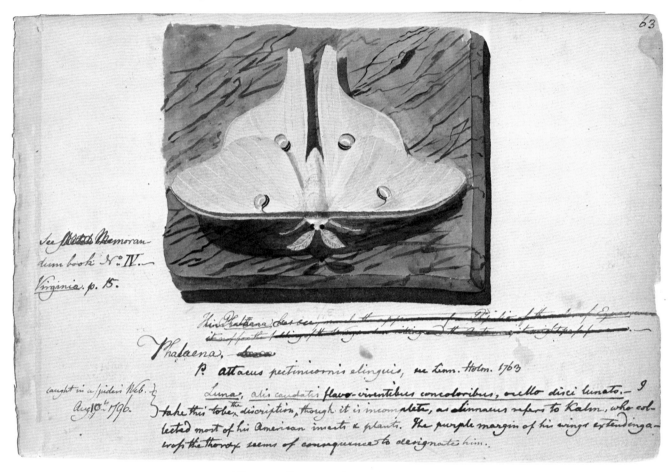

See Abbots Memorandum book No. IV.—
Virginia. p. 15.

caught in a spider's Web.
Aug. 10th 1796.

His Phalaena ~~has been~~ ~~and the appearance~~ ~~Wilio of the~~ ~~Sphinx~~
~~it and for the folding of the wings when sitting. In the Autumn it caught itself.~~

Phalaena. ~~Luna~~

P: *attacus pectinicornis elinguis*, see Linn. Holm. 1763

Luna, alis caudatis flavo-virentibus concoloribus, ocello disci lunato.— I
take this to be the discription, though it is incomplete, as Linnaeus refers to Kalm, who collected most of his American insects & plants. The purple margin of his wings extending a-
cross the thorax seems of consequence to designate him.

Plate 22. Luna moth, 10 August 1796.

of Stone of a good but coarse grit in the style of the Country Gentlemen's houses in England of 50 Years ago. It is a tolerably good house but the taste is indifferent.

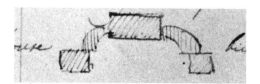

At two the next morning the Stage proceeded. We crossed the Rappahanoc at the upper ferry to a small town on the other side called Falmouth. This town was almost entirely burnt some months ago. The country assumes an aspect more and more bold the nearer you approach the Potowmack. We arrived at Dumfries about 11 o'clock. Dumfries is a small town near the head of *Quantico* bay. The river *Quantico* brings small vessels from thence to the town. Four miles further is Rippon Lodge on the top of a very bold promontory extending to Occoquan bay, a bay formed by many Creeks and Rivers running into the Potowmack between the Occoquan and Neabsco[28] distant four miles from one another. The Neabsco is a small Creek on which Mr. Tayloe's* iron works are situated, the Occoquan is more considerable. The bay as seen from Rippon lodge is accurately drawn in [the] Sketch book [PLATE 17].

Rippon lodge was built by the Father of Colonel Blackburn a Yorkshire Gentleman of Rippon.[29] The buildings are of Timber, and whimsically enough consist of two Houses built opposite to one another. [See FIG. 24.]

On Sunday the 16th of July, I set off on horseback for Mount Vernon, having a letter to the President from his Nephew my particular friend Bushrod Washington Esq. I travelled through a bold broken country to Colchester. Colchester lies on the North Side of the river Occoquan over which there is a ferry. The river is filled chiefly by the back Water of the Potowmac. At the ferry it is 105 Yards wide but extends (nearly the same width) only 2 Miles up the country where it dwindles into a Rivulet. The town is small and scattered. The river is shallow and the convenience for trade not considerable.[30] I breakfasted with Mr. Thomas Mason.* From Colchester to

28. Neabsco Creek flows southeasterly through Prince William County into the Potomac River. It runs roughly parallel to and between Occoquan River and Powell Run.

29. Richard Blackburn (c. 1703–55) emigrated from England in 1725 and built Rippon Lodge shortly after his arrival in America. The home was named after the cathedral town of Rippon (now Ripon) in Yorkshire, Blackburn's native county. Richard Blackburn Black, "Rippon Lodge," *Historical Society of Fairfax County, Virginia Inc.* 9 (1964–65): 23, 29.

30. Colchester was established by the Virginia Assembly in 1753 on Peter Wagener's land on the Occoquan River in Fairfax County. For years after its establishment, Colchester flourished due to its location on the important King's Highway leading to Occoquan ferry. By 1790 it had declined while rival Alexandria thrived twenty-five miles away. Mrs. Robert V. H. Duncan, " 'Fairfax Arms' and 'Colchester,' " *Historical Society of Fairfax County, Virginia Inc.* 9 (1964–65): 21–22.

Fig. 24. "Rippon Lodge," home of Thomas Blackburn, 13 July 1796.

This View explains the situation from whence the former [PLATE 17] was taken. The house on the left hand must have been built near 100 Years ago, as the oldest people now living do not remember to have heard when and by whom it was built. The family make use of both the houses, neither of them being sufficiently commodious of itself. It seems to have been the intention of Coln. Blackburn to have united them by a large Room between the two.

Mount Vernon the road lies through extensive woods. The distance is about ten miles. About 2½ Miles from the President's house is a Mill belonging to him on a Canal brought from the river Dogue.[31] Its neatness is an indication of the attention of the owner to his private concerns. The farm of the President extends from the Mill to his house. Good fences, clear grounds and extensive cultivation strike the eye as

31. Dogue Run flows south in Fairfax County through Mount Vernon estate and empties into the Potomac River.

162

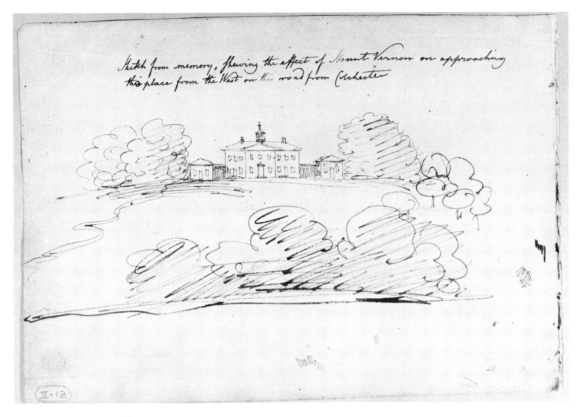

Sketch from memory, shewing the effect of Mount Vernon on approaching this place from the West on the road from Colchester

Fig. 25.   Mount Vernon seen from the west, sketched from memory.

something uncommon in this part of the World but the road is bad enough. The house becomes visible between two Groves of trees at about a miles distance. It has no very striking appearance, though superior to every other house I have seen here. The approach is not very well managed but leads you into the area between the Stables. The general plan of the building is as at Mr. Man Pages at Mansfield near Fredericsburg, of the old School. It is a wooden building, painted to represent champhered rustic and sanded. The center is an old house to which a good dining room has been added at the North end, and a study &c. &c., at the South. The House is connected with the Kitchen offices by arcades. The whole of this part of the building is in a very indifferent taste. Along the other front is a portico supported by 8 square pillars, of good proportions and effect. [See FIG. 26 and PLATE 18.] There is a handsome statuary marble chimney piece in the dining room (of the taste of Sir Wm. Chambers), with insulated columns on each side.[32] This is the only piece of expensive decoration

32. Sir William Chambers (1726–96), English architect, studied in China and Italy and later exhibited his taste for both classical and Chinese architecture in the Kew Gardens. He taught architectural drawing to the Prince of Wales, later George III, and received the position of comptroller of his majesty's works. Perhaps his best known building was Somerset House, which has been described as "the greatest architectural work of the reign of George III." *DNB.*

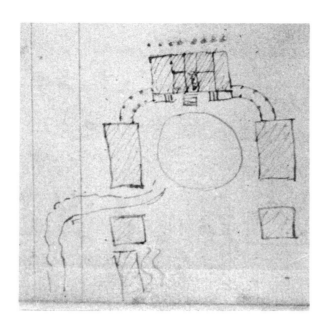

Fig. 26. View of Mount Vernon looking toward the southwest, 17 July 1796.

I have seen about the house, and is indeed *remarkable* in that respect. Every thing else is extremely good and neat, but by no means above what would be expected in a plain English Country Gentleman's house of £500 or £600 a Year. It is however a little above what I have hitherto seen in Virginia. The ground on the West front of the house is laid out in a level lawn bounded on each side with a wide but extremely formal serpentine walk, shaded by weeping Willows, a tree which in this country grows very well upon high dry land. On one side of this lawn is a plain Kitchen garden, on the other a neat flower garden laid out in squares, and boxed with great preccision. Along the North Wall of this Garden is a plain Greenhouse. The Plants were arranged in front, and contained nothing very rare, nor were they numerous. For the first time again since I left Germany, I saw here a parterre, chipped and trimmed with infinite care into the form of a richly flourished Fleur de Lis: The expiring groans I hope of our Grandfather's pedantry.

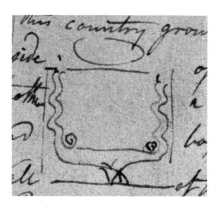

Towards the East Nature has lavished magnificence, nor has Art interfered but to exhibit her to advantage. Before the portico a lawn extends on each hand from the front of the house and of a Grove of Locust trees on each side, to the edge of the bank. Down the steep slope trees and shrubs are thickly planted. They are kept so low as not to interrupt the view but merely to furnish an agreeable border to the extensive prospect beyond. The mighty *Potowmac* runs close under this bank the elevation of which must be perhaps 250 feet. The river is here about 1½ miles across and runs parrallel with the front of the house for about 3 miles to the left and 4 to the right. To the left it takes a sudden turn round a point, and disappears, proceeding to Alexandria and the Foederal City, but the sheet of Water is continued in the Piskattaway which appears at first sight to be the Potowmac, being of the same width. The Piscattaway is in sight to the distance of eight or nine miles and then vanishes at the back of a bold woody headland. This river continues about 15 Miles up the Country a bold Stream, being filled by the back Water of the Potowmac. It is however shallow and at present no object of commercial advantage. An extent of 1500 acres perfectly clear of wood, which borders the river on the left bank on the Virginia side boldly contrasts the remainder of the Woody landscape. It is a farm belonging to the President. The general surface is level, but elevated above all inundations. Beyond this Sheet of verdure the country rises into bold woody hills, sometimes enriched by open plantations, which mount gently above one another till they vanish into the purple distance of the highest ridge 20 miles distant. The Maryland shore has the same character. Opposite to the house, where its detail becomes more distinct it is variegated by lawns and copses. [See PLATE 19.]

After running about 4 Miles to the right, the river turns suddenly to the Eastward but is seen over a range of lowland for a considerable distance. A woody peninsula running to a point backs the silver line of the water, and the blue hills of Maryland just appear above the edge of the trees, beyond the next bend. [See FIG. 26.]

What are descriptions of the Face of Nature good for? They convey just as much an idea of the scene as the description of the features of a Lady does, of her face. The pen and the dictionary of Mrs. Ratcliff has done little more than to tire her reader by setting him to paint imaginary scenes of Landscape that interrupt the story. Descriptions of buildings are more successful in general, and I think she is particularly so in them, though I once endeavored to plan the Castle of Udolpho from her account of it and found it impossible.[33]

Having alighted, I sent in my letter of introduction, and walked into the portico next to the river. In about 10 Minutes, the President came to me. He was dressed in a plain blue coat, his hair dressed and powdered. There was a reserve but no hauteur in his manner. He shook me by the hand said he was glad to see a friend of his Nephew, drew a chair and desired me to sit down. Having enquired after the family I had left, the conversation turned upon Bath to which they were going.[34] He said he had known the place when there was scarce a house upon it fit to sleep in. That the accommodations were he believed very good at present. He thought the best thing a family regularly visiting Bath could do, would be to build a house for their separate accomodation, the expence of which might be 200 Pounds. He has himself a house there, which he supposes must be going to ruin. Independent of his public situation the encreased dissipation and frequency of visitors would be an objection to his visiting it again, unless the health of himself or family should render it necessary. At first *that* was the motive, he said, that induced people to encounter the badness of the roads and the inconvenience of the lodgings, but at present few, he believed, in comparison of the whole number, had health in view. Even those whose object it

33. Ann Radcliffe, *The Mysteries of Udolpho: A Romance; interspersed with some pieces of poetry,* 4 vols. (London, 1794). See p. 153 and n. 19.

34. Bath (now Berkeley Springs), a resort village in Berkeley (now Morgan) County, W. Va., near the Potomac River ninety-three miles northwest of Washington, was famous for its reputedly medicinal waters. It attracted visitors from Pennsylvania and Maryland as well as from Virginia. *Martin's Gazetteer.*

was, were interrupted in their quiet by the dissipation of the rest. This, he observed, must naturally be the case in every large collection of men, whose minds were not occupied by any pressing business or personal interest. In these and many more observations of the same kind, there was no moroseness, nor any thing that appeared as if the rapidly encreasing immorality of the citizens particularly impressed him at the time he made them. They seemed the well expressed remarks of a man who has seen and knows the world.

The conversation then turned upon the rivers of Virginia; he gave me a very minute account of all their directions, their natural advantages, and what he conceived might be done for their improvement by Art. He then enquired whether I had seen the Dismal Swamp and seemed particularly desirous of being informed upon the subject of the Canal going forward there. He gave me a detailed account of the old dismal Swamp [Land] Company and of their operations, of the injury they had received by the effects of the war, and the still greater, which their inattention to their own concerns had done them. After many attempts on his part to procure a meeting of Directors (the number of which the law provided should be *Six* in order to do business), all of which proved fruitless, he gave up all further hopes of any thing effectual being done for their interests, and sold out his shares in the Proprietary at a price very inadequate to their real value. Since then his attention had been so much drawn to public affairs, as scarcely to have made any enquiry into the proceedings either of the Swamp or of the Canal Company.[35] I was much flattered by his attention to my observations, and his taking the pains either to object to my deductions where he thought them illfounded, or to confirm them by very strong remarks of his own, made while he was in the habit of visiting the Swamp.

This conversation lasted above an hour, and as he had at first told me that he was endeavoring to finish some letters to go by the Post upon a variety of business *"which notwithstanding his distance from the Seat of Government still pressed upon him in his retirement:"* I got up to take my leave but he desired me in a manner very like *Dr.* [Samuel] *Johnson's* to *"keep my chair,"* and then continued to talk to me about the great works going forward in England, and my own objects in this country. I found him well acquainted with my mothers family in Pensylvania.[36] After much conversation upon the Coalmines on James river I told him of the Silver mine at Rocketts.[37] He laughed most heartily upon the very mention of the thing. I explained to him the nature of the expectations formed of its productiveness and satisfied him of the probability that

35. The Dismal Swamp Land Company was organized in 1763 to drain and develop 40,000 acres of Virginia's Dismal Swamp. For the Canal Company, see p. 238, n. 54.
36. For the Antes family, see p. xxx, n. 36.
37. Rockett's Landing, on the north bank of the James, below Richmond.

ore did exist there in considerable Quantity. He made several very minute enquiries concerning it and then said, that; *"it would give him real uneasiness should any silver or gold mine be discovered that would tempt considerable capitals into the prosecution of that object, and that he heartily wished for his country that it might contain no mines 'but such as the plough could reach,' excepting only coal and iron."*

After conversing with me more than two hours he got up and said that *"we should meet again at dinner."* I then strolled about the lawn and took the views. [See FIG. 26 and PLATE 19.] Upon my return to the house, I found Mrs. Washington and her grand-daughter Miss Custis* in the hall. I introduced myself to Mrs. Washington as a friend of her Nephew, and she immediately entered into conversation upon the prospect from the Lawn and presently gave me an account of her family in a good humoured free manner that was extremely pleasant and flattering. She retains strong remains of considerable beauty, seems to enjoy very good health and to have as good humour. She has no affectation of superiority in the slightest degree, but acts compleatly in the character of the Mistress of the house of a respectable and opulent country gentleman. Her granddaughter Miss Eleanor Custis (the only one of four who is un-married) has more perfection of form of expression, of color, of softness, and of firm-

Fig. 27. Sketch of a group for a drawing of Mount Vernon. "Nelly" Custis, servant, Martha Washington, and an unidentified youth.

ness of mind than I have ever seen before, or conceived consistent with mortality. She is every thing that the chissel of Phidias aimed at, but could not reach; and the soul beaming through her countenance, and glowing in her smile, is as superior to her face, as mind is to matter.

Young la Fayette with his tutor[38] came down sometime before dinner. He is a

38. George Washington G. G. Motier Lafayette was the son of the Marquis de Lafayette. His tutor was Felix Frestal, an elderly Frenchman. James T. Flexner, *George Washington: Anguish and Farewell (1793–1799)* (Boston: Little, Brown and Company, 1972), p. 261.

young man about 17 of a mild pleasant countenance, favorably impressing at first sight. His figure is rather awkward. His manners are easy and he has very little of the usual french air about him. He talked much, especially with Miss Custis and seemed to possess wit, and fluency. He spoke English tolerably well, much better indeed than his tutor who has had the same time and opportunities of improvement.

Dinner was served up about 1/2 after three. It had been postponed about 1/2 an hour in hopes of Mr. Lear's arrival from Alexandria.[39] The President came into the portico about 1/2 an hour before 3 and talked freely upon common topics with the family. [See PLATE 20.] At dinner he placed me at the left hand of Mrs. Washington; Miss Custis sat at her right and himself next to her about the middle of the table. There was very little conversation at dinner. A few jokes passed between the President and young la Fayette, whom he treats more as his Child than as a Guest. I felt a little embarrassed at the silent reserved air that prevailed. As I drink no wine and the President drank only 3 glasses the party soon returned to the Portico. Mr. Lear, Mr. Dandridge* and Mr. Lear's 3 boys soon after arrived and helped out the conversation. The President retired in about 3/4 of an hour.

As much as I wished to stay, I thought it a point of delicacy to take up as little of the

Fig. 28. Outlines of a group for another drawing of Mount Vernon.

time of the president as possible, and I therefore requested Mrs. Washington's permission to order my horses. She expressed a slight wish that I would stay, but I did not

39. Tobias Lear (1762–1816) was Washington's private secretary from 1785 until 1793. After his first wife died, he married twice more, both times to nieces of Martha Washington. In 1794 he settled in Alexandria, near Mount Vernon, and was elected president of the Potomac Company the following year. He began his diplomatic career in 1801 when Jefferson appointed him consul and general commercial agent at Santo Domingo. He was appointed consul general at Algiers in 1803 and in 1805 signed the Treaty of Tripoli. Forced to leave his post in 1812 by the Dey of Algiers, he returned to Washington to work as an accountant in the War Department. He committed suicide in 1816. *Senate Executive Journal*, pp. 401, 405, 453, 455; *DAB*.

think it sufficiently strong *in etiquette* to detain me, and the horses came to the door. I waited a few minutes till the President returned. He asked me whether I had any very pressing business to prevent my lengthening my visit. I told him I had not, but that, as I considered it as an intrusion upon his more important engagements, I thought I could reach Colchester that evening by daylight. "Sir," said he, "you see I take my own way. If you can be content to take yours at my house, I shall be glad to see you here longer."

Coffee was brought, about 6 o'clock. When it was removed the president addressing himself to me enquired after the state of the Crops about Richmond. I told him all I had heard. A long conversation upon farming ensued, during which it grew dark, and he then proposed going into the hall. He made me sit down by him and continued the conversation for above an hour. During that time he gave me a very minute account of the Hessian fly[40] and its progress from long Island where it first appeared through New York Rhode Island, Connecticut, Delaware, part of Pensylvania and Maryland. It has not yet appeared in Virginia, but is daily dreaded. The cultivation of Indian corn next came up. He dwelt upon all the advantages attending this most usefull crop, and then said that the manner in which the land was exhausted by it, the constant attendance it required during the whole year, and the superior value of the produce of land in other crops would induce him to leave off entirely the cultivation of it, provided he could depend upon any market for a Supply elsewhere. As food for the Negroes it was his opinion that it was infinitely preferable to Wheat bread in point of Nourishment. He had made the experiment upon his own Lands and had found that though the Negroes, while the Novelty lasted, seemed to prefer Wheat bread as being the food of their Masters, they soon grew tired of it. He conceived that should the negroes be fed upon Wheat or Rye bread, they would, in order to be fit for the same labor, be obliged to have a considerable addition to their allowance of Meat. But notwithstanding all this he thought the balance of advantage to be against the Indian corn.

He then entered into the different merits of a variety of ploughs which he had tried and gave the preference to the heavy Rotheram plough from a full experience of its merits. The Berkshire iron plough he held next in estimation. He had found it impossible to get the iron work of his Rotheram plough replaced in a proper manner otherwise he should never have discontinued its use. I promised to send him one of Mr. [Gilbert] Richardson's ploughs of Tuckahoe, which he accepted with pleasure.[41]

40. A small mosquito-like gall gnat, *Mayetiola destructor* Say, the larva of which is very destructive to wheat. There is disagreement among experts as to whether the Hessian troops introduced it to America during the Revolution.
41. BHL wrote to Washington on 22 August 1796 to inform the president that "the plough which you did

Mrs. Washington and Miss Custis had retired early and the President left the company about 8 o'clock. We soon after retired to bed. There was no hint of Supper.

I rose with the Sun, and walked in the grounds near the house. I also took the view [see PLATE 18]. The president came to the company in the sitting room about 1/2 hour past 7 where all the latest Newspapers were laid out. He talked with Mr. Lear about the progress of the Works at the great falls[42] and in the City of Washington. Breakfast was served up in the usual Virginian style. Tea, Coffee, and cold and broiled Meat. It was very soon over, and for an hour afterwards he stood upon the steps of the West door talking to the Company who were collected round him. The subject was chiefly the establishment of the University at the Foederal City. He mentioned the offer he had made of giving to it all the interests he had in the City on condition that it should go on in a given time, and complained that though magnificent Offers had been made by many Speculators for the same purpose there seemed to be no inclination to carry them into reality. He spoke as if he felt a little hurt upon the Subject.[43] About 10 o'clock he made a motion to retire and I requested a servant to bring my horses to the door. He then returned and as soon as my Servant came up with them he went to him, and asked him if he had breakfasted. He then shook me by the hand desired me to call if I came again into the Neighbourhood, and wished me a good morning.

When my youngest Brother [John Frederick Latrobe] was about six years old he went with the family to see the king of England go through St. James's park in State to the House of Lords. Upon being told that he rode in such and such a carriage, he would scarcely believe that the person he saw could be the king; and being assured that he really was so, he cried out: "*Good lord, papa, how like a man he looks.*" The Sentiment

me the favor to say you would try is now ready, and I shall send it . . . by the first vessel that is bound from hence [Richmond] to" Alexandria. Apparently Washington never received the plow. George Washington Papers, Library of Congress; Hamlin, *Latrobe*, p. 285.

42. Maryland and Virginia chartered the "Potowmack Company" in 1785 to improve Potomac River navigation. George Washington was chosen first president of the company and work began on a canal to bypass the Great Falls. The canal was completed in 1802, three years after Washington's death. Alexander Crosby Brown, "America's Greatest Eighteenth Century Engineering Achievement," *Virginia Cavalcade* 12 (Spring 1963): 42, 46.

43. Both Washington and BHL were interested in the establishment of a national university. Some time before 1795 Washington drew up a will in which he left fifty shares in the Potomac Canal Company and one hundred in the James River Canal Company to be applied toward the endowment of a national university. In his Eighth Annual Address, delivered five months after BHL's visit to Mount Vernon, Washington vainly urged Congress to establish such a university. BHL's interest in the idea continued throughout his career. In 1816 he drew up plans for a university to be located at the west end of the Mall, south of the President's house, which he submitted to a committee of the House of Representatives considering the matter. The university was never built. James T. Flexner, *George Washington: Anguish and Farewell (1793–1799)* (Boston: Little, Brown and Company, 1972), pp. 199–200; *PBHL, microfiche ed.,* 266/A3.

expressed by the boy, is, I believe, *felt* by every man who sees for the first time a man raised by merit or reputation above the common level of his fellow creatures. It was impressed upon me, upon seeing one of the greatest men that Nature ever produced, but in a less degree than even when I saw that least-like-a-man-looking-king Frederic the Second of Prussia. Washington has something uncommonly majestic and commanding in his walk, his address, his figure and his countenance. His face is characterized however more by intense and powerful thought, than by quick and fiery conception. There is a mildness about its expression; and an air of reserve in his manner lowers its tone still more. He is 64, but appears some years younger, and has sufficient apparent vigor to last many years yet. He was frequently entirely silent for many minutes during which time an awkwardness seemed to prevail in every one present. His answers were often short and sometimes approached to moroseness. He did not at any time speak with very remarkable fluency:—perhaps the extreme correctness of his language which almost seemed studied prevented that effect. He seemed to enjoy a humourous observation, and made several himself. He laughed heartily several times and in a very good humoured manner. On the morning of my departure he treated me as if I had lived for years in his house; with ease and attention, but in general I thought there was a slight air of moroseness about him, as if something had vexed him.

For Washington, had Horace lived at the present age he would have written his celebrated ode: it is impossible to have ever read it and not to recollect in the presence of this great Man the *Virum justum, propositique, tenacem, &c. &c.*[44]

I returned by the same route that had brought me to Mount Vernon. Near the spot at which the roads to Alexandria and Mount Vernon separate, lives an old man of the age of 85 by his own account. He was born in Yorkshire. His name is Boggis I think. He is tall, rather thin, and rawboned, but perfectly hearty and strong. What is remarkable in him is, that he has for many years past lived upon nothing but *tea*. He drinks his tea three times a day, consuming in it a pound of sugar daily, and a great quantity of the richest cream. A pound of tea lasts him a week. He buys the best he can procure, and makes it pretty strong. It is very remarkable that, *in re venerea ne satyris quidem fabulosis cedit; virtutemque, omnium puellarum pauperum, quae habitationi ejus sunt vicinae, in periculum ducit, largitionibus pecuniae, verbisque, blandulis. Nec in re ipsa perficienda ullus est aut vigoris, aut abundantiae seminis defectus.*[45] My authority for this fact is Captain Huie who has seen and well knows the man.

---

44. Trans.: The man (who is) just and firm in purpose.　　The source is Horace, *Odes*, Book III, 3.1, where the text is *Justum et tenacem propositi virum*.

45. Trans.: In matters of sex he does not yield first place even to the satyrs in the fables; and he endangers

The ferryman at Occoquan ferry, is one of the uncommon productions called *Albinos*. He is one of several who are children of Man and Woman, Negroes brought from Africa, called here Salt water Negroes. I could not get an exact account of his family from him, he appeared ashamed of the Trick dame Nature had played him. He has the exact features of a perfect Black, flat Nose and thick lips and is very ugly. His skin both of his face and body is uncommonly fair and white. His cheeks and neck which is extremely thick are very red and pimpled as if he were a hard drinker. His hair or rather wool is yellow. His eyebrows are white with a yellowish cast, his eyelashes which are very long and almost choak his eyes, are almost white. His eyes are reddish grey. He wore his hat and twinkled as if they were weak, but upon my asking him the question he told me *"he had as good eyes as anybody else."* I suppose he is much pestered with enquiries, and illnatured jokes upon his colour; for he seemed very pettish upon the subject. If his eyes are good he is an exception to Jefferson's general remark in his notes.[46]

FREDERICSBERG, JULY 22D, 1796. Upon my return from Mount Vernon to Rippon lodge the weather became extremely wet and did much injury to the hay much of which is still out, and to the Oats which are cut. It rained violently on Monday night with some very dreadfull claps of Thunder. Tuesday morning, the 19th it was tolerably fair and I went to Dumfries. In the night it rained again violently, and the Roads were extremely slippery and deep. I was disappointed in getting to Fredericsberg by the Stage. I spent Wednesday with Captain Huie and took a transient view of the Creek and Marsh an application having been made to me respecting the improvement of the Navigation of the Place.[47] It rained dreadfully all Wednesday night. On Thursday morning I got onto the Stage.

The *Neabsco* runs under the hill upon which Rippon lodge is built. A range of hills separate that valley from the next in which is *Powell's* run.[48] Dumfries is watered by the *Quantico*. About 5 Miles from Dumfries flows the *Choppo-whamsick*.[49] It was very

---

the virtue of all the poorer girls who live near his house by gifts of money and caressing words. Nor in the accomplishment of the act itself is there any lack either of vigor or of abundance of semen.

46. Jefferson, *Notes on Virginia*, pp. 70–71.

47. The state legislature passed "An Act for opening and improving the navigation of Quantico Creek, in the county of Prince William" on 5 December 1795, authorizing the incorporation of the Quantico Company. BHL's assistance in improving the creek's navigation was never required, however, for the Quantico Company, like most of the river improvement companies authorized by the legislature in the late eighteenth century, never materialized. Shepherd, *Statutes*, 1:394; Joseph Hobson Harrison, "The Internal Improvements Issue in the Politics of the Union 1783–1824" (Ph.D. dissertation, University of Virginia, 1954), p. 98.

48. Powell's Run flows southeasterly through Prince William County and into the Potomac River at Brushy Point. It runs roughly parallel to and between the Neabsco River and Quantico Creek.

49. Chopawamsic Creek, a small creek dividing Prince William and Stafford counties, flows into the Potomac River south of Quantico Creek and north of Aquia Creek.

full and we were obliged to build a bridge of fence Rails over a gulley to enable the Stage to pass. About 5 Miles further runs the *Aquia*.[50] As the ford in the shortest road was supposed impassible we drove a Mile round to the lower ford where is a small Village collected round the Tobacco Warehouses, for there is an inspection at this place. The Water was very deep and rapid, and as a French-Man had been drowned at this place sometime before who was a Passenger in the Stage we were particularly careful to try the ford by riding one of the horses through. We found we could safely pass. The Frenchman had been drowned in attempting to swim across. The Stage, however was at that time floated 1/4 of a Mile down the Stream. We afterwards crossed Olston run[51] and arrived at Stafford court house[52] to dinner. We paid a dollar for very scanty and bad fare. About 2 Miles from the Ct. House is the Ackickeek.[53] Five Miles from Stafford court house and 7 from Fredericsberg is the Potowmac Creek, a bold stream. All their waters discharge themselves into the Potowmac.

FREDERICSBURG, JULY 23D, 1796. While I was at Rippon lodge, I went to Mr. Tayloe's furnace at Neabsco. It is not a work of any very considerable Magnitude. Eight Hands by day and 8 by night are employed in it. It labours under this very great disadvantage, that all the Ore smelted in it is brought by Water from the Eastern shore of Maryland, to the Mouth of Occoquan bay and then carried by Waggons 2 Miles to the Furnace over very wretched roads.[54] It is in blast only every third year. The woods which furnish Charcoal, already begin to feel a deficiency, although some thousand acres are appropriated to the Supply. The Valley in which the Furnace is situated, as well as the Country around in general abounds in Slate. It is not worked though so near to the Foederal City and apparently of such good quality. It is singular that all the lamina stand vertically. I have not met with one instance to the contrary.

---

50. Runs southeast through Stafford County and empties into the Potomac River. Admitting tides from the Potomac, it was navigable by schooner for several miles. The town of Aquia is on the creek at the head of tidewater, and the area was the source of the Aquia freestone used for much of the early building in Washington, D.C., including the U.S. Capitol. *Martin's Gazetteer*.

51. This is probably Austin Run, which flows east below and eventually into Aquia Creek.

52. Small village and county seat of Stafford County located seventy-six miles northeast of Richmond and forty-six miles southwest of Washington.

53. Accokeek Creek, one of the three sizable creeks in Stafford County which admit tides from the Potomac River, flows southwest into Potomac Creek shortly before that stream enters the Potomac River.

54. John Tayloe's (1771–1828) iron furnace was established by his grandfather about 1738 and remained in the family for several generations, though partnerships were formed at times with John Ballendine, Presley Thornton, and John Semple. From its beginning, the furnace was supplied with Maryland ore. The first Tayloe had applied to the Virginia Council for a permit to import iron ore from Maryland duty free. The permit was renewed in 1757 and the furnace still used Maryland ore when BHL visited it in 1796. Kathleen Bruce, *Virginia Iron Manufacture in the Slave Era* (New York: Augustus M. Kelley, 1968/1930), pp. 16–18.

No Country that I ever saw has so much the appearances of having received its present form from the operation of Water [as] this part of the World. All the summits of hills are regularly covered with Pebbles for some way down. From the Summits of the hills many Vallies, narrow and steep, descend, bearing the exact resemblance of the Gullies formed in miniature in the Soft earth by heavy rains. These steep and narrow vallies are very remarkable at Rippon lodge. They descend from the terrace on which the house is built towards the Neabsco to the number of 6 or 7, the hills dividing them are not a yard wide at the ridge, in many places, and the sides are so steep as to render it difficult to walk down them. I dare to say many of them are from 100 to 200 feet deep at the Mouth.

FREDERICSBURG, JULY 24TH, 1796. I have been to take a view of the Falls of the Rappahanoc, in company with Captn. Gray of Culpepper. The River tumbles over a ridge of Granite of a much softer and more laminous texture than that at Richmond or Petersburg. It resembles I think exactly the rock higher up upon the Appomattox which crossed the river at Jeneto and extends through the county of Amelia. The greatest, or most sudden fall is between Mr. Thornton's* Mill and Tide Water. The difference of level is in about 3 Furlongs 22 Feet. Above the Mill a large Island extends near a Mile, belonging to Dr. Mortimer of Fredericsburg. There is no sudden fall on either side of the Island but the river is every where interrupted by single rocks or ledges.

We could not proceed with ease higher than the point of the Island. We stopped there and turned our attention to a nest of the bald face hornet, which was suspended from a twig, and observed the bustle of business that appeared at its orifice. Mr. Thornton the proprietor of the Land on this side of the river, from Tide water a considerable way up the falls, had joined us at his Mill. Having sufficiently gratified our curiosity keeping at a respectfull distance for fear of being stung, we went with Mr. Thornton to his house, a solid but ill contrived brick building; situate at the top of a high hill which commands a most extensive view of the towns of Fredericsburg and Falmouth and of the Valley of the Rappahanoc for many miles down its course. A shower detained us about 1/2 an hour. We then rode to the Allum Springs. About 1 1/4 of a Mile to the West of the river runs a range of hills the basis of which is a calcareous free stone of a good though rather coarse grit. The directions of this hill is NNE and SSW nearly. Their tops are covered with pebbles. The Alum spring runs from under the edge of this rock, where it runs up to Day in an Eastern Direction. A stream, upon which a good Merchant-Mill belonging to Mr. Lewis is built, runs below. The Edge of the rock is covered with Chrystalls of Alum. The spring forms a jet of about an inch diameter. The Situation is beautifully romantic.

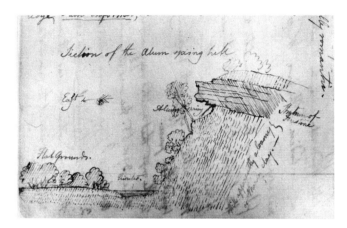

The Edge of the Rock contains a great quantity of Pebbles such as compose the tops of the hills and the beds of the Rivers. They seem to be siliceous in general, but many are pieces of Granite such as it exists in the falls. Great quantities of petrified roots are mixed with the pebbles, and still more holes and hollows impressed with the fibres of wood and the knots of roots and branches. The Rock itself, is full of holes which seem to have contained wood which has decayed and disappeared. To the East of this ledge, *I am informed*, there is no Freestone.

FREDERICSBERG JULY 24TH. *Wasps and Hornets belonging to the Linnaean Class of Hymenoptera, Sphex, Vespa, Apis.*

I believe all insects of this class have more or less ingenuity, from the Honey-and-Wax-making-bee, down to the little Wasp who persecutes the Caterpillars and deposites his eggs in their bodies.[55] 1.) The first Wasp I have observed in Virginia appeared as early as March. He was a long slender black fellow very busy, and I was told that his sting is very acute. He suspends his comb from cielings of outhouses and branches of trees, where I have found them with about a dozen hexagonal cells, and eggs, in the beginning of May. I have not observed them since.[56]

2.) The next that excited my attention was the Mason, see pages [157–60]. He was at work the beginning of June in Amelia and I suppose every where else in this state.

3.) A large *Humble-bee*-looking-insect at the same time attracted my notice.[57] He was at work in an orifice he had made in a piece of timber. I am told their passages are sometimes a foot or two long. Captain Murray told me he had often traced them to that length, but I have never had the means of examining either the insect or his work.

55. Various species of the Ichneumonidae parasitize caterpillars.
56. Our common colonial wasps are species of *Polistes*.
57. These insects, commonly called borers or carpenter bees, are species of *Xylocopa*.

4.) At Rippon lodge, some Wasps were at work in the Bench of the portico in the same manner. I could not get one of them, but I blew up part of their passages with Gunpowder. One of them was full of sawdust at the outer end. Further on seemed to be Chrsyalides which were mashed in being taken out.[58] I followed another for some inches, but it was empty. In appearance the insect resembled:

5.) *The Bald face Hornet.*[59] This dangerous fly is proverbially fierce. If he is disturbed he darts at the face of the intruder with great force and inflicts in a moment a sting, the pain and swelling of which is most extraordinary. He is not so large as the English Hornet, but much larger than a bee. He derives his name from the pale yellow colour of his face. His body is also spotted with straw color, and the two low folds of his Abdomen are jagged with yellow. His sting is black and very long, and thick. A yellow bag adheres to it when drawn. The females as well as Males are furnished with this Weapon, for one of them, whom I was examining, laid an Egg into my hand. Their Nest is strongly wrought into the leaves of a twig by which it is suspended from the branch of a tree. The external covering is composed of a number of their tough flakes resembling parchment, which turn the wet most compleatly. Near the bottom is a hole at which the hornets enter and depart; and the nest may be easily taken and destroyed by stopping this hole in the night with a cork. In the inside are different cakes of hexagonal cells. That which I saw had two. They were placed obliquely and the entrance hole was between them and served both cakes. The young hornets come to maturity successively: many of the cells were empty,

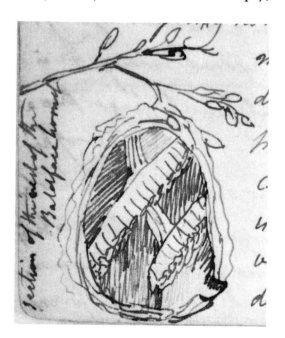

58. Evidently a different species of carpenter bee.
59. The white-faced hornet, *Vespa maculata* L.

having discharged the brood; others contained small, others large grubs; and others were closed and held a chrysallis. The grub is very similar to that of the Mason reversed, having a thick head and a slender tail. See [PLATE 16].

These Nests are sometimes found as big as a Bushel. That which I saw was about as big as the head of a boy of 10 Years old. The food of these furies is, Flies. One of them fell into my butter dish at breakfast with his prisoner. They follow their prey into houses, and are unpleasant visitors, but they do not sting unless provoked.

6.) In the side of a bank at Mr. Thornton's, a swarm of bees was supposed to exist. We went to the attack of them, but found the family very few in number, though there were a great many holes in it. They all escaped. In opening the holes, I found they continued a few inches into the bank perfectly cylindrical and smooth; in one or two was a white grub. I did not see any of the *Bees*, so called.[60]

7.) In searching for these *Bees* we discovered in a neighbouring stump a colony of *Scarlet* Wasps, longer and lanker than the Masons.[61] Their comb was suspended from a jag of the stump, and exactly similar to that of the common Wasp. It was full of bluish worms in different stages.

8.) The Yellow Jacket[62] I have not examined, but he appears to be, when on wing, very like the common English wasp, and, *I am informed*, burrows in the ground in the same manner.

The Bees, the black, the scarlet, and the Yellow Wasps, and the bald face hornet, feed their Grubs in the cells during their growth with *daily supplies*. In this they all differ from the Mason, who in every view, is, I think one of the most whimsical of God's works. The bees have something of his *forethought*, and their materials are more usefull to man, and better manufactured and they are therefore more noticed and admired. But the odd predilection of the mason for spiders, his separate provision for each grub, and his cruelty seem very eccentric instincts. The Spiders of Virginia may truly be said to fear the *blue* devils.

60. This was probably a group of individual nests of some species of mining bee.
61. This was evidently another species, or variety, of the colonial wasp, *Polistes*.
62. *Vespa diabolica* L.

4

Virginia, 3–26 August 1796

RICHMOND AUGST. 3D, 1796. I returned from Fredericsburg on the 24th of July in the Stage. The roads were much better though still muddy with the late very heavy rains which have been particularly so to the Southward.

On the 28th I went in the stage to Williamsburg, where I found horses that carried me to Mr. William Ludwell Lee's* house at Greenspring about 6 miles SW of the city. [See PLATE 21.] Greenspring is well known in the history of the American war having been the Scene of an action between part of the American army under General Waine [Anthony Wayne] and the British under Lord Cornwallis in which the Americans were defeated.[1] The British did no great damage to the building. They destroyed however a quantity of Tobacco which had been housed in a large br[*illegible*] barn, and having hauled out a boat which was also secured in the same place they set fire to it. The barn caught fire from the boat and the horse prevented the negroes from putting it out. This was all the injury done. The massive ruins of the barn remain a proof of the superior value of this plantation and former days when Jamestown was the Capital of Virginia. The principal part of Greenspring house was erected by Sir William Berkeley who was Governor of Virginia the latter end of the last Century.[2] (See Stith's and Beverley's history of Virginia.)[3] It is a brick building of great solidity, but no attempt at grandeur. The lower story was covered by an arcade which is falled down. The porch has some clumsy ornamental brickwork about it of the stile of James the 1st. The Estate descended to the present possessor by Maternal descent. He is just of age. He was born in England, but came out to Virginia very young. He seems activated by a spirit of improvement, and indeed the Estate wants it in every respect.

Greenspring lies about a mile in a strait line from James river. The ground is flat, but might be easily drained. All the watercourses are deep and run very freely and I judge that the lowest ground lies 10 or 15 feet above common tides in James river.

The wetness of the Season, and I may add the badness of the husbandry has much injured the Crop of Indian corn now growing upon the Estate. But where it has had a tolerable chance it is tall and vigorous, although the same land has been in perpetual cultivation since it was first cleared.

1. The Battle of Green Spring was fought on 6 July 1781.

2. Sir William Berkeley (1606–77), who served as governor from 1642 to 1652 and from 1660 to 1677, built the original house prior to 1649. Part of this building probably was incorporated into the second Green Spring mansion, completed about 1680, which BHL saw in 1796.

3. William Stith, *The History of the First Discovery and Settlement of Virginia: Being an Essay towards a General History of the Colony* (Williamsburg, 1747); Robert Beverley, *The History and Present State of Virginia, in Four Parts* (London, 1706).

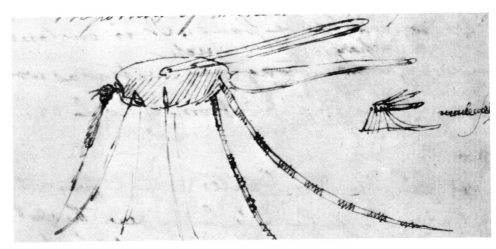

Proportion of the head to the body on a large scale.

The worst circumstance belonging to Greenspring is the swarm of Muskitoes and Gannippers[4] which at this season of the Year torment Men and horses day and night. They rendered my stay perfectly miserable. The Gannippers are about four times as large as a Muskitoe. They are similarly formed but their size exhibits the colors with which they are variegated distinctly. The head is most uncommonly minute compared with their bodies. The back is covered with down stripped with brown and white and their last pair of legs which are nearly an inch long, are alternately ringed with dark grey and white. Half way down their bill extends a brush. Its use I cannot guess, as it is raised, upon insertion of their bill.

The extensive woods upon the Greenspring estate still contain a very large quantity of deer and other wild animals. The vicinity of the two Noble Rivers York, and James river, does nothing towards the improvement of this neck of land. Fish, oysters and wild fowl are in such plenty that most of the proprietors seem content with what Judge Tyler termed his estate on York river in his advertisement, *an excellent* [*stand?*] *for good living*, without thinking of anything further. Poverty and decay seem indeed to have laid their withering hands upon every building public and private between Hampton and Shockoe creek at Richmond.

Greenspring derives its name from a very copious Spring of excellent water which bursts from a gentle knoll upon which the house stands. It is enclosed in a brick house and discharges about as much water as would run through a nine inch pipe from a level with its upper edge.

It is Mr. Lee's intention to pull down the present mansion and to erect a modest Gentleman's house near the spot. The antiquity of the old house, if in any case, ought to plead in the [project?], but its inconvenience and deformity are more powerful advocates for its destruction. In it the oldest inhabited house in North America will disappear for it was built in the Year 16[. .] . Many of the first Virginian assemblies

4. BHL was probably referring to gallinippers, another common name for the crane flies of the genus *Tipula*.

were held in the very room in which I was plotting the death of Muskitoes, and many of their deliberations were directed to the same end in respect of the Indians, and for the *same reason*—they were *weak* and *troublesome*.

On Sunday the 31st I rode over to a Church which was built near Jamestown for the accomodation of the neighboring plantations early after the first settlement. It is a plain brick building well fitted with pews, but in bad repair. The congregation consisted of only four Gentlemen, and half a dozen Negroes. The Bishop of this State Dr. Maddison read prayers. We were too few to deserve a sermon, though Christ has promised to grant his presence to *two* or *three*.

The annual income of Dr. Maddison as Bishop is only £100 Per Annum. This depends entirely upon subscriptions, and will neither afford a Wig nor Lawn sleeves, much as the interests of the Church may be injured for Want of them. But it will do more. It has contributed to the comforts of a Man whose talents, exemplary conduct and liberality, next, I suppose, to Wigs and Lawn sleeves, are of the utmost service to the Cause of Religion. But what would become of such a Bishop in England? A Man who corresponds with Dr. Priestley![5] Luckily however, *"to his own Master he standeth or falleth."*

In the evening I rode with the Bishop to Williamsburg where I slept, and returned to Richmond on the stage on Monday morning.

RICHMOND, AUGUST 5TH, 1796. In accidentally turning over the book entitled, "Elegant Extracts in prose and Verse," I met with a poem entitled "The love of our Country"; a prize poem by Dr. Butson p. 300 of the poetic Volume.[6] After reading this beautifull poem once or twice through, I am utterly at a loss to account for its title. The first 28 lines say merely, that the exploits of the heroes of that day (1772) are equal in merit to any performed either by the Britons or subsequent Inhabitants of the Island of Great Britain. Then follows a most elegant eulogium on the Corsican Paoli, and another upon Sidneys conduct in death.[7] The next passage

5. Dr. Joseph Priestley (1733–1804), English scientist and educator, was a Nonconformist minister and political radical. He emigrated to the United States in 1794. *DNB.* See also p. 381.

6. Christopher Butson's poem was later published in *Oxford Prize Poems; Being a Collection of Such English Poems as Have Obtained Prizes in the University of Oxford, 1768–1806* (Oxford, 1807).

7. Pascal Paoli (1725–1807), Corsican general and patriot, led the Corsican movement against Genoese and French control of the island. After his defeat by the French in 1769 he made a daring escape to Great Britain. During the French Revolution Paoli was recalled to Corsica by the French to rule once more as military commandant. Relations with republican France deteriorated, however, and he sought independence with British assistance. But this attempt failed, and in 1794 he relinquished Corsica's sovereignty to Great Britain. When he was not named viceroy of the island, he settled once more in England. *DNB.*

Algernon Sidney (or Sydney) (1622–83) was executed for treason following conviction for his alleged implication in the Rye House Plot of 1683 to assassinate King Charles II and James, duke of York. Even the duke conceded that Sidney died "very resolutely and like a true rebel and republican." *DNB.*

has the nearest affinity to the subject but is merely a poetical repetition of the duty of concentrating in patriotism all private attachments and the poem closes with the observation that in the private walks of life and literature as much glory may be earned, as in the bustle of the field or court. It ought to bear the title rather, "On Glory."

The passage relative to General Paoli is so applicable to General Washington, as far as the 24th line that I cannot help transcribing it.

> Poor is his triumph and disgrac'd his name
> Who draws his sword for empire wealth or fame.
> For him, though wealth be borne on every wind
> Though some announce him mightiest of mankind
> Though twice ten nations crouch beneath his blade
> Virtue disowns him and his glories fade.
> For him nor prayers are pour'd, nor paeans sung.
> No blessings chaunted from a nations tongue
> Blood marks the path to his untimely bier.
> The curse of orphans, and the Widow's tear
> Cry to high Heaven for vengeance on his head
> Alive deserted and accurst when dead.
> Indignant of his deeds the muse who sings
> Undaunted truth and scorns to flatter kings
> Shall show the monster in his hideous form
> And mark him as an earthquake or a storm.
> Not so the patriot chief who *dar'd* (dares) withstand
> The base invader of his native land
> Who *made* (makes) her weal his noblest, only end
> *Rul'd* (rules) but to serve her *fought* (fights) but to defend
> Her voice in council and in war her sword
> Lov'd as her father, as her God ador'd
> Who firmly virtuous and severely brave
> Sunk with the freedom which he could not save.
> On worth like his the Muse delights to wait
> Reveres alike in triumph and defeat,
> Crowns with true glory and with spotless fame
> And honors Paoli's more than Frederic's name.

Were the 23d and 24th lines (altering the whole passage to the present tense which ought to be done at all events to agree with the presenting lines), changed thus; it would exactly fit

> *Who, when he sees his country's cause succeed*
> *Retires to till the land his valor free'd,*

The last then ought to be perhaps, "*And raises Washington's o'er Frederic's name.*"

RICHMOND, AUGT. 6TH, 1796. Upon looking over some loose papers, I found the following ode written soon after the most melancholy event that can ever befall me.[8] The paper is so ragged, that I [*illegible*].

> *Ode To Solitude.* written Decr. 20th, 1793.

> Oh Solitude! Though sung in fancy's glowing ode
> Strew'd by thy pensive bard with withering flowers,
>   Alas! to me how dreary seems thy chill above
> How weighs the air in these thy silent bowers.
>   Unnerv'd my mind starts from reflection's forms
> Looks round! Ah me! is ought of guilt to fright?
>   Are these of lawless rage the embryo storms?
> That tremble in my breast, and fully reason's light?
> Low on th' horizon burns the evening gleam
>   Clouds thicken o'er the long stretch'd radiant line
> The dank fog glides on day's departing beam
>   Woods, streams and plains in misty tint combine.
>   What sound hangs on the sighing blast
>   Quick let me fly! Ah useless haste!
>   Thy wide dominion, Solitude, extends
>   Far as the low'ring welkin's circle bends:
>   Enthron'd within my sick'ning soul
>   Thy baneful sceptre with'ring every budding smile,
>   Each friendly phantom rais'd, my sorrows to beguile
>   Thou chas'st, kill'st all my infant joys, nor fearst controul.

---

8. BHL's first wife, Lydia Sellon Latrobe, died in November 1793.

Once—ah! how broken is the sullied trace
   On mem'ry's tablet of that lovely face!
Blotted by tears, worn by corroding woe!
   The faint lines smile! the pale cheeks redd'ning glow!
Away! thou phantom. To th' damp vault they bore
   Her lovely corpse, those beauteous arms entwining
   Her pale cold body,—my body,—for she was mine.
Oh! break, my heart!—for she is mine no more!

   See where along the solitary way
To press their father to his dreary home
Clasp'd hand in hand, her orphan children come
   And ask him where,—oh heav'n,—his Lydia stays.

Go! Go! wretched babes, why call your mother's name
   Why of your father's tears the dread occasion seek?
Why fan of fierce despair the madd'ning flame?

   And clasp his trembling knees, and kiss his fading cheek?
She's gone, she's gone! Did ye not hear her knell
   Nor see the sable hearse forsake the door
Weep, weep, poor babes, your mother's passing bell
   Has toll'd,—she's gone, ah! to return no more.

   But come! ye pledges of our spotless love,
   Where the young violet buds upon her sod
   Kneel by your father; there the present God
   To calmer tears his burning eyes may move;
Pour balm upon his widow'd wounded heart;
And strengthen him to act a father's part.

RICHMOND, AUGT. 10TH, 1796. EAGLE TAVERN.[9] Having been pestered by the flies in my apartment on the ground floor, I moved up one pair of stairs. A new enemy has attacked me here, who though not quite so troublesome as the flies, keeps me pretty much upon the *alert*. This is a small red ant, whose dwelling is somewhere under the woodwork of the Windowseat. The flies below tormented me by crawling about me, spotted my drawings and devoured my indian ink. The Ants ramble constantly across my paper, fill my water glass with their dead bodies, and devour my

---

9. The Eagle Tavern, built in 1787, stood on Main Street between Twelfth and Thirteenth streets. It was destroyed by fire about 1839. Mary Wingfield Scott, *Old Richmond Neighborhoods* (Richmond: Whittet & Shepperson, 1950), pp. 131–32.

insects and butterflies. They are indeed thirsty souls, and find particular pleasure in drinking out of a glass. They ascend the slippery side of the Tumbler, turn the edge, and then descend hanging their heads to the Water sometimes 2 or 3 hundred at a time. A slight motion of the surface sucks in a great many, but the greatest number return after filling their little bodies till they become transparent. I have tried several methods to supply them with water without their having occasion to recur to my Glass where they hang to my brushes and are very inconvenient. I poured out a quantity of water close to the chink from whence they issue. Few however chose to drink so humbly while the magnificent reservoir was in view. I then made a *circumvallation* of Water round them. This was effectual for some time, but as a path across it soon dried, I put the glass opposite to this opening and very soon the majority of tipplers marched through it, and used the glass as before.

Mr. Valentine ([Mott] and Lawrence, New York) brought me yesterday morning early a beautiful Phalaena [see PLATE 22]. He had caught it in a spider's web. It was much damaged, but enough remained to make a tolerable drawing; the spurs only being imperfect. It was perfectly alive. I crushed it so that it could not escape, but could not any-how kill it. I then placed it upon my chimney piece which is loose and hangs from the Wall. In the evening I looked at it, and found the body covered with red ants and separated from the thorax. The thorax was hollow, and hundreds of ants were busy in it. The body which was uncommonly full of long and thick down had been bared in some places, and the ants seemed to be employed in heaping the down together near it. I then took the breast and wings and shaking all the ants out of it, till not one was left, I permitted them to retain the body. This morning I viewed them again. The body was entirely a shell, and almost stripped of down. The ants were extremely busy in making two hills of it full of cavities and recesses; in the lowest of which I saw several of them very busy through the thin covering. I am at a loss to conceive how they could lay up this flimsy stuff so as to form arches and chambers with it. But so it was.

The Butterfly itself I fixed to the door, by a pin running through one of the Wings.

This evening the ants have removed every atom of down from the Chimney piece,

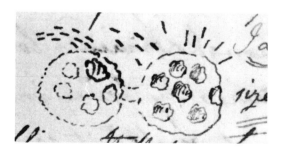

having taken down their hills, and not an ant is to be seen. The room has been locked since I left it, and the key in my pocket. What is still more extraordinary, the breast of the Phalaena, which was hanging upon the midst of a plain door, beyond the reach, as I should have supposed, of any thing that could not fly was again full of ants. Not one could be seen on the Chimney piece, and a violent rain having beaten in, and thoroughly soaked the Windowseat, they had either plenty of liquor below or were drowned, for not an individual was abroad. I cleared my butterfly again, and fixed him to the Wall at a distance from every chink and cranny.

AUGT. 11TH. Without noticing my Phalaena I went out and returned at noon.

I then found it upon the midst of a Cloth coat loosely thrown upon a trunk over which I should suppose no ant of the diminutive size of mine could crawl. The wind had carried it thither, and it was fuller if possible than ever of these little busybodies.

It is truly astonishing with what activity and success instinct furnishes itself with sustinence while reason makes a clumsy hand of it without immense exertions. How these ants found out their prey in spite of all my endeavors to secure it, is to me incomprehensible. It cannot be by scent, for tho they love sugar beyond every thing, they will run by a lump twenty times, and always seem to stumble upon it at last, and express a joyous kind of surprize upon the discovery, by their wriggling. As to centinels, or scouts, or scowering parties the distance they run to finding food is rather against the opinion. I have looked 20 times since the removal of the body of the Phalaena from the Chimney piece, and have waited 10 minutes at a time without seeing one of them. Yet the moment almost it was put there, they covered it.

I put down a drop of lemonade near their drink. Many were then about, and two came to the drop. They tasted and ran off, as if the acid offended them. But the Sugar induced them soon to wish for another sip, they walked slower and slower, and at last put about and ran quickly back. Their draught was now longer, but they suddenly ran off as if frightened, and went hurrying down the chink. I did not see them return nor did any others come to make the experiment. I suppose they held forth, upon their arrival in the congregation, upon the sweetness of the cup of pleasure, and the sour dregs that are in the bottom. Like other preachers, they had tried it themselves; but far more successful were they, if they deterred others from the experiment.

AUGT. 14TH. Since the wetting of my Window seat, I have very few ants to trouble me. They seem to have suffered materially by it.

I find I am not singular in being so tormented by these little ants. Everybody else complains that they abound this summer more than ever.

AUGT. 19TH. After a very warm day my little family has again made its appearance, and 50 or 60 are drowned in my tumbler.

AUGUST 16TH, 1796.[10] Pope says somewhere or other:

> Laugh at your friends, and if your friends be sore,
> So much the better, laugh the more.[11]

If Pope had sensibility capable of feeling friendship (a matter not perfectly demonstrated), yet, I believe he never put this recommendation in practice. I once met with a Mrs. Barett, a most agreeable chatty old Lady in a Stage coach going from London to Townmalling in Kent. She had been much in Pope's family when very young, and as we were alone, I took great pains to get from her every scrap of domestic anecdote with which she was acquainted. She confirmed the opinion which a perusal of the works and correspondence of that constellation of wits which shone in the beginning of this century, had given me—that their vaunted affection and friendship for one another had more of parade than sincerity in it. Indeed I should rather suppose that envy frequently supplanted the pleasure which the admiration of congenial excellence might create. Pope's letters to Swift are evidently studied, and his anxiety to recover them, which I recollect, appears in many of the last of them, shows that he intended them for the public. In one of them—if I remember right what I have not read for Years—he hopes, by the publication of their Miscellaneous works, to walk down to posterity, *hand in hand*, as it were, and leave the book, as an *immortal* Monument of their friendship. The friendship of the heart has none of this Ostentation about it. I suspect that literary friendship is in general a *flimsy affair* (as Dibdin says).[12] Pope's waspishness, though excusable by his ill health was almost proverbial among his friends, and Lady Mary Wortley Montague, has, I dare to say, colored his picture right, though perhaps too highly.[13] *Gay* was a good natured, soft tempered fellow, and might now and then feel the edge of the wit of his poetical friends, but with this exception, I believe it was chiefly employed to the purpose of compliment and often gross flattery.[14] Popes letters to and from these Gentlemen are at all events very little

10. This entry is in its proper place. The two preceding entries were made on the same manuscript page. BHL apparently wished to keep his observations on the ants together.

11. The quotation is "Laugh at your friends, and, if your friends are sore, so much the better, you may laugh the more." Alexander Pope, "Epilogue to the Satires in Two Dialogues" (1738), Dialogue I, lines 56–57.

12. Charles Dibdin (1745–1814), English dramatist and songwriter.

13. Lady Mary Wortley Montagu (1689–1762), known in English social and literary circles for her wit and beauty. When her friendship with Alexander Pope ended in a quarrel, she replied to his criticism of her by writing *Verses Addressed to an Imitator of Horace by a Lady* (1733). *DNB*.

14. John Gay (1685–1732), English poet and dramatist, was the author of *Beggar's Opera*.

less sickening than those of Pliny the younger, and indeed of Cicero to his *amantissimi* and *dilectissimi*, and *carissimi* &c., &c., &c., &c.[15]

But—(for all the preceding is merely by the bye), I do not agree, either in feeling or in reasoning with Mr. Pope upon the subject. Beyond the four first words, the precept ought certainly not to go. It is certainly *bad policy*, to say the least, to hurt the feelings of your friend—to make him sore. The adage, *he would rather lose his friend than his joke*, condemns it most properly and forcibly. The wound made in this way, though it may heal, always leaves a scar behind. I think I would go to the utmost extent in my opinion respecting the impropriety of using ridicule even against the foibles of a friend, though I confess the difference of tempers must render the rule uncertain. But against an irrascible temper it ought never to be employed. Irrascibility and candour commonly go together; serious and friendly reproof cannot in that case fail of being more successful, as indeed, I think it must be in almost every other, where real improvement or correction of error is the object. No man can bear to be an object of ridicule, and least of all to his friend. There is a way however of making a man appear ridiculous to himself, and inducing him on that account to correct that which renders him so to others, without appearing to enjoy the laugh yourself.

It is a very great mistake to suppose that a pettish irrascible temper can be cured by ridicule. Abashed it may be, and perhaps kept under, but the friendship that effects the cure, is destroyed in the operation. Neglect and indifference to its ebullitions is, I believe always more effectual, it acts as a *sedative*, and though such conduct from a friend may vex at the time, when coolness returns, the offence having been of a negative nature, the memory takes no account of it.

There are subjects upon which a friend ought never to be rallied beyond a certain extent. One of these, is *love*. The practice indeed is diametrically the reverse. Most people consider a friend in love as the most legitimate game, with as much right, as a man suffering in the gout never escapes a joke or two being cracked upon him. The titillation of a little gentle ridicule is at first not unpleasant to the object of it, but it becomes a pain, and at last an insult in its progress. If the attachment is respectable and proper, *very little* ought to be indulged, if otherwise friendship ought to exert itself very differently, and in the most serious manner if exerted at all in an affair of so much delicacy.

There are other subjects, which in the amazing scope of conversation which the male sex allow themselves ought not to become *personal* jokes. Perhaps a very little decency will prevent error, but I have seen unpleasant consequences result from too much indulgence of *personal* ribaldry.

15. *Amantissimi:* most loving; *dilectissimi:* most beloved; *carissimi:* dearest.

AUGUST 20TH 1796. RICHMOND.   Today a negro, a notorious thief, was hanged.
An exhibition of this kind is uncommon here. It of course attracted a great crowd
of spectators. For my part I would rather travel twice as far in an opposite direction
than see it, but the detail of the execution was in every body's mouth so that all the
circumstances were told me by twenty different people. It is to the honor of this
part of the World, though it must have been a terrible Shock to the feelings of the
Deputy Sheriff, Mr. Moseby, that no one could be found to undertake the office of
hangman. Mr. Moseby was therefore under the necessity of performing that duty
himself with all its circumstances of blindfolding and tying up the criminal, and
then driving away the Cart, in which he was mounted along with him. Mr. Moseby
is a man of genteel connexions and manners and remarkably lenient in the execution
of his unpleasant office which chiefly consists in levying distresses, and executing
writs. He is on that account much beloved. To such a man it must be a horrid office
indeed, and I understand that he took great pains and offered a considerable reward,
to obtain a deputy, but in vain.

I have always doubted the propriety of inflicting capital punishments in any case
but that of murder. If the philosophical principles, upon which the American revolution proceeded be true, the law that inflicts the punishment of death for any other
crimes, is directly contrary to them. These principles suppose, and very properly,
that in the formation of civil society, all power possessed by the government established
by common consent, can only consist in the concentration of all those *natural rights*
and power which were possessed *in a state of nature* by those individuals who united for
mutual defence and support. The delegated power or right can never exceed that
possessed by the party delegating. In the state of nature (a state, which though
nowhere perhaps existing, theoretically considered, is a correct basis of reasoning)
retaliation is the utmost punishment that ought to attach to any injury of persons
and satisfactory restitution to any offence against property. In cases of property more
than mere restitution ought perhaps to be made, on account of *secondary* inconvenience
and injury that must result from its detention or destruction, but upon no principle
of common sense can the *irrevocable deprivation* of life ever be an equivalent, for that of
property which *may* be restored. In the defence of property, if death be the lot of the
thief, the case is wholly altered. The two parties are then on an equal footing as to
risk, and if one does not fall the other may. Most of the other States have abolished
capital punishment in every case but murder. Virginia is daily improving, and I hope
her laws will be amended in this as well as in other essential respects.

The Negroe's name was William Harris. He was a Slave, and had been used to labour in the Deeprun coal works.[16] After many other villainies committed he was at last apprehended and convicted of having broken open a store in the town. This was the crime for which he suffered. He had always entertained hope of a reprieve or at least that some Gentleman would buy him, as the phrase is, from under the Gallows, in order to carry him out of the State. This it seems is often done. There is a baptist preacher in this town, a Mr. Courtnay,* who assembles a large congregation of Negroes every Sunday upon the hill in a miserable meeting house. He seems, and no doubt is, in very good earnest in his labor upon their souls. He preaches the good old doctrine of heaven and hell, the atonement and justification by faith with Stentorian rhetoric. The criminal of today, had been visited by him in prison, and was so perfect a convert, that he walked from thence to the Gallows, not only with composure but with cheerfulness, declaring his happiness in the prospect of death, and the certainty of *being soon with God in glory*, to use the phrase he so often repeated. He sung psalms during the intervals of his professions of happiness and comfort. At the gallows he called to his acquaintances whom he saw in the crowd, took leave of them, and told the Sheriff once or twice that he was ready. Mr. Courtenay attended him with his pious labours.

What a strange thing the human mind is! How easily might not arguments of undeniable conviction be built upon the effects of religious enthusiasm upon this miserable black. To a cool reasoner it appears very absurd that by some mental chemistry, the polluted soul of a thief should at once be regenerated and entitled to the reward of consummate virtue. Independant of the strange jumble of ideas, by which the *atonement* is placed in the light of a commercial transaction between God and the human race, it seems odd to suppose, even taking for granted the fact, that the debt due to one person of the Deity has been discharged by the voluntary death of another, the subsequent settlement of account with every individual human being, seems a most flagrant breach of divine justice.

But how little respect is it possible to entertain for the means that produce these apparently supernatural effects, when we look to the mischievious and indeed dreadful consequences that religious enthusiasm has inflicted, and indeed *usually* inflicts upon the human race. Its history is a catalogue of greater crimes, and more shocking barbarities than that of the most destructive wars. Indeed it includes within it the most

---

16. The Deep Run Pits were located along Deep Run in Henrico County, six miles north of the James River and twelve miles northwest of Richmond. They were opened in 1760 by Samuel DuVal and later operated by David Ross and James Currie (1788), Francis Hyland (1789), and the business partnership of Henry Heth and Andrew Nicolson (1804). Eavenson, *Coal*, map no. 5, pp. 35, 41, 64. For Ross and industrial slavery, see Charles B. Dew, "David Ross and the Oxford Iron Works: A Study of Industrial Slavery in the Early Nineteenth-Century South," *WMQ*, ser. 3, 31 (1974): 189–224.

murderous and vindictive wars that were ever permitted to depopulate this unhappy planet. Confining our attention to that enthusiasm produced by the doctrines of the so called Christian religion—are its effects more powerfull in the conversion of the negro than in driving the inhabitants of western Europe to a croisade, in making the portuguese and Spaniards submit to the Inquisition, or in procuring the signature of John Calvin to the condemnation of the rational and mild Servetus[17] to the Stake? The only difference is in the effect produced by a different application of the same means. It is impossible not to rejoice in the diminution of the sufferings of the unfortunate black, although it is certain that the dread of his example, the only *real* benefit attending a public execution was almost lost by it. But does not the Mahometan superstition daily do as much, and the Braminical more?

What different ideas of divine justice and mercy must be the effect of a due consideration of the calm and mild religion of Christ, as it ineffably and irresistibly beams through that load of imposture and rubbish with which the fraud and ambition of the world and subsequent centuries have loaded the books of the New Testament.

"Thou shalt love the Lord thy God with all thy might, and with all thy strength, and thy neighbour as thyself, *in this is all the law and the Prophets.*"

RICHMOND AUGST. 21ST, 1796. FIREFLIES.[18] The fireflies made their first appearance this season in the beginning of May. Their light is much more brilliant about dusk than when daylight has entirely disappeared. At least it appears so to me and to all those to whom I have made the remark. The numbers in Amelia were astonishing and almost troublesome. As I have no books here, I cannot determine the genus of Coleoptera to which they belong. They carry the light in their tail like a common Europaean glowworm, but it differs from them in two respects: It is more brilliant, and scintillates perpetually while the insect is alive. The tail is white and fiery alternately, and the light has the effect of being infused from the upper part of the body by jerks. As soon as the fly is much wounded or killed the light remains stationary. I cut off the abdomen of one of them which was dead and as the light still remained I cut it in two. Each part remained fiery from 7 in the evening till 12 when I went to bed, and I have no doubt of it's having continued till it became perfectly dry. There are now but a few stragglers left, that fly early in the evening. They seem to be busiest in damp and rainy weather.

---

17. Michael Servetus (1511?–53), physician and theologian, was executed by Geneva Calvinists for heresy. His unorthodox teachings were condemned by both Protestants and Catholics.

18. The family Lampyridae, of the order Coleoptera (beetles), includes the fire-flies and the glow-worms. The latter are either wingless females or larval stages of the former. Common species of the Eastern United States are *Photinus pyralis* L. and *P. scintillans* Say.

RICHMOND. AUG. 24TH, 1796. I returned last night from Tuckahoe where I
have been since Sunday morning. I got most thoroughly wet in riding thither, and
drinking a Glass of Brandy, to keep out the Cold, I got a three days headach in its
stead. It is a good idea to let ones stomach to the God of fire, in order to keep out the
God of frost, but both of them are troublesome tenants. Mrs. [Gabriella Harvie]
Randolph was confined to her chamber, having had a severe fall from her horse. The
following message procured us the favor of her society with out which Tuckahoe house
is extremely dull:

> Dear Madam, permit me with you to condole
> On your dangerous fall,—yet your bones being whole,
>   I may mod'rate my weepings and wailings
> And anxiously hope that when you are dress'd
> You will hobble downstairs, where we'll all do our best
>   To make you forget all your ailings.
> Your father has comforts so solid and wise
> While Arthur will cheer you with witty replies
>   And Bishop make very fine speeches;
> Mr. Law[19] he will tell how oft he was unhorsed
> But as for myself I shall come off the worst
>   For I'm dripping, coat, Waistcoat and Breeches.

Fig. 29.   Mr. George Law of Barbados.

RICHMOND AUGST. 26TH, 1796. In mentioning the circumstance (see p. [191])
of the Sheriff being under the necessity of performing the office of hangman to the
black lately executed, to General Wood,* he told me that previous to the war, it

---

19. Identified by BHL in his sketchbook index as George Law of Barbados.

became his turn to fill the office of Sheriff. In this state that office is always filled by the eldest magistrate in the county in rotation. The fees of office render it a desireable object and at that time it was usually farmed for £200 a Year, which was the annual sum offered to General Wood, by a man who solicited the Situation of Deputy Sheriff. General Wood would have agreed to the bargain, had the man been willing to engage to take care of any execution which might occur during his Shrievalty. This however he could not be prevailed upon to do nor would any other person undertake the situation of deputy Sheriff upon these terms. Rare as executions were, no one chose to risk their occuring, and on that account General Wood refused to serve, and the office passed to the next in rotation.

General Wood is at present Deputy Governor of this State. He signalized himself greatly during the late war, and led the attack at German town. The British were so little apprized of the intended attack that the outpost with which General Wood first came up, consisting of 3 or 400 Men were asleep in their tents. He ordered his men to push down the tents and put those who did not surrender to the bayonet without firing a shot. Several Women were in the tents, which proves the security in which they supposed themselves. The ill success of that day was chiefly owing to a fog so thick that the American troops frequently fired upon one another by mistake.[20]

Colonel Innes, whom I have mentioned [p. 130] as one of the most eminent lawyers at the bar of this State was at the action at German town commanding as Lt. Colonel a regiment. As his Colonel was much below him in ability, General Washington contrived to keep him away from the army on the recruiting service in Virginia. He behaved with uncommon bravery on that day. After his men had given way, he rallied them several times, and General Wood saw him puffing and blowing upon his horse (for he was then as now, very fat) and endeavoring to encourage his men to face about and make another stand said these words: *"By the immortal God I adjure you, stand your ground, my fellow soldiers."* (*commilitones!*) A address exactly in character with the man.

General Marshall, another most eminent barrister [see p. 133] was a lieutenant at the battle of Brandywine, and was shot in the hand. He behaved wherever he had an opportunity with great bravery and spirit. He was then very young.

Gibbon somewhere observes that the disunion of the civil and military characters in the decline of the Roman empire was most injurious, and considerably hastened its fall. Here we have the military character united with almost every civil distinction from the attorney general to the man who keeps the Eagle tavern who is often Captain, sometimes Major, and now and then Colonel Radford.

20. British troops defeated the Americans at the battle of Germantown near Philadelphia, in October 1777.

5

Virginia, 25 January–3 August 1797

TO GOVERNOR JAMES WOOD

Richmond January 25th. 1797.[1]

Sir,

I have the honor to return herewith the Map with the Loan of which I have been favored, and to express my thanks for your liberality in permitting to me the use of it. I will take the liberty of waiting upon you, on my return to town to request the favor of seeing the Sketches you were so good as to mention in your letter to me.

There is another subject, on which it was my intention to have intruded myself upon the notice of the Executive whenever it should have appeared to me that I could have done so with propriety, namely, to offer my services in the design of the Penitentiary house voted by the last Legislative Assembly.[2] For this purpose I waited till I could obtain information of the Ground resolved upon by the Governor and Council of State, in order that I might have had the means of presenting a design wanting little or no explanation, and adapted to every circumstance attending the building: but as Mr. [Meriwether?] Jones* has anticipated much of what I should have submitted to your Excellency and the Council of State, by laying before You a very rough drawing, intended only to elucidate my private conversations with him; I have now only to express my extreme gratification in the indulgence shewn by the Executive to that plan; and to beg permission that whenever the steps taken by Government shall have sufficiently ripened the business, I may be allowed to lay before them for consideration whatever former experience, or the particular demands of the plans proposed for this State, may suggest.

I have the honor to be with the greatest respect Your Excellency's most obliged humble Servant

BHLatrobe.

1. ALS, State Penitentiary Papers, Virginia State Library, Richmond. The three manuscript journals for the period 27 August 1796 to 12 April 1797 are missing.

2. In December 1796 the General Assembly passed "An Act to amend the penal laws of this Commonwealth," the seventeenth article of which authorized the governor to purchase land in or near the city of Richmond for the construction of a penitentiary capable of accommodating at least 200 prisoners. Shepherd, *Statutes*, 2:5–14. On 25 June 1797 BHL learned that he had won the competition for the design of the "penitentiary house." He supervised construction until his removal to Philadelphia in December 1798, after which Major John Clarke completed the building with extensive modifications of BHL's design during 1799–1806. The prison was constructed throughout of vaulted masonry as a fire preventive; permitted a 180° view of the semicircular range of

199

RICHMOND APRIL 13TH, 1797. Wanley Penson, Vol. II p. 65.[3]
Mrs. Carville's (a widow's) song to her infant

> While on my breast my babe reclines
> Its sighs my trembling heart strings rend
> Whilst round my neck it fondly twines
> Its infant smiles my woes suspend.
> Yes, yes, sweet babe! from thee
> Derive at once my bliss and misery
> A tear! oh me! how is my heart distress'd!
> A kiss!——and mammy's blest!

APRIL 14TH, 1797. I really believe that in leaving 30 behind me,[4] I am growing old—going down hill in opinions and strength of mind. With my health I parted last September, and am become a sort of valetudinarian, and I think my mind and my body coincide very much in their feelings. For a week together I am sometimes in good health, and in good spirits. I am satisfied with men and things, and enjoy my dinner and my company as well as any body. Then again I am bilious and sick. I nauseate beef and society at the same time, I fancy the country I live in worse in every respect than every other, I hate to work and I detest being idle; I cannot draw nor read nor write nor walk nor sit nor talk nor lay down to sleep with any satisfaction. One very dangerous symptom that attends me is a desire for Novel reading. I get hold of some sentimental rhapsody, and presently work myself up into God knows what sort of an impracticable frame of mind: which is fortunately commonly attended with a total inertness, otherwise, were I to go abroad *"in these my lunes,"* I should at once *establish* my character as a lunatic, which is at present only suspected from my strange propensity to read and write.

This and the last page may serve at once as a symptom and a proof of my disorder, and should [I] ever be very violently afflicted my friends may be judge of the probability of procuring me relief by observing that its standing is to be dated from somewhere about the 1st of April 1797.

---

cells from a central building; provided both individual cells and workrooms for communal labor; showed attention to ventilation; and displayed an advanced neoclassical style. As such the design reflected new, international penological and architectural thinking. Nonetheless the penitentiary proved to be an unsuccessful experiment in penology, due primarily to the manner in which it was administered. After numerous alterations, the last traces of BHL's work disappeared in 1928.

3. Wanley Penson, *Wanley Penson; or the Melancholy Man*, 3 vols. (London, 1791).
4. BHL was born on 1 May 1764.

RICHMOND APRIL 15TH, 1797. *Recollection of facts.*

My father in law, the Reverend Dr. Sellon[5] possessed a farm of 200 or 300 acres on the Harrow road, at a village called Halsden, situate in the parish of Willsden. The house which was old and inconvenient was roomy. It was overrun and almost hid by vines, and as no part of it had the least pretence to elegance, the plainness of its furniture, and the unadorned simplicity of its garden was just what it should be. It stood at the upper end of the Village green, at some little distance from the neighbouring cottages, and a row of very fine old Elms so hid the view of them, that it appeared perfectly solitary. The distance from London was five miles. The old Clergyman who regularly spent the summer months in this retreat, had been afflicted by a paralyzing stroke before I ever saw him, and at the time when the smiles of his daughter first led me to Halsden green, his mind and his body had already suffered so much, that I never knew that strength of reason, and that depth of learning, for which he was once so celebrated. The amiable qualities of his heart were however more conspicuous than ever. The mask of prudence was withdrawn; he had no command of his feelings, and whenever they were excited, they streamed from his eloquent tongue in *incautious* expressions, and from his eyes in tears. My first interview with him, was when I went down to Halsden to request his consent to my marriage with his daughter. Concealment, I always thought troublesome, and I therefore told him at once all that he had to expect in his son-in-law, as to character, family, connections, and fortune. The good old man, wept, but could say nothing. He gave me his approbation in a squeeze of my hand; and a long speech could not have said as much. However every thing was not thereby settled. There were aunts, cousins, brothers, sisters, brother's-in-law, and sisters-in-law to be consulted. I omit, a *mother*, because she *willed* only as her daughter Lydia[6] dictated. I was invited to stay all night, and I most willingly complied. I was up early, long before the rest of the family. Lydia had heard me go down stairs and soon followed me. We rambled together round the fields, and returned to breakfast. The family had waited for us. I was too happy to be embarrassed, my mind was made up, and though the approbation of all present was highly desireable, it was by no means *essential* to the resolution of either Lydia or myself. But the breakfast party looked all sorts of sentiments and all sorts of sensations.

5. William Sellon (c. 1731–90) matriculated at Trinity College, Cambridge, in 1751. He was ordained deacon in 1756 and served as minister of St. James and St. John, Clerkenwell, from 1757 to 1790. He was also preacher of St. Giles-in-the-Fields (1758–90) and at Magdalen Hospital, St. Andrew, Holborn (1790), and proprietor and minister of Portman Chapel, Marylebone. John Venn and J. A. Venn, comps., *Alumni Cantabrigienses*, pt. 1, vol. 4 (Cambridge: The University Press, 1927), p. 42.

6. Lydia Sellon Latrobe (1761–93).

The aspects of [the] old gentleman was friendly, of the mother *affectionate*, Mrs. Fraser[7] the aunt looked *spiteful*, Patty seemed chagrined, and *Sophy* smiled archly at her sister. The eldest Son William gave me a distant welcome, Jack the barrister a hearty one, but Joe scowled his ill temper without reserve. Upon the whole I felt more hurt than pleased, and Lydia the expression of whose countenance was electrical felt with me. I had *then* some personal pride, and a spirit not easily daunted. I saw an attempt to separate our seats, but assuming the freedom of an old acquaintance I removed Patty and Mrs. Fraser from their chairs, and claimed the priviledge of an accepted lover.

The tea began to be poured out in silence. I looked at Lydia and saw a tear in her eye. This determined me to leave nothing to *doubt;* I assumed the discourse, and before we had finished breakfast which was prolonged very considerably, the vivacity I had endeavored to keep up, and the laughable turn I had accidentally given the conversation, and never did any family enjoy a laugh more—surprized all but Mrs. Frazer into the expression of a wish that I might soon become a member of their circle.

This happened about the 29th of July 1789. I was married the 27th of Feby. following after having had to combat the opposition of 2 or 3 rivals and of all the Brothers, sisters, first and second cousins, Brother and sisters in law, and the weakness of my reverend father-in-law which gave way to my representations when present but immediately complied with the contrary wishes of my in relations when absent. This change of sentiment was entirely owing to the single circumstance of fortune, for I never heard of a single other objection, and *latterly* both William and John Sellon became my friends.

Lydia was so truly affectionate a daughter and sister, that it was with some difficulty I prevailed upon her to permit me to set all this opposition at defiance, and boldly to demand her of her father, and to fix upon a day for our marriage. I did so however, and succeeded. Mr. Sellon (whose very considerable fortune had grown by the great prudence he and his wife had always practised notwithstanding the almost annual increase of his income from his various church preferment) had given to each of his married daughters, Mrs. White and Mrs. Smith,[8] 200 pounds as a wedding present, but had absolutely refused to promise or to settle any thing upon either of them during his lifetime, always holding out that his estate should be equally divided at his death among all his Children. When I claimed the hand of Lydia in a full assembly of the family, and fixed that day fortnight for the wedding day, I hinted that if her father chose to act on that occasion as he had done on two similar ones I should think myself

7. See p. 205.
8. See pp. 206–07.

highly obliged, but that otherwise the expence of the praeparations should be defrayed by myself. It happened that the whole party were persuaded or surprized into a repetition of their consent given at my first breakfast at Halsden, and the old Doctor gave orders to his tradesmen the next morning to supply the necessary articles of dress. I knew that I was very well able to support my small family at that time in moderate comfort, without the assistance of any profession, and I therefore neither expected nor wished for any further provision from my father-in-law. But he took it it into his head to settle upon his favorite daughter 2000 pounds secured on his Estate in Portman chapel. He was obstinate on this occasion. The whole family were offended at the preference, and took care that the settlement should be such as they knew neither I nor Lydia would accept. When it was drawn it was read to a small family party in the presence of myself and Lydia. It provided as usual for every possible case of survivorship that could happen, but had three very usual but very exceptionable articles in it, which so roused the quick sensibility of Lydia, that she absolutely refused to sign it. These articles were 1. a provision for a separate maintenance, 2. a clause that in case of her death, the fortune should devolve to the trustees for the education of the *children* independantly of their father, and be equally divided among them when of age depriving me even of a life estate in it, and 3. another clause, by which the whole sum of £2000 was to be divided among the heirs of her father, in case she should die without issue *after his demise*, and revert to her father if she should die before that event. This settlement was therefore altered, and rendered very liberal, but a clause was added excluding her from any inheritance with the rest of her father's heirs, unless she should be expressly named in his will. We were married the day after this settlement was signed. The improved settlement was however only for £1000. I refused for some time to hear of any exception of my case to that of the rest of Mr. Sellon's children, but the father was set upon it, and I saw no great harm in complying.

Immediately after the ceremony I left London. I felt no regret at parting with my newly acquired relations excepting my father and mother in law. All the rest had given me more or less cause of vexation at different times and had contributed much to my Lydia's unhappiness for six months. Indeed I ought not to have blamed them. I kept a title and a large fortune out of the family, and had nothing to offer in its stead but very sincere affections and a tolerably good education.

We spent two months in the Country. My happiness needed not the contrast of my present situation to deserve that name.

Upon our return I found that my father-in-law had had another stroke of the palsy and was gone to Bath. I took a house in Grafton street Fitzroy Square, where I lived to my departure for America.[9] Grafton street was at a great distance from the habitations of every one of the members of the family, and as I applied very industriously to my profession, in which I succeeded with uncommon rapidity, Lydia saw more of them than I did. There were circumstances that rendered every one of their Houses unpleasant to me.

It has been disputed with much warmth, whether certain diseases be or be not hereditary. I am well convinced that dispositions are so. The family into which I married afforded to me a proof of this speculation. My father-in-law bore in his manly handsome countenance the index of a noble generous mind. He had inherited it from a father equally deserving. Mrs. Sellon, was once a Miss *Littlehales*. The male branch of that family were similar as far as I knew them, in disposition, and when I say that public report was as industrious in dragging their names into notice, as the individuals of my wife's family were carefull to keep their history from my knowledge I say enough. Mrs. Sellon was, as Mrs. Grumming would say, the best of the bunch. She was properly, what is called a good sort of a woman. But she was the Channel by which the Littlehales disposition was conveyed into many members of the Sellon family, so that it consisted of two sets of Characters wholly different from one another.

My good mother-in-law was once very handsome and retained at the age of 63 very strong marks of former beauty. She was however better provided with external charms and accomplishments than with understanding. Her affections were violent and lasting, and as she never thought deeply, her prejudices were not less so. Her acquaintance with and partiality for Mr. Sellon commenced when he was at Westminster school, and till his death she was so violently in love with him, that the good man never could leave her for a day without throwing her into fits, or into a melancholy that endangered her health. He was extremely fond of her, but it was Lydia's observation, that he always felt, and often showed that he felt, a void in her understanding, and a redundance in her show of fondness, that rendered him incompletely happy.

Considering the strength of character that marked my father in laws conduct upon all public occasions, and also in all family affairs in which his wife was unconcerned, or neuter, I have often wondered that he gave up a most important point to her—the *spoiling* of their children. I have been told, that in the case of his eldest Son, he stood his ground firmly but he had been completely vanquished before his youngest was born.

9. BHL lived at No. 6 Grafton Street.

RICHMOND, APRIL 16TH, 1797. I came home last night too early to go immediately to bed, and took up this book by way of killing an hour in which neither my spirits, nor yet the time, were sufficient for serious employment. It was my intention to tell my Children, if they ever get hold of their fathers scribblings a family story in which more variety of character was displayed, than is usually the case in the common occurrences of human life. But having begun to talk of Lydia I got out of the way, and as I am now in the midst of my very worthy relations I cannot part without some little further ceremony. The story most likely will be at the end instead of the beginning of the book, should this rain continue all the day.

The individuals that composed this affectionate family, for with all there faults they were very affectionate whenever they met, are so numerous that it is dreadful to begin a catalogue of them and their characters.

The eldest ingredient was Mrs. Fraser, the sister of Mrs. Sellon. *Aunt Fraser* as she was called, had eloped very young with a military beau. Her father, old Littlehales, was then very rich and great expectations were entertained of the fortunes of his daughters. His connexions however with Lord Palmerston[10] had so injured his fortune in a few years, that Capt. Frazer found it impossible after a reconciliation had taken place to squeeze any Guineas out of him, and he therefore left his wife, very big with Child, and what was worse loaded with disease, to the mercy of her relations. The Child died very young. She suffered for many years under the consequences of her husbands infidelity, but was supported by her father and her Sister Sellon in a decent way. Her husband, who in the mean time had compleatly ruined himself and had left the army, hearing that she had a tolerable subsistence came to live with her again. She was taken by surprize or she would have fled from him. In a few weeks he robbed her of everything she had collected, and again disappeared. Her family then got her into partnership with a Milliner in the City where She saved enough to support her with very strict oeconomy, and she was never afterwards dependent upon any one. Upon my father in laws building Portman chapel she took lodgings near it and undertook the care of letting the pews, an employment in which she persisted in 1794.

She had been so illtreated and had such ill health that much sweetness of temper could not have been expected to remain with her had nature given her ever so large an original stock. But this was not the case. She was remarkable for her intrepidity in argument, her extremely mean and shabby mode of dress, her fiery zeal for holy mother Church, and her hatred of the marriage of her niece to B. H. Latrobe.

---

10. Henry Temple, second Viscount Palmerston (1739–1802), father of the famous Victorian statesman, sat in Parliament from 1762 until his death. He was known more for his social adventures than for his political career.

William Marmaduke Sellon, the eldest Son was a good jolly openhearted fellow, remarkably handsome in his person and profuse in his expences. His father had funded 10,000 pounds in Mr. Kielings brewhouse, which he afterwards bought and gave to him taking his bond for the 10,000 Pounds.

He had married a pretty fair unmeaning nonentity, so unlike himself in affections and understanding, that their union was productive of very little happiness, although of the finest Children imaginable.

Elizabeth [Patty] the eldest daughter, an uncommonly beautiful woman, was married to the Revd. Dr. White, a relation of the Duke of Newcastle. His elder brother Taylor White of Wallingwells is one of the richest commoners in Nottinghamshire, having an Estate estimated at £8,000 Per Annum. He was the youngest brother of 3, and had no more than £5,000 to begin the World with. Sir Gilbert Heathcote gave him on his marriage the living of Lavington in Lincolnshire and he afterwards got two others from other branches of his family the proceeds of which were £1,200 Per Annum. He had not seen any of his parishioners for 5 Years when I left England. By the death of his aunt Mrs. Priscilla Armstrong he came into a very large property and to his eldest son £40,000, and £200 Per Annum to each of his younger children were also bequeathed by this precious old maiden.[11]

Mrs. White was as notorious for her avarice as her husband for his love of the bottle. The former was always hungry and the latter never sober (always thirsty). The children were half starved and out of 11, four died of the rickets and bad nursing. It was impossible to visit them, there was seldom any thing to eat, always too much to drink, and often a most dreadfull squabble to listen to.

Martha the next in turn, was uncommonly short and plain in her figure and face, had very good sense, a good heart, but a very bad temper. Her health and looks doomed her to virginity.

Sarah, without being handsome, was a remarkably fine woman. Her mind was more beautiful than her person. Her temper equalled her sense, and both were of

11. Stephen White (1750–1824), third son of Taylor and Frances Armstrong White, entered Queen's College, Cambridge in 1769. He received the LL.B. in 1775 and the LL.D. in 1781. White was vicar of Lavington, Lincolnshire from 1774 until his death, and also had livings in Conington, Huntingdonshire, Langtoft, Lincolnshire, and Lidlington, Bedfordshire. He married Elizabeth Sellon on 5 April 1774, when he was given the living of Lavington by Sir Gilbert Heathcote (d. 1785), third baronet, who was M.P. for Shaftesbury. Heathcote's grandfather, also Sir Gilbert, reputed to be the richest commoner in England, left a fortune estimated at £700,000 on his death in 1733. White's eldest brother Taylor (1743-95) entered Lincoln's Inn in 1759 and Queen's College, Cambridge, in 1763. White's aunt, Priscilla Armstrong (b. 1725–26), died unmarried. *DNB;* [John Debrett], *Debrett's Peerage, Baronetage, Knightage, and Companionage* (London: Dean & Son, 1901), p. 36; John Burke, *A Genealogical and Heraldic History of the Commoners of Great Britain and Ireland,* 4 vols. (London, 1836–38), 4:339; J. A. Venn, comp., *Alumni Cantabrigienses,* pt. 2, vol. 6 (Cambridge: The University Press, 1954), p. 440.

the first rank. She had married very young, a *Mr. Smith* who at that time was a Clerk to an eminent attorney. The match was ineligible in every respect. Smith was profligate in his morals, and not worth a farthing. The father opposed the match violently, but at last was obliged to give way to the Mother who could not resist her daughter's entreaties. Smith is a man of good sense and wit. He loves his wife passionately and his children if possible still more. But he is notwithstanding a bad husband. His morals are publickly profligate, and his manner affectedly coarse. His greatest virtue is industry. He has amassed a large fortune, holds many very lucrative places in his profession, and is one of the most eminent practitioners in his line in the North East corner of London. The conduct of Mrs. Smith as a wife and a mother is an instance of the purest affections unshaken by constant violation, of the most correct conduct to her children, unswayed by the most unreasonable paternal indulgence, and her manners have retained elegance and delicacy, though hourly assailed in the Society of a coarse and unbridled wit.

Mr. John Sellon was educated at Merchant Taylor's School and afterwards studied at St. Johns College Oxford. He then devoted himself to the Law under [George] Crompton the Special pleader, and has now arrived at more eminence than most young men of his standing. He has genius, united to application, his heart and his head are equally good. At the bar he is eloquent in spite of his *lisp*, he reasons closely, and his profound knowledge of the Law appears in all his arguments. His *Practice of the Courts*, a book which is in the hand of every lawyer, here, as well as in England, is a proof of his knowledge and application.[12]

Mr. John Sellon married at an early age Miss Dickinson, the daughter of a very rich brewer,[13] who had left her 10,000 pounds at her own disposal. In this choice he rather violated than consulted his inclinations. She was some years older than himself, and extremely ugly. Her manners were very little congenial with his own.

---

12. John Baker Sellon (1762–1835) was admitted into Merchant Taylor's School in 1773 and into St. John's College, Oxford, in 1779. He graduated B.C.L. in 1785. Merchant Taylor's School was established in 1561 by the "Company of the Marchaunt Taylors." As in most eighteenth-century English grammar schools the curriculum stressed the classics. In 1566 Sir Thomas White, a co-founder of the school and founder of St. John's College, Oxford, offered forty-three fellowships tenable at St. John's to the scholars of Merchant Taylor's. Since then it has become a tradition for students of Merchant Taylor's to continue their education at St. John's. After graduating from Oxford, Sellon studied law and was called to the bar from the Inner Temple in 1792. He was the author of *The Practice of the Courts of King's Bench and Common Pleas*, 2 vols. (London, 1792–96); *Analysis of the Practice of the Courts of King's Bench and Common Pleas, with some Observations on the mode of passing Fines and suffering Recoveries* (London, 1789); and *Treatise on the Deity and the Trinity* (London, 1847), a posthumous work edited by W. Marsh. *DNB;* Allibone, *Critical Dictionary;* Howard Staunton, *The Great Schools of England: An account of the Foundation, Endowments, and Discipline of the Chief Seminaries of Learning in England* (London, 1865), pp. 211, 213, 229; W. A. L. Vincent, *The Grammar Schools, Their Continuing Tradition 1660–1714* (London: John Murray, 1969), pp. 19, 78–79.

13. Sellon married Charlotte (d. 1832), daughter of Rivers Dickinson, in 1788. *DNB.*

He was free, generous, and remarkably bold and open in his conduct, she littleminded, and rather vulgar, and her real or affected timidity was extremely ridiculous. However, she was rich; all the family therefore conspired to promote the match, and above all, she was most violently in love with him. After much intrigue of aunts and cousins, Jack at last *submitted* to receive the hand of his inamorata. He is an excellent husband, she a prudent domestic wife. They have 4 or 5 Children.

Lydia was the next in age and the first in merit. She was educated entirely out of her father's house.

Sophia, is like her sister in person and temper, but much inferior to her in sense and health. She is an excellently good girl. She was unmarried in 1795.

Mr. Joseph Sellon, the youngest of the family was in every respect unfortunate. He was a very sickly Child; of course spoiled. At 4 Years old he was Lord of the house. Full of the most unaccountable and unreasonable Whims, not a soul dared to thwart Him. His mother lived only for her dear Joe. The servants had no other master, and his father, brothers and sisters no greater plague. He disliked School, he therefore was permitted to stay at home. He neither learned to read nor to write, for he hated the trouble and restraint of a master, but a hatchet was his delight, and the furniture was at his service. In this manner he grew up, deformed in person, temper, and manners till he was 14. Shame then induced him to have recourse to his own industry to learn to read and write, and he deserves credit for his unassisted exertions, by which he accomplished his end *alone*, for an attempt to teach him excited his most outrageous anger.

When he had arrived at the age of 18, ignorant of the world, of men and of books, he was suddenly seized with an invincible desire to go into the army. He was remarkably short, humpbacked, illfeatured and weak in constitution. At first he seemed unconscious of any personal defect, but when his father found other arguments useless, it became necessary to point out the objections that would be made to his admittance into any regiment, on account of his personal appearance. Nothing could equal his first rage upon hearing so mortifying a truth. He was however not deterred, and his mother was determined he should not be thwarted. His father therefore resolved to use all his influence to procure him a commission, in hopes that military discipline would correct a mind, which domestic indulgence had almost ruined. After 2 or 3 fruitless attempts to get him accepted, in which he was refused with as much politeness as possible, but in a manner sufficiently mortifying, an ensigncy was bought for him in the 13th regiment of which Craddock was Colonel, and which was on the Irish Establishment. He left England shortly before I married, to join his Regiment. As soon as his commission was purchased, he seriously applied himself to such studies,

208

as are in general thought absolutely necessary to a military man. He succeeded in a short time to acquire a very competent, and indeed considering the neglected state of his faculties, a very astonishing knowledge of french, of fortification, and of Geometry.

It is very probable that he met with very severe mortifications while he staid with his regiment. The Officers were, even in Ireland, notorious for their dissolute manners and their drunkenness. The pay of an ensign and the scanty additional allowance made to him by his father would not permit him to follow the expensive dissipation in which his brother Officers were immersed. I have heard that it was with great difficulty he kept from receiving insults of the grossest kind, for some months. It is certain however that he gained and maintained respect during the last six months of his military life; but he most probably found such good reasons to repent of his unadvised choice of employment that he never chose to say a word upon the subject.

After having remained in Ireland about 18 Months he procured a furlough and came home. No one who knew him before, could have conceived it possible that so short a time could have effected so entire a change in his manners. He was polite in his conversation, perfectly attentive to the Ladies, spoke like other men, flew into no unaccountable fits of passion or of sulkiness, and was kind to his Sisters. From having been disliked, he now became the favorite of the whole family, and having sold out of the Army he purchased a beautiful farm at Pinner where he settled with his Mother and single Sisters.

These were the Members of this motley family. They were united by the sincerest affection for one another and the most perfect and well deserved veneration for the father of the family.

About the end of June 1790, Dr. Sellon moved for the summer to his house at Halsden green. He had not been there many days, when he was seized with a paralytic stroke and his life was soon despaired of. On the first news of this misfortune, I went down with my wife, and found the whole family collected round his bed. He was senseless. It happened that *all* his married daughters and daughters in law were in a situation which rendered violent grief extremely dangerous, but nothing could move them from the Chamber of their dying friend. Dr. Potter who attended, was so affected as to be unable to administer those medical applications which were advised by himself, and in fact, I became the only active nurse, and exerted myself for near 24 hours incessantly to recall departing life by friction and various other means. In the mean time all the Ladies were in tears, and his two eldest Sons sat in silent grief upon the Side of the Bed. The youngest was in Ireland and Mr. Smith did not choose to attend. Mrs. Sellon seemed totally torpid evidently overpowered by the weight of her grief. I prevailed upon most of the married Ladies to lie down alternately for a few hours. They all met again in the Chamber very early on the Second morning and a few moments afterwards, Dr. Sellon expired without a groan. I removed Lydia from the Scene as soon as possible into the Garden and succeeded in moderating the expression of her grief. On my return to the bedchamber, I found every one dissolved in tears; loud lamentations filled the room, the men were as intemperate as the women, they were embracing, vowing eternal and indissoluble affection, and invoking the departed spirit of their father to witness the attachment of his Children to one another, and their dutiful veneration for their mother. It was a little overdone, but as they were all beings of warm imaginations, I am sure it was sincere. I had been talking philosophy in the Garden, and was not wound up to the key in which the rest were performing. I kept Lydia out of the room, and by degrees broke up the party and cleared the Chamber. It was intolerably hot, and I was now under the necessity of turning my thoughts to the corpse. The family in the mean time indulged their grief, and their affection in the drawing room. Thus the day passed. Lydia was irritated a little at the reflections thrown upon my want of feeling by Mrs. Fraser and walked with me in a neighbouring copse, not joining much in the lamentations of her family though she felt severely and long. My share of grief would not be great. While I had seen my venerable father-in-law, I had seen him daily sinking under a disease in which his mind suffered more injury than his body felt pain. It was the remembrance of his former abilities and virtues that endeared him to the rest—but I had not known them. But grief is contagious, I felt for the family what I felt not for myself, and I was most exceedingly moved by the romantic attachment that seemed to have melted all the contrarieties of their characters into one mass of strongly cemented affection. Late in the evening I accidentally heard Patty half whisper and half cry to her brother John who sat in the next chair, "My dearest dearest Jack, when when is our dearest father's will to be read?" Tomorrow morning, said he.

We shall have a quarrell in the course of tomorrow said I, to Lydia.

How could she think of the Will, said she, let us go to town immediately, I would not stay to hear it.

The curricle however was returned.

We went to bed early. Before breakfast I was out in the fields with Lydia. At eight we returned and John gave notice that after breakfast the will would be read. This will had been drawn without any consultation with any of the family by Mr. John Sellon the barrister, and was upon the whole a most equitable and elegant production. It had been signed only a few days before Dr. Sellon's last illness, and its contents were unknown to any but John.

The Ladies were in a corner whispering guesses at the probable disposal of their father's effects.

Lydia was shocked and I wished to get away, pleading her ill health; but Mrs. White *would* stay, and had sent away my carriage meaning to take us home in her coach.

Dr. White had got drunk the evening before and was very unwell and not quite sober.

Wm. Sellon had the principal part of the personal estate in his possession and was uneasy least unpleasant arrangements might be made to take the money out of his hands.

Mr. Smith had just arrived and was angry at his wife's evident fatigue and indisposition.

Mrs. White was vexed at her husband, and fretful.

Mrs. John Sellon was frightened least she might have caught a fever, or be overset in going home, and her fears were soon encreased to a panic by a slight thunderstorm.

Mrs. William Sellon, looked ill and began to broad hem a piece of muslin.

Poor Mrs. Sellon wept silently.

There was no kissing, no embracing, no vows, no protestations, an air of suspended discontent reigned throughout the company.

Breakfast was at last got over, and we adjourned to the drawing room.

"In the name of God, Amen, I William Sellon of the parish of Clerkenwell," — &c., &c.

All the chairs moved three inches nearer into the middle of the room, except mine and Lydia's which moved six inches back,

"do give and bequeath,"

Two more inches advance in the position of the chairs,

"unto John Sellon Esqr. my second son, all my real and personal property being" &c., &c., &c.

Then followed an account of property bequeathed in trust, to pay the following annuities and legacies,

To his Widow an annuity of £200 Per Annum and all his furniture and plate.

To each of his Daughters Martha and Sophy an annuity for 83 Years secured on Portman chapel of 60 Pounds.

To John Sellon £1,000.

To Joseph Sellon £600, 400 having been before paid for his commission.

To Mrs. Smith, £50 for 83 Years as above.

To Mrs. Latrobe, nothing but her share of the Residue in consideration of her settlement.

To Mrs. White, only £200, in consideration of her husbands riches, and an annuity independent of him of £200 Per Annum bequeathed to her by Mrs. Armstrong.

To Wm. M. Sellon his eldest son £1000 by way of deduction on paying the bond of £10,000 and interest due by him to the estate. He had before received some thousand pounds besides the brewhouse. No share in the residue.

There were a few more trifling legacies. Each of the seven Children were then to divide the residue share and share alike. Each share is estimated at about 2,500 pounds.

As these different articles were read the Chairs gradually retreated till they were all close to the wall.

Silence reigned for some minutes when John Sellon had done reading.

"I should like to know who drew that Will," said Mrs. White, "and why I am worse off than my Sisters."

"You are much better off," said Martha, "than we who may starve if the estate fail; I think you cannot complain. Our father has been very considerate."

"I am sure I cannot tell how to pay 10,000 out of my business," said William, "without becoming a bankrupt."

"And I am sure," said Aunt Fraser, "the Chapel will not pay all these annuities and Latrobe's settlement into the bargain which is as good as a bond debt."

"I will then give up my settlement," said Lydia.

"That you shan't, my dear," said her mother.

"Don't be a fool girl," said Smith, "but I am sure my wife has charity enough to provide for poor Mrs. White by sharing with her, her revenue of 50 pounds Sterling Per Annum. Don't cry, Mrs. White, I'll find you bread and butter. There's a dear love!"

"Pray hold your tongue you brute," replied Mrs. White. "Ladies!" said Doctor White, "suppose you say no more about it now, but let us have a Glass of wine together and then go home."

"I wish I was safe home," said Mrs. John S. "The roads are very bad and dangerous."

"It was an odd whim," said Mrs. White, "of our father's to give Latrobe that settlement and rob the rest of his Children."

"I cannot hear my wife's father called a robber even by a Lady," said I. "You will therefore be so good as to say you were mistaken."

Lydia left the room.

"Don't talk nonsense," said Dr. White, "you are eaten up with the sin of covetousness. Latrobe come and drink a Glass of wine with me." I did so, Mrs. Sellon left us.

John Sellon then *commanded* in a very elegant and pertinent little speech silence upon the subject of the will, and recommended separation.

The Coach drew up. Dr. White pushed me and my wife in, got in himself, and then pulled his wife in after him.

This was very distressing to me and I was beginning to make some sort of an apology to Mrs. White for getting in first, but she only answered that her father might as well have left her £1,000 besides her share of the Residue, for she should certainly have given it to her Sisters. As for me, it was a shame that I should enjoy my £1,000 on such better terms than any of the rest.

The fact is that I lost about 400 by the arrangement, though my security was certainly excellent. I had even to pay for my wife's wedding cloaths after her father's death, no provision having been made by the will for that debt, and *Lydia* having ordered them.

This most equitable Will thus separated a family, before proverbially affectionate. Whenever they afterwards met there was the greatest show of attachment, sincere, no doubt, for the time, but it was daily growing colder when I left them.

Hadley's Quadrant

EDITORIAL NOTE

In May of 1797 Latrobe wrote a letter to the Reverend Robert Andrews, * Professor of Mathematics at the College of William and Mary, to which he appended diagrams concerning the mathematical proof of Hadley's Quadrant, a surveying and navigational instrument, and suggesting a new way in which it might be employed in measuring distances.[14] As an experienced surveyor Latrobe was undoubtedly familiar with Hadley's Quadrant, which had been developed in the first half of the eighteenth century, and it is certain that a sextant accompanied him to America (see p. 30). The sextant was a more precise and versatile instrument that operated on the same principles as the quadrant. A contemporary English surveyor's manual listed a Hadley's Sextant as one of the instruments necessary for a surveyor.[15]

Why Latrobe chose to discuss a quadrant rather than a sextant such as he owned is a matter of speculation. Quadrants were cheaper than sextants and were more widely used by both American and British seamen, while few, if any, instrument makers on this side of the Atlantic manufactured sextants.[16] Presumably Professor Andrews as well as other Americans acquainted with surveying and scientific instruments had used quadrants but were unfamiliar with the sextant.

With a quadrant a mariner measured the position of the moon, sun, and stars above the horizon, and with the help of published nautical tables determined latitude and longitude at sea. On land a

14. BHL referred to Andrews in his journal entry of 5 April 1796, but it is unclear whether he ever met Andrews either on his trip to Williamsburg of 2–3 April or on a visit he made in July of that year.

15. George Adams, *Geometrical and Graphical Essays, Containing a Description of the Mathematical Instruments Used in Geometry, Civil and Military Surveying, Levelling and Perspective; with Many New Problems, Illustrative of Each Branch* (London, 1791), p. 200.

16. J. B. Hewson, *A History of the Practice of Navigation* (Glasgow: Brown, Son & Ferguson, 1951), pp. 80–84; Silvio A. Bedini, *Early American Scientific Instruments and Their Makers* (Washington, D.C.: Smithsonian Institution, 1964).

surveyor used the quadrant to find angles between fixed objects and, by using geometrical and trigonometric functions, to measure lines of which one or both ends were inaccessible.

Latrobe's first figure (p. 216) indicates how a quadrant functioned. The quadrant had a fixed glass *A*
of which one half was a mirror (the lower half, usually) and one half was clear. The first object *C* was
sighted by the observer through the clear glass with the telescope. A mirror *B* was fixed on the pivot of
an index arm *G* so that when the end of the index arm was located at zero degrees (0°) on the arc *F*
(called the limb), the image of the object *C* was reflected from mirror *B* to *A* and to the observer through

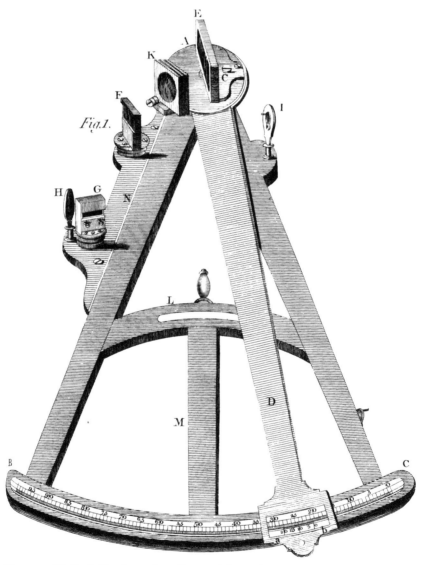

Fig. 30.   Hadley's Quadrant, from George Adams, *Geometrical and Graphical Essays* . . .
(London, 1791).

the telescope.[17] Thus, once the observer had object *C* sighted through the clear glass of *A*, he could move the index arm until the second object *D* coincided with it in the mirror of *A*, then read off the angle indicated on the limb by the pointer of the index arm. By the law of double reflection the degrees on the limb were reduced to half of the true measurement, but instrument makers commonly doubled the calibration of the degrees to eliminate the need to multiply by two on each operation. To avoid confusion, the end of Latrobe's constructed line *CB* will be rendered as *C'*, both in this editorial note and in the transcriptions of Latrobe's calculations on pages 216 and 217.

The first part of Latrobe's appendix to the Andrews letter was devoted to proving the theorem basic to the quadrant's operation: that the angle subtended by *C'* and *D* at the mirror *B* was 2*x*. In other words, constructing *C'B* parallel to *CA* for the purpose of the proof (two parallel lines having the same angle with any other line), Latrobe needed to show that the angle *x* given by the index pointer was actually half *C'BD*.

The proof required the axioms of Euclidean geometry, in addition to the law of geometrical optics which states that the angle of incidence equals the angle of reflection. The theorem proved can be generally stated in these terms: if one keeps the direction of incident light fixed and rotates a mirror through an angle *x*, the reflected ray will rotate by an angle 2*x*. This theorem was well known to mathematicians of Latrobe's time, and was undoubtedly familiar to anyone with a higher education. Latrobe unnecessarily considered a second case of the incidence of *D* (p. 218), for which the proof is actually identical to the first. This need to twice demonstrate the proof may indicate Latrobe's inability to abstract geometrical ideas.

The second part of the journal entry concerned Latrobe's proposal of a new use for Hadley's Quadrant to measure distance. The novel aspect of the idea was that it would permit determining the distance from the observer to a given point with only one sighting of the instrument, whereas two sights (two angles) plus measurement of one side of the triangle or one sight (one angle) plus two sides were normally required. In this case Latrobe proved that the difference from a true parallel (the parallax) of the two mirrors could be used to provide the second angle.

Virtually all quadrants had an index error which could be measured by observing a distant object of small size with the index arm at zero. By finely adjusting the index so that the object as seen in the mirror half exactly coincided with that visible through the clear glass, the slight deviation might be determined. The deviation of the quadrant was often in the negative direction, and was usually provided for on the limb as a small extension of the calibration in the direction from zero not normally used. This extra calibration was the "arch of excess." In precise measurements the deviation was added (or subtracted if it was in the positive direction) to the angle found by the normal method.

Latrobe's final diagram (p. 219) shows the quadrant aligned with an object *C* and adjusted so that the actual and reflected image of *C* coincided perfectly. Given that the angle *x* was indicated on the arch of excess, Latrobe used plane geometry and the trigonometric law of sines to show that the distance of *CB* could be calculated.

Although the proposal appeared sound it was impractical. The accuracy of the standard triangulation method of surveying depends upon making the known sides as long as possible. Yet Latrobe proposed using *AB*, a part of the quadrant no greater than a few inches in length. It is unlikely that the measuring instruments of the time could have found the length of *AB* to an exactness sufficient to make it a reliable constant in surveying calculations. Latrobe's idea for a one-sight measurement of an object's distance lay in an appreciation of the operation of the quadrant, but was not mathematically realistic.

17. Theoretically both the actual object and its reflected image coincided at *A* when the index arm was at 0°. However most quadrants had an index error, a factor which BHL proposed putting to use in a novel way. See below.

The principle of Hadley's Quadrant depends upon proving that the angle X is equal to ($\frac{1}{2}$ b ※ CBD). X is measured on the Limb of the Quadrant, CBD is the angle subtended at B by two objects C & D, the line AE & CB being assumed parallel on account of the extreme distance of the object C & the infinitely minute proportion of its parallax CB to its distance. The proof is as follows:

nexed to a Copy of a letter to M.ʳ Andrews, Professor of

Mathematics in the University of Williamsburg. May 15ᵗʰ 97

There are many modes by which the theorem

may be demonstrated; but the following appear to me

the shortest;—having no books to refer to, I have been obli-

ged to study the demonstration my self.—

$$\overbrace{CBM}$$

given ———— $a + x = CBD - MBD,$ ~~by~~

and ———— $a = 0$

now $x = 0 + MBD$ ergo

$a + x = 0 + 0 + MBD = CBD - MBD,$ ergo

$CBD = 2a + 2MBD = 2x,$ or

$x = \tfrac{1}{2} CBD.$ Q. E D

It may happen that the ray DB may fall above the

Mirror BM in which case the proof will stand

thus:—

Turn

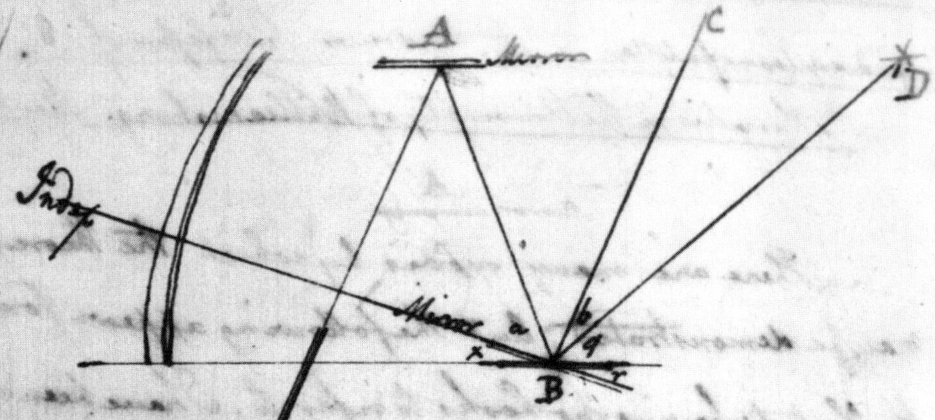

given $a + x = b + q$

and $a = q + r$

now $x = r$, ergo $a + x = a + r$

now as $a + x = b + q$, therefore $a + r = b + q$; and.

as $a = q + r$, therefore $a + r = (q + r + r) = q + 2r$

ergo, $b + q = 2r + q$, ergo

$b = 2r = 2x$ or $x = \tfrac{1}{2}b$ $= $ $= $ Q.E.D.—

It has occurred to me that by a single sight, by means of any Quadrant or Sextant sufficiently accurately & minutely graduated, distances may be measured, and calculated from what may be called the Parallax of the Instrument of the object of a triangle, of which the distance objects or the angle subtended at the Instrument by the center of the mirrors or the horizon center lines of the two mirrors. The following Diagram will explain my meaning.

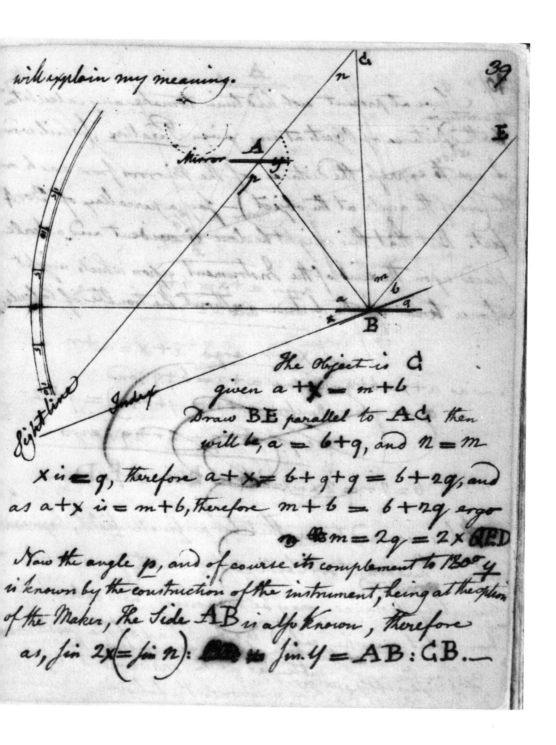

The Object is G

given $a + x = m + b$

Draw BE parallel to AG, then
will be, $a = b + q$, and $n = m$

x is $= q$, therefore $a + x = b + q + q = b + 2q$, and
as $a + x$ is $= m + b$, therefore $m + b = b + 2q$ ergo
$$m = 2q = 2 \times \text{QED}$$

Now the angle p, and of course its complement to $180°$ y
is known by the construction of the instrument, being at the option
of the Maker, The Side AB is also known, therefore
as, $\sin 2x (= \sin n) : \quad \quad \sin y = AB : GB.$ —

I have at present not had time to make any calculation to ascertain the Distance of Objects at any given _Parallax_, (which word I use to express the distance of the Mirrors from each or the Cord of the angle at the object) — say a parrallax of 3 or 4 feet. But that this might be done is evident and a scale placed upon the Limb of the Instrument upon which might at once kread off the distance without the trouble of Calculation

$$AB : CB.$$

MAY 22D, 1797. One of the most sensible and agreeable Women I have ever known, objected to Shakespeares plays in general, as containing expressions highly offensive to Modesty, and to *Othello* in particular, as not only violating decency, in the dialogue but good manners, and even the character attributed to the hero, in the circumstance of his striking Desdemona in a fit of jealousy. It was impossible to deny the *first* charge of indelicacy. Such expressions as fall from the mouth of Iago, Brabantio, and Othello himself are shocking in themselves, and must always have appeared so to the young and the female hearers. But I ventured to *excuse* our favorite poet by stating the great difference between the manners of our day, and those of Shakespeare. It is certainly a great improvement of manners that teaches us to shun the appearance of licentiousness, and to be shocked at its expression, and so far Mrs. W.[18] had certainly had the advantage, had the argument been, whether or no our manners are more favorable to virtue than those of former times; and she was perfectly right in asserting, that to decide upon these expressions as they now appear to us, and especially to those who have not, by long study brought themselves to conceive that they are living in the time and among the contemporaries of the author they are reading; we must at once condemn them as highly indecent, and improper to be read or heard.

By degrees however the field of discussion enlarged itself. I found it necessary to attempt the proof that Shakspere did not so much violate the decency of the manners of his age, as ladies of the correct delicacy of Virginia may suppose.

The Merry Wives of Windsor was written in the days of Queen Elisabeth. The Bible was translated in the reign of James the 1st perhaps 20 Years after. I mean no disrespect to that Book when I say that the translators, who were men of great piety and learning, and in such a work, published for the correction of morals and manners, would no doubt be as cautious as was necessary, not to give offense to delicacy, have every where used language consonant to the original no doubt, but highly repugnant to our present ideas of delicacy. They certainly might have avoided it, by circumcumlocution, or a different arrangement of expression; for it happens, that every language with which I am acquainted is on no subject more ductile than when common expressions are to be rendered equivocally allusive to indelicacy; or natural functions, unfit to be *plainly mentioned*, are to be *intelligibly* hinted. How little care has been taken to soften the necessary mention of these things by the translation of the Bible Leviticus and Ezekiel can fully show. The fact is, I believe, that the manners of the time admitted all the freedom they took, and no one was offended thereby.

I was proceeding to quote Beaumont and Fletcher, Dryden, Congreve, but Mrs.

---

18. Jean (Moncure) Wood, wife of Governor James Wood.

Wood very properly observed that during the reign of Charles the II and some time afterwards the stage partook of the profligacy of the manners of the court and she might have added that even to the moral authors of *that day*, whose delicacy of expression when they necessarily mention indelicate subjects is no ways conspicuous, the stage appeared to use a most unjustifiable licence of language, and that it was thought highly disreputable for a young modest Woman to appear at the theatre.

Delicacy, however, admits of many degrees, and is subject to fashion. Xenophon tells us, that a persian lost his character entirely, and became almost infamous if he were heard to cough or seen to spit. They did not, I presume, chew tobacco. In Virginia this seems ridiculous. The Hindoos never use the right hand for any *indelicate* purpose. It would be profaned and rendered unfit for feeding themselves or for performing any honorable function were they accidentally to make a mistake in this respect. And yet their modest Women, and no women are more scrupulously so, publicly worship their Priapus, *Lingam*, the grossest of all emblems of the fertilizing power of the deity. Every married woman wears the *Taly*, a small representation of the same deity. The dress of the Greek Ladies would appear *loose* to a modern belle. A Prostitute would scarce dare to wear it publicly. That of the Men was very little short of nakedness. I need say nothing of their naked statues, for we moderns equal them in our apathy at beholding them although in Virginia the infant State of the Arts renders them rare. The Egyptians were not less delicate than the Greeks in their morals, and yet the Worship of Priapus was a thing of course. As to the Romans, the delicacy of their Matrons, and the *pudicitia*[19] of the young women has been held up as an example to the modern World, and yet the rites of Venus, and many other parts of their divine Worship would appear shocking to us. It may be taken for granted, I think, that the *best* comic poets of every Nation, though they may extend the *licence* of language to the utmost limits, will not go beyond it in any gross degree. Many have called Horace an impudently licentious poet. I think it might be proved that the Romans did not think him so, and Virgil was never suspected by them of licentiousness. His *modesty* has been even praised and the line quoted: *Speluncam devenere in unam*,[20] which is by the bye as loose a one by its necessary consequence as he could have written. Horace says plainly: *Multorum ante Helenam fuit cunnus caussa bellorum*[21] and speaks as plainly in many other places. Virgil's eclogue in which his hero,

19. Modesty.

20. Trans.: They came into one cave.   The source is Vergil, *Aeneid* IV, 165–66: *speluncam Dido dux et Troianus eandem / deveniunt*.

21. Trans.: The vagina of many before Helen has been a cause of war.   The source is Horace, *Satires*, 1.3.107–08: *nam fuit ante Helenam cunnus taeterrima belli / causa*.

formosum ardebat Alexin[22] is still worse: And his Girl who *fugit ad salices et se cupit* **ante** *videri*,[23] was a very good delicate creature, though in Virginia she would have been inadmissable. *Juvenal* is grosser than any modern poet, even Swift, dared to be. I am however convinced that the delicacy of the Romans, I mean of the modest Romans, was not at all shocked, as is ours, by the expression, in which he says of the Vestal virgins, that if they were not violated by the beaux of the day, *quod si recusent, clunem submittunt asello*.[24] I did not, of course, insult Mrs. W. with all this indelicate Latin, but *generally* stated what I knew and believed of the manners of the ancients, and as I have no books, I even now quote scantily and perhaps incorrectly. But I believe it might easily be proved that many things said, done and written, as we think, licentiously and indelicately among them, had no effect upon the moral character of the people; because the *fashion* of delicacy was then different.

In order to make out my point, which had grown into the general assertion, *that though much of the moral character of every nation depend upon its manners, it is in a much less degree than should be imagined:* I then had recourse to what I had myself seen of the manners of different Europaean nations. A very modest Italian girl called her old uncle and guardian an old *buggeroni:*[25] the expression she perhaps did not understand —I mention it merely as having struck me, I may say shocked me, in the mouth of a young lady, whose modesty was not affectation. She must have heard it from her *Mamma* who was a woman of high and deserved respectability, and indeed any other would have used it. An Italian Lady at the table of Sir Wm. Hamilton, where french happened to be spoken, speaking of the Buffalo cows, and addressing herself to a *Gentleman*, said, *N'est il pas un circumstance tres singuliere, qu'elles ont leur petite incomodite chaque mois comme nous autres.* Mrs. Hart, now Lady Hamilton, could scarcely keep her chair.[26] The Italians felt nothing. (I disbelieve the fact, by the bye.)

The French ladies are known to receive visitors in bed and in their dressing rooms. I never heard of an instance in which these visits had produced infidelity or even the slightest indelicacy *beyond the fashion*. In London there is more attention to external decorum, but, I am well convinced, not a whit less real licentiousness.

22. Trans.: Was in love with the fair Alexis [a boy; *formosum* is masculine]. The source is Vergil, *Eclogue* II, 1: *Formosum pastor Corydon ardebat Alexin.*

23. Trans.: Flees toward the willows and desires herself to be seen first. The source is Vergil, *Eclogue* III, 65: *et fugit ad salices et se cupit ante videri.*

24. Trans.: Which if they (men) refuse, they (women) place their buttocks under a donkey. The source is Juvenal VI, 332–34: *hic si / quaeritus et desunt homines, nulla mora per ipsum, / quominus imposito clunem summittat asello.*

25. *Buggeroni* is plural; the singular would be *buggerone*. In Italian the word denotes one who cheats, swindles, tricks, but BHL apparently assumed that the girl was using an Italian equivalent of buggerer, or sodomite.

26. Sir William Hamilton (1730–1803) was British minister at Naples from 1764 to 1800. Emma Hart (1761?–1815) became Sir William's mistress in Italy in 1786 and married him in England in 1791. *DNB*.

"*It seems however impossible that such opportunities, as the manners of Europe give, should remain neglected.*" But the fact is, that *opportunities* of actual intercourse of an improper kind are not more common *there*, than *here*. In Italy, Spain and all the Southern parts of Europe, the single Women are narrowly watched. It is impossible almost ever to have a chance of being alone with any of them. *Here*, there is not a young Lady who would not trust herself alone even with a stranger. Jealousy does there what habit does here, and the effect is the same. In france the toilet and the bedchamber are open to all visitors. They cannot therefore become places of assignation. And if an assignation be intended, there is no corner of the earth that does not furnish convenient retreats for lovers.

But I can appeal to the experience of almost any one who is past thirty as to a very great Change that has taken place in the fashion of delicacy among ourselves. Look at your Mother's pictures and ask yourself whether you would expose to any painter what is there exhibited?

But you answer, that was the licence of the painter! I believe not. Hogarth in his scenes from real life, every where exhibits the bosom of his most modest women. But admitting that it was the licence of the painter would any painter use it now, or if he did would you hang the picture up. The fashion of delicacy has taken a different turn. Had a Lady dressing herself in Muslin, without stays, her waist short as nature intended it should be, the soft pliability of her lovely person appearing in every motion, her bosom however modestly concealed—had a lady so dressed appeared by the side of a beauty of the Year 1750, cooped up in a Whalebone barrel, commonly called Stays, her waist, where the most considerable swell of her body ought to be, pinched and drawn up into the form of an inverted sugarloaf, her hips extended on each side by a preposterous hoop a Yard at least; her feet appearing from under the ample canopy of her petticoats tottering upon the points of her toes and a pair of heels 3 inches high; her face spotted with sticking plaister like that of a leopard; her bosom naked, and endeavoring to escape from its whalebone prison—would not the former have been branded with every epithet that could designate wantonness, indelicacy, and indecency. Neither of these fashions are overcharged, the painter has preserved the latter, and will immortalize the former.

In this way we might carry our reasonings almost to any length, and at last be tempted to conclude, that *indelicacy*, as far as it is free from vice is an artificial idea, and that delicacy is a *relative*, not a *positive* virtue.

To state the extreme cases, I would only compare the *naked* and modest African who never dreams of *adultery*, and rarely indulges in wantonness of any kind, with the wanton, libidinous Chinese muffled up in coverings to the tip of her nose and the end of her fingers.

We are children of habit herein as in almost every thing else. You tell me, and I agree with you most cordially, that the Virginian ladies are *delicate* in the highest degree. This I discover'd very soon after my arrival among them. I prefer their manners without exception to those of the Women of any country I was ever in. Were I to chuse a Wife by manners I would chuse a Virginian, and yet let me tell you there are things done and seen in Virginia which would shock the delicacy of a bold Englishwoman, a free Frenchwoman, and a wanton Italian.

What do you think, Madam, of the naked little boys and girls running about every plantation. What do you think of the Girls and Women, waiting upon your daughters in presence of Gentlemen with their bosoms uncovered. What think you of the known promiscuous intercourse of your servants, the perpetual pregnancies of your young servant girls, shamefully exhibited to your children, who well know, that marriage exists not among them?

Oh but who minds the blacks; you surely are aware of the difference between them and the whites. Our Girls never think of these things; they appear to them as a different race, neither objects of desire, nor actuated by the same *refined* passions with themselves!

You are right, Madam! Poor wretched Blacks! You are indeed degraded; not even considered as better for virtue, or worse for vice! Outcasts of the moral, as of the political world! Your *loves* on a level with those of the dogs and cats, denied protection to your affections, and deemed incapable of that sentiment, which, refining sexual desire into love melts soul into soul with a union not less rapturous than the embrace of wedded and *virtuous sensuality*.

You are certainly right: our Girls never think of these things. Neither do the french-women think anything of toilet visits, the Bostonians of bundling, the Kentish peasants of pregnancies previous to marriage, the Hindoos of the Worship of Lingam, or the Mindingo and Dahomy negroes of assemblies of the Naked of both sexes.

Jottings on the Opera "Alceste"

EDITORIAL NOTE

A gifted amateur from a family of accomplished musicians, Latrobe found pleasure and relaxation in music throughout his life. He played the clarinet and the pianoforte, demonstrated a wide knowledge of the acoustical qualities of various types of musical instruments, and wrote a dedicatory hymn for St. John's Episcopal Church in Washington. Latrobe's knowledge of classical music must have been considerable as his father, Rev. Benjamin Latrobe, the Moravian educator, was a close friend of the great music historian, Dr. Charles Burney. The elder Latrobe may have assisted Burney in the translation of the German authorities Burney used in writing *The Present State of Music in Germany, the Netherlands and the United Provinces* (1773), and other works. Burney is best known, however, for *A General History of*

Music from the Earliest Ages to the Present Period, 4 vols. (1776–89). Latrobe and his elder brother, Christian Ignatius, who was to become "a great collector of religious music and a learned hymnologist," were frequent visitors in the Burney home, where they must have heard of the dramatic changes taking place in classical music.[27]

It is not surprising, therefore, that his journal entry of 29 May 1796 contains some jottings on the famous opera *Alceste* (1767) by Christoph Willibald Gluck (1714–87).[28] What is surprising is that Latrobe incorrectly attributed the libretto to Pietro Metastasio (1698–1782) rather than to its true author Ranieri de' Calzabigi (1714–95). Three factors may have caused Latrobe's confusion: Metastasio, one of the most prolific of Italian librettists, dominated the entire field of operatic libretto until 1762, when Gluck turned from him to Calzabigi (a collaboration which revolutionized the art of dramatic music with *Orfeo ed Euridice*); Latrobe probably knew of Dr. Burney's *Memoirs and Letters of Metastasio*, which had appeared in 1796; and there was a character named Alceste in Metastasio's *Demetrio* (1731).

On each page of the following journal entry Latrobe wrote several measures of music followed first by lines of Italian and then of English verse. The first scraps of music and verse are from the end of act 2, scene 2 of Calzabigi's libretto.[29] The Italian is a nearly perfect transcription of the concluding aria of that scene sung by Alceste. Latrobe's translation was poor, but it caught the spirit of the Italian and was only intended to have "been adapted to the expression of the song."

Neither the music nor the Italian lines on p. 228 are in Gluck's original score or Calzabigi's libretto of *Alceste*. They are from the aria of Alceste in act 2, scene 3 of the French libretto by François Louis Lebland Du Roullet, first performed in Paris in 1776.[30] Du Roullet's effort was a translation of Calzabigi's original, probably with some modifications.[31] Du Roullett was an enthusiastic admirer of Gluck, as well as French attaché at Vienna, where the composer had settled in 1750 at the time of his marriage. Du Roullet successfully set in motion a plan which culminated in Gluck's composition of *Iphigenie en Aulide*, first performed in Paris in 1774.[32] Latrobe's concluding English verse appears to have been unrelated to the Italian verses or to the corresponding French of Du Roullet's libretto.

It is impossible to say whether Latrobe had a score or libretto before him when he made his 29 May 1797 journal entry. He may have relied on his memory, which was musically accurate.[33] This could

---

27. Hamlin, *Latrobe*, pp. 19, 604, 6.

28. *Grove's Dictionary of Music and Musicians*, 5th ed., s.v. Gluck.

29. For the music see *Alceste, Tragedio. Messa in Musica Dal Signore Cavagliere Cristoforo Gluck. Dedicata A Sua Altezza Reale, L'Arcidura Pictro Leopoldo Gran-Duca Di Toscana*, Etc., Etc., Etc. (In Vienna Nella Stamparia Aulica Di Giovanni Tomaso De Trattnern. MDCCLXIX), p. 104. The libretto is in Calzabigi, Da Ponte, and Casti, "L'opera per musica dopo Metastasio," ed. Mario Fubini and Ettore Bonora, appendix in Pietro Metastasio, *Opere*, ed. Mario Fubini, introd. Luigi Ronga, in *La letteratura italiana; storia e testi* (Milano; Napoli: Riccardo Ricciardi Editore, 1969), XLI, 860.

30. *Alceste: Opera en Trois Actes*, Paroles de du Roullet; Musique de G. C. Gluck; Edition Conforme au Manuscrit de L'Auteur; Partition Chant et Piano; transcrite par L. Narici (Paris: Edition Choudens, [1904]), p. 132.

31. For a composer's opinion on the transformation of *Alceste* from the Italian to the initial French version that supports this view, see Hector Berlioz, *Gluck & His Operas with an Account of Their Relation to Musical Art*, trans. Edward Evans (London: William Reeves, 1940), p. 76.

32. Gluck played his new work for Dr. Burney when he visited Vienna in 1772.

33. Evidence of BHL's excellent musical memory can be found in a manuscript music book which has recently come to light in Colonial Williamsburg's collections. In this book, BHL noted at the beginning of his transcription of the aria "Moi non soi" by Giuseppe Sarti (1729–1802), that "the English Words [were] by B. H. Latrobe, the music written from memory," and at the conclusion that "The Original is longer." The music book, which bears

explain why he confused Metastasio with Calzabigi, for a libretto probably would have identified its author. Still, Latrobe's transcription of the first Italian passage argues for his access to that portion of Calzabigi's libretto. But then what of the second passage, which was not part of that libretto but appeared in the first French libretto? Certainly Latrobe did not use an Italian retranslation of the final French libretto of *Alceste*. By then, the opera's structure and the rhythm of its verse had been altered so radically from the 1767 version that not a line of the original Calzabigi text remained.

MAY 29TH, 1797. Translation of an Air in Metastasio's *Alceste* for the music by Chevalier Gluck, adapted to the expression of the song.

Non vi turbate no
pietosi dei
Se a voi m'involero
Qualche momento.
Anche senza il rigor
Di voti mei
Io moriro d'amor
E di contento.[34]

---

a title in John H. B. Latrobe's hand, *Old-Fashioned-Songs and Hymns Copied by B. H. L. Senior*, includes about thirty examples of music, often with accompanying words. The pieces are excerpts from longer works such as arias from operas, hymns, songs, and waltzes. Although there is no provenance for the music book, physical and internal evidence argue for its compilation in America, and suggest that BHL and his wife, Mary Elizabeth (Hazlehurst) Latrobe, who also transcribed some of the music, assembled the book for their amusement and for their children's musical instruction.

34. The same passage is found at the end of act 2, scene 2, of Ranieri de' Calzabigi's *Alceste*. See Appendix, Pietro Metastasio, *Opere*, 860:

Alceste

Non vi turbate no
pietosi Dei,
se a voi m'involeró
qualche momento.
Anche senza il rigor
de' voti miei,
io moriró d'amor,
e di contento.

Still, still kind powers stay
Your fatal Mission
One moment's sweet delay
Is my petition.
'Tis love that points the dart
The vow I've taken
Although it pierce my heart
Remains unshaken.[35]

Sepur cara e a me la vita,
Se per te mio dolc'amor &c.[36]

If e'er to live, I were desirous
'Twere for thee to draw to my breathe
Thee to save, ah! if the Gods require us
Now to part!—then, welcome death.

35. The following is a free English translation of the Italian passage above:

Don't be disturbed
merciful gods,
if I disappear from your sight
for a few moments.
Even without the severity
of my vows,
I will die of love,
and will willingly do so.

36. The following is a free English translation:

If life is at all dear to me
It is to show you my sweet love.

The corresponding passage in French is found in the Choudens edition of the opera. See *Alceste: Opera en Trois Actes*, 132:

Je n'ai ja_mais chéri la vi _ e,
que pour te prouver mon a_mour.

Leaning firm on thy affection
I descend to deaths dark bower
Safe in love's benign protection
I shall triumph o'er his power.

RICHMOND, JUNE 29TH, 1797. On the 6th of June I went down to the Dismal
Swamp, being engaged in a survey of the property of the old Dismal Swamp
company. My transactions and observations on that trip I have written down in the
IXth Vol. of Memorandums.[37] On the 25th I received a letter from the Govr. of
Virginia informing me, that my plan of the Penitentiary house was adopted by the
Executive, and desiring me to return immediately to Richmond to direct the first
steps for carrying it into effect. I set off the next day, and arrived through Portsmouth
&c. and Petersburg at this place on the 27th. Today I was admitted to an interview
with the board of Council, and received their instructions.

EXPEDITION TO THE DISMAL SWAMP

SUFFOLK, JUNE 10TH, 1797. About the beginning of the Month Mr. Macaulay,* merchant of York, the acting director of the *Old Dismal Swamp Land* Company,
engaged me to go down to the Swamp, to survey the Boundaries of the Company's
property, and to point out such improvements as might occur to me as a professional
Man.

On Tuesday the 6th of June we intended to go down to York by the Stage and
having staid there a day or two, to cross the James river to Smithfield, and then to
proceed to Suffolk. But by some mistake the Stage set off without us. We therefore
resolved to go to Petersburg and take the South side of the river. Our companions
in the carriage were Mr. Geo. Hay* of Petersburg and Mr. Parker* of Smithfield. We
breakfasted at Osbornes and arrived about 11 in Petersburg.

Soon after our arrival at Bob Armstead's a tall well looking young man introduced
himself to me, and presently entered into a very lively conversation upon [horses,]
their diseases, the best mode of treating them, gave me a very intelligent account of
an extraordinary marsh upon his estate in Lunenburg county, and was so witty and

37. This account, comprising a separate manuscript journal, follows below.

good humor'd, that I thought his acquaintance an acquisition. He dined with us, became equally acquainted with Mr. Macaulay and seemed to be the life of the whole company. He procured our names and gave us his, which was *John Mason.*

I spent the evening at Mr. Hay's and returned to the Inn about 9 o'clock.

The company had just sat down to Supper, and Mason was one of the Party.

As soon as he saw me he called out, "*Walk in* Billy Keely." I thought him drunk. He then introduced me to the Gentlemen sitting to his right and left.

"This is Mr. Jones, a very honest humane little Gentleman, as you may tell by the shape of his nose, and this is Mr. Brown, as quiet a good soul as you'll meet in a thousand, and this, Sir, is the true *Billy Keely.*"

"Pray Sir," said I, "is Billy Keely, a title of distinction or a Noun proper."

"*Sir,*" said he, "let me tell you, who *Billy Keely* is. The *Billy Keely's* are a numerous family, and by the cut of your gib, or your physiognomy as the learned say, to which by the bye, I have taken a very particular fancy, I know you are one of them. Billy Keely is a soft, humane, quiet accomodating gentleman; suiting himself to dispositions, tempers, circumstances, and times. He never contradicts roughly, never finds fault, never is out of humour, never quarrelsome. His opinions are right, correct and virtuous. You think he converses, while he argues, you think you have convinced him, but he has changed your own opinion. You think you have conquered, but he has triumphed. Mankind is a great deal the better for *Billy Keely.* He relieves the distressed, comforts the sorrowful, and makes all sad faces put on a smile."

"You do me much honor," said I, "to adopt me into this family of Billy Keelys, and I am very happy to find so many of my relations in this circle for I observe that you give them all the same name." "They are all good fellows," said he, "all Billy Keelys, and we will drink a bottle together." He then ordered a bottle. Some of it was drank. He ran on for above an hour in the same eccentric mad way till I and he were the only members of the Billy Keely family left. In the course of the evening he discovered my fondness for natural history, and immediately turned the conversation to the subject of Dr. Greenaway's* studies. He had been educated by that very extraordinary man, and this explained his acquaintance with learned terms, and subjects. I thought him excessively drunk, though every thing he said was very rational. But it was wildly arranged, and he started from one subject to another without any apparent connexion.

I hoped by his means to procure some books left by the late Dr. Greenaway, and which his widow wishes to sell. It was with difficulty I escaped from him to bed.

June 7th. About 1/2 past 6 I came down stairs and found my friend Billy Keely waiting for me. He had just prepared a Mint julep. "Sir," says he, "you do not drink spirit, I know, but still we may take this julep together. I will drink the spirit, you take the botanical part. I am a Virginian dram-drinker, you a disciple of Linnaeus."

I was very sorry to see him appear so drunk, and hoped to escape from him by going to breakfast with Mr. McAulay to Mr. Geo. Hay's. But it was in vain. He had fastened upon me like a Leach, and he declared he would accompany us. He did so, to the utmost distress of the excellent family. However, he was so witty, his observations were so shrewd and original, that he kept us exceedingly merry till it became necessary to return to the inn in order to proceed by the Stage. It would be impossible to follow him through four minutes duration of his eccentric talk. Like the plays of Reynolds,[38] which depend upon unexpected incident, stage effect, the humour of the performer, and the very *ridiculous* effect of his selection of words, the conversation of Mason would perhaps appear extremely insipid if *read*.

On our return, there happened to be a Gentleman in the porch, unlike Mason in every respect but his extreme fondness for talking, Mr. Tom B————g. As soon as he saw him, Mason proceeded to the attack. He introduced him to me under the most ridiculous though indecent name, Σκαρλετκοδs.[39] "Sir," said he, "this is a very particular and entertaining friend of mine, a *very* distant relation of Billy Keely, a great talker, almost as bad as myself, and above all, let me tell you, a most honest man, the most honest man, I may say in Petersburg. For you must observe," continued he turning to me and speaking in a half whisper, "there goes a great deal of very strong sense, to make a great rascal." Tom had not sense enough to understand him.

About 12, the stage was ready. After we had got in, I was distressed to see Mason follow us. He declared he would go one stage with us. I contrived however to persuade him to deliver two letters for me at the post office, and while he was doing it the stage drove off.

During the whole time during which this unfortunate man attached himself to me I did not discover the slightest trace of insanity, and was astonished to hear from Mr. Hay just as I was leaving him that not only he but his father and other members of his family are insane. He *spoke* more like a drunken than a mad man and acted soberly enough. After hearing that he was insane, I could however plainly perceive

38. Frederic Reynolds (1764–1841), an English playwright, produced over one hundred tragedies and comedies during his career, but only a few of them enjoyed even temporary popularity. His plays were criticized as concentrating on slight and transient issues and having no lasting value. *DNB.*

39. Scarletcods.

231

that he is conscious of the light in which he is considered. He is in the highest degree jealous of every look and whisper amoung those with whom he is conversing; he often repeated the words; "They say that both my father and myself are mad, but notwithstanding, let anyone try to gain his ends with us on that supposition."

John Mason is just mad enough, or which comes to the same thing, he acts and speaks just enough out of the common road, to be extremely troublesome, without being injurious to Society. He drinks hard, and it seems probable that in time he may bring himself into a State of mind in which the law concerning lunatics may reach him. At present there is so *much method* in his madness, that he must be permitted to take liberties, which men in their senses dare not attempt. He lives for instance upon the tavern keepers without paying them, torments their company without their daring to turn him out, or to caution them against him. Both he and his father are accused of having pleaded their insanity in order to violate contracts, and make void imprudent and injurious engagements. All this rendors him less an object of pity.

The company in the Stage besides Mr. Mcaulay and myself, were two Frenchmen who could not speak English, and seemed to belong to Barney's[40] armament, Mr. Parker, and Mrs. West the wife of West the Comedian.[41]

After watering horses at Prince George Courthouse[42] we got down to Geary's tavern a little after 3 dined, changed horses at Cabin point, a small declining village, and arrived at Macintosch's, or Cross roads,[43] as it is commonly called about 7. We had a good Supper, but were miserably off for beds. Six of us slept in a miserable, low, hot Garret. Several Gentlemen went to the Court house (Surry) opposite to the inn, and slept on the Ground. At 1/2 past 2 (June 8th) we proceeded. Our two Frenchmen left us and Mrs. Reddick Mrs. Bradford and Miss S. Richardson joined us. We arrived to Breakfast at Smithfield a small town on Pagan creek. The Creek has 9 or 10 feet of water up to the town but is navigable only for small boats higher up. The place is famous for the beautiful and fast sailing pilot boats built here. It is a small town without much trade at present. The bridge being entirely decayed we crossed

40. For Barney, see p. 242 and n. 58.

41. Margaretta West (d. 1810), well-known tragedienne, was the wife of Thomas Wade West. *Norfolk Gazette & Public Ledger*, 6 June 1810; Sherman, "West," p. 10. For Mr. West see p. 334, n. 14.

42. County seat near the center of Prince George County about five miles east of Petersburg on the stage road. It was created in 1784 when Blandford, the previous county seat, became incorporated into the city of Petersburg. William H. Gaines, Jr., "Courthouses of Charles City and Prince George Counties," *Virginia Cavalcade* 18 (Summer 1968): 10.

43. The lands of Robert McIntosh at the Cross Roads, sixty miles southeast of Richmond, became the county seat of Surry County in 1797, shortly before BHL visited there. The courthouse (completed in 1797) was constructed opposite McIntosh's tavern, where BHL stayed. A. W. Bohannan, *Old Surry: Thumbnail Sketches of Places of Historic Interest in Surry County, Virginia* (Petersburg: Plummer Printing Co. Inc., 1957), pp. 41–42.

the river in a ferry boat, and the Marsh over a very good Causeway. The high land
is about 20 feet above the Marsh and river. The Marsh is of very considerable extent,
and winding with the River among the woody hills has a very pleasant variety of
Landscape. We had a very indifferent breakfast at Taylors tavern. Our company was
encreased by Mr. Barber whose politico-religious disquisitions, if they contained no
wit were however the cause of it in others. I observed that the Rock upon which the
Clay and sand Stratum lies which forms the Soil of the neighbourhood of Smithfield,
is exactly the red loose shell Rock of York (see Vol. VII p. [. .]).[44]

We changed the horses at a cottage, the extreme neatness and cleanliness of which
were a strong contrast to the dirtiness of most of the little houses in this part of the
Country. A very neat woman furnished such of us as would alight with milk and
whortleberries, and with some very rational conversation.

We got to Suffolk about 10 o'clock, much fatigued by heat dust and sleeplessness.
Suffolk lies on Nansemond river, and has up to the town from 7 to 9 feet of water.
It is [a] neat town and some Years ago had a very great trade in tar, pork, and lumber.
It is now declining, the N. Carolina people carrying their produce more generally
through Albermarle Sound to Norfolk and the more northerly ports. The tar trade,
and the shingle and Lumber trade of the Dismal Swamp are however still very considerable and employ many hands and vessels. The former is not very profitable, and
the latter is at present very dull, the Westindia market being much interrupted.

The town consists of one street running at right angles with the River. It was laid
down N5° W so that every house in it is badly situated as to aspect, facing East and
West. Although the street is upon Ground elevated 15 or 20 feet above the Marsh
and River, yet it is surrounded on every side but to the NW with still higher woody
levels, and the light airs of Summer are compleatly excluded. These two circumstances
make it very hot and unhealthy. Four physicians find employment in it, although the
inhabitants cannot exceed 600. There are only 5 in Norfolk, none of whom are in the
road to Wealth.

On Friday, soon after Sunrise, on June 9th Mr. Macaulay, Mr. Swepson* the
company's steward, and myself, set off the first in a chair, the two latter on horseback
to begin our view of the Swamp. We got down to the Company's Plantation 6 miles
from Suffolk in a direction SSE by 8 o'clock. Here we met Mr. Reddick the Overseer
of the Plantation. We had brought with us bread and cheese, and with the addition
of some Milk we made a very good breakfast. This Plantation was purchased with a
view to raise a sufficiency of Corn and Rice for the support of the Company's Negroes
who were at Work in the Swamp. Few hands are at present employed in it, but for-

44. Volume VII is missing.

merly it was an object of some importance. The Land is very rich yet, though it has without ceasing been called upon for more than 30 Years without rest or manure. From the plantation a Canal or Ditch has been dug, chiefly for the purpose of draining the high Land, to the Lake in the Swamp, called *Drummond's Pond*. This canal is about 5 Miles in length 10 feet wide and was in common seasons 3 feet deep. It was likewise useful to bring out a great quantity of Lumber and Shingles, although the Plantation was no very convenient place from whence to cart them to navigable water.[45]

Having breakfasted we descended to the Swamp. The upper part of the Canal was dry and we walked about a mile upon a causeway made by the Earth thrown up in digging the Canal. The Soil is a white Loamy Sand. After the first mile the Soil becomes black and the bank invisible having apparently sunk into the Earth. Here we found several Canoes. Mr. Macaulay, as the Man of most weight went with a Negro to paddle him into one, Mr. Swepson and myself with another Negro into another. The Water was for 3 miles so shallow, that to get the Canoe along was the work of much time and labor. Millions of Muskitoes surrounded us. Mr. Swepson, who was very thinly cloathed was cruelly stung. I was better equipped in Buckskin Pantaloons and halfboots and had only my face to defend. I therefore took the Paddle and helped to work through the mud. I believe we were three hours employed before we reached deep Water near the lake. The Wood on each side consisted all the way of immensely large gums, maples, and Elms, interspersed with a few very large *Cypress* and *Juniper* trees,[46] and a great abundance of younger and smaller trees of all the above descriptions. The canes[47] at the entrance of the swamp were small and low but before we had got down 2 Miles encreased much in size till at last they formed a most beautiful semi-circular Arch over our heads in many places; and compleatly prevented our seeing 10 Yards into the Swamp on either side. The Canal which is perfectly straight, till it arrives within half a mile of the Lake, then takes a gentle turn to the right and under an arch of Canes shows at once the entrance into the Lake. [See PLATE 23.]

---

45. The canal, now known as Washington Ditch, was used extensively until 1810, when the longer Jericho Canal was built. *Virginia Cavalcade* 4 (Winter 1954): 26. See n. 50 below.

46. Gums: here probably *Nyssa biflora* Walt., water gum, but see p. 122, n. 82. Cypress: *Taxodium distichum* (L.) Rich., bald cypress. Juniper: here probably *Chamaecyparis thyoides* (L.) BSP, white cedar, in swamps and bogs. See p. 84, n. 15.

47. Canes: *Arundinaria gigantea* (Walt.) Chapm. See Joseph and Nesta Ewan, *John Banister and His Natural History of Virginia, 1678–1692* (Urbana, Ill.: University of Illinois Press, 1970), pp. 89–90; William Bartram, *Travels Through North and South Carolina, Georgia, East and West Florida, the Extensive Territories of the Muscogulges or Creek Confederacy, and the Country of the Chactaws* (Philadelphia, 1791), pp. 231–32; or Ronald M. Harper, *Economic Botany of Alabama* (Geological Survey of Alabama, Monograph 9, pt. 2; also publ. Washington, D.C., 1928), pp. 72–77.

The first view of this magnificent sheet of Water through so narrow and so singular an opening cannot well be described. It was as smooth as glass when we entered it. The Lakes of Switzerland and of Westmoreland in England, have a character of Magnificence and intricacy, depending upon the Lofty mountains with which they are overhung and the infinite variety of forms and of objects that crowd upon the eye. They produce a sensation of confused and somewhat embarrassed astonishment, a sensation too big, too inexplicable, too unintelligible to be placid, and perfectly easy. I have *sometimes*, when such scenes have suddenly burst upon me, felt an astonishment not entirely pleasant. It has required time to expand the organ of comprehension to the object, as it does to enlarge the pupil of the eye to an encreased light, and in both cases the process is not agreeable. But upon opening upon Drummond lake, one simple idea, one immense object, uncompounded of heterogenous parts, fills the eye, at once and satisfies it. A vast circular surface of Water which appears perfectly circular, bounded by a margin of the most gigantic trees in the world (so gigantic that on entering the lake, the barkless stems of trees that have died, appear on the opposite side at the distance of 8 Miles, as objects of very large size) at one view opens to the eye. It absorbs or expells every other idea, and creates a quiet solemn pleasure, that I never felt from any similar circumstance.

We had not long contemplated the beauty of the lake, before we observed a very black cloud hovering over the opposite shore. We had put off a little into the lake, and had landed on the right shore in order to take, and give our negroes, some refreshment. But the storm rose so rapidly, that it soon seemed to have reached the lake, and though not a breath of air was stirring where we were, the roaring of the Wind and of the Waves at a distance soon became tremendous. We immediately got into our Canoes and endeavored to reach the Canal. We had scarce got into it before the Wind reached us. We landed, and dragged the largest Canoe on shore. The ground was however so soft that I sunk more than once up to the top of my boots into it. We tried to raise the Canoe and to support it by the paddles, having first overturned it, in order to make it a shelter against the rain. We had scarce lifted up one end, before the rain arrived. It fell in torrents and we all left the Work and ran in among the Canes. They were scarce any defence, and in a few minutes we were all wet through. For about 1/2 an hour the rain was tremendous. It then abated, we launched our canoe and returned. It rained the whole way back. We worked hard and at last arrived at the Plantation without a dry thread upon us.

Mr. Reddick had provided us an excellent dinner. We made a roaring fire of some dry Juniper, the smell of which was delightfully aromatic, and dried our cloaths as well as we could. After dinner we returned to Suffolk the Evening having proved very fine.

The Canal which is about 2 feet 6 inches deep was quite dry at the Plantation; and full (*within* 6 inches) at the lake. As the depth is every where nearly equal and the bottom parrallel with the surface of the Swamp we may fairly suppose that the Lake lies two feet lower than the West side of the Swamp *at the plantation*. I have been told by many, that in wet seasons a very gentle current may be observed draining towards the lake. Immediately after the very heavy rain with which we met at the lake there was a pretty strong current from the lake towards the high land. This is easily accounted for. The Lake rose with every drop of water which fell. The Swamp absorbed or detained it. Though therefore there seems to be no doubt that the Lake lies lower than the *West edge* of the Swamp at the Plantation, the difference of level must be extremely minute, perhaps, as I have above supposed, only 2 feet in 5 miles. I shall have occasion to show however when I *more* minutely examine Jericho mills, that the whole of the *West edge* of the Swamp cannot lie higher than the lake, although it seems undoubtedly to be the case at the Plantation.

The Canal was dug with the view of draining the low lands of the Plantation, as well as for the purpose of getting out the Shingles. It seems odd that the Plan should have succeeded; no level was previously taken, and good luck guided the projecter to perhaps the only spot where the scheme would have had effect.

Besides the Cane, and a very large and beautifull species of Fern,[48] I saw nothing that was new to me in Botany. We met only with two Snakes. I have however heard from many Gentlemen, that they sometimes appear in very great numbers. There were many black Tarapins on the Banks, and many very large grey Owls among the Trees who did not appear shy.[49] As we approached the Lake the Muskitoes and the Flies became much less numerous and troublesome, and there were none on its edge.

JUNE 10TH, SATURDAY.   I rode with Mr. Macaulay to Jericho Mill; it is a small Grist Mill. The Mill pond is supplied by two streams from the Swamp, and one from the highland. They are all so dry at present that the Mill does no work.[50]

48. Probably *Woodwardia virginica* (L.) Smith.

49. The terrapins and snakes may have been any of several species. The owls were probably the northern barred owl, *Strix varia varia* Barton, which Murray more recently has found to be abundant in the Great Dismal Swamp. See J. J. Murray, *A Checklist of birds of Virginia* (Virginia Society of Ornithologists, 1952). The great horned owl, *Bubo virginianus virginianus* (Gmelin), is also a possibility.

50. On 30 June 1801, the Dismal Swamp Land Company directors authorized Thomas Swepson, the Company's agent, to "open a road from Jericho Stream into the timber, and also to cut a canal from Jericho towards" Lake Drummond, according to the plan Swepson had proposed three years earlier. The directors also "resolved that a saw mill with two saws and a corn mill of one pair of Stones be erected at Jericho as soon as the canal shall be cut far enough to render it effective." A new Jericho Mill was built later that year, but it was unprofitable as it was frequently damaged in storms. Thomas Swepson to John Brown, 31 August 1798, and Minutes, meeting of Directors of the Dismal Swamp Land Company, 30 June 1801, Dismal Swamp Land Company Papers,

From Jericho Mill we proceeded to Colonel Robert Reddick's* house on the Edge of the Swamp. He has converted it at present into a Smallpox hospital and it was full of Patients in different Stages of the disease.[51] He is a widower. Having lived all his life at this place, and being a great hunter in the Swamp, his advice and assistance will be of importance to me in my expedition. We then called upon a man of the name of Benjn. Baker* whose knowledge of the Swamp renders him the fittest companion I could have. He was from home. Returned to dinner.

The wild animals that inhabit the Swamp are called by the People here *Vermin*, which they pronounce *Varment*. Deer, bears, wild cats, opossums, Rattlesnakes, and mokkason's, are all *Varment*. The Swamp is very properly termed the *Desert*, and pronounced with the accent on the last Syllable, the *Desàrt*.

Colonel Reddick had the good fortune to kill the largest specimen of *Varment*, last winter that has been known here. It was a young bear of immense size.[52] I could not procure its dimensions, as it had not been measured. Its paw was 7 inches wide, and its weight 3.75 Cwt. Its skin covered a barn door, which must be about 9 feet high and about 6 wide. The animal was very lean, and Coln. Reddick supposed that if it had been as fat as the She bear that he shot at the same time, it would have weighed 6 Cwt. The Colonel, in ranging the Swamp, observed the track of a Bear leading to some Oaks which were full of Acorns, and that the Branches of the Trees were much broken. He went out therefore in the Evening and secreted himself near the spot. He had not been there long, before he observed the largest of the two Bears. He shot him, and soon after the She-Bear appeared and he shot her also. The next morning he got them out of the Swamp by means of a yoke of Steers.

Mr. Lamb Reddick* encouraged by the Success of his relation went a few nights afterwards into the Swamp in hopes of similar good fortune. He had not long hid himself before he heard a rustling among the Canes. He got his musket ready, and soon an immense black *Varment* made its appearance among the canes. It was very dark, however he fired and the animal fell. It is not always safe to attempt to skin or carry away a bear directly, least he should not be compleatly dead, and perhaps in his last exertions kill the huntsman. Mr. Reddick therefore contented himself to mark his rout by breaking branches of trees and beating down the canes. The next morning he roused the neighbours, and having collected a considerable party and

---

Duke University Library, Durham, North Carolina; Robert H. Reid, "History of the Dismal Swamp Land Company of Virginia" (M.A. thesis, Duke University, 1948), p. 47.

51. These were patients who had been innoculated with live smallpox virus. Edward Jenner was introducing vaccination for smallpox at this time in England.

52. The common black bear, *Euarctos americanus americanus* Pallas, which is known to reach a weight of six hundred pounds.

got a Yoke of Steers and a Chain he soon found out his track. The huge black *vermin* was seen at some distance among the canes. The company arrived at the spot. But what a metamorphosis! Lamb Reddick's enormous bear was changed to a poor woman's black cow! The raillery of the company, and the disappointment of the young huntsman were not the worst part of the business. The cow was necessary to the existence of the Woman, and another was to be purchased. Lamb Reddick has now to answer frequent enquiries, "*Whether he has lately killed a bear.*"

SUNDAY, JUNE 11TH.   Having engaged Mr. Baker to go with me, we set off in the evening for Norfolk intending to stop and view the Company's Mills on the East Side of the Swamp, called Smith's Mills[53] in our rout. We hired a horse, and a horse and chair. I rode. The chairhorse was blind and so old and poor, that having reached Shoulder's hill on the North Edge of the Swamp 14 miles from Suffolk, we found it impossible to get further. The stage stops at this petty tavern. We had good beds, but were plagued with Muskitoes.

MONDAY. JUNE 12TH.   Set out early having breakfasted with the stage passengers for Smith's Mill. It was excessively hot. We arrived there about 10. It is 14 Miles for Shoulders hill. Mr. Sheppard* an intelligent young gentleman manages the Companys affairs here. Unluckily he was under the necessity of attending a Courtmartial at Portsmouth, and we were left alone the rest of the day. In the evening we walked along the old shingle road to the *Canal*. It was quite dry.

This Canal has been carried on not only without any judgement, but with great injury to the proprietors of land and Mills. The Water is entirely cut off from Smiths Mill, and it has been unable to do any work for these 2 Years. It is however the intention of the D. Swamp Company to redress themselves, by cutting into the new companys canal.[54]

53. The Dismal Swamp Land Company acquired "½ of Smith's or Shepherd's mills houses &c. for £450" in an agreement of 1 January 1796 with Thomas Shepherd. Dismal Swamp Land Company Papers, Duke University Library, Durham, North Carolina.

54. The Dismal Swamp Canal Company was chartered by both Virginia (1787) and North Carolina (1790) for the purpose of connecting the Elizabeth and Pasquotank rivers. George Capron, who worked for the Canal Company, cut off the water that supplied the Land Company's mills, thus rendering them useless. For this action the Land Company intended to "bring Sute against the Dismal Swamp Canal Company." In addition, Capron further aggravated the Land Company by purchasing "at least One Million of Shingles" that poachers had cut from the Land Company's timber. Thomas Shepherd to John Brown, 11 April and 29 August 1799, Dismal Swamp Land Company Papers, Duke University Library, Durham, North Carolina. See p. 236 and n. 50.

TUESDAY, JUNE 13TH. Mr. Sheppard had arrived in the night. After breakfast, we all went to the Mills. They are a Saw Mill of 2 Saws, and a Grist Mill of 2 pair of Stones.

Both wanted repair. I directed many improvements to be made, especially to the Sawmill. And in the evening set out for Norfolk in order to prepare for my expedition.

WEDNESDAY, JUNE 14TH. I ordered the necessary articles, but there was so much delay that my stay was necessarily prolonged beyond my expectations.

RICHMOND, JUNE 28TH, 1797. By a great variety of delays in the different people who were to furnish me with the articles I wanted, and by the necessity of waiting the arrival of Mr. Macaulay, I staid in Norfolk till the 25th when I received a letter from the Governor informing me that my plan of the penitentiary house was adopted, and desiring my immediate attendance in order to set the work agoing. I therefore went the same night to Portsmouth where I slept, and setting off on Monday the 26th at 3 o'clock arrived at night at Macintoshes. The next morning the driver called us all up by mistake at 1/2 past twelve instead of 2 o'clock. We arrived too early at Cabin point to breakfast, proceeded therefore to Moody's, breakfasted, got to Petersburg about 11, dined at Osbornes, and arrived at Richmond about 1/2 past 5 o'clock. It is my intention to return as soon as possible.

[RICHMOND, JUNE 29TH, 1797, CONTINUED.] I spent the morning of yesterday at Colonel Jo[hn] Mayo's house about 1 1/2 Mile from hence on the Western road. The Wasps called *Dirtdaubers* or *Masons* were very busy behind the framed prints in his dining-room. [See pp. 157–60 and PLATE 16.] I have described the Blue Wasp Fig. 1. in Vol. [. .][55] of my memorandums pretty accurately. This Mason whose Cells are joined longitudinally and form one tube seems to be the most common of the two. The proverb, "*Two of a trade can never agree*," does not apply to these two species of *Spider catchers*. I have found both species at Work behind the same picture.

There is a considerable difference however not only in their manner of constructing their Cells, but in the structure of their bodies. The *Sphex caerulea*, No. 1 of the Sketchbook is of a very blue color, the other (which is not described by Linnaeus) is quite black, and spotted on the Thorax and thighs with yellow. The former has a petiolated abdomen, but the petiole increases gradually from its union with the thorax, the petiole of the latter is of equal thickness till it suddenly swells at its union with the

55. This is a reference to a description and sketch in a missing manuscript journal.

abdomen. The nose of the former is somewhat pointed, of the latter it is broad, emarginate, and slightly turned up.

In lifting the picture from the Wall, I injured several of the Cells of this industrious Workman; the dirt sticking to the Wall being torn off. I held up the frame a little and he soon returned to work, bringing with him a round lump of Dirt. He had just begun a new Cell, but seeing his former work disturbed he ran rapidly over the cells, seemingly doubtfull what to do. At last he put down the lump upon one of the holes I had made, and began spreading it with his nose, pushing it out before him, with the action of a hog who is rooting. While he did this he made a shrill buzzing noise. Having plaistered up the hole very compleatly and neatly, he flew away. In about 4 minutes he returned with another lump of Dirt. He put this down upon another hole, and stopped it up in the same manner, and thus he employed himself 4 times. The fifth time he brought his dirt to his new Cell, and was proceeding to go on with it, having compleated his repairs, when I pressed the picture to the Wall, and thus caught him.

I then opened his Cells beginning with the lowest, and being curious to ascertain in what manner the quantity of Spiderflesh collected for the Worm is ascertained, as the size of the Spiders is very various, I weighed them and found the result as follows [see p. 241].

From this trial it appears that the quantity of Food collected for each Worm is nearly the same in weight, about 7½ Grains notwithstanding the difference of the Spiders in number. The Cell *number 3*, must have contained 22 or 23, and that No. 2, only 18 spiders, and the difference of weight was only proportioned to the consumption of spiders in each. It also appears, that the Worm, whose weight at his first escape from the egg scarce amounts to the 5th part of a grain, weighs at his full growth about 1/2 as much as the food that reared him.

The whole class of Insects called by Linnaeus *Hymenoptera*, seem indowed with singular modes of oeconomy, and with much ingenuity and almost reasoning faculties. The Ichneumon lays his eggs in the bodies of other insects or animals. The Sphex is a careful provider of subsistence through the life of his young progenys. The *Vespa*, is an architect, the *Apis*, follows many trades building, making wax, and collecting honey &c. and &c. The ingenuity of the Formica, the ant, exceeds perhaps that of all the others.[56]

56. There are several genera of insects known as Ichneumon flies. *Sphex* was an old genus name for the mud-daubers, now in *Sceliphron* and *Chalybion. Vespa* is the genus of the yellow jacket and the white-faced hornet; *Apis* of the honey bee; and *Formica* is a genus of ants.

Plate 23. Entrance to Lake Drummond from Washington Ditch, Dismal Swamp, 9 June 1797.

FROM THE SKETCHBOOKS

Coming to Richmond in the stage.

The appearance of the rainbow was for about 10 minutes nearly like the drawing. The Rays then began to play very much like those of the Aurora borealis. They appeared to be rather occasioned by a luminous, perhaps electrical fluid, than by the reflection of the solar light. However the center of the Rainbow was also the center from which they diverged.

I observed this Rainbow the more particularly, as all the passengers in the stage were obliged to get out, on account of a Waggon which stopped up the road down Church hill. One of the horses, had fallen down in convulsions and was to all appearance dead. He was dragged from under the pole, but the negroes attempting to throw him into a gulley, one of them laid hold of his tail to pull him away. In a moment however he revived, and trotted up the hill the Negroe still holding fast by his tail, lest he should escape.

Plate 24. Extraordinary appearances in the heavens and on earth, 2 August 1797.

the size of the spiders is very various, I weighed them and found the result as follows

The lowest Cell N.º 1 contained 19 Spiders, and a small Worm who seemed just hatched and had eaten nothing. The spiders weighed —— 9.ⁿ 7½

worm N.º 1

N.º 2 contained 17, spiders, and one empty skin — 6½

the worm weighed ½ a gr.

N.º 3, contained 19, very small spiders & a few skins weighing 5¾
the worm weighed ½ a grain —— ½ } 6¼

N.º 4 contained a few empty skins of spiders
the worm was just beginning to spin, but appeared very much leaner than usual, he weigh. — 3¼

N.º 5, contained an involucrum in which was a Grub not yet turned to a Sphex fallis. the involucrum & worm weighed being heavier than the last worm alone, } 3½

The 6.ᵗʰ & 7.ᵗʰ were open at one and the Wasp having made his Escape.

When my *Sphex* saw the dilapidation I had occasioned in his cells, he must have *thought* and *reasoned* upon what he should do. The mischief was done in his absence. The mud he brought on his return, was intended to build a new cell. But seeing the injury done to the old ones, he altered his plan and before he proceeded to build the new ones he thoroughly repaired the former.

I conjecture that this Sphex is the *Sphex Pensylvanica*[57] of Linnaeus, although his description does not exactly suit him.

RICHMOND, JUNE 30TH, 1797. While I staid at Lindsay's Hotel, Norfolk, I had constant opportunities of seeing and conversing with *Commodore Barney*,[58] who is, in the present uncertain state of politics, grown into an object of attention. He is certainly a man not destitute of abilities, and as a seaman, I believe he is equal to the most skilful American Navigators. His personal courage is also not to be doubted. But there are many traits in his character and habits that appear to me to unfit him for the situation in which the French republic have placed him. There are not many men, upon whom *command* fits easy, unless they have been inured to it for a considerable time. There is an ease about an old General, Admiral, or Minister of State, let him be ever so haughty and despotic, that is to be acquired only by habit. Barney has not yet acquired it. He appears to be in a situation to which he may perhaps be equal, but to which he is unused. On that account he is not loved by his Crews. Frenchmen have been particularly accustomed to a polite and easy though rigid discipline in their officers of the old School, and must easily detect the deficiency. There is something diametrically opposite to the condescending haughtiness of a French officer, in the plain roughness of an English or American Sea Captain. Barney has much of the latter left, although having made himself tolerably perfect in the rudiments of french shrugs and gesticulation, he is perhaps on the road to acquire the latter. Another cause of dislike to him, originates perhaps in his scarce ever going on board his Ships. In the System of Liberty and equality, this seems a strange neglect. Besides this he never permits his men to come ashore but on particular occasions, altho' by the rules of the french navy, one tenth of the Crew have the right to go ashore *daily* in rotation, when in port.

But the most exceptionable part of the Commodore's conduct, as a *public functionary*, seems to be, the want of reserve with which he expresses himself upon his objects and intentions as Commander of a military force. Should his openness however be supposed to be merely assumed, and intended as a Cloak to his real plans, it has this bad effect, that it lowers the opinion entertained of his prudence. In these free communications however he is not very consistent. Having got the *Medusa* frigate thor-

57. *Sceliphron cementarium* (Drury).

58. Joshua Barney (1759–1818) served in the American navy from 1776 until 1796, when he was appointed commodore in the French navy, where he served until 1802. During the War of 1812 Barney privateered against British shipping, and in 1814 he was placed in command of a flotilla to protect the U.S. Capitol from the British. He was ordered to disembark and retire to Washington, where he led his naval forces in the heroic but unsuccessful Battle of Bladensburg. He was appointed naval officer at Baltimore after the war. *DAB*.

oughly repaired, he has dropped below the fort almost as low down as Crany Island.[59] He sometimes pretends that he will leave this station on the first dark night with a fair wind. Then he means to go up the Bay. At other times, he thinks he is of service to the french cause by keeping a Superior British force idle in the Chesapeak. He says that he blockades the English, and that it is of little consequence whether he detain them by lying within, or without them. He gives his opinion upon the probabilities of the War, lays open his ideas of his own situation as it respects his french or his american citzenship, and reasons upon the conduct he may pursue in case of a rupture to any one who will listen to him. The natural effect of this conduct must be, and indeed is, to produce an idea that no important confidence, ought to be entrusted to him, and that the French directory will not long continue to employ him.

He makes no Secret of his being deeply engaged in commercial pursuits at Norfolk; and I heard him say, that if he were kept in port long enough he should make 200,000 dollars. He is indeed a little given to boast of the property he has acquired in the French Service.

At Lindsay's Hotel he constantly meets officers of the British fleet, and they converse together with great ease, and perfect good humor. He is indeed not an unpleasant man, and his conversation, though it betrays no very great depth of understanding, and runs too much upon indelicate subjects, is not wholly unentertaining.

A midshipman from the *Topaz* (british frigate), a boy about 15 Years old, being in his company, requested Colonel Hamilton[60] to point him out to him. The Colonel did so. The young midshipman having surveyed him for a few minutes turned round and said, "A damned good looking fellow, by God, I should like to see him along side of our frigate."

RICHMOND, JULY 12TH, 1797. Since my arrival I have been entirely engaged in setting out the foundation of the new Penitentiary house, and in getting forward the provisory steps for its erection. Although so near Richmond, and so much frequented by Cattle, the steep gravelly knoll upon which the house is to stand, abounds in snakes and *scorpions* (as a poisonous lizard with a red head and green body is here improperly called).[61] These reptiles found the brick kiln before it was set fire to, a

59. A small island at the mouth of the Elizabeth River five miles from Norfolk, where in 1813 Americans defeated British attempts to capture Norfolk, Portsmouth, the *Constellation*, and the Gosport shipyard. Wertenbaker, *Norfolk*, pp. 111–13.

60. Colonel John Hamilton was the British vice-consul in Norfolk. Stationed there at least four years before BHL mentioned him, Hamilton was still "Brittanic counsul" in Norfolk as late as 1807. *CVSP*, 6:375, 9:545; Wertenbaker, *Norfolk*, p. 92.

61. There are neither scorpions nor poisonous lizards in Virginia. Possibly BHL referred to the harmless blue-tailed skink, *Eumeces fasciatus* (L.), but the description is dubious.

Fig. 31. "Hermitage," home of John Mayo, 10 July 1797.

very convenient lodging house, and those who attended the burning of the brick, told me that as soon as the fire and smoke began to incommode them they left their retreats in great numbers and were seen crawling round the top of the Clamp till the fire put an end to their misery. In clearing the ground several mockasons, and *Scorpions* have been killed, of which I saw some.

Two days ago the following singular circumstance occurred of which Major Quarrier,* Colonel Burnley,* and myself were witnesses. The morning was extremely hot, there had been a meeting of several members of the Executive upon the Ground, and we were returning down the side of a hill when we heard a violent screaming of birds in a small low bush. We stopped, and saw two of the birds, called the *French* Mocking bird,[62] furiously pecking at, and fighting with something which was hid in the bush. I got very near them and perhaps disturbed them, for presently the birds flew up the hill, close upon the ground, and a large black snake followed them. They alighted upon a tree very near us and seemed in great agitation. Of the Snake we

62. The brown thrasher, *Toxostoma rufum* (L.), not our common mockingbird, *Mimus polyglottos polyglottos* L.

244

soon lost sight. On examining the Bush we found a young mockingbird alive but wounded severely in the back and bleeding much. I took it up. It screamed, and was answered by the old one in the tree. I therefore put it down again, went away and presently saw the old ones descend to its assistance. It should seem that the snake had been robbing the Nest during the absence of the old birds. This is a very striking instance of the strength and courage inspired by parental affection.

RICHMOND, JULY 23D, 1797. After the longest drought remembered for several Years, we have had for the last Week past heavy rains almost every day. The first fell on the 15th. Yesterday the day opened with heavy low Clouds all round the horizon. It was sultry, and about 10 o'clock it rained a little. About 12 a very severe thunderstorm arose from the Southwest attended with a deluge of rain. It was succeeded by another which came from the East. A continued succession of Thunder clouds from different quarters arose till about 1/2 past 1. I was sitting in my room writing, when a sudden flash of lightning almost blinded me, and in a moment it was succeeded by a tremendous crack of Thunder, resembling the sudden fall of a heavy building. It was short, and unaccompanied by the usual long roll at the end of it. The horses and animals in the Inn Yard were terribly frightened by it, they ran about in confusion for some minutes, and all the Children set up their pipes. It afterwards continued Thundering very violently, and successive clouds arose and passed over till I went to sleep at 12 o'clock.

The severe clap mentioned above had struck the house of Colonel John Mayo, on Councilchamber hill in a very singular manner. The hill is the first and most prominent point on the West side of the Shockoe Valley, and has in different places been very frequently struck by Lightning. The house is rather low being only one story. Coll. Mayo having removed to the Hermitage [see FIG. 31], and Mr. McCrea* who has hired the house not having as yet taken possession of it, it was quite empty even of furniture, excepting two Looking glasses in gilt frames, one between the Windows of the front, the other between those of the back parlor.[63]

The lightning appears to have first struck the Chimney the top of which it had entirely thrown down. Half of the bricks, had fallen to the front, half to the back of the house. A small part of the Shaft which remained above the ridge was most singularly shattered, the bricks being taken out in holes, and those which remained, standing in the most whimsical and critical positions. At the Chimney it appears to have divided. One part struck the roof and tore off all the shingles a considerable way

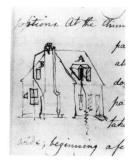

63. An account of the lightning damage to Mayo's house was recorded in *The Virginia Gazette & General Advertiser* (Richmond), 26 July 1797.

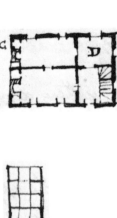

down, leaving however in one place a patch of three courses. The shingles were taken off in a straight line about 2 feet wide; beginning a few feet below the ridge, and ending about 4 feet above the eaves. At *B* the lightning passed through the roof and entered a closet. It forced open the door, and struck it into the sloping cieling with such force that it could not be moved. It seems to have followed the edge of the door and the door-post, guided perhaps by the hinges. All this edge was shattered, and one part was much burnt. Almost all the panes of Glass in the Window of the room were broken, most probably by the expansion of the Air. From this closet the lightning descended to that below at *C*. It there compleatly demolished the Sash, and part of the frame, and broke down the boarded partition between it and the room. The architrave of the door was torn off and forced into the opposite Wall of the room, where it stuck so fast in the lath and plaister as to be immoveable. All the wooden dressing of the chimney piece, and all the other wood work of that side of the room was torn down and dashed to pieces about the floor nor did a whole pane of Glass remain in any of the windows. A large nail, which seemed to have belonged to the frame of the Closet Window, was taken out and stuck fast in the Closet door, so that it could not be drawn. Thence the lightning seems to have proceeded to the back door in the lobby *D*. The door, which was locked and bolted was forced open and the handle of the large key which was in the lock snapped off short, nor was it to be found. All the windows of the Lobby were broken. Further, the effects of this part of the flash were not traced.

The other part of the flash, entered the dormer window *A*, broke all the glass and took out one of the sash rails (bars) compleatly. It left several marks on each side of the window and then descended into the room below making a hole in the paper and plaister near the cieling. It then struck the corner of the looking glass frame, burnt up the gilding leaving a sulphurous smell, and acted upon the surface of the glass, so as to leave upon it a slight indenture filled up with very small particles of glass. It seems then to have leaped to the center of the glass on the lower side where it pulverized the surface in the same manner and then descended along the ornament to the Wall tearing away the paper in an irregular line, and making a hole in the plaister. It passed through the floor, but I could not get into the Cellar to trace it further.

At the same time the lightning seems to have struck the Capitol, although there are two Franklins[64] upon the Roof: for one of the Modillions of the wooden cornice was found torn off upon the Ground, and a young Gentleman (Mr. Allen) who was in it, complained of an uneasy sensation on his left side, as if it were covered *with Cobwebs*, as he expressed himself.

64. Lightning rod invented by Benjamin Franklin.

A Man was also knocked down in the Main street and remained senseless some minutes.

JULY 24TH, 1797. The following inscription for the Cornerstone of the Penitentiary house was drawn up by me on Thursday and approved by the Executive without alteration.

The Legislature
of the Commonwealth of Virginia
having abolished the ancient sanguinary criminal Code
This first Stone of an Edifice
the Monument of that Wisdom
which would reform while it punishes the Criminal
was laid on the 7th day of August
in the Year 1797, and of American Independence the 22d
by Jn. Wood Esq Governor
_____Gr. Master of Masons
Deputy   ditto
Lodges No. 10, 19.

_____ ⎞
_____ ⎟
_____ ⎟ Council
_____ ⎟
_____ ⎟
_____ ⎠

RICHMOND, AUGST. 3D, 1797. On Saturday the 29th I went down in the Stage to Williamsburg and from thence to Greenspring to Mr. Ludwell Lee's house. He has entirely pulled down his old mansion, and he wanted me for the 3d time to give him a *new* design to proceed upon. I did so, but as his meanness seemed to grow upon him daily, I found it impossible for me to bend my ideas, to a compliance with his mode of procedure with his workmen. I therefore declined any further connection with him and returned to Williamsburg on the 31st. I spent that day and the next in visiting my friends in that charming village, and returned to Richmond by the stage on the 2d. The weather has been very tempestuous and raining for some time past, and was so on my journey home.

About 3 Weeks ago the drought had so entirely destroyed all prospect of even a moderate crop of corn, that no subsequent rains were expected to be of any great service in recovering. It has however turned out differently and on all tolerable good lands the most astonishing growth has taken place, so that a most plentiful crop may reasonably be hoped for. On poor and sandy [land] the plant was too much injured to recover and many fields still look miserably; but in general this is not the case. A stalk of corn which I observed in a garden in Richmond, grew seven inches and 3/8ths in 24 hours.

When on my return to Richmond I arrived in the stage on the top of Churchhill[65] all the passengers were obliged to get out, as the road was stopped up by a waggon. This gave an opportunity of observing a Rainbow the most perfect and singular I ever saw. It was spread like a fan the circumsference being in many places connected with the center by many broad and luminous rays. In Sketch book No. III is a very rough but exact representation of the phaenomenon [see PLATE 24]. The rays played like those of the Aurora borealis. They were almost colorless. The Rainbow was also rather whiter than usual. A second luminous arch was very distinctly seen without any interruption.[66]

A very ludicrous scene which happened is represented on the same page.

65. Church Hill was one of the two hills (the other is Shockoe Hill) upon which the city of Richmond was built. The two hills were divided by Shockoe Creek. Stanard, *Richmond*, p. 71.

66. Dr. George S. Benton of The Johns Hopkins University has offered these observations on the rainbow: "Multiple arches are well known. I have personally seen a rainbow with two distinct luminous arcs. However, the angular distance between the two arcs should, I believe, be greater than that shown in Latrobe's sketch.

6

Virginia, 6 August–5 September 1797

The story of Miss Charlotte Hoissard.

We pay so little attention in general to what is going forward on the scene on which we ourselves are actors, that when now and then a real story, unadorned by fiction is presented to us in the succession of its circumstances, we are very apt to fancy it too full of incident and contrivance to have passed on the theater of *real* life. I have more than once made this observation in reading my old journals of trivial transactions, which had indeed very little but truth to recommend them. In this respect we are like the actors of dramatic scenes, who are so engaged with their own parts, that they hardly ever study the performance of others. We wait till our own cue comes, and then go on, as we have accustomed ourselves to do.

I have often intended to make the recital of some of my own adventures an amusement of my leisure, but whenever I have attempted it, the appearance of *fiction* has accompanied many of the most positive facts. Indeed the general rage for Novels, which most frequently recite very common occurences, but which we know to be invented, throws a false reflection upon every relation which at all steps out of the common road.

In the following story I was a subordinate actor and with all its circumstances I was intimately acquainted. I shall relate therefore nothing that I do not know to be true, although the whole of it may appear the production of fancy.

About 50 to 30 Years ago lived at Hackney near London, a physician, who was either then, or has been since, knighted, and is now Sir John Silvester. He was an eminent practitioner in his day, but whether fashion or skill gave him that eminence I know not, for he belongs now to former times, although he "lives and moves and has his being." He has I believe outlived all his patients, having never taken medicine himself.[1] His Son, I believe his only son, John, was educated at Oxford, and afterwards studied law. Nature, in denying him genius, gave him two qualities infinitely more valuable, industry, and the best of hearts. He was very young when his usual residence became the house of his father at Hackney. Sir John, was a widower, hale, hearty, and rich, and was turning his eyes to a second wife, after his daughter had married Captain Carteret, the adventurous companion of Admiral Wallis in the dis-

---

1. Sir John Silvester (d. 1789), physician to the Army in the Low Countries (1744), was knighted in 1774. His son John (1745–1822), a lawyer and recorder of the City of London (1803–22), married Maria Hoissard. His daughter Mary-Rachael (1741–1815) married Philip Carteret, rear-admiral in the Royal Navy. John Burke and John B. Burke, *A Genealogical and Heraldic History of the Extinct and Dormant Baronetcies of England* (London, 1838), p. 484. Although BHL's statements are not entirely clear, he apparently thought Silvester was still alive. BHL quoted from Acts 17:28: "For in him we live, and move, and have our being; as certain also of your own poets have said, For we are also his offspring."

covery of Otaheite.[2] He had fixed his hopes upon Mrs. [Maria] Hoissard, the widow of a Mr. Hoissard, formerly a very rich merchant of Lisbon, who had left her a good fortune and eight Children.

Mrs. Hoissard was the Sister of two very extraordinary Men, Peter and George Livius. The former is well known as the incorruptible Chief Justice of Canada, and the opponent and prosecutor of Governor Haldimand; the latter exhibited his excentricities in the East Indies, and still continues the admiration and astonishment of his friends in England, where he has married a first cousin of my brother-in-law, Mr. Foster.[3] *She herself* thought more brilliantly, and expressed herself more oddly than most Ladies, though her conduct was perfectly consistent with the manners and laws of society, and infinitely more correct and amiable than that of more common wives and mothers. The family character seemed however to consist in a rapid and fiery imagination, warm affections, and a great contempt for the quiet, prudent and cold manners that are so safe a road to fortune and respectability.

Mrs. Hoissard had so much beauty, wit and address, that her 8 Children were forgotten, and she was the toast of all the young Widows[4] of Hackney. Sir John Silvester was so smitten by her charms, and so persuaded of the irresistible powers of himself and his riches, that he felt himself secure in his prospect of becoming her husband, nor was he convinced of his mistake till he one morning was informed that she had about half an hour before married—his Son.

The disappointment and rage of the knight may be easily imagined. The new couple with their large family were every where admitted but at his house. Sir John quitted Hackney and went to Bath, and Mr. Silvester began to apply himself indefatigably to his profession. The practice of the old Bailey is the least respectable in London, but it is perhaps the most lucrative; unless it be that of a few whose talents or long experience enabled them to set their own price. Mr. S. had neither, but his attention to his clients, and his extreme industry, soon brought him sufficiently into practice to enable him with the assistance of his wife's fortune to support his family in a comfortable and rather genteel manner, and by degrees to keep a carriage. He never had any children by his wife, and her sons were sent abroad. Tom went to the

---

2. Samuel Wallis (1728–95) sailed to the Pacific in 1766 in the *Dolphin*, accompanied by Philip Carteret (d. 1796) in command of the *Swallow*. In the Pacific, Wallis discovered numerous islands, including Tahiti. *DNB*.

3. George-Peter Livius, commissariat-general in the East India Company, married Mary, the daughter of Joseph Foster Barham. They had seven children. Peter Livius, chief-justice of Quebec, married Anne-Elizabeth, the daughter of John Tufton Mason. They had three daughters. *Burke's Landed Gentry*, 3:204. Sir Frederick Haldimand (1718–91), governor and commander-in-chief in Canada (1778–85), was prosecuted after his return to England for false imprisonments made during his term of office. *DNB*. For the Fosters, see p. 268 and n. 11.

4. In the eighteenth century "widow" could be used for either sex. *OED*.

East Indies, Daniel to Lisbon. Both these made fortunes. Tom sent to England to the care of *my* Mother, a most beautiful little half Hindoo Girl, whose dispositions and talents were as perfect as her form, and to whom she gave a very excellent education. He soon after died leaving her all his fortune. Daniel died single at Lisbon many years afterwards. What become of the others I do not remember, excepting the three eldest Girls, Matilda, Charlotte, and Anna. Anna lived to be one of the finest Women I ever saw, and one of the wittiest, but died of a consumption, and in the Year 1786 when I came to England, the family was reduced to Mr. and Mrs. S. and Matilda, and Charlotte Hoissard. My father's family were then the most intimate friends they had.

Matilda was not a regular beauty. She had however a good figure, was remarkably tall, and added to many other accomplishments a most wonderfull talent for painting and embroidery. Her performances in Worsted and Silks were among the best that have fallen under my observation. Though most perfectly good hearted, and good tempered, there was an apparent haughtiness in her manner that left the Men at a distance. Her pride swam all upon the surface of her behavior for her heart seemed not to feel it.

Charlotte was a great contrast to her sister. Less handsome in face and person, she appeared to much greater advantage in mixed company. She was much marked by the Smallpox, and yet her face had so much vivacity and wit in its expression, she had such fine teeth, and exposed them so often by her smiles, that at first sight she took all notice from her more handsome Sister. She was too lively to apply to any study. She had just picked up a *little* of all her Sister had *learned*, and was incomplete in the acquisition of any thing but dancing. A more amiable giddy heart, however, never existed. All the poor children of the neighbourhood were her pensioners in cloaths, and the mothers in soups and candle. Her mother was divided between her anxiety for and her admiration of this wild child who seemed to have too little design of her own, to detect the views of others, and to be eternally exposed to temptation and danger. Matilda's prudence seemed a sufficient guard to her. The united care of the father and mother appeared scarce sufficient to protect the careless innocence of Charlotte. But they were mistaken.

It was Charlotte's birthday. She was just nineteen. The family breakfasted about 1/2 past nine, and every chair was ready to be filled but Charlotte's. She was not come down. They waited a few minutes, and then sent up a servant to call her. Her room was deserted, and no appearance even of her cloaths lying about. Her Sister flew up, and her Mother followed. Every thing but the furniture was removed. All the chests of drawers, and wardrobe were empty. A sealed note lay upon the toilet. Matilda took it up trembling, and read

> My dear parents and sister
> Forgive and forget forever
> Charlotte Hoissard.

The despair and anguish of the Mother and sister cannot be painted. The feelings of such moments are scarce understood by the Sufferers. Her father felt doubly. She was the darling of his soul, and he was the husband of her wretched mother!

The first suggestion was to enquire whether any one had been married that morning at the Chapel of the Rolls, the Chapel to which that part of London belonged, as to matrimonial registry, Mr. S.'s house being in a street which is *extraparochial*.

The enquiry was fruitless. In his distress her father came to our house. My father and mother, my sister Louisa [and] myself were seated in the drawing room. He entered, and unable to speak, he sat down. My father saw his agitation, and enquired after the health of his family. He wept, and my mother retired, beckoning to me and my sister to follow. Soon however I was called in, and having promised secrecy, my father told me the unfortunate story, and desired my active assistance in the search after the fugitive.

There was not the smallest cue to guide us. However it was supposed, that she might have been married in one of the numerous churches of the immense cities of London or Westminster. I proposed searching the West end of the town, while *John*, the faithful old Coachman enquired at all the Eastern Churches.

Honesty is the same principle in a Minister of State and in a menial Servant. Its value varies, according to its polish and setting, but the Jewel is the same. John possessed it of the first Water. Its coat was rough. He had been servant in the family of Sir John when his present Master was a Child. He had attached himself to and followed his fortunes. He was an old *Man*, and was allowed and practised the priviiledge of an old domestic in its fullest extent. He was the tyrant of the kitchen and servants hall, and the monitor and counsellor of the parlor. The present distress of the family put him into great activity, and his intimate knowledge of the town rendered his assistance highly usefull.

I thought it highly improbable that any one who had had a design to elope with the daughter of a man so well known as Mr. Sylvester would chuse to acquire a residence in a very near parish to his house, in order to entitle him to the banns or a licence of marriage. *Mary, lebone*, the most distant, and the most populous, seemed to me more likely. If she had been married in London, it must have been by banns, as she was under age, and could not obtain a licence without her parents consent. So many banns are published from the Pulpit of Mary lebone every Sunday that no one attends to the names, and the Church is in noisy motion all the time they are read. Many a *private* and *clandestine* match is by this means publickly proclaimed and yet wholly unknown, till all is over.

I therefore made the best of my way to Mary lebone stopping by the way only at St. Georges Bloomsbury, St. Ann's Soho, St. George's Hanover square, and Oxford chapel. I was however disappointed. I then turned to the South, examining every church till I came to St. Johns, Westminster. I then went to Lambeth came to the Abbey, and coming up the Strand examined St. Martins, the Savory, the New Church, Covent garden, and about 5 o'clock came to St. Clements Danes close to Mr. Silvesters house, for he lived in Cary-street Chancery lane. I was so completely fatigued that I passed the Church intending to dine at St. George's coffeehouse, for I had tasted nothing since the morning. However I turned back and enquiring for the Clerk he went with me to the Vestry-room when to my astonishment I at once saw the names of *William Osborne* and *Charlotte Uzzard* married that morning, by publication of banns on the 3 preceding Sunday's. She had it appears permitted the Clerk to spell her name wrongly both in the Banns and the Entry, although she had signed it rightly herself, but so indistinctly that the difference was not evident at a first examination.

I enquired of the Clerk into all the circumstances attending the marriage. The names for the publication of banns were delivered to him by some one whom he did not recollect. The Lady when she came to be married, got out of a Hackney coach, was dressed in plain muslin, with a large close plain muslin bonnet which hid her face, and a long black cloak. She seemed unwell and was much agitated. She could scarce go through her part of the ceremony, and the Clergyman was so struck with it, that he hesitated for a moment to proceed. When the ceremony was over, the fees were to be paid. The husband however had no money. After a moments hesitation the Lady put her hand into her pocket, and pulled out a very elegant purse full of Guineas. She had drawn off her Glove, and showed a beautiful white hand and arm at that part of the ceremony at which the ring is given by the husband. This had excited the Clergymans surprize and the purse confirmed it. He suspected something extraordinary to belong to the match, and said: "Good God, Madam, I have made you miserable this day for the rest of your life, whoever you are! Pray to God to forgive you, it is too late to go back." She fainted at this involuntary exclamation of the reverend old man, and there was some bustle in the Church before she recovered, but no one knew her. She drove off in the Coach that brought her. The Clerk gave me so exact a description of *William Osborne*, that if he had ever visited in Cary street, I was sure to find who he was.

RICHMOND, AUGST. 6TH, 1797. *Continuation of the Story of Miss Charlotte Hoissard.*

With this account I returned to my father's. We agreed to wait the return of *John,* before we mentioned my success to Mr. Silvester. My father had spent the whole morning in endeavors to console the mother and the Sister of the imprudent girl; who dreaded more that she might not be married at all than that she might have married improperly. He had just returned when I came in, and John soon entered with an account of his unsuccessful search. John was a sober, discreet and wise man, not given to swearing.

"Pray, John," asked my father, "do you know a Gentleman of the name of William Osborne?"

"A Gentleman," said John, "a Gentleman? May all hell open to swallow such a Gentleman and his Master along with him! A Gentleman, Sir, he is no more a Gentleman than I am, and may I be d_____d if I would stand in the shoes of such an eternal scoundrel for the whole universal world and all its kingdoms!"

"But who is he then, and who is his Master?"

John then gave an account of the adventures of William Osborne from his first coming to London as a country clown, getting as a helper into a stable Yard, becoming a Hackney coachman, a groom to a Woman of pleasure, a Coachman to an old debauchee, from thence being hired as a footman into Mr. Silvester's family, being turned out of it for impudent behavior, and at last being hired as Coachman to some old Rake with whom he at present was supposed to live.

The description I had obtained of the Clerk exactly answered that which John gave of him. Short in stature, with a weatherbeaten face, squint-eyed, and bow legged, wearing his hair combed down to his eyes in front, and curled close to his head all round behind in a very small strait curl; his whole head well plaistered with pomatum and thickly powdered; just as it was then the fashion for the smartest order of Coachmen to dress.

Upon the mention of William Osborne it was impossible for John to conceive that his young Mistress had married him himself. He only supposed he had contributed to an elopement with his Master, the old Rake. But upon hearing that she had married him, neither the respect due to my father's character, to the family of Mr. S. nor to the delicacy of a woman kept him from bestowing upon him and her a volley of language of the coarsest and most unbridled kind; neither expostulation nor anger could quiet him, till at last he threw himself into a chair, and cried like a child. It took some time to make him think and act rationally. It was late in the evening before my father returned to give the family the melancholy account of the nature of the loss they had suffered.

We all feel and judge relatively: A slight headach is troublesome, but could be a happy relief from the tortures of the Gout. The mind feels in the same way. Her unhappy mother who could scarce support existence under the dread that she might be debauched, felt relief from the fatal news that she had *married* even *William Osborne*.

I leave it to the Ladies to account for the fact. All I have to do, is to tell it. Without supposing insanity, there is scarcely any thing to pity in the case of poor Charlotte, if her act be taken for the deliberate resolve of misplaced affection. But from hints that were *once* given, I believe that she did not leave her father's house quite innocent, but that she had been the prey of arts, while Osborne was in the family, too horrid and detestable for any modest pen, and that having lost her purity by means of the abominable *potions* of a villain, she threw away her happiness and character, preferring the disgrace of having made choice of such a *husband*, to the most intolerable infamy of surrendered chastity to such a *man*.

The next morning Mr. S.'s family left London, in order to hide as much as possible the Chasm that was made in it. To discover the unfortunate fugitive was a task of new difficulty. My father kindly offered his assistance, and to the prudence and benevolence of so zealous a friend, they intrusted the entire direction of their affair.

London is the sink and hiding place of every species of vice and misery. It is vain to search without some clue. But in the present case it seemed impossible to find one. *John* knew something of Osborne's connexions, but he himself was so well known to them, that he could not expect to gain any information which Osborne wished to be kept back.

There was a poor, but very good and honest Woman, whose family of little Children had been cloathed and almost supported by the kindness of Charlotte, from her own pocket money; and she herself had been set up in a little Milleners shop by the joint assistance of the whole family. Her name was Williams at that time, she having lately married a second husband, a carpenter, whom I was endeavoring to push into business. Charlotte was particularly attached to her and made her a sort of confidante. I sent for her husband, and examined him without his perceiving it upon the visits that his wife might have lately made in Cary street. I found he knew nothing of the affair. I therefore told him what was necessary, and desired him to sound his wife. The poor woman was almost distracted at hearing the news, and plainly showed that she was innocent of any connivance or assistance in the business. I saw her myself soon afterwards. She told me that she had observed that Charlotte had been very pensive and unhappy lately when she had found her alone, and that she seemed to assume more gaiety in company than she felt, and also that she had got all her Cloathes into very good order a few weeks ago. All this proved a design which had been laid for some time. She knew Osborne well, and thought she remembered a particular attention in him to Miss Charlotte, but had not seen him for some weeks. She told me accidentally that she had carried something for her to the Peacock in Grays-inn lane, but seemed not to suspect the possibility of an intrigue, as the errand was of the most plausible nature, and seemed perfectly undesigned. This gave me however an idea which I immediately put into execution.

The Peacock was a house of very low character at that time, the receptacle of thieves and loose women, and famous only for very excellent Burton ale which was sold there, and which drew together now and then some more respectable characters.[5]

The Peacock was some short time afterwards exalted into a house of much higher Character by the visit of the Prince of Wales, who in a drunken fit went thither and spent there a riotous evening.[6] The circumstance was soon generally known, the Land lord put up the sign of an enormous gilded peacock, called himself Purveyor of Burton ale to His R. H. the P. of Wales, and it became the ton to go thither to drink Burton ale. Another infamous house next door then arose which took off the rascals.

It [the Peacock] was kept by a Yorkshireman, and was much resorted to by North country people on that account. It occurred to me that Osborne most likely might frequent the house, or might have formerly frequented it and be known there, as he was from Kendal in Cumberland. The message to the house, though it seemed to bear no relation to a correspondence with him or any one there, might be a mere contrivance of secrecy.

John would have been the best person to have followed the scent I had found. He was extremely shrewd, and his manners were best adapted to gain confidence there. But he was too well known to avoid suspicion. I therefore got myself well instructed in all he knew of Osborne and his connexions, and undertook the task myself. I washed all the powder out of my hair, and platted it into an awkward sort of a tail. I got a coarse shirt, and was dressed in a coarse drab colored suit with heavy ill made boots and dirty buckskin breeches. Thus equipped with a thick Oak stick in my hand, I went about 8 o'clock that evening to the house. I was perfect master of the Yorkshire dialect, and endeavored to assume as clownish a gait as I could.

All I could do that evening was to scrape a tolerable acquaintance with the Yorkshire landlord (whose name I forget) and a better with his wife, pretending I came from Cumberland where I had been doing business as a horsedealer.

5. The following paragraph was inserted as a footnote by BHL.

6. George IV (1762–1830) may well have visited the Peacock in Gray's Inn Lane while he was Prince of Wales. He and his clique were well-known visitors to many of the London pubs, where he incurred huge debts and gained a reputation for riotous living. *DNB*.

The next evening I returned in the Same dress and was recognized by my new acquaintance, and asked into the bar.

I then asked if none of my country folks were
Aw thien ax'd if nun o' me cuntry fauk wurn't
there for I'd be glad to see some of them in
thur, for aw'd be fiain to see sum on 'um ith
this great town of London.
this girt tahn o' Lunnun.

The good natured Landlady told me that many came to the house, and if I would stay, "*I should mayhap laght o' wun o' t'uther on um* (light upon one or other of them)."

I soon heard a voice (which I immediately discovered to be a Cumberland man's) call for a pot of ale.

About 5 or 6 Men had just come in and had placed themselves in a box that was empty, at a distance from me. I got up and sauntered about the room a few times and then taking my pot I came to their table and putting it down, I feigned to be drunk and sat down saying

Nu offence, I huap, gentlemen!

I was however mistaken in my party, they were as unacquainted in London, as I pretended to be, and I left the house late almost despairing of meeting with any one who knew Osborne.

I resolved however to go again the next night, and see what I could do with the Landlord. I went into the bar, sat down, and by degrees introduced a conversation about Kendal in Cumberland, and at last asked him if he knew any body from thence. He at once told that a man of the name of Osborne now and then came to the house but that he had not seen him for about a week past, and that he heard he had married the daughter of some rich man. I now almost gave over the hopes of meeting with him or finding out any of his comrades who might be in the secret, as it appeared highly probable that Charlotte would influence him to stay at home, and the Landlord knew nothing of his residence. John had discovered that he had left his last place about a week before his marriage, and no one knew where he was.

I did not go to the Peacock for some days after, when I resolved to go again it was almost without hope of succeeding. I sat down in a box and as usual called for a pint of ale. Many very ill looking men came in and went out, while I sat just opposite the door till past 9 o'clock. I was just going, being sick of the business when a little man came in whom I did not particularly regard: he sat down in the next box with his companion, a hackney-coachman, and they called for a pot of ale.

Blast my liver, says the coachman, Bill, you are a damned lucky dog!

Damme, said the other, so I am, she's a nice tit,[7] by god.

Nu offence, gemmen, I huap, said I, putting down my pot and tumbling into the box by their side.

Ah! countryman!, said the Coachman, I see as how you loves a good drop of stuff, tip's your daddle; when did you come to tahn?

Nobbut t'uther dea, said I, what's this nace tit yur talking on, is shu out to crack on; aw'l swop, please ye, an aw fancy hur.

Ye'll swop, says the Coachman laughing, swop indeed swop your wife if ye got one, by G'd, Damme if there be'n't many a man who'd swop his wife, aye and his brats too, by G-d.

Whoay, said I, I thought shu'd been a filly, you wur talking on. But no matter, no offence, I huap.

This occasioned a violent laugh from both my companions; I had heard all I wanted, and had distinctly surveyed my little Man whom I found to answer the clerk's and John's description exactly to be *William Osborne* himself.

It was my wish to have dodged him home, but my dress was so remarkable that I must have been observed, and I therefore agreed to a Game of Cards, that was proposed. The Game was new to me then, and I have forgotten it since. The Hackney Coachman undertook to teach it to me, and I played till I was cheated out of near three Guineas. I saw the Tricks played me. They were very gross and adapted to my pretence of drunkenness. I let them pass, as my object was to make another appointment, and tempt them to it.

After losing and paying as much as I thought proper I said I had no more money, but would *tack* my revenge next night, to which both agreed, and we parted.

I attended the appointment, having got Mrs. Williams to muffle herself up (for she had become a most zealous and necessary instrument to the object in view), and to sit with an oyster-barrow and candle at the alehouse door, selling a few oysters. As soon as she saw Osborne go out she was to follow him, wheeling her barrow into the street and leaving it if he walked too fast for her.

I sat long, and had almost given them up, when Osborne the Hackney coachman and another man appeared. I pretended not, to be drunk, but insisted that they had not played fair the evening before. I wished Osborne not to stay late, however I agreed to play. I soon found that there were some Cards in the packs longer than others, and knowing a few tricks upon Cards myself, which I once very dearly purchased of Breslaw; I cheated them out of all my money back again, and of 4 or 5

7. In the seventeenth and eighteenth centuries, "tit" was sometimes used as a term of affection or admiration. *OED.*

Guineas besides which to my astonishment they paid. I then suffered them to play their own way, and lost about a Guinea back again. I then got up, swore they were a pack of *Lunnun rogues*, and *oafs* into the bargain to pretend to cheat a Yorkshireman, and striking a most violent blow on the table with my stick, I threatened to crack their skulls if they did not move off. However, though this sent Osborne home alone, as I intended it should an afray ensued in which I got and gave some very hard blows, and was glad to get home alive, and undiscovered. I was obliged to keep my bed all the next day, I was so much bruised.

As soon as Mrs. Williams heard the quarrel, she was so frightened, that she left her barrow standing took to her heels, and in her fright ran *up* Gray's inn lane. Had she taken her right road home, *down* Gray's inn lane, all my scheme would have miscarried. She had not got 50 Yds. before she recovered from her fright and turned back. As she turned round Osborne stood immediately before her, going up the lane. She let him pass and followed him, and at last saw him go into a mean lodging house in Pitt Street, Tottenham court road, a neighbourhood infamous for poverty and vice.

She approached the house after the door was shut, and listening attentively she heard in an upper room the voice of *Charlotte*.

She arrived at my father's soon after me. I was gone to bed. My father came up to me, and told that he meant to go to see her the next morning.

Mr. Silvester was an exception to the general conduct of step-fathers, equal to a thousand. Few fathers ever have shewn that tender affection to their own Children, that zeal to promote their happiness, that he did to his adopted offspring. They therefore loved him as a father, but Charlotte seemed to feel an attachment to my father and a reverence for him superior to her regard for Mr. S. It was returned on his part, and the anticipated feelings of their meeting affected him to a degree that I never saw on any other occasion. To the best and tenderest of hearts, he united a strength and firmness of mind seldom equalled, and impossible to be exceeded; but then it seemed to give way a little, and he poured out his feelings to me in a manner, wholly to overpower me. However recovering himself, he closed the conversation with the most eloquent admonition upon the ruinous effects of unrestrained passions.

About 10 the next morning he went to Pittstreet in a Hackney coach taking Mrs. Williams with him. The Coach drove up a few doors off to prevent alarm. The house door was open, and as the light and voice on the preceding evening was on the second floor, my father walked up without stopping to enquire, and opened the door of the room. Mrs. Williams followed him close. Charlotte was sitting alone leaning her head on her hand with her back to the door; and my father had walked up to her before she turned and saw him. She shrieked and fainted. With some difficulty Mrs. Williams restored her to her senses. As soon as she recovered, she fell at his feet, tore her hair, and implored his forgiveness with frantic cries. My father was melted to tears; she would not for some time permit him to raise her up. At last he said, *My daughter, I forgive you!* Her joy was then no less immoderate. Mrs. Williams who told me these circumstances, feared that she had lost her senses, and added, *And, faith Sir, I thought it was well she had, for, Lord have mercy on her, poor soul, a mad house is a better husband than Will Osborne.*

As soon as Charlotte was somewhat composed a long conversation took place between her and my father alone, the substance of which I never knew. At the end of it Mrs. Williams was desired to go to 3 or 4 Alehouses in search of Osborne. At one of them she found him, and brought him home.

Independent of her father and Mother Charlotte had only £600 in the funds. This became the property of her husband upon her marriage, but my father acquired such an ascendancy over the mind of Osborne, that he agreed to vest it in the hands of Trustees by way of settlement upon her and her Children should either of them die. My father, Mr. John Reeves (since so well known in the politics of England)[8] and myself were the Trustees. Osborne had frequently in the course of these negociations called upon us. He was indeed the meanest looking rascal I ever saw. His manners were below vulgarity, and disgustingly civil. Mr. Silvester went so far as to give him the lease of a farm he possessed at Sewardstone, near London where it was proposed they should settle. My father did not press an interview, and was content with the disposition of conciliation he had produced without urging the matter further for the present.

When all the papers were prepared, the lawyers, Osborne, his wife, and the trustees met at our house, and thence proceeded to the bank to make the transfer of the stock, and it was proposed to execute the Lease upon our return. It was necessary that Osborne should sign his name to the Transfer in the book. The shame of Charlotte and of all parties is not to be described when instead of his name he made his mark, a clumsy crooked kind of an O, and having filled his pen too full he added a huge blot underneath which attempting to wipe off with his sleeve, he spread over half the page, and miserably sullied the Transfer book. She ran out of the Office and hid herself in the Coach. I walked home with Mr. Reeves. Taking a short cut through the paved Courts, we got home first, and on opening the door the servant gave me a dirty ill folded note, nearly as follows:

8. John Reeves (1752?–1829), lawyer, politician, and pamphleteer, published a number of works on law and politics. One of his best known pamphlets was *Thoughts on the English Government, addressed to the quiet good sense of the People of England in a series of Letters: Letter 1,* published anonymously in 1795. *DNB.*

Honerd Sur,

God be with us hears new horrad villune about Wilm. Osborns who desarves hanging worser then any horcesteler. i gust hears of Tom Sandwist as how hees gotten too wiffes god be praced and so I hop hell be hanged for bigmummy as Tom says, and my jung Misses will get quitt of him at last. Havn't told nobody yet because I wanted to lett you no furst, and dont no wether it will plece or fret my Missis, she taks so hujele on about the afare so no more at present from yours to command Your hble Servant

John Fresh

I stais over at Bonds stable till you sends for me.

I read the letter several times scarcely believing its contents possible; so cooly had Osborne acted since I first saw him, and so well did he seem inclined to come into every proposal of establishment that was made for him. As soon as the Coach arrived I took my father aside and showed him the letter. He reflected a moment and then went into the drawing room where the parties were assembled, and taking up the Lease he read it silently, and calling Mr. Reeves, gave him John's note watching him as he read it. As soon as he perceived him near the close, he addressed him, and said, "Don't you think Mr. Reeves we had better postpone the signing of this lease till tomorrow when I may perhaps induce Mr. Silvester to be present, and send these good folks home. We have done business enough today." Mr. Reeves agreed, but Osborne objected. However he was overruled and the company broke up and went away, excepting Mr. Reeves. Charlotte was melancholy, and bitter repentance was painted upon every feature of her face. It was the first time I had seen her since her fall. We had been playmates when very young. Her eyes avoided mine. It was a melancholy meeting. My sister went home with her, but neither could speak tho' they remained together some hours.

As soon as they were gone, we sent for John. He told us, that *Tom Sandhurst*, an intimate crony, and countryman of Osborne's, who at present filled the honorable station of porter to the Duchess of Cumberland, had informed him, and was ready to take *his bible oath* to the fact, that Wm. Osborne had a wife at Kendal who was living within 6 Months.

It was proposed to send for Sandhurst, but as privacy was of more importance than expence, I offered to go immediately to Kendal by the Stage, and to bring up this first Wife, if she existed, with her marriage certificate, to London. John was directed to get from Sandhurst all the intelligence he could, but he had already done so, and had found the maiden name of the Woman to have been, Susanna Kedgely.

My father, knowing my youthful eagerness of temper would not agree that I should go without John. He therefore went to Cary street and settled matters so, that John was permitted to accompany me.

I have said nothing about the wretched family in Cary street. What they felt can easily be imagined during all this unhappy time. Half of every Novel labors to put into words feelings, of which sensibility wants no hint, and which will ever remain unintelligible to selfish apathy. Sensations to which the news of *Charlottes marriage* to Osborne could give relief, and which could now again be somewhat alleviated by the prospect that that marriage might be void, must have been excruciatingly keen.

I set off with John that night and travelling day and night, arrived on the third day at Kendal about 300 miles from London.

Having taken some refreshment and slept a few hours, I went that very evening to the parish Church. The Clerk accompanied me. He was a good plain blacksmith with a stentorian voice, and infinitely elevated with the importance of his office. After about an hour's search, I at last found what I wanted. It was very late, and as the Clergyman was not at home, I was obliged to wait till the next morning for a copy of the Parish Register. The Clerk informed me that Sue Osborne was in the Workhouse, being an *idle Strapper*[9] since her husband had run away. She had once been to London after him but had not been able to hear any thing of him in that immense hive of Vagabonds. She was taken up there by the Police officers and passed back to her parish of Kendal, where she had since been confined to the Workhouse.

As soon as I was up, I got a Postchaise and went 10 Miles across the Country to the house of a Mr. Smith, where the Parish Minister (whose name I have forgotten) was visiting. I found him an elegant pleasant Man. He received me most politely, introduced me to Mr. Smith, and I dined there. Before dinner, I told him the object of my journey, he promised me every assistance and returned with me in the Postchaise that had brought me. Having procured the marriage Certificate, he sent the Clerk to the Workhouse for Mrs. Osborne. In about an hour she appeared decently dressed. She was a tall athletic, and not unhandsome woman. I could scarce understand her, so coarsely did she speak the Cumberland dialect. However, upon an examination we found, that she had never had the least intelligence of Osborne since he left her, and was ready to go any where in search of him, if she could but find him, in hopes of having a *proper lick at the rascal*. I staid a day at the Clergyman's house, and am ashamed of my memory in letting slip a name attached to so much learning, hospitality, and elegance of manners. John in the mean time took care to equip *Sue* with a few decent cloaths, and to make her a more decent companion "*for a Gentleman in a Postchaise.*"

About 5 o'clock in the morning the postchaise was at the door which was to convey

9. Strapper: a "strapping" or tall and robust person, one above the average stature and strength of build (chiefly applied to women); a seasonal laborer. *OED.*

the very curious trio towards London. When I came down stairs ready to go, I found John and Susan waiting for me at the Chaise door. John bowed, and Susan dropped a very low curtsy, expecting me to get in first. I begged the Lady would precede me but she curtsied, and hoped she knew better manners. I entreated her not to distress me, but to permit me to hand her in. She curtsied again to the ground and gave me her hand. All the waiters, chambermaids, hostlers, the Landlord, and John, burst into the most violent fit of laughter, and I could scarce help joining them. *Susan's* delicacy was shocked. "Concarn ye all," said she, "are ye mad?" John stood nearest to her and she made his old head ring with the blow she gave him. I begged her *to moderate her passion*, and pushed her into the Chaise! I then ordered John to get in, but he begged not to sit next to her. I was however positive, not chusing it myself. In getting into the Chaise he contrived to tread upon her toes, and a new scream and squabble arose. I could not help laughing excessively, got in, the door was shut and we drove off amidst the hooting, and hallooing of the people in the inn yard.

While we were at breakfast at the next stage, the Stage Coach drove up. I was glad of the opportunity of extricating myself from my company, took a seat for London, and ordered John to proceed, following the stage at a short distance, and to stop at Highgate where I would get out and await them. When they got there, I found that they had been quarrelling the whole way, and I believe fighting some part of it. I got into the Chaise, as soon as it became dusk and arrived in London about 8 o'clock. I left Sue to the care of John, who got lodgings for her, and went home.

A long consultation now ensued upon the steps to be taken at which Mr. Silvester attended. It was resolved to bring Osborne and his wife face to face as soon as possible, and in the mean time to get a warrant to apprehend him. The only difficulty was to break the matter to Charlotte. This last task my mother undertook. The next morning I carried a note to Pitt Street to Charlotte begging her to be at home with her husband in the evening, as my father would call upon them. Having arranged matters completely, my sister and mother and myself went about dusk in Mr. Silvester's carriage to Pitt street and drew up to the door. My father followed with John, Sue and a peace officer in a hackney coach and staid a few doors off.

I got out as soon as the carriage stopped, and the street door being always open, I ran up stairs. There were two rooms occupied on the second floor by Osborne and Charlotte. I perceived a light in the Bedchamber through a wide crack in the door. I could not avoid looking through it. I there saw the elegant figure of Charlotte leaning over the Chair of Osborne, while her beautiful hand guided his coarse fist in which he had a pen. She was teaching him to write. I stopped some minutes to look at this most affecting scene, and saw the tears trickle gently down her cheeks and drop upon his shoulder. The contrast of character in the two faces was not less striking than that of the two figures. Soft and gentle grief was elegantly painted upon her expressive features, while his brown and wrinkled visage spoke stupid and vulgar impatience. At last he threw away the pen, damned the plague of writing and swore he couldn't tell the use of making pot hooks and hangers, instead of learning to write at once.

I immediately knocked at the door, which Charlotte opened. I left her no time to say anything, but taking her hand told her that my mother and sister were waiting below to take her to our house, and then desired him to stay above, as my father was coming up to speak with him about moving into the Country. I led Charlotte down just as she was and she did not resist. I put her into the carriage which drove off and immediately ran up to Osborne who was coming down stairs. My father was in an instant with us, and we all returned to his room.

After a few words of conversation, I went down stairs and having enjoined the strictest silence upon Mrs. Sue I led the rest of the party up stairs. I pushed the Woman in first, and followed her. She immediately fixed her eyes upon Osborne, hesitated one moment and then flew like a fury upon him. She scratched, struck, bit and shook him more like a tiger than a human being, and it was with the utmost difficulty that our united strength could separate them. For a war of words we were prepared, but had not expected any thing like what happened. Osborne bled most violently at the nose and blubbered like a great schoolboy. His wife was almost as much hurt though not by her husband, but by John, who had dealt his blows upon her most liberally in endeavoring to separate them. The people of the house hearing the noise came into the room, and I could scarce get rid of them when all was over. Osborne said little but his wife bellowed and swore most furiously. My father exerted himself, and at last we got all quiet again. The constable then executed his warrant on Osborne, and he was put into the Coach and carried to Newgate. He shewed none of that courage that had enabled him to conceive and execute so villainous and difficult a plan as that which put Charlotte into his possession.

During my absence in the country, Mrs. Williams had been engaged by Charlotte as her maid and lived with her. We left her and her husband, the carpenter, in possession of Charlottes apartments.

While Osborne was travelling towards Newgate, his wife was put into a postchaise, and a bribe of one guinea, and twenty Guineas in prospect prevailed upon her to go with an old female Servant of my mothers to Hounslow where we proposed to detain her, till her evidence against Osborne might be wanted.

Charlotte in the mean time came to our house with my mother and sister.

After much preparatory conversation, the secret was at last disclosed to her. She fixed her eyes on my mother, and asked "Is this true?" "It most certainly is," replied she, "here is the certificate." Charlotte read it. She then drew off her wedding-ring and threw it into the fire. She could not speak. My Mother told her, that lodgings were prepared for her in a quiet neat court in Fetter lane, and that my Sister would stay with her for the present, if she would permit it. She seemed not to hear it. My father returned. He spoke much and kindly to her but she remained silent. It struck eleven o'clock from a time piece that stood over the fireplace. She was roused, and fell upon my Sister's neck. The carriage had remained at the door. She made signs to go, my Sister led her down stairs, she looked at my father and mother but said nothing. I got up behind the coach, and directed it to her new lodgings. We had to walk up the Court. I knocked at the door. It was opened and the Ladies walked in. Mrs. Williams had come, and every thing was ready. My sister wept much, I kissed her, and said a few affectionate words to her. Charlotte looked sternly at us. I took her hand and putting it into my Sisters, said, "Suffer Louisa to share your grief." But she drew it away, and walked upstairs. My Sister followed her, and I went home. She threw herself immediately upon the bed, and neither the tears nor the expostulations of my Sister could make her say one word. The next morning she was delirious and in a high fever. She continued so for about 9 days. When she recovered she seemed to have forgotten every thing that had happened but her having treated Louisa unkindly. But by degrees the complicated wretchedness of her situation arose in her memory. She gained strength very slowly. She saw nobody during all this time but our family.

Her mother, Sister and father would now gladly have visited, for they had forgiven her, had it not been feared that she might be discovered, as Mr. Silvester and his family were extremely well Known in that neighbourhood. In the course of a little while it was discovered that she was with Child. This was a new and extreme aggravation of her wretchedness. She was therefore moved to Hommerton about 4 Miles from London. Her family there regularly visited and attended her, and my sister devoted great part of her time to her unhappy friend. She was there brought to bed of a son, who was immediately put out to nurse under my mother's care. It was a sickly child. It lived four years afterwards, but when my mother died, I heard no more of it, and know not whether it be still alive.

Osborne was in the mean time confined in Newgate. It was an embarrassed consideration what to do with him. Had he been tried he might certainly have been hanged for bigamy, but that would have proclaimed the dishonor of Charlotte's family. Another course was therefore pursued. He agreed to go to the East indies, the almost certain grave of such adventurers, as a common soldier in the [East India] Company's service. I have never heard of him since.

Upon this arrangment his wife was sent back to Kendal. I sent a letter with her and twenty Guineas to the Clergyman, for her use. He was so kind as to take the charge of keeping her from returning, but had she ever come back she could never have found out the places and persons she had seen but by accident, for she never knew the names either of myself, my family or Mr. Silvester, and care had been taken that she should not know where in London she had lodged, or had been conducted. I know not what is now become of her and it has ceased to be at all material.

Soon after Charlottes removal to Hommerton my father died. In him she lost a father and a friend, but my mother still remained to protect and to intercede for her. On his death bed, my father had requested Mr. Silvester to promise to forgive and if possible to forget all that had happened, and the goodness of his heart rendered the performance easy. As soon as my father's affairs could be settled, my mother removed to her house in Yorkshire. My eldest Brother[10] had arrived from the Continent. We took a house together, and Louisa staid with us till Charlotte was well enough to be removed. Mr. Silvester in the mean time hired Mr. Gott's seat at Calverley near my mother's for Charlotte. An old servant of our family and his wife entered into her service, and Louisa accompanied her to Yorkshire. There she was unknown, and by degrees she recovered health and spirits. Her own benevolent disposition, her kindness to all the poor of her neighborhood, her correct conduct, and her genius, won her the friendship of all the neighboring Gentry, and her intimacy with my Mother raised her character above suspicion. My sister Louisa about 12 Months afterwards married Mr. [Frederick] William Foster, the eldest son of Mrs. [Dorothy Gale] Foster of Jamaica, who had an Estate at Bedford. Mr. George Livius the uncle of Charlotte married about the same time Miss Foster Barham, the first cousin of Mr. Foster who also lived at Bedford.[11] Mrs. Silvesters health had most cruelly suffered from her grief at her family misfortunes, and she died about the same time. About two years after my mother also died. Charlotte's eldest Sister Matilda then went to Yorkshire and lived at Calverley with her sister. Mr. Silvester found himself so solitary in London that he purchased a house at Carrington[12] a few miles from Bedford for his daughters to which they removed. Mr. Daniel Hoissard was in the mean time taken very ill at Lisbon. His sister Matilda's health was become also precarious. It was therefore thought better that she should go to Lisbon not only to attend her brother, but to endeavor to recover her own health.

Charlotte thus remained alone at Carrington. Her father was as much with her as his leisure would permit. She was in the midst of her friends, and regained cheerfulness

10. Christian Ignatius Latrobe.

11. William Foster (1722–68) of the Bogue Estate, Jamaica, married first Elizabeth Vassal and second Dorothy Gale, daughter of Isaac Gale; they had six children. His son, Frederick William (1760–1835), a bishop of the Moravian Church, married Anna Louisa Eleanora Latrobe (d. 1824), BHL's sister, on 15 May 1791. Frederick William and Louisa (Latrobe) Foster had two sons and one daughter. Three generations later the name La Trobe was incorporated into the Foster family name. *Burke's Landed Gentry*, 1:816.

12. BHL was referring to Cardington, Bedfordshire.

and good looks. In Yorkshire she had become extremely fond of riding, and of horses. She was the first horsewoman, and drove 4 in hand better than any Lady in the county of Bedford. She carried this amusement perhaps a little too far, and it might have made her an object of much observation, had not her uncle Geo. Livius exhibited daily excentricities close by her side that were ten times more remarkable. His mode of living, his dress, his equipage, his conversation, his house, and his grounds, all exhibited new appearances. He drove six pied horses in a black and white carriage, his house was more contrived for the luxury of a Nabob, than an English country Squire. He had his hot, and cold, his vapor and tepid baths, his perfuming and smoking rooms, his drawing room surrounded with sofas, and his antichamber filled with bamboo chairs. His grounds were full of painted Hogsheads for seats. His dresses at home were silk gowns covering many folds of flannel, and abroad you might smell him for half a mile. The strongest understanding, and the most frivolous levity chequered his conversation; he was always either lavishly profuse, or meanly parsimonious. But upon the whole he was a pleasant and entertaining man.

Carrington was the property of Mr. [Samuel] Whitebread the great brewer, whose son Samuel acts at present so splendid a part in the British parliament, and of the great Mr. Howard, whose benevolence and unremitting activity has near modelled the criminal code of almost all Europe and of part of America. The philanthropy of two such men could no where be idle within the sphere of their power. It had rendered Carrington the neatest and most delightful Village I ever saw. It formed a Square round a venerable Gothic Church shaded by ancient Elms. All the cottages were rough-cast, whitewashed on the outside, and in the inside nothing could exceed their cleanliness and neatness. All the poor Children were neatly dressed. A school was established in the village to which they regularly went at stated hours and returned in order and quiet. Little rewards were distributed among the most deligent.[13] In the evening they played on the green under the eye of the Older inhabitants who decided their disputes, and encouraged their cheerfulness. The Children did not alone enjoy the attention of the benevolent proprietors. The cottagers themselves were rewarded by small but distinguishing priviledges in proportion to their cleanliness, their industry, or their care of their children. Health the reward of temperance and exercise, and chiefly of cleanliness had fixed her abode at Carrington, and the evils of poverty kept at a distance.[14] Charlotte in establishing herself there, found new employment for the active goodness of her heart. She became the queen of the Village, and the distributress of the bounty of Mr. Howard and Whitebread, and added her own contribution. She joined her share to that of my Sister Louisa, and established

13. Obsolete form of diligent. *OED.*
14. John Howard (1726?–90) was a philanthropist and prison reformer; Samuel Whitbread (1720–96), the

a little separate school for girls under a certain age and amused herself often with teaching them herself. Whoever saw her so amiably and usefully employed could either not believe that she ever had erred, or must have thought it impossible she could ever err again.

I had in the mean time married, and spent many a happy day with Louisa and with Charlotte, whose affection for my wife became very great. Daniel Hoissard died at Lisbon, and Matilda returned. Mr. Silvester married Mrs. Speed a young very rich widow, and I lost my Lydia. After the last event I saw very little of any of my former acquaintance for two years. The world had altered its appearance to me, the charm that made it pleasant was broken. Once or twice a Year I visited Mr. Silvester's family. Charlotte had again become a regular Member of it, and was Miss Ch. Hoissard.

About six Months before I left England, I was sent for by the Miss Hoissards to breakfast. After scolding me for my absence they begged me to go into the country with them for the day. I did so. It was to give my professional opinion upon a house and Estate they meant to buy in Essex. Danl. Hoissard had left them each a very independent fortune, and they disliked their Mother-in-law, who was a prim, notable, smart, half genteel body. Their scheme was to live together, and their father had consented. I gave them with great pleasure my assistance and altered the house for them into a very snug and rather elegant retreat. I became by this means very intimate again in their family. Mr. Silvester took every delicate Method to hint that the house might perhaps become not an unpleasant residence for myself. I believe he alluded to his wishes for Charlotte. Matilda was too haughty, altho' her prospects and hopes had been much lowered by her Sister's conduct. But I had not forgotten Lydia. Charlotte kept my little Girl for two Months with her and was very kind to both my little orphans.

When I was almost ready to sail for America, my brother who was also married, and was daily in Mr. Silvesters house, or at Tanton-hill, as the Miss Hoissard's house was called sent for me. His note was strangely worded and excited much curiosity in me to know what he could want with me. I found a postchaise at his door. He made me get in, and would not tell me where we were going, only saying that I should not believe mine own eyes when we got to the end of our journey. We went on to Ware in

---

brewer, was M.P. for Bedford from 1768 until 1790, when he was succeeded by his son, Samuel (1758–1815). Both Howard and Whitbread owned estates in Cardington. Around 1758 Howard erected model cottages on his Cardington property, providing elementary education for children of all sects, and encouraged the individual industry of the villagers. The close relationship between Howard and Whitbread is evidenced in the disposal of Howard's Cardington estate. When Howard's son died in 1799 the estate passed to Samuel Charles Whitbread, grandson of the brewer. *DNB; Burke's Landed Genrty,* 3:311–12.

Hertfordshire, and from thence struck across the country and stopped at a small farm house. A good looking rosy faced man came to the door; we got out. His features were prepossessing and his figure handsome.

"Give me leave," said my brother, "to introduce you to Mr. Talbot." I shook hands and bowed. We walked into the parlor. A Lady rose on our entrance.

"Give me leave," said my brother with an archness entirely his own, "to introduce you to Mrs. Talbot."

I did scarcely *believe mine own eyes*, it was my old friend Charlotte.

I stared, but wished her joy, and immediately saluted her. She was excessively embarrassed, and said, "for God's sake don't look so satirically, let us be friends still."

I then turned to her husband and recognised the smart groom of Mr. Whitebread who had always attended me at Carrington, and who was farrier, and inspector General to Charlottes horse establishment in that village.

"Upon my word," said I, "I am very happy to see an honest and sensible man, and a most amiable benevolent woman united," and assumed a rattling kind of manner which being joined in by my most witty brother passed off the day very well.

"You see," said my brother to me in a whisper, "how matters stand, pray which of the two bride*grooms* of our friend Charlotte do you like best?"

Charlotte had this time however acted an open and fair part. Whether she courted Talbot, or Talbot her, she never told me. She sent to my brother about a week before her marriage, and told him that she intended to marry a man whom she knew to possess, except education every thing necessary to her happiness, a good temper and an honest heart. That she was miserable since her father's marriage, that she had no right to hope for a brilliant establishment, and felt that she stood in the way of her Sister's being married. She therefore begged him to lay the affair before her Step-father. He did so. Mr. Silvester was at first enraged, but soon recollecting himself, he said that if Talbot could hire a good farm, he would assist him with money, and give his consent.

Mr. Whitebread immediately gave him the lease of the farm near Ware, where I saw him, and they were married as soon as the house was got ready. My brother gave her away.

Talbot will be as happy as goodness of heart, conscientious discharge of her duty, and strong sense can make him, he will be as miserable as unequal knowledge, unsteady temper, and the spectres of former folly conjured up perhaps by very trifling excentricities can render him.

Dispositions surely are more hereditary than diseases or family features. How necessary is attention to this in the marriages of our Children.

RICHMOND, AUGST. 15TH, 1797. After a drought which began on Easter Tuesday [18 April] and lasted till the 15th of July, we have had a constant succession of very heavy rains, and short spells of fair weather. James river has swelled considerably, and is beyond all example muddy. This is easily accounted for. The Ground has been parched and reduced almost to dust for 3 or 4 feet down. It was therefore in a state in which it *washes* and is carried off most easily. A circumstance has occurred for which people variously account. Innumerable fishes have died. They are principally mullets. They float in shoals upon the Surface of the Water, and as the River has retired they are left in great numbers upon its banks. I think the extreme muddiness of the Water may be the cause of this *murrain* among them.[15] An old negroe however has given me another very ingenious solution of the difficulty. The *Asmart*[16] which grows plentifully in all the wet places, and on all the shores of the river and creeks, is a well known Poison to the fish. It is very common for the negroes, when the tide retires, and in the low country leaves lakes or ponds of water full of fish, to throw in a Basket full of bruised Asmart and stir it about. The fish soon come to the Surface in a torpid state and are easily taken. All the waters of James river, and the river itself having been for some Months uncommonly low, this herb has grown almost across many creeks, and is every where observed to have spread itself in uncommon luxuriance. The sudden rains having rapidly swelled the Stream, has thrown the Water and the fish upon the beds of *Asmart*, where they *may* have been poisoned in great numbers, and perhaps the Water itself has imbibed some deleterious quality. At New York and Philadelphia there is an epidemic among the Cats.

AUGST. 17TH, 1797.[17] When I wrote the inscription for the Cornerstone of the Penitentiary house, and sent it to the Executive for approbation, I accompanied it with an inscription in Latin to the same effect, proposing that it should be engraved on the other Side of the Plate, or perhaps be the only Inscription adopted. The Council however voted that the Inscription should be in English only. I think this is a very inhuman, and barbarous vote. They had their choice of burying a *dead* or a *living* language, and they chose to inter that which was *living*.

15. Fish kills are well known in the rivers of the Atlantic Coast. They appear more frequently to involve the alewife, *Pomolobus pseudoharengus* Wilson (*Alosa pseudoharengus* [Wilson]), than the mullet, *Mugil cephalus* L. Abrupt changes of water temperature are suspected of being the cause.

16. Asmart: *Polygonum hydropiper* L., early introduced from Europe, or the native *Polygonum sagittatum* L. or *P. hydropiperoides* Michx. Now called smartweeds, in earlier days "Arse-smart," and in Jefferson, *Notes on Virginia*, "Arsmart."

17. On this day BHL submitted his "Report upon the State of the Works at the Penitentiary House at Richmond, in Virginia." The manuscript is in the Virginia State Library, Richmond. See also *PBHL, microfiche ed.*, 156/C6.

The Tale of Sir Osbert

EDITORIAL NOTE

Latrobe's fictional tale of Sir Osbert, which he entitled "A Fragment," was "occasioned by a conversation at Mr. Orris Paines." From the text itself it is evident that the generative topic of conversation at the Paine household was the doctrine of the sensate life of plants, similar to that set forth, for example, in Erasmus Darwin's *Zoonomia*, a work with which Latrobe was familiar. Section XIII of that treatise, titled "Of Vegetable Animation," aimed to demonstrate, in the summary of Thomas Brown, "that vegetables are indued with irritability, sensibility, voluntary, and associability, and, therefore . . . that they are *animals*, in the strictest sense of the term."[18] This doctrine had already been adumbrated literally in the notes and figuratively in the poetry of Darwin's two-part georgic poem, *The Botanic Garden*,[19] which Latrobe admired considerably. In the notes and additional notes to *The Botanic Garden*, Darwin cited several later eighteenth-century works of experimental and speculative biology that supported and amplified the theories presented in his poem and also contributed to the formulation of the summary generalizations regarding the sensate life of plants in his later prose treatise *Zoonomia*. Latrobe may well have been familiar with any number of these works as well.

Brown, in his critique of the doctrine as set forth in *Zoonomia*, rejected it on methodological grounds. To prove the animation of vegetables, Brown noted that Darwin "contents himself with stating phenomena, to the production of which he conceives it to be necessary,"[20] and this reasoning by paralogism is not scientifically acceptable.

In contrast to Brown's criticism, the focus of Latrobe's critique is on the absurd implications for human action that serious and sentimental adherence to the doctrine of the animation of plants would have. Toward that end, Latrobe invented a central character, Sir Osbert, a knight of exquisite sensibility, who "has taken it into his head" as his all-too-insensible squire Basileo put it, "that every thing such as trees and stones, and sticks and stocks, and Lord bless me, I don't know what all, can feel as well as we Christians." The "Fragment" consists of a series of narrated episodes in which "our enraptured knight" and a variety of "his matter-of-fact companions" proceed to the mansion of Theodora, Osbert's beloved. The language, dialogue, and event of the episodes are purposely ordered to make evident both the unreasonableness of the doctrine as a basis for human action and the essential vanity of an overly active sensibility that would embrace such a doctrine further to indulge itself.

Latrobe borrowed from antiromantic literature in general the structural principle of deflation through exaggeration and reductive contrast. This principle is evident at every level of the "Fragment," from the contrast between the inflated diction of Osbert and the vulgar speech of the other characters to the contrast between Osbert's fine and elevated sentiments on viewing the prospect before Theodora's village and the gross enthusiasms of his companions, priest and squire alike, for food and drink.

From antidoctrinal satire, such as Voltaire's *Candide*, with which he was apparently familiar, Latrobe borrowed the structural principle of satiric attack on a doctrine through the narration of an adherent's misadventures and misfortunes. In contrast to Candide, however, the catastrophes that befall Osbert are less violent and more homely: damage to a farmyard after a storm, a fallen door, a runaway horse, companions who mock his sentiments, and a beloved who takes him seriously enough to point out the suicidal implications of his sensibility.

---

18. Darwin, *Zoonomia; or, The Laws of Organic Life*, 2 vols. (London, 1794–96). Brown, *Observations on the Zoonomia of Erasmus Darwin* (Edinburgh, 1798), p. 248.

19. Part two, "The Loves of the Plants," was published in 1789; part one, "The Economy of Vegetation," in 1791.

20. Brown, *Observations*, p. 248.

Finally, from the Quixotic tradition Latrobe borrowed the narrative device of enraptured knight and all-too-human companions, as well as the bittersweet tone of a reluctant condemnation. This last feature is, perhaps, the most important of Latrobe's general sources. It corresponds to Latrobe's own stance, which is, apparently, that of the reluctant satirist who identifies himself in part with that which he mocks in his characters.

As a considerable man of letters, Latrobe was familiar with the achievements of the eighteenth-century satirists, as his references to Swift, Pope, Fielding, Gay, Smollett, and Sterne make clear. There is also other evidence throughout the journals that Latrobe employed satire as a literary mode. Before composing "A Fragment," Latrobe had written a mock-elegy and a number of epigrams.[21] Not long after "A Fragment," Latrobe wrote *The Apology*, a hastily composed satire on the Federalists, especially Hamilton and William Cobbett ("Peter Porcupine").[22] *The Apology*, which was performed in Richmond in January 1798, employed both parodic techniques (it was a takeoff on Hamilton's published apology for his affair with Maria Reynolds) and direct satire (the character of Vaucamil attacks Hamilton while the character of Skunk attacks Cobbett). His criticism of the Scriblerian satirists, particularly Pope, suggests his preference for what predecessors in the art would have called "toothless satires."

This preference for the genial critique, laughing rather than lashing at the satiric object, is carried through in the Osbert tale. Indeed, the manner of Theodora, as she gently mocks Osbert at the end and wins his reformation, fulfills perfectly the advice Latrobe offered all satirists: "There is a way . . . of making a man appear ridiculous to himself, and inducing him on that account to correct that which renders him so to others, without appearing to enjoy the laugh yourself."

Latrobe's "Fragment" was composed at four sittings. The first, on 20 August 1797, produced an introduction, the episode of Osbert's expostulation on the effects of a storm, the episode of Gundy and the fallen door, and the episode of Basileo's retrospective narration of his search for Caballobeato, Osbert's runaway splendid nag. Composition continued on 31 August with the introduction of Friar Ximenes and the debate between him and Osbert on the extent of sensate life. This debate began a shift away from a dramatic narrative toward a more static, expository presentation of the satiric subject. That shift was continued in the next segment, composed on 4 September, which offered further exposition of Osbert's "condition" through the interrogation of Basileo by Ximenes. The last section of the "Fragment," composed on 5 September, narrated Osbert's arrival at the mansion of Theodora, their conversation, and Theodora's mild but firm exposition of the rationale for satirizing Osbert in the first place: that the supposition of the sensate life of plants raises an insurmountable barrier to the achievement of humanity.

With Theodora's exposition and her introduction of the letter from Henry to her friend Lydia "before their union," the satiric fiction all but dissolved. This letter was presumably written by Latrobe to his wife Lydia Sellon before their marriage in 1790. It gave an account of his coming upon the doctrine of vegetable sensation and of his mixed reaction to that doctrine. He was charmed, it seems, with the pleasant fantasy of a sweet pea's grateful address to his beloved. He was also impressed with the recognition that there were vegetarians whose practice arose from "a benevolence of intention," though that practice would be complicated by the fact of vegetable sensation. It seemed plain to Latrobe that "unless suicide be the *only* virtue, the sensibility that feels too much for the corporeal sufferings of other animals—I had almost added vegetables—is not meritorious, for it is unnatural."

Latrobe did not return to Osbert. The manuscript ended with Henry's letter to Lydia, but in a final paragraph Latrobe noted that he was "happy in having had my own doubts resolved by two very

21. See pp. 146–48, 156–57 above, 302–03 below.
22. See p. 333 below.

sensible, humane, and candid Sisters, Mrs. Paine and Miss Betsy Hay, both of whom agree that the said sensibility is very ridiculous."

AUG. 20TH, 1797 RICHMOND. *A Fragment*, occasioned by a conversation at Mr. Orris Paines.[23]

. . . Having risen early in the morning, Osbert thought to set out upon his journey. The scanty herbage around the miserable inn which had given him a shelter from the horrors of the tempestuous night lay prostrate upon the ground. The scattered remnants of the blast whistled by fits, in the surrounding forest. A fringe of livid red began to hang from the thick purple clouds of the east, they were the livery of the morn. Osbert stood on the shattered threshold, and saw the havock of the tempest strewed in heaps around the hovel. The lacerated Limbs of trees venerable for their age and the torn twigs of shrubs pitiable in their tender youth. Here tiles, whose long protracted protection deserved gratitude, broken to sherds, and forever torn from the roof to which they had so faithfully adhered—there unfortunate hencoops, topsy turvy, shattered, and bruised, and more unfortunate chickens, cruelly ejected from their hospitable confinement! The pride of the tow'ring ladder laid at length across the yard, and a cow crib overset! The humble Haystack dripping wet, and shivering in the bleak wind! O ye miserable Shirts and stockings that hang on yonder line! Was it not enough that your bodies wore the scars of old, and felt the pain of present wounds in every part, but ye must be left by the merciless hag under whose tyranny ye exist, to wave in the less ruthless storm, to be drownd by the chill rain, and to be shredded by the whirling wind!

Osbert had a soul!

Say, ye powers, who compounded this inexplicable, this various this contradictory being, Man—Say, was it in love or anger that ye gave him his bliss, his torment—sensibility? Surely not in anger, for ye also gave him—tears.

Osbert wept.

The balm of the wounded heart poured itself from his eyes, and soothed his pang. He gently moved his manly face from the shirts and the stockings, from the prostrate cow cribb and the fallen ladder. The half drowned chickens and their shattered coop, the soused and shiv'ring haystack, the tattered shrubs, the dismemberd oaks, and all the supine thistles, docks, and nettles partook of his pitying smile! The Sun also peeped through a wet cloud, and seemed to smile upon his benevolence!

Osbert's heart was full. A mixture of gently thrilling sentiment, the luxury of

23. Orris Paine, Richmond merchant and owner of coal pits west of Richmond, sold lime to BHL for the Virginia State Penitentiary and later became his close friend. *American State Papers. Miscellaneous* (Washington, D.C., 1834), 1:808; Hamlin, *Latrobe*, p. 125n.

pitying sympathy vibrated upon its strings. Rapture—not of the bouncing, throbbing, blustering kind, but quiet, soft, silent—somewhat saddened, and a little gladdened, possessed him! It was a tone of soul fit to slide into Elysium.

Once more he turned towards the door. The old woman who had opened, still held it; partly to keep it from falling, for it hung only upon its lower hinge, partly to shut it when he should have left the threshold.

Age had not visited *Gundigunda*[24] without bestowing upon her those tokens of his presence of which he is never parsimonious. Her mouth, puckered like the hard drawn purse of the miser, shrunk from the kiss of the libertine into a deep cavity, armed at its entrance by the sharp and connected points of her chin and her nose. Her eyes in perpetual briny streamlets bewailed the loss of their color and their fire. Her temples were adorned with radiated furrows and her forehead with the deep lines of experience and care. A few surviving hairs escaping from her cawl[25] straggled round her temples. Her withered neck and palsied fingers contrasted not each other, their color and their wrinkles were in perfect harmony.

Osbert turned from the objects of pity exhibited in the Yard of the hovel. The humble waiting figure of *Gundigunda* caught his eye. Attuned to softness, could the soul of Osbert behold *a female* without emotion!

Let me, pour out the effusion of pity upon thy lips, said the Chevalier, let me, I beseech thee imprint the tenderness that dissolves me, by a kiss for thou *wast* fair, and art still *a woman!*

God bless your honour, replied *Gundigunda*, haven't had such good luck this many a year.

He stooped, and Gundigunda stood a tip-toe. Already had the blooming mouth of the fair Osbert passed the promontories of Chin and Nose and were within an inch of the lips of Gundigunda when, alas, the door fell flat into the hovel. Alas, poor Gundy! Of the daughters of Eve how many before thee, have been, and how many after thee will be betrayed from their duty by a kiss! Oh that thou hadst but kept thy hold of the door, then had not thy toe been crushed, nor had the only hinge of the faithful guardian of thy hovel been destroyed! Then had not the venerable portal received a fall, nor hadst thou ruffled the surface of thy temper.

Thou shalt pay for the hinge and the doctor! This comes of thy fooling, screamed the enraged hostess! Oh my toe, my toe, my toe!

24. The name was adapted from Voltaire's character Cunégonde, beautiful daughter of Baron Thunder ten Tronkh and beloved of the naïve optimist Candide, who finally returned to her after his adventures only to discover that she had become ugly.

25. Obsolete form of caul, a close-fitting cap worn by women, a net for the hair. *OED.*

Alas! said Osbert, crushed by the strife of the elements, how many murdered herbs lie on the breast of their mother earth, dead, dead, and unpitied but by me! Accuse not Osbert of want of sympathy, thou matron of the suffering hovel! Think not the miseries of the door, stunned by its downfall, nor the anguish of the lacerated hinge escape my impassioned commiseration. What then must be my distraction to see thy trembling nerves convulsed with the pain of thy crushed toe. If the balsam of pity were a medecine in the dispensatory of the learned physicians, I would search the world to bring it to thee. But see it springs in my breast, and flows from my eyes.

Curse your kissing and your crying too, said Gundigunda, what good can they do to a poor old woman, who has to buy victuals. All I wants is a little money.

A piece of gold was already in the hand of Osbert, it slipt silently into hers. "The sand," said he, "that drops to the bottom of the boundless ocean, and is now and then washed upon its shores is no part of its essence. That sand, is money. Pity is the inexhaustible, clear, world embracing element."

"God bless you fair knight," replied Gundy. "I got no great hurt thank God. Damn the old crazy door." The knight stept from the Threshold.

You forget the kiss, called Gundy. You're a sweet Gentleman, I could kiss you myself for all my modesty.

Osbert moved slowly on! *Damn* the old crazy door, thought he, then, why *kiss* the old crazy woman? Oh! the unfeeling world, can there be a *female* breast untenanted by compassion?

Scarce had the Chevalier walked four steps from the hovel when the clattering of hoofs was heard behind him. He turned round, and saw his faithful Basileo in pursuit of him.

And where said Osbert didst thou hide thy grey head from the cloud of torrents that burst upon the forrest in the last terrific night, how didst thou recover my wandering steed, how didst thou trace the steps of thy melancholy Knight.

Good Lord stand by us, replied the Squire, could a body get a mouthfull of victuals in this hogstye? Bless me what a bad thing it is to be hungry. Gracious heavens, I am ready to die with hunger, for gods sake lets have a thimblefull to drink before starting: my blessed lady, I am plaguy wet, for the love of mercy, lets get near a fire to dry ones self. Lackadaysie what a night it was—faith! I'm heartily glad to see your worship, Odsbodikins this is good luck again, plague take me if I thought I should ever see you, goodness me how glad I am I've found you out, I dare swear you staid all night in this rascally hut——

Do not talk so rapidly, interrupted Osbert, alight, and rest thyself, as for food I fear thou wilt be disappointed.

Basileo had already entered the hovel, and was demanding of the old woman fire, victuals and drink.

Gundigunda stared, not knowing whether her guest was a squire, or a knight, a receiver, or an expender of Cash. Osbert returned to the house, and gently requested her to provide Basileo with fire, and to set before him whatever the house contained of eatables. To be sure, said she, bless your honor, if his worship can take up with such homely fare as we have got here.

In a short time a few dry sticks furnished a scanty warmth, and some coarse bread and a little goats Milk a frugal breakfast. Basileo was not very well contented, but the knight moderated by gentle words the expressions of his dissatisfaction. And now, said he, tell me by what fortunate circumstance thou hast traced me to this lonely cottage through the mazes of this intricate Wilderness.

Why, replied Basileo, God bless us all, but as I never swear, plague vex me if I can give you a proper account of the matter. For, by my troth, and that your honor knows I wouldn't say if it wasn't true, it was enough to make a parson swear. Now your honor knows, and may I be _____, but I never swear, that when your honour alighted to replant the vine which the goats had torn up by the roots, and your honor's horse, curse light on him, ran off, and he turn'd and turn'd, and jump'd and kick'd first this way and then that, Lord save us, running right on, and then to the right and then to the left, ding dong, dash thro' the mire, splash out again, up hill and down, in among the trees and the brambles, snuffing and snorting, and scuffling away like the devil himself, mercy on me, and I after him scampering like wildfire, and, God in heaven knows if I was not a good horseman, aye as good as any in Christendom though I say it, who shouldn't, but your honor knows it as well, and if your honor speaks the truth, as the Lord knows your honor like a true Christian knight always does, you will testify that it is true; for plague take me if there be any, under the rank of a true knight, be he who he may that can sit a horse like your squire Basileo, let him caper, kick, curvet, up with his heels down with his nose, rear again as upright as a lance down smack and up behind, plunge forward, stop short, up in the air with all fours, start sideways, run back, play devil tricks of all sorts new and old, if I cant tame him, sit tight to the saddle, close with my knees in with my toes, all square and upright, may I never get into a saddle again. Mercy on us, your honor's knows its as true as the sun. More fire, old Lady, do you hear?

"Heaven," replied Osbert mildly, "has given thee to me as a companion, in order to strengthen my patience. But if thou will proceed straight forward in thy narrative and tell me concisely how thou foundest me at this place it will be acceptable, as I will fully allow thy merits in horsemanship."

278

Lord bless us all, said Basileo, must I not follow the horse—gracious heavens, did I ever lose sight of him, *dash* he went into the thickest forest—that won't do, said I, in after him by St. Jago, close up all the way! Lord have mercy, how your honor stares at me—in, I say he went into the wood, isn't it true—to be sure it is, and I after him—well then, plague take it—I see your honor wants the end of it all in a hurry—why then we came, after riding and galopping this way and that way, to the right and the left, why then we came to a river. In went Caballobeato![26] Oh ho! thinks I, you won't like that fun long. He swam about, and to make short o' the matter he came out again, and I caught him.

Thank you, good Basileo, now you have caught my horse, bring him hither as soon as you can.

Why there again, continued Basileo, if your honor would but give me time, and have patience; mercy on us for our Lady's sake; who can tell a story, does your honor think, all of a heap as you may say, and have done with it. Bless my soul, it must have a beginning; then the devil's in it, if it mustn't move on quietly and slowly and just as it happened; or by the living Gingo, it will never be like the thing you're talking of. Look ye here now, that story I was telling your honor t'other day about my Grandmother's—no not my Grandmother—zounds, faith, I believe it was my old Aunt Winifrid, God's mercy, that is very odd, that I should forget—well its no matter—Oh Lord—now I think on it, it was about my fathers old mule—no indeed it wasn't that story neither about my mother, that I've told you a hundred time over. Well, well, well, here old Lady, get some fire, this bread is plaguy musty. Mercy on us, had your honor had no better fare . . . .

AUG. 31ST. Very fortunately for the reader there is here a Chasm of several leaves in the old manuscript, and the next part of the Story that is legible proceeds thus:

. . . For my part, replied the friar, give me the bacon well boiled and I'll never think of the screaming of the hog under the butchers knife, and as for the Sallad, your Honor must be very much inclined to be merry, if you could stop your meal to pronounce a Mock elegy over it.

"It is perhaps *folly* as you term it to quarrell with that system of pain and destruction," said Osbert, "which we see every where in force. It should seem as if it were part of the great plan by which the universe is kept agoing. Myriads of sensitive beings swarm round us, whose power of existing under terror and pain appears to

---

26. The name is compounded from the Latin *caballus*, meaning nag, pack horse, hack, or jade, and *beatus*, happy, prosperous, blessed, fortunate, excellent, or splendid, the combination making this horse a fitting beast to bear the burden of Sir Osbert.

belong to them for no other purpose but that they may be frightened by the pursuit, and suffer in the jaws of their enemies. The ox stung by the bite of the muskito is scarcely freed from his tormentor before he is revenged by the voracious Muskito hawk (Neuroptera).[27] No sooner has the latter devoured his victim, but he is torn to pieces by the nimble Swallow. See how she skims upon the surface of yonder lake—hark, she screams! A Hawk is tearing her to pieces. But short is the victory. The peasant has drawn his bow, the arrow flies, and the destroyer of his poultry dies in agony. Nor does the machinery of providence stop here. The peasant groans under the tyranny of a more cruel tyrant than the hawk. He is the slave of Don Quimbarino, the lord of yonder castle. [Flies?] torment the Muskitoes, and thus begins again the round of pain and misery, busy and ceaselessly revolving, like the wheel of Ixion.

Well, well, my noble friend, said father Ximenes, then just let things wag on the old way. Why should you plague yourself more than comes to your share? Do you think I should have grown so jolly had I been all my life fretting and fuming about partridges whose legs are shortened by the Scythe, flies caught in spiders webs, trees whose limbs have been blown off, old foundered horses thumpt to market by old purblind women; or rotten sheep dying in a ditch. No, no, my good friend, let's live merrily while we may, take things as they come, make the best of 'em, and enjoy a bottle and a friend when we can meet one.

"I was just revolving in my mind," answered Osbert, "that if we turn from this dark side of the question, we may also consider what a fund of happiness and pleasure belongs to the mutual dependance of all the species of sensative beings upon one another. For instance, in a melon or cucumber bed, what pleasure the beautiful male flowers must enjoy in the conversation of the delicate females, carried on by means of the sweet honey thigh'd bee. In a grove of trees of various kinds, what a variety of ideas must be mutually communicated, how every observation must be marked by character. The strong and manly sense of the Oak softened by the delicate and refined remark of the Larch and embellished by the flowery expressions of the Tulip tree[28] while thousands of delightfully singing birds intermingle their melodies."

Our lady of Loretto save us and be merciful to us cried the monk, leaning quite back onto the rump of his mule and crossing himself, what is it you say, pray heaven and San Jago di Compostella keep your noble senses from oversetting! May St. Francis be mercifull and intercede for you with the holy Virgin!

I return you many thanks for your very good wishes said the knight smiling, you

---

27. BHL was referring to what we today call a dragonfly. These are now placed in the order Odonata, rather than the Neuroptera.

28. Tulip tree: *Liriodendron tulipifera* L. This is the tree which the Indians called "The Tree of Peace" (Jean Bernard Bossu, *Travels*, trans. Forster [London, 1771], 1:349).

suppose I am mad, because I am not so illiberal as to imagine that we two legged animals monopolize all sentiment and all reason. No, believe me, I have too high an opinion of our common Creator to admit a doubt of his having given the power of enjoyment to every one of his creatures. That beautifull Sun, and this humble Earth, are, I believe two *beings*, you may call them *animals*, of an order higher and greater beyond conception than ourselves, but equally endowed with sensations and affections. Although we cannot prove positively that this *is* the case—for it is a matter above our grasp—is it not more probable that it should be so than otherwise. How regular are not all their operations. Is there anything more rational, or more apparently the effect of motive in my waking 16 or 17 hours and sleeping 7 than in the diurnal rotation of the earth. How uniform my daily employment! I rise, I eat, I move about, I eat again, I converse, I write, I work—how little does what I do amount to! I am fatigued, I go to bed.

What, go to bed without supper, exclaimed Ximenes, go to bed without supper, surely that's enough to turn any man's brain. Now d' ye'see, I sup, go to bed, and rise in my senses. I advise you to follow my example. But pray go on, I declare it is very new and entertaining.

I was saying, continued the knight, smiling in pity upon father Ximenes, that my daily operations are so alike that I cannot think the annual progress of the earth round the Sun (and we may suppose *a Year* to be *a day* to so large an animal as the earth) has in the least more of uniformity in it, than the daily history of my own life. I mention this because we are so apt to consider the heavenly bodies merely as wheels in a Mill—a vile vulgar mean idea—that any other mode of considering them is scarce admitted without a smile of contempt. Look at the Sun! Does he not rather appear a mild beneficent parent to his children the planets who live round him in a family of six. Look at the moon his granddaughter the child of the *Earth*, what a sweet smiling damsel she is. Jupiter has 4 Saturn 5 or six Children equally dear to their grandfather. Mars, like every soldier is better without a family, and the loose life of Venus easily accounts for her barrenness. As for Mercury, he seems but a child as yet. We are not to suppose that the present number bounds the fertility of the Sun, or of any of his family. Look at the earth. What convulsions must she have been in. How the living beings that she entertains have been tost about. The bones upon our own Rock of Gibraltar, shells upon mountains, and trees at the bottom of mines! We stare at these appearances and think the change of situation astonishing. It is nothing to the magnitude of the Earth. What is it to my appearance whether my beard be a little longer or shorter or a few hairs be cut off and either fly away or adhere to my mantle? Just as much is this shifting of material, to our mother Earth. Perhaps it happened when she was brought to bed of the Moon. Who knows but on the awful day which the Holy Church teaches us to expect, she may be delivered of another, perhaps of twins. But not to dwell upon our own Planet much longer, look at the spangled sky! What a goodly company of sensitive beings. Of glorious depositories of life, motion, and affection, of rapturous friendship, and extatic love. Our poor little earth, in such an assemblage of Great, powerful and wise beings, may be compared to a little sparrow hopping about in the court of a palace on the day of a royal banquet![29]

Good Lord have mercy, *Kyrie eleison, Christe eleison Kyrie Eleison,* said the Monk! crossing himself! Beelzebub fly hence! *O Maria, ora pro nobis!* May St. Francis for the Sake of his five holy wounds, which you know he had the honor of receiving the prints of, on account of his peculiar sanctity he being the founder of our most holy order, which is by far the most holy of all the orders, although I do not much approve of his embracing a Lady made of Snow, nor of his being such an enemy to good wine— but Lord amercy these Saints do strange things, I have no ambition of that sort. Good Basileo, thats your name, I think, lets have a drop of some of the wine which the good old Lady gave us. Bless her soul, she is a very good Christian indeed, I love to drink the health of such good holy women. So heres to the lady Quatlelca del Saragossa.

SEPTR. 4TH.   Osbert was so lost in the Grandeur of the subject of his conversation that he scarce heard the pious ejaculations that broke from the friar, who really thought he had fallen in with a madman. He rode on and was soon separated from his companions near 50 Yards before they thought of following him; Basileo having alighted in order to fill a Goblet of Wine from one of the Skins which were borne by the Sumpter Mule, for the Priest and another for himself. They then jogged on after him slowly.

"My very good friend Basileo," said the friar, "This is very good wine. Very good wine and a very good friend are two very good things. But pray tell me who is this Master of thine! May St. Francis keep his senses. Surely he is not quite right in the

29. The following extract was bound into the ninth volume of the manuscript journal between pages 61 and 62 (page 281 of this volume). BHL's citation is inaccurate. The quotation is from the first part of the *Botanic Garden*, "The Economy of Vegetation" (Canto I, lines 103–08), rather than from the second part, "The Loves of the Plants."

Botannic Garden
Doctor Darwin's Poem   the Loves of the Plants   Novr. 9th 1797
Canto I. L. 103. Let there be Light, proclaim'd th' almighty Lord
Astonish'd Chaos heard the potent Word
Through all his realms the kindling Ether runs
And the Mass starts into a Million Suns
Earths round each Sun with quick explosions burst
And second planets issue from the first.

main point. Keep a good look out after him. Try to dissuade him from drinking Water. Water is a sad windy beverage. It flies into the brain. Wine strengthens the heart. It is the oil that makes the Wheels of life run glibly. Thy Master ought to indulge. Good meats, good wine, good cooking and good company, commend me to these four cardinal points. And now pray satisfy my curiosity and inform me who this courteous and gentle knight is, that thou hast the good fortune to serve.

Lord have mercy upon us, replied Basileo, what a deal I should have to tell you, if I were to tell you all. So for shortness sake, d' y' see, as I am a sinner, I cant tell you any thing about who he is. But I can tell you who I am. You must know then—

Tell us that another time, said the Friar, we have not much time now, how didst thou and he meet.

Upon the road d' ye see, returned the Squire, he picked me up like a good pious Gentleman as he is, in the forest. I had been robbed and left for dead. He came by accidentally, took me up behind him, naked and bloody as I was and got me to the next inn. He staid a week till I recovered. As I was a poor man, and did not know how to get home, he bought a horse, clothed me, and now, d' ye see, I am just jogging on with him wherever he chuses to go. Sometimes he travells but a few miles in the day, sometimes, we get a good way forward. In fact our horses are our masters. We stop when they are sluggish or tired, and proceed only when the road seems pleasant to them, for he would not for the universe hurt a living creature. Nay, for that matter, I believe it goes to his very soul to trample upon the road for fear he should hurt it, so tender hearted is he, and he has taken it into his head that every thing such as trees and stones, and sticks and stocks, and Lord bless me, I don't know what all, can feel as well as we Christians. However he's a mighty good man in the main, and if you let him have his own way, a kinder and better master never lived.

And whither said the Monk is he now travelling.

Why, replied Basileo, that's a kind of a secret. But I believe its to—Lord a mercy on my foolish tongue, I had near popp'd it out—Well, bless me, if I ever swore, I would take a vow against telling anybody about it. But by all the holy prophets and Vangilists, I protest I didn't mean to tell a human being. So, good master parson, don't you now ask me a word about the matter, for by the Lord, d' ye see, I wont tell ye.

My son, said father Ximenes, keep thyself from sin, and honor the holy Church. Confess to each other, saith St. Paul, and St. Francis hath said, put thy confidence in the holy friars, and keep not thy secrets from them, for they have the keys of heaven, and act as attorneys for St. Peter upon earth. If therefore thou revealest not this secret unto me, most assuredly thou sinnest, and thou shall go to perdition—give me another Cup of Wine, good Basileo.

Basileo having again alighted, and having drank himself and given the friar a flowing cup of Wine they again proceeded, just keeping the knight within view, who was riding gently along, lost in deep meditation.

And now, continued Ximenes, I am ready to hear thy confession, tell me therefore truly, whither travelleth thy master.

Grammercy, I shouldn't tell neither, said the squire, and yet I should tell too, by the Lord, as your worship's a priest. Now that's very odd I think, that I should do right to break a promise, which you know is doing wrong, because you're a father confessor. Bless my heart, I'm sadly puzzled. But out it must I suppose—why then, he's going a courting.

Poogh, poogh, poogh, is that all. Going a courting indeed. Ha! ha! ha! Sun, moon, and stars all going a courting with him! Now I understand the trim of it! Let him alone, let him alone, my good Basileo; let him drink water, he has his cure before him, marriage will cure him of all his fine tender, languishing, thrilling, hyperbolical, fantastical, rhapsodical, sentiments. That's a proper cooler. That brings a man down to matter of fact. *Squalling brats* are then found where *smiling pledges of love* were expected. A badly cooked dinner where the feast of love was hoped for. A bed visited by headach and rheumatism, in spite of Cupid and Hymen. Dull harangues, and stupid replies in the place of the *converse of hearts* and the *flow of soul*. Let him alone boy. He is the first Madman that voluntarily went to Bedlam, but I'll answer for it, his cure will be compleat. St. Francis be praised, and this Cawl, No such folly for me.

The priest and Squire now trotted briskly along with the two Sumpter Mules, and soon overtook the knight who was proceeding in deep meditation.

The forest was thick, the trees overhung the road. Already had the Sun sunk beneath their lofty summits, and trembled, among their busy leaves. The cool breeze of the Western sea waved the spangled boughs. Freshness was wafted upon its Wings. A thousand sweet feathered throats warbled to the scene of enjoyments. Even the hoarse note of the cold frog, and the caw of the rustic rook, mingled in pleasant contrast with the varied melody.

For a moment a thicker shade of aged cedars envelopes our enraptured knight, and his matter-of-fact companions. The road gently turns to the right. He stops! The forest is behind him! The ocean bounds the view.

O thou beneficent being whose finger of power and of love hath spread this feast of wonders before us, give me strength to bear the extacy that fills, swells, and overwhelms, my soul and all its faculties. Thus exclaimed Osbert.

The priest stared. "A fine prospect no doubt," said he, "a very pretty prospect, but lets jog on to some place of entertainment, I begin to be hungry, methinks a roast duck might not be amiss. As I find we are so near the Sea, don't you think we might stand a Chance of good fish, and shrimp sauce, or of a good roasted lobster. Now of all things I love crimped Cod, provided the fish was well alive when he was crimped. However, if we can't get that, we may no doubt be sure of fried eels, fresh from the Water. Oysters I know to be plenty in this neighborhood and very good muscles, and as for wine, thank the holy mother of God, we have plenty of good liquor along with us."

The pencil of the great Raphael D'Urbino might in its happiest efforts perhaps have planted a *hint* of Osbert's face. Fixed upon the sensual friar, his eyes flamed indignation at his insensibility, and fierce anger at his cruel voracity. But soon they softened to an expression of commiseration, as the fluttering duck under the knife of the cook, the convulsively gasping fish, the shrimp boiled and the lobster roasted alive, the Cod trembling under the crimping knife, the twisting and flayed eels, and the lacerated oyster and muscle, moved in slow procession before his imaginaton, like the miserable victims of superstition in the pageantry of an Auto de Fé. The charm of the Landscape was dissolved for many minutes. Basileo saw the wretchedness of his master. He whispered silence to the friar.

Lord a mercy what's your honor about, exclaimed he. Look but what good Luck we have. Here's a fine sight for you, and just such a one as your honor says that the Lady Theodora lives in. Wont your honor ride forward.

I Thank you, good Basileo, said the Knight, it is true. We are now not very far from the habitation of the gentlest soul that ever inhabited a beauteous body. See how the drooping Sun smiles upon the turrets of her seat. The friar was slowly going down the hill. The knight had stopt his horse upon the brink of its declivity just where the road emerged from the thick forrest. An epitome of a kingdom was stretched out before him. In vain did the numberless objects that composed the Landscape croud through the eyes, the imagination could not contain them.

From the Verge of the forrest, several of whose most majestic trees stepped forward into the foreground, a green slope descended for a mile towards the Valley. Its grassy side was covered with innumerable herds of Cattle attended by their piping shepherds. The tinkling sound of the sheepbells was heard to the right and left, till it vanished in the breeze. At the foot of the hill, the winding road entered the village. The neat cottages interspersed with shady trees surrounded the venerable church which towered above them, like a reverend father above his playful offspring. Rich cultivation encircled the busy spot. It was a garden spread around by cheerfull industry. Another village with its varied spire, another with its square tower, still another and another succeeded on every side. Embosomed in trees and glittering in the golden sunbeam they seemed to repose upon a carpet of the richest verdure, varied by the most beautiful tints, and mellowed into one mass of softest harmony. The purple curled margin on each side bounded the view, but opened new prospects to the delighted imagination. Among the beauties of the scene the silver stream wound its mazy way. Now gliding behind a gentle knoll, then starting again into view, hid now among the shady groves, and presently reappearing a broad mirror of resplendent light, it at last emptied itself immediately in front, into the boundless ocean. The boundless Ocean! The mind paused upon its ample bosom. The playful beam danced in a radiant line upon a thousand ripples, to the sound of the murmuring surf. The fleet of the villages of the bay, a multitude of fishing boats, glided upon its surface appearing to a distant beholder like so many dark moving spots upon the purple expanse.

Oh! for a pen powerfully and softly expressive like the creative pencil of Claude Lorraine.[30] Immortal painter! thou darling child of Nature, thou magic inspirer of the canvass! Soft soft beneath the light earth that hand which nature, embracing, sweetly guided o'er the lifeless pannel, till it glowed with the fervor of a summer sky, shedding its vivid light oer a thousand valleys rich in verdure, and chequered in magnificent architecture, or till it smiled, the soft influence of the evening breeze waving the play-full branches, and courting the careless shepherd to the song. Oh! for such a pen, then might I paint the feelings which thy works inspire, and speak what the memory of thy genius demands. Then might I describe what our knight beheld when he issued from the gloomy forest.

The friar had proceeded half way down the hill when turning round he still saw the knight gazing from his horse upon the beauties of the scene. He grew impatient, for he had discovered the Sign of the Village inn glittering among the trees below.

Osbert was pointing out to Basileo the mansion of Theodora. It was a white square spot rising above a grove of Oaks at a small distance from the village. At each angle was a tapering turret. There said he, dwells what long has quitted this bosom, the heart of your master. Possessed by the gentlest of her gentle sex it dwells with Theodora. Haste let me visit it.

He rode down the hill. The Monk rejoiced. The knight is generous thought he, the fish is excellent, the ducks, and the crimped cod is divine, we will eat our fill and Osbert will pay.

He was soon overtaken; for Osbert was going to Theodora. In riding along, he

30. Claude Lorraine (1600–82), the best known French ideal-landscape artist, tried to portray nature in a more perfect state than it actually existed. He was especially influential in England between the mid-eighteenth and mid-nineteenth centuries.

expatiated to the friar upon the beauteous Landscape, and the happiness of the innocent Villagers. The plough had just stopped at the end of the furrow, and the shining share reflected the declining sunbeams. Industry was preparing for recreation and rest. The sturdy ox carried his harness to his stable, the peasant followed to the evening dance. The sheep hastened to the fold, and the sweet breathing cow bore home her milk to the dairy, lowing to her imprisoned calf. The reddening light of day swam upon the glittering wave—he seemed to delay for a moment to behold the joyful scene—and sunk to rest. Quickly brightened the horned Lamp of Diana, silvering the rising mists.

Our travellers had now arrived at the inn. The friar had alighted, and the croud of curious villagers surrounded the Strangers. Your honor, said Ximenes, will no doubt alight and refresh yourself. After the fatigue of the day, the pleasures of the evening are appointed to man. For my part, religion causeth me to refrain, but let the layman enjoy the good gifts of God, with thankfulness, while the holy saints procure by this intercession a blessing.

I do not mean to take up my abode here to-night, replied Osbert. But you Basileo remain here with my equipage, and wait upon this holy father. Father! I crave your prayers.

The Monk bowed assent, happy in the absence of so acute an observer of hypocrisy, whose practical religion under the garb of a Cavalier, spoke to the heart, while the sensuality of the friar was but ill concealed by the monastic livery.

Osbert rode slowly through the village, and turned his horse at the end of it, to the mansion of Theodora. He soon reached the Gate.

SEPTR. 5TH.   The gate was covered with ivy which rambled unconfined over its battlements. It was inhabited by an aged servant, whose attention to the visitors at their entrance was repaid by ease and affluence, if the gratification of every desire deserve that name among the poor as well as the rich. Osbert struck the bell and the gate opened. The quiet mansion appeared at the end of a long vista of aged Elms. The faithful domestic knew him. Osbert alighted to embrace him.

My good old friend, said he, tell me. . . .

A long chasm.

. . . When that hour comes, my dear Theodora, when life trembles upon the unstrung nerve, like the flame of an expiring candle upon the consumed wick, then even shall I think of thee! That thought, too strong, too full of affection, and of longing desire, will break the thread of life, will impress itself upon the soft substance of my departing spirit, will become part of its essence, and mould its form in the world of harmony and bliss to which it will wing its way. It will stamp me a faint, an imperfect image of Theodora, it will be my passport to heaven my claim to the love of angels.

My faithful Osbert, replied Theodora, how gratifying, how flattering is the love of so much tenderness, so much sense, so much virtue as you possess. I would tell you how my heart feels and returns it, I would indulge myself in acknowledging all my weakness as your beloved. But I feel for you, what ought to be more valuable to you than the love of such ill-judging youth as mine. I feel for you the truest friendship, and if you would promise me upon that honour which you hold so Sacred, to permit me to talk to you as a friend; instead of hearing your tender, and I believe heart dictated speeches across the room, I would call you to sit by me on this Sofa, and hear me laugh at one half of your sensibility, while I love and respect the other.

Osbert rose, he sat by her, and promised to hear all she had to say with patient gratitude.

Don't you think, though, said she, that the weight of both of us must rather incommode this tender sofa?

Osbert sprung up. Good heav'ns, cried she how you trample upon the soft texture of the humble carpet. Pray have mercy upon it, my dear sympathizing friendly Osbert!

He sat down again. He looked at her. A satirical but kind smile dimpled her cheeks. He felt ashamed.

You carry this too far, said he, the eagerness of your manner surprized me into folly. You have succeeded in making me appear ridiculous to myself as well as to you. But you mistake my conjectures for my real opinions. I do not by any means devote every thing to uselessness, because I think it capable of sensation. Where I suspect that pain *may* be felt I would avoid being the author of it.

Now pray then [said she], to prevent mistakes between us, let me a little into the Secret of your system. I should have ordered supper, but when Sebastian asked me what I would have and at the same time announced your arrival, I was utterly at a loss what to do. Fish, chickens, meats—oh these were all inadmissible. What tender compassionate Soul could possibly exist by the destruction of life. Fruit next occurred. What? rob the fair appletree of her children, pluck the bleeding grape from the fragrant vine, tear the pomegranite from the parental boughs, or the fig from its leafy family, to be crushed to pieces alive by voracious teeth. But milk may be innocently enjoyed. Aye, by the calf, for whom wise nature and the motherly cow intended it. But should we turn robbers of the infant cattle who cannot redress their wrongs? No, no, no, my dear Osbert, let's go to bed supperless rather. But alas! what can we do tomorrow morning. Shall we suffer that merciless tyrant, hunger, to trucidate[31] the tender offspring of our souls, compassion. Poor Osbert! you must consider the matter over again.

Surely you are very cruel, interrupted the knight—no! let father Ximenes cater for you, let your lobsters be roasted alive, your cod be crimped, your hogs *barbecued*,[32] and your eels skinned the moment before they are thrown into the pan, but spare me the cruelty of your ridicule.

The cruelty of my ridicule! said Theodora, does the smile, the manner, and the accent with which I repeat your ideas, make the System on which they are founded tremble? Had your solemn voice pronounced the very speech I have now finished, and your solemn face sanctioned it, would its subject have been more true? And after all, why would you be miserable upon suppositions.

Yes, Theodora, the *suppositions* even—as you call the principles upon which I speak, and endeavor to act—these suppositions which guard and fence in the line of humanity are at any rate deserving of attention, on account of their good tendency. But they are more than suppositions.

Nothing more, be assured my good friend, replied Theodora. The line of humanity wants not fences so insurmountable, so thorny, and so choaking to the path, that it is impossible to walk in it. Had I the wit, the inexhaustible vivacity in which satire and good humour, in which the most winning address, and the most invincible sarcasm were so blended and mixt, that the subject of ridicule departed the best pleased of her hearers, that animated the conversation of my friend Lydia,[33] how would I rally you into the enjoyment of a life that may be so useful to the world and so full of happiness to yourself. Then should you not solicit in vain that I would reward your attention to my lectures—alas! I could never reward it as she did the love of her Henry! But she is gone, and now no doubt, he is as miserable as you would be if you knew how, but with less cause!

My adorable friend, cried Osbert, if my conversion would obtain the reward of *your* love, what system, though entwin'd into the very essence of my understanding, and bound there by the straightest chains of prejudice, would not yield to the magic touch of your hand and quit its hold forever? But you have often mentioned your friend, and her eccentric husband, did his ideas ever fall into that train which you think so ridiculous in me.

I will read you a letter [answered Theodora] which I have in my pocket-book and if

31. Trucidate: to cruelly kill or murder. In a humorous context, such as this, the word means "to slaughter." *OED.*

32. BHL added the following in a footnote: "formerly barbecuing meant to whip a hog to death before roasting."

33. BHL's first wife, Lydia Sellon.

you will subscribe it as your rule of faith and not go beyond it, I will thus far indulge you. Here it is. It was written by Henry to Lydia before their union. I will read it.

My dearest Lydia,

I have nothing to say. Pray, you dear satirist, let yourself down to my level. Be not so kind all at once. Spread your eloquence over a little more paper. Dilute your wit with a spoonfull more of ink. Write with a worn pen that I may read more slowly and not receive at one rapid draught such a flow of goodness, of mirth, of sense, of elegance as you have poured upon me in your last letter. I could *look* what I feel, I could imprint it in kisses upon your lips, I could pour it in tears of joy into your bosom, I could interweave it into a grateful life of years, but I cannot write it, nor could I say it. I must take a new subject.

I have been reading a strange book. It contains experiments which have been actually made by a learned and honest man, and which prove beyond a doubt that almost *all plants have sensation*.[34] Behold a new subject for your wit! But let me explain myself. Philosophers all agree that motion (the outward sign of life) is communicated to the muscles of all animals by means of the nerves. Vessels similar to nerves have long been discovered in the plant. In animals, all live nerves are electric (galvanic). You know the meaning of that term. This property is lost in the dead animal, but if communicated by art, the limb assumes a temporary life. This new discovery goes to show that the nerves of live plants are also electric, and that the same artificial life may be infused into them. It seems therefore probable that plants may *feel* though certainly in a degree inferior to animals, and the gradation we see in nature from animal to vegetable life, through the Polypus, the whole class of Zoophytes, and the sensitive plant, seems to confirm the truth of the experiment.[35]

I read the book just as I was going to rest. I shut it, my mind turned to my Lydia, and the sigh her absence excited lulled me into a soft Sleep. I dreamt, you walked with me into your father's garden. I believe every thing the poets have so sweetly described, the twittering birds, the fragrant flowers, the murmuring stream, the smiling face of the earth, and the serene countenance of heaven were there to make me happy. I know not. But *you* smiled, *your* hand returned the pressure of mine, nor did your eyes refuse to look upon me, and happiness was around us. As we walked a sweet pea invited you to stoop.

34. The "strange book" may have been Tiberius Cavallo, *A Complete Treatise of Electricity in Theory and Practice; with original experiments* (London, 1777; 3d ed. London, 1786).
35. See caption to PLATE 5, n. 2.

The blushing flower—I thought it a silly ungrateful flower when your soft hand approached it—fluttered its purple wings, left its stalk, filled the air with fragrance, and perched upon the twig of a cherry tree. All the other flowers of the plant fluttered away. Prodigies never frighten a dreamer. Neither you nor I wondered. Nor were we surprized when the little flower began to speak.

You beautiful Orb of happiness, said the pea, who smilingly movest in thy allotted path by my habitation, and daily with the return of light and heat, refreshest my nerves with showers, glittering now in clouds of blue, veiled now in white, but always beaming from those two bright black spots in thy most distant part, happiness upon me, art thou thyself happy? Alas can I think that thy so regular approach and departure is a mechanical operation, that thou enjoyest not life and sensation and powers of pleasure to which my quickest and most accute feelings are the dull senselessness of this cherry tree. No, sun of my bliss, let me, though called a rhapsodist, in derision, hug the sentiment to my heart, and believe that he who put motion into these little wings of mine, and sensation into this breast, left not so large nor so beautiful a world as thou art void of feeling and of happiness.

Now you must know—lest you should not be able to dream as fast as I did— that this sweet pea was adressing my dear Lydia, who regularly every morning watered the plant, and whose beautiful black eyes watched and smiled upon its growth. Was it not a philosophic little flower, my love; and like a philosopher, it got itself ridiculed?

The confusion of happiness that filled the rest of my dream with your image, lasted till morning when I awoke. But even then the speech of the Sweet pea hung in my mind, and I rubbed my eyes several times to be certain that I was awake.

After all, thought I, I have heard less rational sentiments from the rostrum of a university, and less pious ones from the pulpit of a bishop, than were uttered by my sweetpea from the Cherry twig. We may smile at such reasoning, but are we sure that some higher being does not *laugh* at our smile? The knowledge of every species of beings seems so to be fenced in by ignorance of the state and system of every other, and so filled with the *vanity* of thinking that they are the highest in rank of created creatures, that we scarcely admit by way of hypothesis the possibility of a comparison of other animals with ourselves. As to vegetables, I see you smile at the absurdity of the idea. But I am getting quite away from the leading idea that struck me upon reading the experiments of professor Valli,[36] and the fanciful theory that I thought might be built upon the harangue of the sweetpea.

The Hindoos, the Peguans[37] and Siamese (at least the cast of Priests) abstain from every thing that has had life, and eat nothing but vegetables. There is a benevolence of intention in this practice that is very amiable. And altho' I cannot include this abstinence in my theory of morality, I think the goodness of heart that originally dictated it, is rewarded by the health of body, and the serenity and clearness of mind that the *vegetablist* enjoys. I have tried it myself for three or four Months, and I am sure I never felt more cheerful, more light, and more capable of mental exertion. Perhaps my courage was less in proportion, and I might not have so easily fought a duel.

But how grossly are the Bramins and the Talopins (the Siamese priests)[38] deceived. I recollect a story either from Father Loubere, Tavernier, or Bernier, of a Bramin to whom a drop of Water was shewn through a miscroscope, and who upon seeing the million of living and nicely organized animals that inhabited it, was rendered so miserable as to starve himself, or at least to despair of attaining the purity proposed as the end of his humane religion.[39] What would he have said on discovering the probability of sensations in plants: That pain and death is inflicted when the corn is cut, the apple plucked, and the grape gathered. It is indeed an unpleasant reflection, and one that adds a little to the disagreeable sensations excited by our total ignorance of the intentions of God in the permission of moral and physical evil.

It may be weakness, but I assure you I would rather live and act so, as that no other sensitive being should dread or hate my existence. I would rather live entirely on vegetables, but professor Valli tells me they feel my voracity as much as the sheep does the butcher's knife. I may therefore as well at once follow instinct in my diet and leave it to him who gave me canine teeth to settle my account with the animal, and to him who gave me grinders, with the vegetable world. We have no business to quarrell with our Creator. "I am as

36. Eusebio Valli, *Experiments on Animal Electricity with their application to Physiology and some Pathological and Medical Observations*, trans. W. Moorcroft (London, 1793).

37. Peguans were inhabitants of Pegu, a division (and the former capital) of Lower Burma.

38. Talopins (Talapoin): "a Buddhist monk or priest, properly of Pegu; extended by Europeans to those of Siam, Burmah, and other Buddhist countries." *OED*.

39. The story is probably from Simon de la Loubère, *A New Historical Relation of the Kingdom of Siam . . .*, 2 vols. (London, 1693). François Bernier was the author of *The History of the Late Revolution of the Empire of the Great Mogul . . .*, 4 vols. (London, 1671–72). Jean Baptiste Tavernier was the author of *The Six Voyages . . . through Turkey, into Persia and the East–Indies . . .* (London, 1677). See p. 509 below.

God made me," is the vulgar excuse for deformity. There is wisdom in the reply.

From these considerations it seems very plain, that unless suicide be the *only* virtue, the sensibility that feels too much for the corporeal sufferings of other animals—I had almost added vegetables—is not meritorious, for it is unnatural. I mean to say, that the physical *existence* of every individual being in the world, depends upon the *destruction* of some other being, and the happiness of each upon the misery of some other, and that the world is so constituted that it cannot be otherwise. A sensibility therefore, that would accomplish its purpose of existing, if not for the happiness, at all events without occasioning the misery of another, would soon starve its proprietor. As to *moral* happiness, we must discuss that another time. . . .

Whether the letter contained any more, or any better arguments against that sensibility that extends its pity from mutton and beefstakes to boiled potatoes and roasted apples, I know not. The manuscript ends here. But I am happy in having had my own doubts resolved by two very sensible, humane, and candid Sisters, Mrs. Paine and Miss Betsy Hay,[40] both of whom agree that the said sensibility is very ridiculous.

40. Margaret [Hay?] Paine (d. 1805) was the wife of Orris Paine (see note 23). Elizabeth Hay died in Richmond in 1811. *Virginia Argus* (Richmond), 5 October 1805, 17 June 1811.

... The public Buildings are, the Church, the Courthouse, & the Playhouse. The former is uncieled, unplaistered & unpave half the squares of Glass in the Windows are broken, & the misera bowlegged turret is tumbling down. — The Courthouse is a p mean building, with a meaner spire. The playhouse is a cent & better than either of the former. — I had almost forgotten the Market house, the irregular position of which is in harmon with its filth and deformity. — The stile of the houses of private ge tlemen is plain & decent, but of the fashion of 30 years ago. — The ne however kept very clean & independent of papering, which not universal, fitted up much in the English style. — The inferio houses are chiefly framed & weatherboarded, & the sort of doubl roof, called by the french un Mansard, (from the Architect wh first employed them in france) — by the English Carpenters, a Curbroo are very common. — I suspect that they may have been introdu by German builders, after the fashion of Saxony, and most of parts of Germany. — All the buildings are covered with shingles, a ligh & durable covering, but dangerous in a country where fires are not provided against by any regulations of police, and where wood it most common fuel. — The shingles are plain pieces of board rou at the edge, & nailed on in the manner of tiles, not groved in to one another like the German shingles. — The river is crowded with nu gill looking weatherboarded Warehouses, upon log Wharfs twi into every direction of obliquity. The said Log wharfs des description more than imitation; but they answer the purpose